Clean Streets

NEW PERSPECTIVES IN CRIME, DEVIANCE, AND LAW SERIES

Edited by John Hagan

Clean Streets
Controlling Crime, Maintaining Order, and Building Community Activism
Patrick J. Carr

Gender and Crime
Patterns in Victimization and Offending
Edited by Karen Heimer and Candace Kruttschnitt

Clean Streets

Controlling Crime, Maintaining Order, and Building Community Activism

Patrick J. Carr

NEW YORK UNIVERSITY PRESS
New York and London

NEW YORK UNIVERSITY PRESS
New York and London
www.nyupress.org

Library of Congress Cataloging-in-Publication Data
Carr, Patrick J.
Clean streets : controlling crime, maintaining order,
and building community activism / Patrick J. Carr.
p. cm.—(New perspectives in crime, deviance, and law series)
Includes bibliographical references and index.
ISBN–13: 978–0–8147–1662–5 (cloth : alk. paper)
ISBN–10: 0–8147–1662–8 (cloth : alk. paper)
ISBN–13: 978–0–8147–1663–2 (pbk. : alk. paper)
ISBN–10: 0–8147–1663–6 (pbk. : alk. paper)
1. Gang prevention—Illinois—Chicago—Citizen participation.
2. Crime prevention—Illinois—Chicago—Citizen participation.
3. Beltway (Chicago, Ill.)—Social conditions. I. Title. II. Series.
HV6439.U7C349 2005
364.4'3'0977311—dc22 2005012896

New York University Press books are printed on acid-free paper,
and their binding materials are chosen for strength and durability.

Manufactured in the United States of America
c 10 9 8 7 6 5 4 3 2 1
p 10 9 8 7 6 5 4 3 2 1

All photos courtesy of Michael Smyth

For my parents, Paddy and Olive Carr

Contents

Acknowledgments

Bringing this manuscript to the brink of publication has been a marathon of sorts, and over the course of this metaphorical run, I have had the assistance of a great number of people. I used to think that I would eschew the formality of thanking people by name and be truly iconoclastic in the matter of acknowledgments. I fear however, that my debts are too large to warrant such a posture, and so I return to the comfort of the traditional salutations.

My academic mentors, first at University College Dublin and later at the University of Chicago, have trained, cajoled, infuriated, inspired, and molded me as a scholar and as a person. My closest advisers, whom I still call on for assistance, continue to make me, and my work, better than I, or it, ought to be. Tom Inglis, at University College Dublin, has always been a far greater influence on me than he would care to publicly acknowledge, and his sharp wit, fine mind, and good heart continue to inspire me. Rob Sampson and John Laub get bundled together because they seem always to intellectually double-team and browbeat me in equal measures. Individually and collectively, they have influenced my work, and their career-long commitment to top-drawer, theoretically engaged research is the example I set myself to follow, always. Bill Wilson has influenced me, and my work, in a more profound way than I can possibly convey in a few short sentences. He is the mentor I aspire to be, the scholar I strive to be, and one of the people I most admire. In 1993, Bill Wilson took a chance that an Irishman with a Mohawk could bring home the ethnographic bacon from Beltway. I hope he has not been disappointed. There are others at Chicago and at Saint Joseph's who have provided encouragement, inspiration, and the atmosphere to do my work. I would be remiss if I didn't mention Richard Taub, who guided the Comparative Neighborhood Study, and did so with intelligence, vigor, and candor. I especially thank him for his patience with a cocky, know-it-all fieldworker.

At Saint Joe's, Claire Renzetti and Raquel Bergen have been fans of this work for several years and have always believed in it, even when it seemed that it would never see the light of day. I thank them for their support and faith, and I hope the final product is worth the wait.

My family has been the primary socializing force in my life, and, even though they are still in the dark as to what I do, I appreciate their encouragement and their faith in my ability. My parents, Paddy and Olive, to whom this book is dedicated, taught me well and encouraged me to follow my instincts. My sisters, Caroline and Barbara, and their respective children are constant sources of support and love. I hope they read, understand, and enjoy this book.

My editor at NYU Press, Ilene Kalish, is either a visionary or a masochist. She has signed this book twice; the first time didn't take for a variety of reasons, and it has been her steadfast belief in *Clean Streets,* not to mention the idea for the snappy title, that has suffused me with the confidence and belief to complete it. Ilene is too good an editor for the likes of me, and I am mystified and overjoyed that she continues to work with me. Ilene's assistant, Salwa Jabado, makes my life easier and always seems to have answers for my many questions. I thank her for her patience and forbearance.

The people of Beltway, many of whom are still doing favors for me long after I left Chicago, are precious to me as friends first of all and as participants in this endeavor. I hope that what I have written here does justice to their efforts, as well as to my own, and that I have accurately represented their lives, opinions, and experiences. Two people who deserve special mention are Linda and Judy, without whom this project would never have happened.

I have benefited from the careful critique offered by several scholars as I revised this work. I am indebted to the anonymous reviewers for their comments on an earlier draft. Deanna Wilkinson is worthy of very special mention because when I was at an impasse she provided me with a meticulous and insightful critical reading, and her wonderful suggestions have helped this work enormously.

The devil is always in the details, and in terms of the charts and maps herein I am hugely in debt to Carol McLaughlin, at the Saint Joseph's University Press. At excruciatingly short notice, Carol conjured up the map of Beltway and all of the charts and tables herein. I am extremely fortunate to be able to call upon such expert assistance.

My longtime roommate and collaborator Michael Smyth is responsible for all of the photographs published here. Though he spent but a few days in Beltway in the summer of 1999, Mickey captured the essence of the place in the inimitable style of his that is so much more than the mere designation of social documentarian.

The Comparative Neighborhood Study was supported by grants from the Ford Foundation, the MacArthur Foundation, and the Rockefeller Foundation. Saint Joseph's University provided support, in the form of a summer research grant, to conduct follow-up interviews in 1999. These funders, big and small, helped me complete this work.

Some of the work herein was previously published in the *American Journal of Sociology*, and is reproduced here by kind permission of the University of Chicago Press.

My final nod to the convention of acknowledgments is to put my immediate significant others last. Maria Kefalas is my partner in crime, in conformity, and in child-rearing. My work is better, my days and nights are more interesting, and my life is richer because of her. No mere words can truly convey the debt that I owe her in love, life, and happiness. My daughter, Camille, is the other love of my life. She makes every day better than the previous one, and I treasure every moment I spend with her. Camille's baby brother, PJ, arrived just in time for this draft of the acknowledgements, and his cheery and impish presence, while distracting, is as welcome as sunshine after rain. I am thrice blessed, and I know it.

1 Introduction

National Night Out—August 1999

Tuesday, August 3, 1999, was a typical hot August evening in Chicago. The air was heavy with the heat and humidity of the day, and in the Beltway neighborhood, many residents went about their business as usual. Some mowed, watered, or preened their precious patches of lawn, while others lolled about their porches listening to the White Sox game on the radio; children played in the side streets and parks, while some dog owners, still in their work clothes, walked their pets after returning from their day jobs. At the Beltway Public Library, the usual early-evening patrons borrowed books and videos, read the day's newspapers, or surfed the World Wide Web on one of the library's public access terminals.

Just after 6:30, the normal routine of the library is augmented by the arrival of a few dozen local residents. They do not arrive together but trickle in at a steady pace, shunning the books and periodicals stacked on the shelves to go into the main meeting room of the library. It is National Night Out, and the local neighborhood watch group, the Beltway Night Patrol, is marking the occasion by gathering its members and any other interested residents to march from the library to the Hastings Elementary School.[1] There are two banners that will be carried at the head of the march. One bears the legend "Beltway Night Patrol: *Your* Neighborhood Watch Group," and the other is the generic National Night Out plastic banner, replete with the corporate logos of local sponsors. There are other, smaller cardboard National Night Out posters stapled together and mounted on wooden poles for participants to carry, and they are distributed to anyone who wants to display one. Over on a side table, there is a cake to mark the occasion; it is inscribed with the legend "Welcome to National Night Out from Beltway Night Patrol." The cake is covered to keep it fresh because it will serve as a treat after the march.

As the members of the Night Patrol arrive, they are warmly greeted by Bernadette Boniek, the president of the BNP; by Lydia Donovan, the head librarian and Night Patrol officer; and by Kitty Kelly, the team leader for the group. Both Bernadette and Kitty work full-time, and they have come more or less directly from work to the library. For Lydia, the library is her workplace, and she delights in combining work with civic activism. Bernadette, Lydia, and Kitty know everyone who comes into the room, and the atmosphere is one of uncontrived joviality. Bernadette and the other core members of the BNP are excited because there is a rumor that the new commander of the local police district will be attending "their march." The local police district covers a large area, and there are several competing marches elsewhere. If the new commander does decide to march in Beltway, it will be a feather in the cap of the BNP, a fact not lost on any of the assembled members.

The local beat officers, Charles Simpson and John Straka, pull up to the library in their cruiser at about five minutes to seven, and they confirm to the BNP that Commander Riordan will be joining them for the march. The mood is now one of barely suppressed excitement, and Bernadette and her husband, George, tell people to gather outside the library in the parking lot for the march. The BNP members have now been joined by three people who represent the local Civic League, and by Father Rooney, the pastor of the local St. Martin's parish. There are about twenty Beltway citizens present; most are active members of the BNP, while others are there because they have been recruited specifically for the National Night Out march. People are gathered in small clusters of two and three in the parking lot, and they chat as they await the word to march.

Commander Riordan pulls up to the parking lot a little before seven o'clock. He is an imposing figure, standing over six feet tall. The police officers present, now numbering five, are careful and courtly with their new boss. Bernadette and George usher people around one of the police cruisers for a photograph before they set off, and people pose with their placards and banners. Pictures taken, the BNP march for National Night Out begins.

Scarcely half a mile separates the Beltway library from the Hastings Elementary School, and the route chosen for the evening is suitably scenic and typical of the neighborhood. Once the group members leave the library they turn left on to Ridge Avenue, a busy north-south artery, and from there people walk the three blocks to the edge of Hastings Park. Hastings Park is a large expanse with several baseball diamonds, a multipurpose field used for soccer and football, and a newly renovated state-of-the-art fieldhouse. We turn right and walk along the edge of the westernmost baseball diamond toward the school, which is located at the eastern edge of the park. As we pass by, two Little League teams are warming up for their evening game. The sun is sliding down to dusk, and at this time of the year there are about ninety minutes of daylight left. Still, the evening is bright, even as the shadows cast by the pristine bungalows lengthen across the grass. The BNP members mostly stay on the sidewalks, although two police cruisers are escorting us. Commander Riordan eschews the comfort of the cruiser and walks with the BNP members. While most of the people walking do not seem intent or purposeful, there is a very specific purpose to the march and the route we take. The group passes the Hastings Park Fieldhouse, and a few interested spectators ask what people are marching for. Lydia explains that it is National Night Out and that the BNP is the local neighborhood watch. The inquisitive citizens nod and wish Lydia well.

Soon after the group passes the fieldhouse, the Hastings School looms into view. A black wrought iron fence surrounds the yellow brick building. On the southwestern edge of the schoolyard, there are three midsize outdoor basketball courts. Weeds and tufts of grass poke holes in the gray concrete of the yard, and the hoops are rusted and worn. Only one of the hoops has a net, and it is tattered and ready to fall off. A lawn borders the eastern edge of the school grounds, where the front door to the school is located. In stark contrast to the neat, green postage stamps that typify the rest of the neighborhood, the grass that borders the Hastings school is less lush and more unkempt. A forty-foot-high flagpole that serves as a monument of sorts dominates the southeastern corner of the school. The flagpole, and what it represents, is our destination. The flagpole proudly displays the Stars and Stripes, and it commemorates not the memory of the many Beltway residents past and present that served their country in the armed forces or those who were killed on active service. This monument is dedicated to the memory of two thirteen-year-old girls who died yards away from this spot a little less than four years ago.

The memorial to Melissa Harvey and Teresa Powell is spartan and stark. Scarcely an hour before the march, the small stone bearing their names that sits at the base of the flagpole was overgrown with crabgrass and weeds. On hearing about this, Lydia Donovan dispatched someone to make sure it was cleaned up before the march. Despite the hurried attempts at pruning, the simple block of polished granite and its surroundings betray an air of neglect. There are no flowers there, and the small privet bush that borders the back of the flagpole is in need of trimming. In fact, if you did not know that there was a memorial there, you would pass by unawares. Though small and hard to find, the monument, and what it commemorates, has great relevance for the Beltway neighborhood and for the present story of crime and social control.

Melissa Harvey and Teresa Powell were shot and killed as a result of a dispute between two rival gangs. Both gangs, the Black Knights and the Regal Vikings, claimed Beltway as their turf. The membership of the Black Knights was made up primarily of local Beltway youths, while the youth that were in the Regal Vikings did not hail from the immediate area. Both young women were eighth graders at the Hastings School at the time, and they died because they were sitting in a van, which was parked outside the school, with members of the Regal Vikings. One of the Black Knights, fifteen-year-old Richard Lindstrom, walked up to the passenger side of the van and fired six shots. Melissa, who was sitting in the passenger seat, and Teresa, who was sitting in the rear of the van just behind Melissa, were shot in the head and died almost instantly. Now, four years later, a few dozen Beltway citizens were walking in the heat of an August evening to the monument erected to the memory of these two teenagers.

As the group gathers around the monument, the jocular air of earlier is replaced by a somewhat more somber tone. Although almost no one present knew the girls personally, one of the teenagers who had come along professes to knowing Teresa and Melissa in passing, everyone joins Fr. Rooney in a short prayer that focuses on remembering the young women and pledging to keep the children of the neighborhood safe from danger. The silence as people stare at the monument is reverent and palpable. It is as if the BNP members are determined to remember the young women; their grim expressions underline this mood.

After Fr. Rooney finishes the prayer, people stand around quietly for a few moments before trekking back to the air-conditioned comfort of the library. The walk back is less purposeful than the earlier march to Hastings, and the group splinters into twos and threes. The conversation among the BNP members is slowly returning to more mundane topics—the record high temperatures of the previous weekend and the toll the heat has taken on people's gardens, the latest shenanigans in the local Ward organization, or upcoming vacations that some plan to take. There is no overt mention of the two teenage girls, or of the silent prayers each person petitioned as they stood by the monument. This lack of reflection may seem strange, but it is in keeping with the stoic sensibilities of Beltwayites. There are no candlelit vigils, no flamboyant eulogies, but the resolution is the same as it would be in any other neighborhood that loses its children to gang violence: never let this happen again.

The rest of the evening at the library is more relaxed and upbeat. The BNP celebrates its third National Night Out with the commemorative cake, and for the group members it is a chance to reflect on some of their past accomplishments and, importantly, to impress the new commander. Commander Riordan does not stay long, as there are other calls to make, other neighborhood groups like the BNP to visit. Increasingly, the lot of the policeman, especially those in positions of authority, is intimately bound up with the citizens they serve. Community policing initiatives that seek to stimulate partnerships between citizens and police have been implemented in various forms in many major U.S. cities. Chicago has had one of the most enduring and widespread community policing programs in the form of the Chicago Alternative Policing Strategy (CAPS), which has been the model employed in the city since 1993. Thus, while it is not unusual for patrol officers, sergeants, and even commanders to socialize with community groups, a number of officers, particularly those who joined the Chicago Police Department before CAPS originated, still betray signs of unease.[2] The beat officers, by contrast, seem at home chatting with BNP members, and Officer Simpson, in particular, is well respected by the watch group. Simpson often attends the BNP monthly meetings to give an update on any notable criminal activity in the area, and he seems genuine in his efforts to partner with the group.

After Bernadette thanks people for coming to the march and the cake is sliced and distributed, people begin to file away from the library. The police officers are among the first to leave, and one by one the members of the BNP exit the library, leaving Bernadette, Kitty, and Lydia to clean up and to turn out the lights in the meeting room. While they are somewhat disappointed by the turnout for the march—the BNP has an active member list of about thirty-five people—the women are happy at how the night's events have gone. Most of all, they are pleased that they have had an opportunity to impress the new commander as one of the more active neighborhood watch groups in the district. On the whole, the BNP officers are satisfied with a job well done.

National Night Out in Beltway was on the surface an unremarkable event. But the event itself, and what it represents, is critically important for the story of crime and its control in the neighborhood. Why, then, did the BNP decide to march to the memorial for Melissa and Teresa for National Night Out? The choice that the BNP made to march to the Hastings School is no accident. Rather, it was an action that gives us the opportunity to give a context to the group, the neighborhood, and the struggle that many citizens face to keep their communities free from crime, violence, and disorder. Civic activism is more often stimulated by concrete events than by lofty ideals, and so it is in the case of the neighborhood watch group in Beltway.

The BNP exists in part because of the Powell-Harvey murders; the group was formed a little less than a year after the two young women were killed. On a mundane level, perhaps, on National Night Out the BNP wanted to commemorate the young women, and they used the occasion as a platform to do so. On a deeper level however, the BNP wanted to remind its members why they patrol each month, why they log every instance of graffiti and agitate to have it removed. Certainly, the murders marked a turning point in the neighborhood, the point at which residents had to confront the harrowing fact that five teenagers from their streets, from the same bungalows in which they themselves live and raise their own children, had committed this callous and brutal act. The murders were not only a turning point; they were a touchstone for the re-creation of community activism in the neighborhood. There were community activists in Beltway long before the Powell-Harvey murders, but the event gave a particular shape and form to what people did. It was no longer a case of being active in the PTA, whose goals are specifically school-based, or in the local Civic League, which deals more generally with country and home.[3] The BNP and groups in similar neighborhoods usually form in response to specific threats and problems, and, while many fold within a year or two, some groups, as is the case with the BNP, persist beyond the first few years.[4] At a time when levels of civic participation are lower than they have been in several decades, the BNP is somewhat of an anomaly in organizational terms.[5]

However, as I think the story of Beltway shows, the BNP is far from anomalous in terms of its raison d'être or for what it is trying to do. The desire to keep one's neighborhood free of crime is one that is shared by citizens across class, race, and national boundaries. Few people would dissent from this basic aspiration, but for many it remains just that, an aspiration that most people do not act upon. Some citizens shun inaction or free ridership and actually attempt to actively keep their communities safe and crime-free. While this action can take many forms, it is important that we understand it not only as an intellectual exercise, but also as a way to examine how ordinary citizens try to keep crime and disorder at bay.

Beltway: A Story of Change

The following story is an account of just one neighborhood and its struggles to control crime and disorder. It is not simply the story of the BNP; the narrative itself begins a full three years before the BNP was formed. Rather, this book is about how the citizens of a typical neighborhood respond to crime and disorder. Beltway, while not typically a law-and-order community, has, over the five years I've studied it, succumbed to challenges and tragedies and to moral panics about youth violence that erupted and fizzled out before any lasting change could take place. In essence, this is a story of change, as Beltway went from a neighborhood that was immune to the violence that was commonplace in many Chicago communities to a place where the worst could happen. The story of change is not simply about the emergence of a gang problem in Beltway but about the changing social conditions that led to this development. Moreover, change in Beltway encompassed the response to the gang problem, and this work charts the difficulties residents faced trying to rebuild social control in their neighborhood.

I explain the change that has altered both Beltway's ability to control youth and the shape and configuration of its response to the Powell-Harvey murders in terms of the factors that have impacted community-level or parochial social control. I argue that what led to the gang problem is the diminishing ability of family and community to enact effective social control, in the traditional sense of collectively supervising local teens and intervening when trouble occurs. So, too, the community response to gangs and crime must be mindful of the changes that have rendered traditional controls toothless and find new ways to efficaciously control crime and disorder. I call this new, hybrid form of community social control "the new parochialism," and in what follows I draw on five years of work, from 1993 through 1998, to illustrate the conditions under which this new parochialism emerges. Further, I assess the implications of the new parochialism for how we think and talk about community control of crime and disorder. Before summarizing the contents of the chapters that follow, I think it is important to flesh out my concept of the new parochialism and to elaborate what I mean by informal social control.

Crime, Informal Social Control, and the New Parochialism

Crime is an inescapable part of life in many American cities, but most people would rather not live under these conditions. Circumstances vary from place to place, but nearly everyone shares the desire to live in an area free from crime.[6] This was particularly true in the early 1990s, when I started my work in Beltway, because crime rates at the time, particularly those for youth crime, were peaking, and, in the city of Chicago, youth gangs were very much the folk devils of the time.[7]

However, in 1993, Beltway did not have a great deal of crime generally, and almost no violent crime. Indeed, the neighborhood ranked among the bottom 10 percent of Chicago community areas in terms of violent crime rates, as it also does today. Over the course of my fieldwork there, however, homegrown youth gangs began to appear, and the neighborhood experienced several gang drive-by shootings, culminating in the double homicide of the two local teenage girls in 1995. All of these events were extreme and atypical for the neighborhood, but crucially they illustrated that Beltway could fall prey to gang crime in its most violent form. The neighborhood reaction to the events of the mid-1990s and the efforts of ordinary Beltwayites to restore order and exert a degree of control in their neighborhood form the basis of this story. I believe that by understanding how informal social control functions in Beltway, or how ordinary citizens act to control crime and disorder, we can learn a great deal about the role and impact of residents in community policing initiatives and, more generally, about civic engagement in an urban neighborhood.

Citizenship is often held up as essential to maintaining order and reinforcing agreed-upon norms and rules of behavior in society. However, often it is left up to the police to keep the peace and enforce the rule of law. The role of police as the primary enforcers of law and order is one that has evolved since the first police force was organized under Sir Robert Peel in London in 1829.[8] The professional or crime-fighting model was the most prevalent type of policing in the late twentieth century in most U.S. cities. In this model, the police react to crime, enforce laws, and arrest suspected wrongdoers. At the center of the professional policing model is the 911 emergency response system, which dispatches police to deal with calls for service.[9] The upshot of the professional model is a diminished role for citizens, as police take on the sole responsibility for fighting crime. Recently, there have been efforts to introduce variants of community policing, which is touted as the counterpoint to the professional model. Community policing aims to involve ordinary citizens directly in day-to-day efforts to reduce crime and disorder. Some advocates of community policing argue that having an increased role for citizens signals a return to the roots of organized policing.[10] One of the basic tenets of the new models of community policing is the idea of empowering ordinary citizens to help police maintain order.[11] In other words, we, as citizens, are entreated to do our bit, to be the "eyes and ears" of the police, and thus to help keep disorder and crime at bay. Whether or not community policing works and whether the police themselves believe the rhetoric of the programs they represent is another issue.[12] What is important is that citizens are told that they are vital cogs in the order maintenance machine, which also implies that ordinary people have a responsibility to engage in activities that contribute to informal controls. Just what people are willing to do to promote the common good is a fundamental question, and one that has attracted a great deal of attention over the past decade.

Perhaps one of the most influential and controversial studies in social science in recent years has been the book *Bowling Alone: The Collapse and Revival of American Community,* by the political scientist Robert Putnam. In this impressive survey of the landscape of civic participation and volunteerism in America, Putnam discusses declining civic engagement in America, and he laments the fact that citizens are not as involved as they were in previous decades in a range of activities, among them informal control of crime and disorder.[13] Putnam draws on a vast array of data culled from national surveys to bolster his thesis that Americans no longer volunteer with the frequency they once did or spend time involved with bridge clubs or civic and community groups. However, Putnam does offer the caveat that, while traditional forms of civic engagement are disappearing, other forms of activism have arisen, and he suggests that this is a heartening development. It is against the backdrop of declining traditional forms of activism and the appearance of new hybrids of activity that the story of informal social control in Beltway takes place.

The term most often used to describe the range of behaviors that ordinary people engage in to keep crime and disorder at bay is "informal social control." Perhaps the best definition of this concept is the one proffered by the sociologist Morris Janowitz when he stated that informal social control is what he calls "collective self-regulation."[14] Put simply, informal social control requires that we, as a group, monitor and regulate one another's behavior in order to preserve order and promote the common good. The collective nature of informal social control is crucial because it underscores the fact that there are agreed-upon rules of behavior and that informal social control works best when it is not simply a case of one person acting to control another's behavior but rather when that person acts for the community as a whole. Some rules are universal, such as prohibitions against crimes against property and person. Other rules and informal norms of behavior have a distinctively local flavor. Such rules and norms, such as the tolerance for loud music or boisterous juveniles, can vary from place to place. Certainly, it is the individual citizen who enacts informal social control, who pursues strategies that help maintain order, or who enforces norms of civility and curbs unwanted behavior. The person who admonishes the teenager skateboarding in the store, the neighbor who watches your house while you are on vacation, the resident who intervenes in a street fight, the woman who sits on her stoop and watches over the small children playing in the street are all practitioners of informal social control. These activities are numerous, but all are distinguished by the fact that they are performed by the ordinary citizen, the man from down the block, the woman from across the street, and it is these acts, which on the surface may seem inconsequential, that are, in fact, the bedrock of community responses to crime and disorder.

Informal social control is important because it is a barometer of neighborhood health. The ability to solve our own problems without having to contact the police or government officials is indicative of how effective and efficacious a neighborhood can be.[15] The converse, where a community cannot control deviant behavior or does so with great difficulty, illustrates one of the basic problems of many urban neighborhoods, one that is exacerbated by the changing nature of the drug trade and the crime and violence associated with that change.[16] Increasing our knowledge of informal social control may help us gain an insight into how these behaviors may be stimulated in areas where they are absent or waning. Moreover, examining informal social control can tell us whether the process is all that it is cracked up to be. After all, simply theorizing that it is good for citizens to informally control crime and disorder glosses over the possibility that what may pass for informal social control may in fact be a persecution of those who are different from the majority. For example, the assaults on Arab Americans, Muslims, and even Sikhs in various parts of the United States in the wake of the September 11, 2001, attacks on the World Trade Center and the Pentagon illustrate the dark underside of informal social control.[17]

The story of Beltway helps us understand how ordinary citizens in an ordinary neighborhood work to keep crime and disorder at bay. In writing about the events, the trials and tribulations, of the five years I spent there, I depict informal social control as an active living process. By doing so, I explain how self-regulation works, and I illustrate the critical role that local residents play in controlling crime and reducing disorder.

There is considerable variation from neighborhood to neighborhood in terms of the capacity to solve problems of crime and disorder. It would be a mistake to assume that every place is equally efficacious, and there are many factors that constrain individual and collective abilities to engage in informal social control. For example, the question of whether working people have the time to engage in activities that reduce crime and disorder in their communities is particularly pertinent. And if they don't have the time, what happens? Do residents who have more time on their hands step in and make up the deficit in terms of activities to reduce crime and disorder? What are the consequences of decreased levels of informal social control? And, importantly, what does the future hold for this most important of tasks? It is interesting that the current push to involve people in the informal control of crime and disorder, mainly through community policing initiatives, is occurring at the same time that demands on families' time and resources are arguably at their zenith.[18]

The Beltway case study offers a detailed picture of how neighborhood residents engage in self-regulation, and it illustrates what makes for effective social control generally at the neighborhood level. This ethnography adds to our theoretical knowledge of informal social control and suggests avenues for further empirical investigation. In this regard, the extended case method employed here addresses the issue of generalization by using what the sociologist Michael Burawoy calls a "genetic" explanation of particular outcomes.[19] Burawoy argues that the extended case method can derive generalizations by reconstructing existing theory, which it does by investigating the implications of the case study for society, thereby uncovering how the local situation is affected by wider societal processes. Crucially, the extended case method tests and refines theory by working "outward and upward to identify the contexts relevant to understanding that case."[20] Beltway is a single case, but the problems that Beltway residents face are widespread. The story of informal social control in Beltway can tell us a great deal about the process generally, and at this crucial time for middle- and working-class America, it can provide an illustration of what this one fairly typical neighborhood does to control crime and disorder.

Levels of Control and the New Parochialism

The sociologist Al Hunter provides perhaps the most useful way to examine informal social control at the neighborhood level.[21] Hunter proposes that we visualize how people engage in self-regulation in terms of an interplay among three distinct levels of control, what he calls the private, the parochial, and the public. For Hunter, the private level of control is grounded in intimate primary groups such as family and friends. The parochial level refers to relationships among neighbors and is based in broader local networks and institutions, such as stores, schools, churches, and voluntary organizations. The public level of control focuses on the ability of the community to secure goods and services from sources outside the neighborhood, such as the city and the police department.[22] In terms of Hunter's model, effective control at the neighborhood level requires that all three levels articulate with one another. Interestingly, I found that Beltway residents engaged in effective strategies of informal social control when all three levels of control were not working perfectly together, a finding that prompts a reassessment of Hunter's schema.

Specifically, I think that what explains this finding is what I call a "new parochialism," in which diminished private and traditionally parochial forms of social control are replaced by a set of behaviors that combines parochial and public controls. For instance, instead of providing supervision and direct physical intervention in disputes, which are private and traditionally parochial forms of control, Beltway residents engage in behaviors that are more secure and that are facilitated by actors from the public sphere of control. For example, the actions of the neighborhood problem-solving group, described in chapter 6, that used the local politicians and city bureaucracy to close down a tavern that was notorious for creating crime and disorder illustrates this new parochialism. Residents who engage in these actions want to control crime and disorder, but they also fear repercussions from their personal involvement. Beltway residents want to engage in secure activism, and while Beltway does not have a high crime rate compared to other neighborhoods in Chicago,[23] many residents there are afraid to involve themselves directly in informal social control.[24]

The new parochialism, then, is that set of practices that creates solutions at the parochial level but that owes its existence and its efficacy to the intervention of institutions and groups from outside the neighborhood. Beltway residents are not closely tied to one another, and this may be one of the reasons that traditionally parochial forms of control—collective supervision of neighborhood children and intervention in disputes, for example—are rare. However, while people who are not closely tied may not supervise or intervene, they may engage in other behaviors designed to help them live in an area free from crime.[25] In fact, the dearth of close ties may be partly responsible for some residents' fear of reprisals if they get personally involved in informal social control. Involvement in a neighborhood organization offers a solution for those residents who want to be civically engaged but who would prefer to do so as part of a group, not as individuals. The new type of parochial control is certainly more formal than the hand-to-hand immediacy of collective supervision and intervention. Beltway residents have a buffer between themselves and young people.[26] They can call 911 to report miscreant teens, they can monitor local wrongdoers through a court advocacy program, and they can involve the Liquor Commissioner when they have a problem with a local tavern. The new parochialism thus allows for a more formalized and, for some residents, a more secure type of activism.

Why is this a *new* parochialism? It is certainly accurate to say that residents in neighborhoods that resemble Beltway, especially white ethnic communities in Chicago, have always used ties to the public sphere to solve their problems. However, the partnerships in Beltway between parochial and public agents of control are formed specifically to enable Beltwayites to engage in self-regulation, a process that by its very nature has always been internal to the neighborhood. It is not as if Beltway residents have outsourced the control of crime and disorder; rather, a new hybrid organization for self-regulation has arisen in response to local, citywide, and national changes.

Later, I explain how the confluence of increasing rates of labor force participation among women, rising rates of youth crime and fear of youth gangs, changing neighborhoods, and a new brand of policing provide the backdrop against which the new parochialism emerges. Certainly, in Beltway, the Powell-Harvey murders were the immediate stimulus for action, but the particular brand of action was formed and shaped by the wider social and historical context. The new parochialism is hastened by developments that render what we have traditionally known as parochial control difficult to enact. If people are not around to supervise or are afraid to intervene because they fear teens or don't really know their neighbors, then the new parochialism is a viable and attractive option in terms of informal social control. In the chapters that follow, I detail a number of case studies, some of which illustrate how the new parochialism functions to support successful informal social control efforts.

The Organization of the Book

In chapter 2, I describe the Beltway neighborhood, using the most recent census data. I also give a brief overview of the history of the area and of the study itself. Chapter 3 profiles the state of organization in Beltway and presents two case studies of civic engagement in action. The activism surrounding the opposition to the Chestnut Court condominium development and the campaign to oust the Hastings Local School Council[27] illustrate what was possible for Beltway residents to achieve for the neighborhood generally and, more important, the resources upon which they could call. Chapter 4 focuses on the first signs of a serious gang problem in the neighborhood, particularly the drive-by shooting of a local gang member, in April 1994, and on the subsequent neighborhood reaction. I profile three separate responses to the drive-by, none of which achieved its goals or endured, and I speculate as to what factors prevented these strategies from achieving success. Chapter 5 describes the events surrounding the Powell-Harvey murders, in December 1995, and I detail the reaction to the tragedy. Here I illustrate the difficulty that Beltway has in coming to terms with the deaths and in beginning to reinvigorate informal social control. Last, in this chapter I explain the circumstances that led to the Powell-Harvey murders in terms of the diminished levels of private and traditionally parochial controls in the neighborhood. Chapter 6 traces the formation of the Beltway problem-solving group and the Beltway Night Patrol neighborhood watch group and describes their ongoing activism in the neighborhood. I show how the intervention of formal control agents was crucial in providing the necessary resources and linkages that maximize the chances for success in the group's campaigns to shut down a local tavern and to tackle the graffiti problem. In essence, this chapter showcases the new parochial strategies in action and indicates how they come about. Chapter 7 summarizes the main findings of the Beltway case study and suggests how the Beltway case has application beyond its specific context. Specifically, I argue that there are examples of new parochial control in other neighborhoods and cities, and I assess the contribution of this work and suggest areas for future research.

2

Welcome to Beltway

As you drive west through the neighborhoods that make up the city of Chicago, along the bustling thoroughfares that traverse the city north and south of the central Loop area, you cannot but be struck by the sheer variety of the areas you pass through. Some neighborhoods are so-called ghetto areas marked by scarred landscapes, where decades of blight have ravaged once-proud settlements. Buildings are in disrepair, businesses are abandoned, and broken glass litters the ground. Other neighborhoods seem to be in transition; they are ethnically or racially turning over, and they exhibit the hallmarks of such change, a plethora of for-sale signs, and, in some neighborhoods, stores that become *carnicerias*[1] almost overnight. Still other neighborhoods seem the epitome of working- and middle-class stability and respectability; in these areas, well-maintained Chicago bungalows stand on pristine green lots, and order abounds. Given this diversity of neighborhoods, if you were charged with choosing one to tell a story about how citizens in a community work to prevent crime, maintain order, and exert social control, you would perhaps choose one of the ghetto neighborhoods, or even a neighborhood in transition, because here the signs of crime and disorder flourish. The odds are that you would not choose a neighborhood that *seems* the epitome of stability. Surely you would learn nothing about crime, disorder, and social control by spending time in such a neighborhood. However, that is precisely what I did, spending five years doing research in Beltway, a typical working- and lower middle-class neighborhood at the edge of the city.

If you did not have a reason to go to Beltway, you might never spend any time there. You might pass close by, but you wouldn't go there. Acquaintances of mine who know of my work in Beltway express vague familiarity with the area. They nod and say that, sure, they know the kind of place it is, and they do, in a general sense. They may never have been to Beltway, but they have been to many other places like Beltway, and they may even have grown up in a similar neighborhood. Many of us have spent time in neighborhoods that could pass for a Beltway. These areas are stable, and generally are good places to raise children; many people own their homes and work hard for a living, crime is mostly confined to petty burglaries, and disorder is almost nonexistent. The fact that Beltway is inhabited predominantly by whites comes as no great surprise. The majority of neighborhoods like Beltway are white, but there are also African American Beltways whose residents have more in common with their white counterparts than either may like to admit. And, increasingly, there are Latino Beltways as second- and third-generation immigrants become upwardly mobile and move away from neighborhoods that served as ports of entry for their parents or grandparents.[2] In all of the neighborhoods like Beltway, residents face the same problems: maintaining their social position, making ends meet, and, if they have children, making sure that they grow up right.

As much as there is common ground shared by the various Beltwayesque neighborhoods across America, there is also the distinctiveness of the local neighborhood. A native Chicagoan called Vinny, from whom I bought a loveseat, once told me that the only way to understand Chicago was to appreciate the uniqueness of each neighborhood. Chicago is not alone in having vibrant, identifiable neighborhoods, each with its own story to tell, and certainly Vinny's insight would not rock the foundations of the sociological community. But, like most astute observations, its profound nature is masked by its simplicity. Specifically, as I sit down to write about the history and place of Beltway in the metropolitan landscape of Chicago, I am reminded of Vinny's maxim. But neighborhoods do not develop in a vacuum, either. Even distinctive neighborhoods that have storied histories and vibrant local culture and tradition are shaped by outside forces. Laws and ordinances are passed in Congress, state capitals, or city halls, the economy booms and slumps, wars are fought, crime rates rise and fall, and people move in and out. It is no small wonder that neighborhoods can retain an identifiable character in the face of such fluid influences, but they do.

Any person who wishes to portray life in an urban neighborhood must describe the distinctiveness of that place, while at the same time noting the wider forces that have shaped the area. This is what I hope to do while describing the Chicago neighborhood of Beltway. Beltway is an identifiable Chicago neighborhood, one that has been part of the city for the better

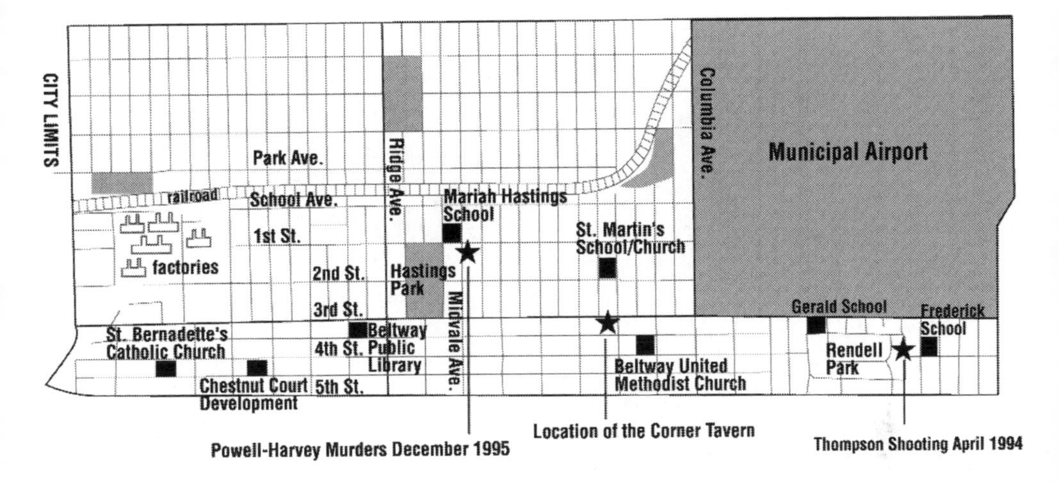

MAP OF BELTWAY

part of the past century, and the Beltway of the 1990s, where I spent five years researching this story, was the product of a distinctive set of sociohistorical forces.

A Short History of Beltway

Beltway is situated at the edge of Chicago, and its location marks it out as an "almost suburb." Indeed the physical layout of the neighborhood, long blocks made up of dispersed, low-rise, single-family homes, more resembles a suburb than it does that of the teeming streets of a city neighborhood. While it does possess some of the characteristics of the typical suburb, Beltway predates many American suburbs, and it owes its initial existence not to post–World War II changes and the age of the automobile but to the economic expansion of the late nineteenth century.[3] Beltway was officially incorporated as a village in 1912 and was annexed to the city of Chicago in 1915.[4] The community was initially a small settlement based largely around the railroad clearing yards to the south of the neighborhood. Beltway's present boundaries reflect further additions of land in 1917 and 1923, at which time most of the land that houses the current population was undeveloped prairie. The first Beltway residents were mainly European immigrants who came to work initially in the railyards and later in the factories that were built by the Beltway Industrial District after the railyards were sold in 1912.

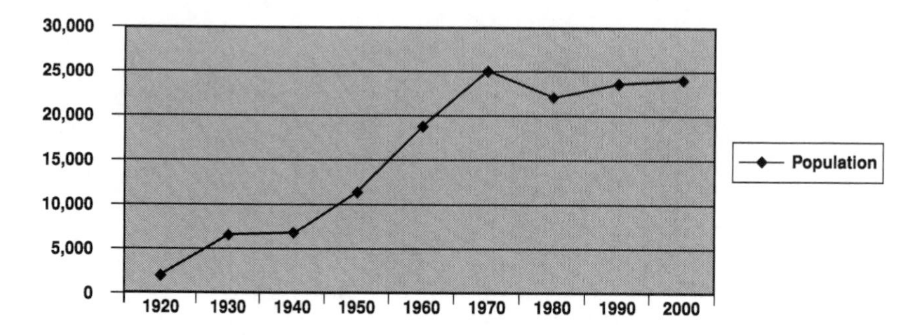

Figure 2.1. Population Changes in Beltway, 1920–2000.

The changes wrought by development in the 1920s influenced Beltway for decades to come. Following on the heels of the establishment of the Beltway Industrial District (BID), Municipal Airport was opened in the 1920s, and, as jobs in the area became more plentiful, the population almost tripled, from about 2,000 in 1920 to almost 6,000 in 1930 (see figure 2.1). As more people settled in Beltway, there was a construction boom, and the infrastructure of the neighborhood improved as roads were paved and amenities provided. The Great Depression did impact Beltway, but, by and large, the industry that was the lifeblood of the area survived. Moreover, the BID served as the economic anchor of the neighborhood during this period, on one occasion bailing out the local bank by preventing a run on its assets. The Depression years saw little population increase in the neighborhood, and, while the neighborhood escaped the worst of the ravages of the period, some things had changed by the end of the 1930s. For example, the number of multifamily housing units tripled in this decade, and renters outnumbered homeowners by 1940.

A second major economic expansion in Beltway occurred around the war years. The existing industry grew in this part of Chicago, as factories labored to supply the war effort. Residential construction in Beltway increased as a result of this industrial growth. Municipal Airport, which had grown steadily during the 1930s, assumed great importance during and after the war, growing to be reputedly the busiest airport in the world in the late 1940s. At this time, the population of the neighborhood was still solidly blue-collar, with the majority of the workforce employed in manual occupations. The 1940s saw the population of the neighborhood almost double to close to 11,000 people, and, as returning local GIs, along with many others who came to work in the factories, settled in the area, the land in the western part of the community was built up in a systematic fashion. The loan guarantees of the GI Bill helped fuel this expansion of Beltway, and the number of houses in the neighborhood almost doubled in the 1940s. By 1950, homeowners outnumbered renters two to one, reflecting the dramatic change of this decade.

The rapid pace of development in Beltway continued in the 1950s, and the population almost doubled again between 1950 and 1960, when it approached 19,000. The number of houses also doubled, and homeowners outnumbered renters four to one by 1960. More than half of all the houses in Beltway today were built in the 1950s and 1960s. At this time, there was also some noticeable change in residents' education levels and in what they did for a living. The people who were settling in Beltway in the 1950s were more educated than their predecessors, and they were also more likely to have white-collar jobs. Slowly the neighborhood was changing from a predominantly blue-collar community to one where workers with blue and white collars lived side by side (see figure 2.2 for a comparison of blue- and white-collar employment trends over time).

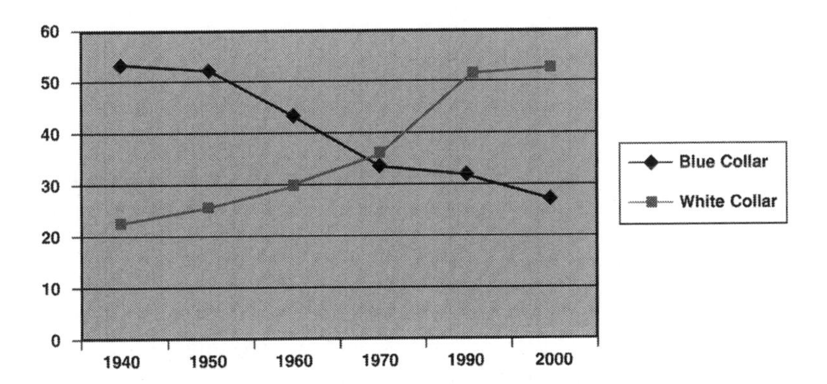

Figure 2.2. Comparison of the Percent of Blue-Collar and White-Collar Workers in Beltway, 1940–2000.

In the 1960s, the neighborhood saw continued growth in population and in the construction of new houses. Population grew by a third to close to 25,000 in 1970, while the number of houses also increased. Beltway was finally stabilizing after decades of expansion and change, and the U.S. Census for 1970 indicates that almost two-thirds of Beltway residents had lived in the same house for five or more years. It was at this time that patterns of activism and the discourses Beltway residents used to explain the world also seemed to solidify.

The Beltway residents who formed the Beltway Civic League (BCL) in 1960 were for the most part first-generation homeowners intent on preserving home and community. These bootstrap Chicagoans had moved to Beltway from old working-class neighborhoods that had served as ports of entry for their parents and grandparents. The movement of these whites to Beltway was part push and part pull. Some Beltway residents had fled neighborhoods that were changing racially as the African American population expanded beyond the historical boundaries of the Black Belt,[5] while others were attracted to Beltway because there they could own their own stand-alone home. Whether it was flight or a step up that brought people to Beltway, they shared a common aim of building and maintaining a strong community. A trawl through the archives of the BCL from the 1960s illustrates some of the preoccupations of the time.

Possibly the two biggest issues that the BCL tackled in its first decade as an organization were a zoning proposal and a plan at the state level to integrate housing. The zoning issue that concerned the BCL centered on a proposal to locate new factories in proximity to housing in the neighborhood, which residents said would endanger their children because of the increased volume in traffic. The BCL organized a series of protests, including one at a zoning meeting in downtown Chicago, to underscore its opposition to the new construction. Several hundred residents were involved in this demonstration of "people power," and it is the first evidence of issue-centered popular activism in the community.

The 1960s were also a time of racial strife in Chicago, epitomized by Martin Luther King's march on Marquette Park. Coming on the heels of school desegregation, and at a time when many neighborhoods in Chicago had gone from having a majority white population to having a majority African American population, sometimes in less than a decade, race relations in the city were volatile. Many whites resented the changes they experienced, some firsthand, in the neighborhoods where they had grown up, and many were fearful that such change could happen in their new communities.[6] Beltway's whites were no less fearful, and when the Illinois House of Representatives proposed a plan for integrated housing, in 1965, the BCL sent representatives to testify in Springfield against the bill. A local newspaper report from June 1965 quotes the testimony of Ethel Burkard, a BCL member, who said,

> I am speaking for all the people in our community that are on the same level as myself. We are afraid of such laws as HB257 and any other housing bill that may be passed. We worked hard for a place in our community and society. We worked to earn our property, constitution, and civil rights, as well as to belong to a circle in society of our own choosing.

Integrated housing did not come to Beltway, but the issue and the way that it was framed crystallize some of the themes and preoccupations that have persisted to the present day. The BCL was also active in opposing the busing of African American children to area schools, and the integration of the public schools in the area was not a smooth process. In the early 1970s, there were a number of race riots at Carver Heights High School (which serves the Beltway area), and many residents vowed that they would not send their children to the school.

Overall, the 1970s and 1980s were decades of stability for Beltway. After increasing for sixty years, the number of residents actually declined to about 22,000 by 1990. The postwar building boom subsided, and the only new structures being built were new blocks of condominiums (figure 2.3 illustrates the number of housing units in Beltway over time). Most residents owned their homes, and many had lived in the same house for more than five years. A hint of change did occur in the 1980s when a Latino population began to settle in Beltway. By 1990, Latinos accounted for about a tenth of the Beltway population, by the 2000 Census, the proportion of Latinos in the neighborhood had doubled, and Latinos represented a fifth of all residents. By and large, the Beltway Latinos are second- and third-generation Mexican Americans, the vast majority of whom speak English "very well"[7] and for whom Beltway, as for the white ethnics that moved there several decades before, is a step-up neighbor-

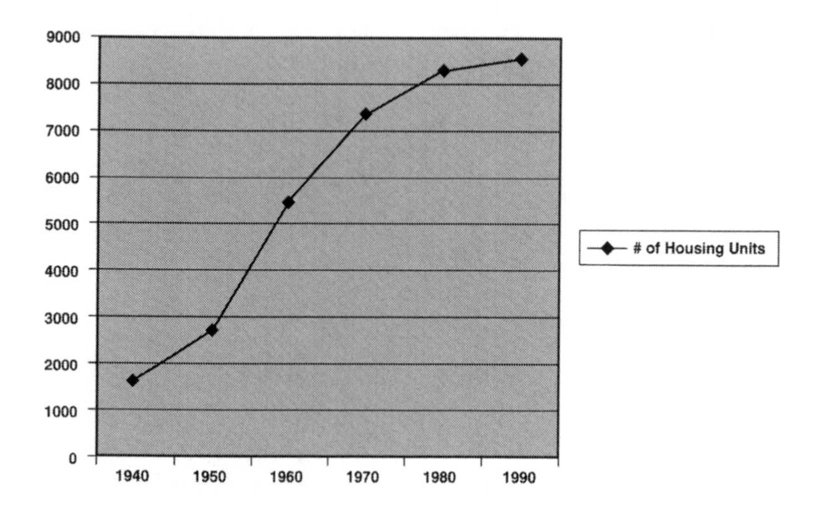

Figure 2.3. Number of Housing Units in Beltway, 1940–1990.

hood. Latinos in Beltway are as educated as their white counterparts; they own their own homes, and some get involved in neighborhood institutions.[8]

Beltway workers, who have historically depended on the nearby factories for work, are now in predominantly white-collar occupations. In 2000, more than one-third of the workforce had "Sales/Office" occupations; a little less than a fifth were in "Service" employment; and slightly more than 20 percent were in "Managerial/Professional" positions. Blue-collar occupations accounted for only a quarter of all occupations (figure 2.2). In terms of earnings, the median household income in the neighborhood was approximately $45,000, which is similar to that for the city of Chicago as a whole; with respect to poverty, about one in fourteen residents in Beltway lives below the poverty line. Many Beltway residents are employed by the City of Chicago, which has an ordinance that prohibits city workers (for example, people who work at City Hall, Streets and Sanitation workers, Chicago police officers, Chicago firefighters, and Park District employees) from living outside the city limits. Beltway is thus home to many city employees, especially police officers and firefighters.

The Beltway that I entered in the 1990s had come a long way from the railroad clearing yards of a little over a century ago. It had endured almost a century of growth and expansion and had stabilized into a place where several generations of working white Chicagoans had raised their families. The neighborhood was not standing still, though. If I had learned anything from Vinny and during my time in Chicago, it was that change is an immutable feature of the Chicago landscape, much like Lake Michigan, ever present but unpredictable. So, even armed with all of the information about the history of a place or how many people do what type of work, I found that it is hard to really take the pulse of a neighborhood without spending time there and, most important, getting to know its people.

The Beltway Study

How I came to tell the story of informal social control in Beltway is, like all good tales from the field, not entirely straightforward.[9] Indeed, my research in Beltway did not begin as a study of informal social control. The work was initially part of a larger comparative study of four neighborhoods in Chicago. The Comparative Neighborhood Study (CNS) was directed by the sociologists William Julius Wilson and Richard P. Taub, at the University of Chicago. The CNS focused on four working-class and lower-middle-class neighborhoods in Chicago: Archer Park, a predominantly Mexican community; Beltway, a white neighborhood; Dover, a neighborhood in transition from white to Mexican; and Groveland, an African American neighborhood. The CNS set out to study the social organization of each neighborhood, with an emphasis on the role of race, racial discourse, and culture. The neighborhoods were chosen on the basis of their ethnic and racial profile, their income level, and, after extensive periods of reconnaissance, their general level of activity.[10] I was hired to conduct some of the initial reconnaissance work on white middle-class neighborhoods, and, after narrowing the field down to two possible candidates, Wilson and Taub chose Beltway as the white middle-class neighborhood to be studied. I began research for the CNS in Beltway in the summer of 1993 and continued working there until the summer of 1998, even though the CNS research was completed by September 1995.

I like to think that this work in some ways continues the great tradition of the Chicago School ethnographies, although the first part of the research was conceived in a slightly different fashion.[11] While the first two years of work were directed at answering a specific set of questions for the comparative study, we were not restricted to doing fieldwork with a narrow focus. Our goal was to immerse ourselves in neighborhood life and to see how a neighborhood lives and breathes. Within this context, we were to find out how people spoke and felt about race and how this played out in public forums. In many ways, this project harkened back to the golden era of Chicago School ethnography, when Robert Park sent his students out to become, in the words of the historian Fred Matthews, "reporters in-depth" so as to thoroughly document the social processes they encountered.[12] The main point of departure is that our study was a comparative piece that attempted to link the disparate contexts of four neighborhoods. To facilitate this linking process, the CNS held biweekly field meetings for the four research teams, and each researcher read the fieldnotes from each neighborhood. Together the researchers discussed the themes that were emerging from the fieldwork. This reflexive approach helped shape the CNS research as much if not more than the initial guiding questions, and this approach allowed themes and new questions to emerge from the field research. At the conclusion of the CNS, I decided to remain in Beltway to study how people attempt to control crime and disorder, which had emerged as a theme during the CNS research. At the time, I felt that I did not have enough data to really tell the story, and I decided to make up for this deficit by concentrating specifically on activities, strategies, and narratives surrounding informal social control.

The second phase of my research, which lasted three years, was more directed than the first two years of study in that I had narrowed my focus; in this sense, this study more closely resembles the early Chicago School ethnographies than the CNS. My work emulates the Chicago School in that I illustrate the process of informal social control as it reveals itself over time in this one neighborhood. Informal social control is not a property that is present or absent in an absolute sense; rather, it is a complex process that can wax and wane over time, and my goal in this work is to chart this complexity. The difficulty, however, with trying to capture a process is that the researcher must be sufficiently intimate with the site to be able to depict the object of study, in this case informal social control.

The two years of the CNS research enabled me to get to know the neighborhood and its residents, to establish myself in the field, and to build the trust and friendships that are stock in trade for the ethnographer. I tried at all times to maintain a critical distance from the neighborhood, as it is all too easy for ethnographers to get too involved in the neighborhoods they study; the phrase the discipline has for this is "going native." At the same time, I tried to integrate myself as best I could into the neighborhood to better report on the events described here.

I can truly say that the people in Beltway gave me red-carpet treatment, and they were, with only two small exceptions, truly welcoming. I immediately was made to feel comfortable and that no question was too inane. The Beltwayites to whom I spoke were aware at all times that I was doing research, and all interviews were undertaken with the full consent of the interviewee. I have no idea what people thought of me, but I assume that many were bemused at "the Irishman writing the book about us," as one resident succinctly put it. After the first two months of fieldwork, Maria Kefalas was hired to work alongside me in Beltway. Maria was originally trained as an economist and graduated from Wellesley College in 1989. She came to study sociology at the University of Chicago in 1992, and her avid interest in urban neighborhoods led her to work on the CNS project. The CNS principal investigators felt that, if possible, each neighborhood should have male and female researchers. I consider myself extraordinarily fortunate to have had the opportunity to work alongside Maria Kefalas, whose keen ethnographic instincts and gift for enabling people to give voice to their concerns, hopes, and fears informs my work as much as it does her own.[13]

The strategy of having a female-male research team helped overcome the very real problem of access to gender-specific arenas. I was not explicitly prohibited from playing bunco with the dozen or so Beltway women who convene each month in one of their houses to chat, throw dice, and just hang out.[14] If I had decided to attend the "bunco squad" gatherings, I believe my presence would have made the women slightly uncomfortable and more self-conscious and thus would have affected the natural balance of the setting. In any case, they would probably have wondered what kind of man I was to want to play dice with a bunch of women in the first place. So, too, I cannot imagine Maria faring any better at the male counterpart—watching a pay-per-view prizefight or a having a few beers watching the Bulls in a local tavern. I know that the time Maria spent with the women of Beltway facilitated my own work with them, and I hope that my work with the men achieved the same for her. It should be said that we were not confined to gender-specific arenas; in reality, I spent more time talking with women over the five years than men. Rather, it was the fact that we could access our respective gender inner sancta that helped our work significantly. That Maria and I were married a year into the fieldwork also helped in that we were not simply a research team but a married couple. This helped us relate to people not just as researchers but as a couple, and it made us also seem less threatening. Perhaps the best illustration of our changed role after our marriage was the fact that some of the more mischievous members of the Beltway Civic League decided that they could now tell us dirty jokes.

Every person that took time out of his her life to speak with me has contributed in some way to this work, and my understanding and depiction of the neighborhood are dependent on its residents' candor and openness. My five years in Beltway were enjoyable, frustrating, challenging, and fruitful. At times I felt that I could never really get a handle on what I was trying to capture and that unless I suddenly became omnipresent I could never really illustrate the process by which self-regulation takes place. Other times, I felt that I was getting so much information so quickly it was tantamount to using a straw to sip from a fire hydrant. It was very difficult for me to stop collecting information and start telling the story. After leaving Chicago, in the summer of 1998, to start my first job as an academic, in Philadelphia, I returned to Beltway in the summer of 1999 to complete some more interviews. Moreover, part of me would like to do even more research there. In the end, however, the wisdom of Gerry Suttles, a gifted ethnographer and sage teacher, prevailed. Suttles always told his students that if you don't think you have enough data, you probably have too much. In the thousands of hours of fieldwork and almost one hundred in-depth interviews and many newsletters, newspaper clippings, and documents I have amassed, there is more than enough material to discuss what people do to control crime and disorder. Perhaps the local librarian, Lydia Donovan, was right, after all. The first time that we met Lydia and told her we were going to do a study of Beltway, she joked that there was enough material in the neighborhood for several volumes. For now, I content myself with trying to tell this one story of how Beltway residents control crime and disorder, and, as with any work of this sort, I am solely responsible for the interpretation and analysis that follow. I try assiduously to remain faithful to my sources, and I fervently hope that Beltway residents and people who live in all the other places like Beltway can pick up this book and see themselves in it.

3

Getting Things Done

Civic Engagement in Action

Introduction

This chapter attempts to set the scene for a larger discussion of informal social control by surveying the community activism landscape in Beltway. Informal social control cannot take place without community engagement, and it is worthwhile to assess the community health of Beltway in the early 1990s. For the most part, as I illustrate, Beltway at the time was a place where issue-driven community activism happened episodically. The two cases that I detail, and the contrasting personalities that came to embody the respective concerns, reveal how successful community activism happens, while at the same time indicating some necessary and sufficient conditions for the new parochial strategies of informal control.

Community activism often needs a champion, someone to lead and personify a cause. Both examples here have such people, and they offer a useful contrast in terms of personality and levels of involvement in community affairs. Barbara Cremaldi is a soft-spoken mother of three who lives in the western part of Beltway. She is a stay-at-home mom, and, being quite reserved, is not what you might typically call a community activist. Jane Pratt looks and sounds more like an activist. She has a busy style, is constantly on the go, and is a regular contributor to public meetings in the neighborhood. Jane knows that sometimes to get things done for your neighborhood you have to go to meetings, organize petitions, muster support, and be prepared to slog it out with administrators, politicians, and bureaucrats. In terms of the archetypal activist, then, Barbara and Jane are different. Despite the contrast, the two women have a great deal in common. Both are mothers of young children and, as such, are emotionally invested in making sure that Beltway and its institutions serve the community well. Both women are passionate about the causes they believe in, and both are willing to go the extra mile in pursuit of their goals. The stories of their personal crusades to get things done in Beltway can tell us a great deal about the neighborhood in the 1990s, and these narratives serve as a backdrop for the story of crime and its control.

Successful grassroots activism is rare without assistance from established institutions and individuals who can parlay people power into a positive outcome. With this in mind, it is useful to take an inventory of what kinds of institutional support were available to activists in Beltway in the early 1990s.

Organizations in Beltway

I have alluded earlier to the fact that Beltway is replete with organizations and is well served by local politicians. The people in the neighborhood can take advantage of ties to two aldermen and their ward organizations, as well as area residents who are city workers in the police department, municipal services, fire department, or park district. In addition, at the time, a U.S. congressman lived nearby and served as one of the ward's Democratic committeemen.[1] Also in the early 1990s, the other ward committeeman was acknowledged as one of the most powerful men in Illinois state politics. Community activists often call on the assistance of aldermen, a friend in the police department, or congressmen for support with a project. For example, the commander of Police District H, Henry Rusnak, talked about how well the local political machine works and how he utilizes the aldermen in his area in order to get things done:

> Now over in Beltway you have two aldermen, young men, both smart. Now if I have a problem that I need their help getting done, like it would take me for ever to do it through the channels downtown, I just call 'em. Once I have to get some new lights put in at Fairfield Park, there's a lot of gang activity there and they figured that if there were more lights there, [if] it was lit up more at night, then the problem would go away. Now if I call up the electric company department and say that one of my officers has a bright idea [*sic*], they'll just sit on it and do it whenever. Now I call up [Alderman Gaudio] and say: "Can you get this done for me?" He says: "Sure, in about three or four days." And it's done, no fuss. That's the way it should be.

Rusnak's comments demonstrate how it is possible in Beltway to tap into local and citywide political structures. Beltway residents who are skilled in utilizing these formal channels are more likely to be successful in their endeavors.

In addition to the strong ward organizations, residents can avail themselves of the Beltway Civic League (BCL), the Beltway Business Association, the park advisory councils, church groups, the Beltway Public Library, and four local school councils, all of which are active within the neighborhood. The sociologist Robert J. Sampson has suggested that when we examine how neighborhoods socially organize, we should ask for what purpose are they organized?[2] For Sampson, social organization is not simply a laundry list of local civic groups, institutions and politicians but rather what actually gets done in the neighborhood. Social organization is thus constituted by action, and the central questions become who are the activists and what do they do to maintain their communities? The following two case studies illustrate social organization in action in Beltway and foreshadow the later discussion of crime control.

People Power and the Chestnut Courts Condominiums

Early in 1992, the Chicago developer John Murphy drafted a plan to build eighty-four condominiums on a two-acre vacant lot on Fourth Place, in the western part of Beltway.[3] That particular section of the neighborhood is populated by neat rows of Chicago-style bungalows and manicured lawns, all of which are single-family homes. As I noted earlier, condominiums were about the only dwellings being built in Beltway in the 1980s and 1990s, and most of them were located on the southern boundary of the neighborhood, overlooking the factories on Fifth Avenue. The condominiums that had been built attracted a mix of residents, ranging from retirees looking for a smaller, more manageable homestead to single white-collar workers who wanted to purchase their own place but had no need for a larger dwelling.[4] The condominium complexes are, by and large, well maintained, and many occupants play an active role in the wider community. Indeed, many long-time residents of Beltway move into condominiums when they can no longer maintain their houses. These long-time residents are joined there by ethnic whites from neighborhoods near Beltway, and so there is a distinctive cultural congruence between homeowners and condo dwellers. Some condo blocks even become places where new social ties are forged. Kitty Kelly, who owns a condominium, recounts in the following excerpt both the movement of ethnic whites into the condos and how she got to know her neighbors:

> When I first moved here nobody talked to each other, and I came from a neighborhood where we were porch sitters. After ye ate dinner, you'd go out and sit on the porch, talk to your neighbors, and get in their business. And I came here and I sat on the porch and there was nobody out. And then, little by little, the neighborhood changed a little bit, and people from the older neighborhoods [moved in] here. I've always had a dog and they were always talking about the dog, and the next thing I knew all the dog walkers. Pretty soon we'd sit out on a Friday night and have a beer and then somebody who was a non-dog-walker would come along. I know quite a few people on the block. They seem to ring my bell when they have trouble with the police. I'm glad to get to know people and with the block parties [there's an opportunity] to know even more. I like to know who belongs here.

For the most part, then, the condos and their inhabitants are integrated into the landscape of Beltway physically and socially. However, when Murphy proposed his development, he met with unexpected resistance.

Barbara Cremaldi was living across the street from the proposed condo site, and, at the time of the proposal, she had been in her house for eight years. She knew the neighborhood well, having grown up in nearby Carver Heights. Cremaldi and her family have to live in the city of Chicago because her husband, Tom, is a city worker. When the condo proposal first surfaced, she set about organizing opposition because she felt that the development would have a negative effect on the neighborhood. Cremaldi did not oppose condos per se. What she objected to was the location of the development on the part of Fourth Place that was made up exclusively of single-family homes. The logic was that property values could be negatively impacted and that quality of life generally would suffer because of added strains on space, parking, and even water pressure. Cremaldi was not alone in her opposition to the proposed development. Many of her neighbors also had misgivings, and together they decided that they would attempt to get the development stopped. In the waning months of 1993, Cremaldi went to the local alderman, John Puchinski, to enlist his support. Puchinski told her that the developer would have to obtain a zoning permit in order to break ground on the complex. In most parts of Chicago, zoning approval is obtained through the City Council Zoning Board. Alderman Puchinski explains how zoning works and the crucial role that the alderman plays:

> In the city of Chicago if someone wants to change the zoning from manufacturing to commercial or commercial to residential or whatever the case may be, they go directly to the alderman. And the alderman will say yes or no because it goes before the City Council [Zoning Board] and so on. Based on what the alderman wants, the committee votes [that way].

However, in Beltway there is an additional layer of bureaucracy that has to be navigated by anyone wanting to change a zoning designation, namely the local zoning board. The zoning board is an integral part of the local ward council that was set up in Beltway in the early 1970s. The ward council is made up of various local stakeholders, including representatives of the civic league and the business association, and the council works with the alderman to troubleshoot local problems. Puchinski describes it as a "a fact-finding or problem-solving group to help the alderman." Puchinski explains how the local zoning board operates:

> The applicant, before he even goes down town to file anything, will go before my local zoning board. The local zoning board will make their recommendation, and they will hear what the applicant wants to do with his drawings and his statistics on why this is good for the community. The local zoning board will vote it up or down and come back to me, and 99.9 percent of the time I will follow the local zoning board's recommendation downtown, if that applicant chooses to go downtown.

The first encounter between John Murphy and the residents who opposed him would take place at the local zoning board meeting, which was scheduled for March 1994.

Barbara Cremaldi became the de facto organizer of the opposition to the Chestnut Court condos, and she began to collect signatures from residents in the immediate vicinity of the proposed development. More important, Cremaldi knew that she would have to enlist the help of other community groups and individuals who could offer support for her campaign. The first major step that Cremaldi took was to approach the Beltway Civic League for assistance. The BCL has a history of becoming involved with zoning issues; indeed, the stimulus for the formation of the group, in 1960, was a zoning matter. However, in this instance, neighborhood activists were fighting a condominium developer instead of a chemical manufacturer. Even though Cremaldi had not been an active member of the BCL and did not participate in the group before or after the fight with the developer, when she needed the Civic League's political connections and resources, she became a member and attended meetings regularly for several months. Specifically, Cremaldi knew that she would need the support of the BCL representatives on the local zoning board.

At the first BCL meeting she attended, Cremaldi asked to make a statement to the group. She prefaced her comments by proclaiming, "I'm proud to be in this group." Appealing to the common values that the working-class residents of Beltway would recognize and appreciate, Cremaldi went on to explain why the condominium development should be stopped. First and foremost, she argued that the density of the housing project would decrease the property values of the single-family homes in the area. It is no surprise that for working-class Chicagoans, any threat to the value of their homes symbolizes a threat to a lifetime of earnings.[5] Next, Cremaldi went on to claim that the new units would put a strain on the already overtaxed sewage and water systems, an argument that was meant to appeal to Beltwayites' sense of proprietorship over the neighborhood and their concern about the quality of services in the neighborhood. Finally, she concluded by reminding Civic League members that "eighty-four new dwellings means eighty-four dogs," suggesting that more people means more trash, more cars parked on streets, more noise, and more opportunity for decay and disorder. Cremaldi went on to add the disclaimer that while she did not oppose all condominiums in the neighborhood, she believed that multifamily housing should be put out on Fifth Avenue "near the factories" and that the area near Fourth Place should be reserved for single-family homes. At the root of this distinction between single-family homes, or "the bungalows," and multi-unit dwellings is the conviction that multi-unit housing could ease the way for lower-class populations to move into Beltway. Condominiums are mostly owner-occupied just like the single-family homes, but the fact that some are rented out to tenants serves to lend credence to the conviction that multiple-family dwellings are potentially detrimental to the neighborhood.

As Cremaldi spoke at the Civic League meeting, people nodded their heads in agreement. Stable property values, the possible proximity of lower-income populations, the quality of city services, and the specter of disorder and decay, are all profoundly important issues to the white working-class residents of Beltway, and the concerns she had raised clearly resonated with her audience. Indeed, shortly after Barbara Cremaldi's first appearance at the BCL, the local zoning board voted to stop the development, and, soon after, the Chicago City Council also voted down the proposal. Approximately fifty concerned residents attended the meeting of the City Council Zoning Committee to speak out against the condominiums. Barbara Cremaldi commented to the local paper: "We're just elated [the proposal] was turned down. We couldn't afford lawyers or other expensive tactics. All we had was people power. This is a good example of what can be done when the people get together with their alderman and work on something."

Barbara Cremaldi's career as an activist was short-lived but boasted a 100 percent success rate. Though she had no real experience before the Chestnut Court campaign, she quickly learned to utilize the resources at her disposal. One might speculate that the road might not have been so easy for Cremaldi in a neighborhood that is not as well served as Beltway. For example, the fact that there is a local zoning board greatly expedited the mobilization against the condos, but, importantly, Cremaldi and her supporters used the resources available to them to get things done. It is also noteworthy that the group mobilized around a single issue that required a short-term investment of time and energy. If the Chestnut Courts Condominium was a tightly bounded short-term affair, it was in sharp contrast to what was transpiring at the Hastings Elementary School around the same period.

Parents for Hastings and the Hastings Local School Council

I first met Jane Pratt at the conclusion of a stormy Local School Council meeting at the Hastings School in February 1995. At this particular meeting, there was a heated debate over how to spend a one-time safety and security grant. The principal, many of the teachers, and a majority of the parents present at the meeting wanted to use the money for a new door security system to protect the school from unwanted intruders. However, the ruling faction on the Local School Council (LSC) had other ideas and wanted to use the money to have school staff undergo CPR training. When the matter came to a vote, the ruling faction, led by three members of one family, voted for the CPR training, much to the chagrin of the principal and almost everyone else at the meeting.

Jane Pratt had been very vocal at this particular meeting. She stood at the back of the room behind a video camera mounted on a tripod. She later explained that she had to videotape the proceedings at each LSC meeting so that what people said could not be taken out of context or distorted. Though she was initially wary about speaking with me, she later explained that she was always tense on such occasions because the meetings usually degenerated into shouting and finger pointing, which had certainly been the case that night. Jane recounted that her husband was one of the members of the LSC who voted independently, without heeding the self-appointed oligarchy, and she herself was active in trying to restore the vox populi. Clearly we had walked into the middle of a minefield. Over the next several months, we got to know many parents, teachers, and community members who would unite around the issue of the Hastings School LSC and form the group Parents for Hastings (PFH).[6] The activities of PFH provide a second example of getting things done in Beltway.

The PFH was formed in early 1995 because many parents and teachers at the Hastings School felt that their LSC no longer represented the interests of the majority of parents. Ironically, LSCs are the product of a 1988 Illinois school reform bill that attempted to devolve control of local schools from a central bureaucracy and into the hands of teachers, parents, and local community representatives working together as a team. In the case of the Hastings School, control had been devolved, but the LSC was neither a team nor truly representative. From its inception in 1989, the Hastings LSC had been led by Thomas Barker, a local resident and Chicago firefighter, along with a number of his family members and friends. The Hastings LSC Majority, as the group came to be known in the community and local press, constituted a visible power bloc on the council. Thomas Barker, who held the chairmanship of the LSC from 1989 until 1996, had become increasingly dictatorial in style as the years wore on. For example, he had moved to disband the Parent Teacher Council (PTC) despite opposition from the principal, teachers, and other parents.

The Parents for Hastings group formed out of the ashes of the PTC and issued its first newsletter in January 1995. In the first weeks of February 1995, the controversy over the allocation of the $5,000 safety and security grant first surfaced. The PFH supported the proposal for a front door security system, which had the overwhelming support of the teaching staff and of other parents. A stalemate had been reached, and, predictably, when a vote was called for, the Barker faction proposal for CPR training won by six votes to five.

The controversy did not end with the vote at the February meeting of the LSC. There was a flurry of activity by what was fast coalescing as an anti-Barker group. A petition, signed by more than 160 parents, teachers, and community members, asked that the money be spent on a door security system. Despite the groundswell of support against the allocation of the grant for CPR training, the Barker group stood firm on its proposal.

However, the anti-Barker group did not give up. On April 28, 1995, Pam Preston and Denise Pawlikowski staged a "security breach" at the school. Preston asked a teenager who was neither a student nor a community resident to walk into the school and wander around. While he walked past classrooms, lockers, and washrooms, no one spoke to him, accosted him, or asked him for identification. Preston videotaped the incident and gave the tape to the LSC. At the LSC meeting on May 2, 1995, when the tape was shown, parents again urged the LSC to rescind its earlier proposal and to reallocate some of the money for a front door buzzer system. After two votes, the first of which failed due to abstention on the part of the Barker faction, a motion was finally passed to reallocate $1,500 of the original $5,000 for the buzzer system. The anti-Barker group had won its first victory.

The initial core members of the PFH were now joined by a number of other parents and community members who disliked the Barker group's tactics on the LSC and who wanted significant parent input on issues. The PFH had existed for a few months, but as relations between parents and teachers on one side and the LSC majority on the other continued to deteriorate, it began to formally organize as a viable group. Beginning in June 1995, "the LSC Majority," as the Barker faction had now named itself, began placing paid advertisements in the local newspapers telling its version of events. One of the first actions of the PFH in its campaign was to solicit support from others in the neighborhood who were not familiar with the problems at the Hastings School. Pam Preston called Ron Zalinsky, the president of the Beltway Civic League, and asked whether the PFH could deliver a statement to the monthly meeting. Ron Zalinsky agreed, and so Pam Preston and Marie Coombs, a local parent, attended the June 1995 BCL meeting. Marie Coombs addressed the meeting in much the same way that Barbara Cremaldi had done several months earlier. She said,

> Hello, my name is Marie Coombs, and I'm a parent of a child that goes to Hastings Elementary School. Recently you may have read about a number of issues that have been going on at the school. The Local School Council, which is supposed to look after the interests of the school and the community, is being dominated by one group. This group is led by Tom Barker and includes his brother and his sister-in-law. They vote together and have a monopoly over the running of the LSC. Recently, they did not pass the School Improvement Plan, which directly affects our children. As parents, we are concerned that we have no real voice on the LSC. This group always votes together and ignores the wishes of the parents and the teachers. The principal, Mrs. McCreesh, is trying to run the school, and this group of people will not let her do the job she is there for. The group was elected, and according to the LSC bylaws they cannot be removed until the next election. So we came here tonight to ask for your help, your guidance, and your support. We have a petition, which we are going to send to Mayor Daley and to Alderman Romanoski[7] and Alderman Gaudio asking them to do what they can to remove these people from office.

The women then passed around a petition, and some of the BCL members asked questions and offered advice to the women from the PFH. When Coombs finished speaking and answering questions, she received an enthusiastic round of applause.

As the PFH organized, it continued to make connections with other Beltway organizations. It successfully enlisted the help of the BCL and the local aldermen. In all, the group gathered more than 600 names on its petition, but no immediate action was taken to remove the Barker faction members. In August 1995, the PFH organized a picnic for parents, teachers, children, and community members at Hastings Park, which was attended by more than 150 people. The PFH's ties to the school, the BCL, and the local political machines would prove fruitful in the following months. While the PFH was organizing, the council limped from one crisis to another. In late May 1995, the Barker-led majority refused to approve the School Improvement Plan (SIP), which jeopardized the funding status of the school. Eventually, the SIP was passed at a hastily convened LSC meeting that none of the Barker faction attended. The Barker faction continued to place paid advertisements in the local paper berating the administration of principal Laura McCreesh. Specifically, Barker asked for a Board of Education inquiry into alleged misconduct by McCreesh. The Board of Education quickly exonerated McCreesh of any wrongdoing.

Meanwhile, late in August, the PFH began sending letters to Paul Vallas, the newly installed head of the Chicago Public Schools, requesting that he remove the Barker faction from the LSC. Initially, the Board of Education did not want to involve itself in the Hastings matter, as such involvement could be construed as running counter to the spirit of school reform. At the beginning of the 1995–1996 school year, PFH organizers sent a petition with almost 800 names to the Board of Education demanding the dissolution of the Hastings Local School Council. After this, in October 1995, Vallas and ten members of his "management team" actually came to the neighborhood and spoke to residents about the problems at the Hastings School. At the meeting, Vallas joked about the gigantic folder on his desk filled with letters, faxes, and petitions from the neighborhood. While Vallas expressed concern about the situation, initially he was unwilling to disband the council. He explained that he felt that the school was not "in crisis," the only real criterion for action in such a case. However, as many people in the crowd of more than 150 reiterated their demand that the LSC be disbanded, Vallas did vow to investigate the charges made by anti-Barker parents that the group had violated the Open Meetings Act and had been abusing its position. Instead of focusing on the dissolution of the LSC, Vallas encouraged the community to use the elections scheduled for April 1996 to make the changes it desired.

The monthly LSC meetings continued to be characterized by acrimony and heated debate. Matters came to a head in January 1996, a month after Teresa Powell and Melissa Harvey had been shot dead outside the school. Both young women had been eighth graders at the school, and their murders were to play a pivotal role in the drama surrounding the Hastings LSC.

In the aftermath of the shootings, Barker and his supporters tried to use the murders to discredit the principal, Laura McCreesh. In a paid advertisement that appeared in the local newspaper, the "LSC Majority" claimed that McCreesh's refusal, at a May 1995 council meeting, to release the names of Hastings students disciplined for gang involvement and drug use had somehow led to the girls' deaths. Soon afterward, Barker and his supporters tried to use the murders to fire McCreesh. Then, at the January 1996 Hastings LSC meeting, Barker called for a vote, in a closed executive session, to remove Laura McCreesh as principal. At the meeting, when Barker tried to announce the council's decision to remove McCreesh, an angry crowd of about 100 people jeered and booed so much that Barker and his supporters were forced to walk out. At one point during the meeting, Barker and one of the parents at the meeting nearly came to blows. Representatives from the school board were in attendance at the January meeting, and an official from Vallas's office spoke to the crowd and assured frustrated residents that Mrs. McCreesh could not be fired without the approval of the Board of Education. The next day, the Board of Education received more than 400 phone calls demanding that the LSC be dissolved. A few days later, on January 24, 1996, accepting the recommendation of investigators from the Board of Education, Paul Vallas deemed the Hastings Local School Council "nonfunctioning" and recommended that the council be disbanded.

The proposed dissolution of the Hastings LSC generated a controversy of its own. Many of the pro-school-reform groups in the Chicago area criticized the move, arguing that such action ran counter to the spirit of school reform. Specifically, they maintained that the central Board of Education should not wield its influence in such a heavyhanded manner. Other stakeholders felt that Vallas had overstepped the bounds of his position by disbanding a duly elected council and viewed the decision as symptom of Vallas's aggressive and autocratic corporate management style.

Due process for the Hastings LSC meant that there had to be a hearing about whether the council was nonfunctioning. The hearing was held at the Board of Education's headquarters on Pershing Road late in February 1996. Many PFH members testified at the hearing about Barker's abuses of power while in charge of the LSC. Jane Powell, the mother of Teresa Powell, one of the murder victims, also testified. Powell spoke out against Barker for placing the advertisement that attempted to blame Laura McCreesh for the shooting. Pale and still visibly shaken by her daughter's death two months earlier, she approached the podium slowly and in a quiet but determined voice said, "I don't need someone on the LSC to find someone to blame for the death of my child. The ads have taken the focus off the fifteen-year-old boy who did this and put it on the principal as if she did it. [Barker] is using my daughter's death as a tool in a fight with Principal McCreesh." The emotionally charged testimony of Powell, along with accusations from parents and teachers from Hastings, combined to seal the fate of the Barker faction. The Board of Education voted unanimously to uphold the decision to disband the Hastings LSC. Though the odds had been stacked against the PFH in its campaign to get the LSC disbanded, it had succeeded, thanks in no small part to the actions of Barker and his cronies. The only task that remained for the PFH was to ensure that Barker and his faction could not be reelected at the upcoming April LSC elections.

The PFH realized that the dissolution of the LSC was truly only half the battle, and it knew that it had to run a successful election campaign to oust Barker, who did have some supporters in the neighborhood. The PFH planned a series of strategy meetings at the house of Jim and Jane Pratt. Jim Pratt was planning to seek reelection, and he was joined on the ticket by five other parents—Pam Preston, Marie Coombs, Tom Lally, Bill Bates, and Jack Johnson, all of whom had been active in the PFH. The PFH felt that it should try to win all the positions on the LSC and, in Pam Preston's words, "start with a clean slate." To achieve a clean sweep, it still needed two community representatives. The PFH had approached the two local aldermen, Bill Romanoski and Anthony Gaudio, for support in the months preceding the dissolution of the council. Initially, Romanoski and Gaudio had refused to criticize Barker and his supporters publicly in order to avoid the appearance of "taking sides." However, after Vallas dissolved the council, he had become a target for Barker and his slanderous leaflets and advertisements. Soon after the advertisements appeared, Vallas asked aldermen Romanoski and Gaudio for their assistance. Romanoski made a brief statement to the local news supporting Vallas's decision to dissolve the council, and he then gave the PFH slate two of his best precinct captains, Tom Nugent and William Krantz, to run for the community representative seats on the Hastings council. The overt intervention by the local political machine was notable for a number of reasons. First, the PFH now had organized political muscle behind its campaign. Second, the PFH was further legitimized in the eyes of community members by having the endorsement of the alderman. Third, the incident illustrates how the various arms of city government are interconnected. Paul Vallas reported directly to Mayor Daley, who runs the Chicago Public Schools, and Alderman Romanoski is part of the Daley coalition at City Hall. Vallas knows that if he asks Romanoski for help, the alderman cannot really refuse.

The PFH was now armed with an organization that pledged to bring out the community vote. It set about making sure that a majority of parents also voted for its candidates. The group continued to hold strategy meetings at the Pratts' house and settled on the moniker PRIDE for its slate of candidates.[8] The PFH sponsored a Candlelight Bowl fundraiser at the nearby Barzini's Bowling Alley. The group campaigned vigorously in the leadup to the election, calling parents and community members and distributing leaflets. The PFH hung posters throughout the neighborhood, painted giant signs and banners for the day of the election, canvassed the neighborhood door to door, spoke to the press, and campaigned at meetings throughout the neighborhood.

In response to the PFH's aggressive grassroots effort in support of the PRIDE candidates, the Barker-led faction retaliated by spending thousands of dollars distributing fliers throughout the neighborhood and placing advertisements in the local newspaper proclaiming itself "the voice for the community." The advertisements attacked Hastings principal Laura McCreesh, the assistant principal, Frank Costello, the PFH and its leadership, the PRIDE candidates, Paul Vallas, and even the commander of the local police district, Henry Rusnak. The PRIDE group decided not to retaliate in the war of words, resolving to concentrate on the election instead. In this respect, the help of both of the local ward organizations (the Hastings School's catchment area spans both wards) was invaluable to the PRIDE candidates. Gaudio's and Romanoski's ward organizations worked the election as if it were an aldermanic race. Both aldermen had their precinct captains canvass the neighborhood and distribute leaflets for the PRIDE slate in the weeks before the campaign, and, on the day of the election, the precinct captains were told to bring in the vote.

The Hastings LSC election, on April 17, was an excellent illustration of the ward machine in action. In the election, parents, teachers, and community members could select up to five candidates to fill eight seats, made up of six parent representatives and two community representatives. The PRIDE slate had eight names; to avoid having people vote for the first five names on the slate, the PFH had a number of different palm cards printed, each with a different combination of candidates. In addition, the precinct captains had been instructing their voters on which five people to vote for, concentrating on those candidates they thought were not that well known in Beltway. Aesthetically, too, the PRIDE slate put a great deal of effort into the election: it used yellow as its color of choice and had been distributing yellow leaflets in the neighborhood for a number of weeks. On the day of the election, there were a number of yellow banners, yellow palm cards, and yellow balloons outside the school, and PRIDE supporters wore yellow t-shirts and baseball hats. Jane Pratt even had her nails manicured in yellow for the occasion. PRIDE also had two Spanish speakers working outside the school, Paul Preston and Jose Rodriguez, who chatted freely with Spanish-speaking parents and community members. The crowning achievement for the PRIDE group and the PFH was the actual mobilization of the vote. The turnout at the Hastings School was officially 1,036, about five times higher than it had been at the previous election. At various points during the day, the line to vote snaked through the gymnasium, where the voting was taking place, out into the street. Tom Nugent continually called the West Ward office, updating officials on the numbers of people voting and, in some cases, asking for precinct captains to get more people out to vote. The Barker faction, by contrast, was notable for its absence for most of the day.

Just after 8:30 P.M. word came that the PRIDE slate had all been overwhelmingly elected. The PRIDE slate had decimated the Barker faction at the polls and had succeeded in distributing votes evenly among its eight candidates. On hearing the result, PRIDE candidates and their supporters danced and sang and cried. Everyone retired to Denise Pawlikowski's house, located just down the street from the school, for a celebration party. The PFH had won a marvelous victory.

Discussion

The upshot of the two case studies outlined here is that each of the activists mentioned at the outset achieved her goals, Barbara Cremaldi with her single-issue coalition and Jane Pratt with the more multidimensional parent group. On the surface, it seems like these examples are textbook illustrations of grassroots activism. Both instances show how it is possible to tap into the local power structure and leverage support. In each case, the civic league and local ward organizations were key players. In such terms, then, these examples of activism in Beltway are comfortably familiar. The sociologist Thomas Guterbock detailed in his study of the Chicago ward system how the organization functions to get things done.[9] More generally, there is a great deal of research on grassroots activism that demonstrates how small groups can achieve their goals by mobilizing the necessary resources.[10] Certainly, the two case studies here illustrate the use of established channels for mobilizing resources in Beltway; at first glance, the examples of the PFH and the mobilization against the Chestnut Courts development seem to contradict the notion of the new parochialism presented in chapter 1. After all, what Barbara Cremaldi and Jane Pratt did was simply use the tried and trusted method of getting things done in a neighborhood like Beltway—they tapped into the local political machine. Cremaldi and Pratt were successful in part because they had an available stock of what sociologists have termed social capital.[11] Social capital exists in the relations between people and can be activated to achieve goals. Social capital is important because it is what inheres in the connection between a person and her political representative, for example, making it possible for a favor to be asked and granted.

In each case, the activists sought assistance both within the neighborhood and outside Beltway. Cremaldi took her grievance to the local alderman and organized her fellow residents to attend the zoning meeting downtown. The PFH case is even more striking in its use of extraneighborhood resources. The PFH activists received crucial support from the Board of Education, partly as a result of their direct appeals and partly as a result of communication from the local aldermen to the board. Securing support and resources from the public sphere is an important underpinning of the new parochialism, and in this respect the Chestnut Courts and the PFH case studies illustrate the channels that existed in Beltway between people and formal organizations.

In another important respect, the case studies also tell us a great deal about the state of community organization in the neighborhood. In both instances, and as I show in the coming chapters, civic activism and participation are limited and reactive. It is not uncommon for people to get involved in grassroots activism simply because they feel strongly about a particular issue. Parents of children in school may get involved for the sake of their son or daughter, as was the case with many of the PFH members. Homeowners may protest when they feel that the value of their property is being threatened. After the LSC election, few of the PFH activists, save for those actually elected to the council, remained as involved as they had been. They had defeated the Barker faction, and so they settled back into their routine. In essence, the need for their continued community service had diminished. Barbara Cremaldi also disappeared from the local scene. While she remained active in her local Roman Catholic parish, she did not attend any BCL meetings after the Chestnut Courts proposal was scuppered.

Overall, voluntary participation is episodic for many Beltway residents. The groups associated with the local schools—the LSCs and the PFH, for example—experience high turnover among their volunteers, which is understandable, as most volunteers are parents of school-going children, and their association with school-based groups usually ends when their children graduate. The BCL, which is an organization that deals with multiple issues, boasts a large paper membership estimated at more than 500. However, the active membership of the group is roughly between twenty and thirty, and attendance at monthly meetings averages twenty-five people.

The episodic nature of Beltway residents' participation in ongoing voluntary groups and activities is not altogether unusual.[12] Most people in Beltway do not volunteer their time regularly for local organizations. On the basis of the interviews I conducted with residents, I estimate that fewer than one in eight people volunteers at a local organization on a regular basis. For those who do volunteer, however, activity is usually marked by involvement in multiple groups. In the interviews I conducted with neighborhood activists, defined as people who regularly volunteer their time with at least one local group, the average activist was involved with slightly fewer than three groups and spent approximately eight hours a week involved in activities for these groups. Beltway does not have a high rate of voluntary participation in terms of the percentage of people who volunteer their time; the estimate of fewer than one in eight is much lower than the nationwide figure of one in five adults, as reported for the year 1989[13] in the Current Population Survey.[14]

For every Jane Pratt, whose activism was sparked by her experience with the PFH and who has remained involved with several groups in the neighborhood, there are two or three Barbara Cremaldis, who are content to melt into the background once their issue has been resolved. Pratt speculates that perhaps people don't have enough time to devote to ongoing community efforts, using the allusion to declining porch sitting to underscore her point:

> The people [who live] on my block—we used to sit on our porch and talk and if the kids were playing, [neighbors] would stop and talk. They're not doing that much anymore, and the people on my block surprise me cause they were never that busy and I don't know all of a sudden why they're so busy.

Whether Pratt is invoking a mythic past is perhaps beside the point.[15] The demands on the time of people who live in neighborhoods such as Beltway have been well documented.[16] The basic truth is that for many middle-class Americans, routine activities involve choices about what they can do in the limited free time they have after work.[17] If citizens are going to volunteer their time, they may want to do so for only a short while, and so a single issue with a limited time frame can be very appealing.

Perhaps more important for the present story of crime and informal social control than the limited nature of civic involvement may be the fact that when people are moved to do something for their neighborhood, it is usually in reaction to an event that has already happened. As we see in the coming chapters, the same is true for events that deal specifically with crime and disorder, which is hardly surprising. However, the fact that people basically react to events, especially when those events involve the delinquent or criminal behavior of local youth, implies that there is little in the way of ongoing involvement with, and monitoring of, the young people in the neighborhood. The sociologists Robert J. Sampson and William Julius Wilson argue that one of the key components in local organization is the extent to which residents of a neighborhood assume personal responsibility for neighborhood problems and the extent to which local youth are collectively supervised.[18] The theme of personal responsibility is important to the story of informal social control in Beltway, as I demonstrate in chapters 5 and 6. In general, Beltway residents do not assume personal responsibility for many neighborhood problems, preferring instead to hold others accountable. The readiness of many Beltway residents to look for others to blame for local ills can impede efforts to solve community problems. However, it is the theme of ongoing collective supervision that is fundamental to informal social control efforts.

The overall picture in terms of collective supervision is that Beltway residents for the most part engage in collective supervision, but they do so only in specific situations. The main point to note is that supervision is age-graded: children up to the teenage years receive the vast majority of supervision, while teenagers are left to their own devices in many cases. For example, at the numerous block parties that punctuate the summer in Beltway, young children are collectively supervised as they bounce on jumping jacks, play Frisbee in the street, or swim in a neighbor's swimming pool. The supervision is expected and unconscious. The nearest parent or adult usually takes care of a group of children. The same collective supervision is also evident at the many school-sponsored activities; concerts, sports events, and picnics are staffed by parents and teachers who keep a watchful eye on the children. Supervision at school activities tend to be more structured than block parties, with each adult given specific responsibilities; in less structured activities, the collective supervision is more sporadic and irregular. Importantly, the day-to-day supervision of teens is rarely a collective enterprise. People tend not to stand on street corners; while some residents sit on their porches, many porches are uninhabited during the summer months. I suggest that there is a crucial distinction that should be made here between supervision as an act of surveillance and supervision as potential intervention. In the case of the younger children, supervision is both surveillance and intervention: if one child is up to high jinx in the swimming pool, the adult in charge will reprimand the child. However, in the case of older teens, the supervision may simply entail keeping a watchful eye on the six or seven teens walking down the street, that is, surveillance without intervention. If the teens walking down the street are engaged in delinquency, people are more likely to call 911 than to intervene. Lydia Donovan, when asked whether people in Beltway engage in collective supervision, replied,

> Yes and no. They usually have a group of kids that they know through friendship ties of their own children, and then if they are the kind of house where the kids come over, then they would supervise in that situation. Sometimes if people are out on the street they may choose to comment depending on the situation. Nobody wants to deal with teens, that's where everybody drops out. They don't want to deal with teens at all. I think part of it is an age perception, a single old adult does not want to go up against a crowd of youth.

The phenomenon of assuming personal responsibility for community problems is more difficult to assess. Generally, responsibility goes hand in hand with participation in voluntary organizations. In other words, those Beltway residents who are likely to assume personal responsibility for community problems are more likely to volunteer their time in community groups. There is not a direct correspondence, though, because some problems, such as the existence of local youth gangs, are difficult to assimilate for some residents. For some Beltwayites, admitting that there are serious internal problems in the neighborhood is a painful exercise. Thus, the step to assuming personal responsibility is one not all neighborhood residents, even activists, take easily.

The story of informal social control in Beltway is bound up with and inseparable from the general tenor of social activism in the neighborhood. The social organization of a neighborhood, or how things get done, and how a neighborhood engages in self-regulation are intimately linked. The Chicago School sociologists Clifford Shaw and Henry McKay, in their extensive study of juvenile delinquency in early-twentieth-century Chicago, were among the first to delineate a connection between how a neighborhood is socially organized and the level of crime and delinquency in the area. Specifically, Shaw and McKay argued that when a neighborhood is socially disorganized, that is, when it is unable to realize the common values of its residents or to solve community problems, there is a consequent diminution of social control.[19] Put simply, when a neighborhood lacks the capacity to do things for itself, it will not be able to control the behavior of its residents. Cut loose from internal controls, then, local youth are free to commit crime.[20] For Shaw and McKay, social disorganization occurs in areas where socioeconomic status (SES) is low and the rates of residential mobility (the number of people moving in and out of the neighborhood) and the level of heterogeneity (the number of different racial and ethnic groups represented among area residents) are high. The logic of the theory is that a neighborhood where residents are poor, where people are constantly moving in and out, and where different groups live cheek by jowl, often in competition for scarce resources, will not be able to spawn vibrant local institutions. Moreover, people simply do not live there long enough or become sufficiently invested to engage in any kind of community activism. With respect specifically to crime and disorder, there is no agreed-upon set of rules for behavior, and, consequently, internal controls are weak. The proof of Shaw and McKay's theory is that when they examined different types of delinquency data, they found that delinquents were concentrated in the same neighborhoods over time regardless of who lived there.[21] They concluded that delinquency had nothing to do with a flaw or failing on the part of the individual but rather was caused by the conditions in the surrounding community.

Shaw and McKay's social disorganization theory was not without its critics, and over time it became less popular and influential as an explanation for crime and delinquency.[22] The theory was reinvigorated by a number of scholars in the 1980s. For example, Robert J. Bursik acknowledged some of the problems with the original formulation of social disorganization theory, and he argued that the essential thrust of Shaw and McKay's thesis concerning the importance of internal neighborhood controls remains pertinent.[23] Similarly, Robert J. Sampson argued for a reconceptualization of the concept of social disorganization that emphasizes the centrality of informal social control.[24] Thus, although social disorganization theory has received its fair share of criticism, many studies have sought to specify the nature of neighborhood processes and their relationship to crime and delinquency. In particular, the social disorganization framework has been recast in terms of the systemic theory of control.

The systemic theory is based on the work of John Kasarda and Morris Janowitz, who state that "local community is a complex system of friendship and kinship networks and formal and informal associational ties rooted in family life and ongoing socialization processes."[25] The complex of network social ties mediates between neighborhood structural variables (e.g., length of residence) and outcomes for the community, among them the informal control of crime. Janowitz specifically links the concept of informal social control to systemic theory when he argues for a return to what he considers the classical usage of social control, namely the capacity for a group to engage in self-regulation.[26] Self-regulation is achieved through the dense array of neighborhood social ties that mediates among the structural variables of poverty, residential mobility, and ethnic and racial heterogeneity and crime rate.[27] Neighborhoods that have a high rate of residential instability or population turnover have difficulty establishing the stable relational networks that serve as the foundation for informal social control. Conversely, residentially stable neighborhoods, with dense and widespread friendship and associational ties, have greater potential for informal social control. The systemic theory redefines social disorganization "as the regulatory capacity of a neighborhood that is embedded in the structure of that community's affiliational, interactional and communication ties among its residents."[28] In other words, communities in which people know their neighbors and who interact frequently with them should do better at controlling crime and disorder.

So if we utilize the social organization/disorganization framework and its advances in terms of the systemic theory, we can speculate that areas such as Beltway that demonstrate a high level of social organization should have strong social controls and low levels of delinquency. However, as the case studies in the following chapters illustrate, the relationship between social organization and informal social control is more complex than the theory allows. The assumption that there is a direct relationship between social organization and informal social control is misleading. Instead, we should perhaps ask whether a high level of social organization necessarily leads to a high level of social control. The recent work by Robert J. Sampson holds that, in looking at social organization in a neighborhood, we should investigate the focus of the organization, that is, for what is the neighborhood organized?[29] Two recent ethnographies of Chicago neighborhoods also point to the variability of social organization and outcomes for informal social control at the neighborhood level.[30] In one of these studies, Mary Pattillo-McCoy, in her ethnography of the Groveland neighborhood, notes that a local gang leader is heavily involved in informal social control in his neighborhood, even while he pursues his own criminal enterprise. Pattillo-McCoy explains this apparent contradiction by illustrating how licit and illicit networks overlap in Groveland, underscoring the situational nature of the relationship between social organization and social control.[31]

Perhaps the most fruitful way to delineate the interplay between the social organization of a neighborhood and its degree of self-regulation is to use what Sampson and his colleagues term "collective efficacy." Sampson defines collective efficacy thus: "Just as individuals vary in their capacity for efficacious action so too do neighborhoods vary in their capacity to achieve common goals . . . in this view neighborhood efficacy exists relative to the tasks of supervising children and maintaining public order."[32] Thus, Sampson argues that it is not social organization per se that matters but rather what communities can do for themselves, particularly with respect to living in an area free of crime.

The present work examines what ordinary people do to control crime and disorder in their neighborhood. As such, it is rooted in the social disorganization perspective of examining what happens at the neighborhood level. However, I go beyond the somewhat static assumptions of the social disorganization approach, which assumes that depending on whether a neighborhood is organized or disorganized, it is either able or unable to control the behavior of its youth. Rather, building on the insights of the systemic model and the recent arguments that have pointed to the centrality of collective efficacy, I investigate the circumstances under which, in what seems like a socially organized neighborhood, informal social control is successful.

Conclusion

The two case studies that form the backbone of this chapter reveal much about social organization in Beltway. In each case, there were committed activists, crucial issues (at least as defined by a significant number of residents), and successful outcomes. Also, in each case activists took similar paths to successful action. The residents who took up the campaigns against the Chestnut Court condominiums and against the Barker LSC majority enlisted the support of local civic and political leaders and then parlayed that support into a positive result. Both cases also involved contact with the wider city bureaucracy, the City Council Zoning Board and the Board of Education, which was facilitated by the local ward organizations. One could simply conclude from this that Beltway is a socially organized, well-connected neighborhood that can tap into an abundant reservoir of social capital and get things done in an efficacious manner. The story is not at all unlike the way things have traditionally been done in white ethnic neighborhoods in places like Chicago.[33] The logical conclusion in terms of how Beltway engages in self-regulation then would be "Very well, thank you." However, as we see in the coming chapters, having well-established procedures for getting things done does not automatically lead to effective informal social control. The notion of collective efficacy implies that the methods neighborhoods use to get things done, and their success at realizing common values of residents, can vary from case to case. Moreover, living in a neighborhood like Beltway, where there is a tradition of civic activism and where there is a well-developed local political structure, can actually serve to mask local problems, because residents become complacent in the belief that theirs is a neighborhood that can deal with any problems that arise. However, as we shall see, controlling crime and disorder once they have arisen can be difficult for any neighborhood, even one where collective efficacy is high.

The next three chapters detail case studies that explore crime, disorder, and informal social control in action. It is useful to bear in mind the general atmosphere of social activism in Beltway illustrated in this chapter, because there are continuities and disjunctures in the case studies that follow. When the matter is crime and disorder on your doorstep and the specter of local youth gangs wreaking havoc on the last garden,[34] often what is required in response is more difficult and less straightforward than stopping a condominium development or ousting a despotic LSC.

PARK
SHOPS

4

Looks Like Trouble

Early Signs of Gangs and Violence

Introduction

On Thursday, April 14, 1994, John Thompson, a nineteen-year-old Beltway resident, was walking in the area beside Rendell Park, in the eastern part of the neighborhood, when a car containing four men drove by. One of the men in the car jumped out, yelled gang slogans, and opened fire, allegedly taking five shots at Thompson. One of the bullets struck Thompson in the thigh. The shooter and the other three men escaped westbound in their car. Thompson later told police that Frank Smyth, a twenty-three-year-old Beltway resident, had fired the gun. Smyth was later arrested and charged in connection with a gang-related shooting.[1] At a time when youth gang violence was peaking elsewhere in the city of Chicago, Beltway had its first recorded gang shooting.[2]

The report of the incident that appeared in the local weekly paper is important because it sets the scene for the events that were to follow. While such shootings, and indeed a great deal more gang violence, were a regular occurrence in neighborhoods to the east, gang-related violence was almost unheard of in Beltway at that time. Long-time residents spoke of gangs that had existed when they were growing up, but, according to these Beltwayites, such gangs were different. Melanie Thorpe, a thirty-five-year-old city worker who has lived in Beltway for about fifteen years, explains how she thinks gangs have changed in the past two decades:

> Yeah, because I remember when I was a kid, like there was groups that hung out, but they never were into like shootings or anything. The only thing you ever heard of was those Black Panthers over on the East Side. But even the Latin Kings, like some of them would say, "I'm in the Latin Kings," but all they did was just hang out together. They didn't you know, go destroying [property] or shooting and stuff. I think that all just kind of came about in the last twenty years.

The language of the newspaper report of the Thompson shooting is significant because the incident is described as "gang-related," the protagonists are said to be "gang members," and the shooting itself is depicted as a "drive-by." These phrases connote gang violence in its most extreme form, something that most Beltway residents thought they would not have to contend with in their neighborhood. Indeed, one of the reasons that some people move to Beltway is to escape gang violence.[3] However, it is sufficient to note that after the Thompson shooting there was a definite perception on the part of some residents that gangs were taking over their neighborhood, and, for most residents in and around the Rendell Park area, there was at least a sense of a growing threat.

This chapter describes the early gang-related incidents and the reaction they provoked in Beltway. Specifically, I focus on the two neighborhood patrol groups that were formed in the wake of the Thompson shooting and the boxing program begun by other concerned residents to help keep young men from joining gangs. In essence, the story of the reaction to the Thompson shooting illustrates how difficult it can be to establish effective informal social control, and I speculate as to the contingent factors that prevent communities from organizing successfully to combat crime and disorder.

Beltway Reacts

In the days immediately after the Thompson shooting in the spring of 1994, a group of people living in the area around Rendell Park got together and sent fliers to many of the houses in the area. The flier, drafted by longtime residents John and Brenda Belinski and Maria Causio, urged people to attend a meeting of the Local School Council (LSC) at the nearby Gerald Elementary School, due to be held the following Wednesday, less than a week after the shooting. The flier promised that the recent shooting and gangs would be discussed at the meeting, and it exhorted people to come along "to voice your concerns about the neighborhood." I had attended Gerald LSC meetings before the shooting; usually, about eleven people attended. However, this LSC meeting was different.

When I arrived for the meeting at the Gerald School shortly before six o'clock, I noticed that a large group of people had already gathered outside the classroom where the meetings were usually held. Before the Thompson shooting, the Gerald/Frederick LSC had arranged to have a police officer come to speak to them at this particular meeting about police-community relations and the impending implementation of the Chicago Alternative Policing Strategy (CAPS) program. The LSC members looked slightly bewildered at the large number of people who wanted to attend their meeting. The room where the meeting was about to take place quickly filled to capacity, as did the hallway outside. In all, approximately 150 people attended the meeting. It was decided that, instead of conducting the normal business of the LSC, since the majority of people were there to hear about the shooting, the police officer would have the floor first. Jean Sidwell, the principal of Gerald and Frederick Elementary Schools at the time, thanked people for attending and tried to reassure the crowd by stating that "even though this situation is disturbing, we need to stay positive." Sidwell then introduced Officer Kelly from the District Neighborhood Relations Office.

Officer Kelly was clearly prepared to give a well-rehearsed pep talk about the impending introduction of the CAPS program, and he was not prepared to bear the brunt of residents' anger and frustration about the shooting of Thompson and what that prophesied about the neighborhood. After talking for a few minutes about the CAPS program, Kelly said that he would take questions from the floor.

The first volley of questions from the floor was accusatory in tone and had the effect of riling up the audience. People asked why the police had not come to investigate when residents had reported that their garages had been covered with gang graffiti. One man complained that the police did not respond when he called 911 to report that he had heard gunshots. Officer Kelly attempted to regain control of the meeting by trying to steer the discussion back to the CAPS program, but his comments about future accountability did not sit well with the residents at the meeting. Kelly then went out and apparently called District Commander Henry Rusnak, because, soon after, Rusnak arrived at the meeting and took over for Kelly. The genial tone of Officer Kelly, which had done nothing to assuage the anger of the residents in attendance, was replaced by Rusnak's confident, direct, and, at times, didactic style. Rusnak lives in Beltway just several blocks west of the Gerald School, and he was considerably more skilled at handling the meeting than Kelly. A number of people stated their complaints, and he told them to speak to Officer Kelly after the meeting and that the police force would have someone "look into it." The subject of the meeting then shifted from complaints about general police incompetence to a discussion of the shooting itself.

People requested more information about the shooting and about the presence of gangs in the neighborhood. Rusnak told the meeting, "If you are so upset about the shooting, [you] should go to court. If the judge were to see all these people standing in his court, that would mean something." A local man asked about the level of gang activity in the neighborhood and what ordinary citizens could do to help reduce gang activity. Rusnak replied, "Is there gang activity? Yes. It is nowhere near the levels of other communities. You have to solve it in your own house. There are a hundred people in this room, and there are a lot of things that you people can do." He went on to say that to combat crime, citizens should keep their lights on, make a point of sitting out on their porches when the weather got warmer, remove graffiti, and organize community watches. These suggestions were greeted with sarcastic comments from the crowd. When Rusnak told people to sit out on their porches, one man replied, "Why? So we can get shot?"

The meeting was in disarray at this stage, and one man asked whether there were gang members at the meeting. In fact, Thompson himself was present at the meeting, hobbling around on crutches. According to a story published in one of the local papers, Thompson stated that the shooting had stemmed from a fight he had gotten into with a member of a rival gang two years before the incident. He added, "I told [the other gang] that no one wanted them around so they didn't have no business hanging around. That's why they shot me. . . . As much as [the community] want to blame me, it's going to continue even after I'm gone."

While the meeting was tempestuous and most residents who attended were angry, two significant interventions were made toward the end of the evening. The first occurred when Sean O'Rourke, a Chicago firefighter who lives near Rendell Park, addressed the meeting and exhorted residents to come to a meeting of the Rendell Park Advisory Committee. O'Rourke stated that local youth had little to do and that things would improve only if people got involved. O'Rourke's intervention was the first time the theme of collective responsibility was raised at the meeting by someone other than the police commander. He would later volunteer his time and money to start a boxing program at Rendell Park.

The second noteworthy development occurred just as the part of the meeting with Commander Rusnak and Officer Kelly was coming to a close. Before people filed out, two local residents, Brenda Belinski and Maria Causio, who had earlier circulated the flier urging people to attend the meeting, passed around a sign-up sheet for people who might be interested in forming a neighborhood watch group. In all, more than fifty people signed up.

These two events signaled the beginning of the neighborhood response to the gang problem. The nascent strategies of social control are the first examples of reactive informal social control in Beltway during the 1990s. It is worth underscoring the key elements in the public discourse surrounding the shooting of Thompson. In the first place, there was clearly a great deal of panic around the belief that gangs were taking over the neighborhood and that it was therefore not safe to walk the streets. The second element of the discourse espoused by many residents was the desire to find someone to blame for the gang problem. The search for accountability included lax parents, poor police service, and bad public schools. By its very nature, finding someone to blame leads people away from seeking community-based solutions to the problem. I return to these points later in the chapter. The LSC meeting at the Gerald School was a watershed of sorts, as it did spawn some community action.

"We Have to Do This Ourselves": The Rendell Park Patrol

There was a meeting at Rendell Park later that month, and about thirty people attended. Two local police officers were present, and the residents who showed up decided that they would form a patrol that would concentrate on Rendell Park and its environs. Rendell Park is located in the center of the area known as "the Village," in east Beltway. The streets in this part of the neighborhood make an oval around the park. The park has a large softball field, a mid-size outdoor basketball court, a small fieldhouse, and a kids' playground area. Rendell Park is not the prettiest park in the city of Chicago, but it is well maintained and gets a great deal of use. The group set a meeting date for early the following month to institute procedures for the patrol.

At the next meeting, the number of residents in attendance had dwindled to about seventeen people. The fieldhouse at Rendell Park is old, and the meeting space is small and cramped. Sean O'Rourke sat at the front of the room along with two local residents, Jeff King and Laura Donlon, both of whom were also active in Rendell Park. At that time, Laura had been chairperson of the park advisory committee for several years. The audience was made up of area residents interested mostly in volunteering for a neighborhood watch.

The meeting itself was somewhat haphazard in terms of what we had become accustomed to in Beltway. In contrast to the meetings at the Beltway Civic League (BCL) and the Local School Councils (LSCs), there was no recitation of the Pledge of Allegiance to start the meeting, no agenda to follow, no Robert's rules of order, no motions, and no real pattern as to who spoke. The emerging consensus was that those in attendance felt that there should be a patrol based in Rendell Park, but people were divided on when this should take place and what would constitute the objective of the patrol. For example, Donlon stated that problems occur when kids from other neighborhoods come in "lookin' to cause trouble," while others were focused on a more ill-defined grouping of "gangbangers." A local resident, Monica Medina, suggested that it might be a good idea to join up with the other group that was forming at the time in the area, called Save Our Neighborhood (SON), and she added, "I think that you all should get together with this other group and try and put all your stuff together." Laura Donlon responded that she didn't think this was a good idea; she explained, "We had started this up long before those other meetings took place." By this, Donlon communicated a pointed unwillingness to pool resources or join forces with other neighborhood groups, perhaps because she did not relish the prospect of sharing power or perhaps because she felt that she had more experience dealing with neighborhood issues. Whatever the reason for Laura's resistance, the idea of amalgamating the two groups was dropped, and the remainder of the meeting focused on figuring out the actual mechanics of the patrol. The meeting was deteriorating when Sean O'Rourke finally said that there was a sign-up sheet for anyone who was interested in joining the patrol. However, nobody seemed anxious to take charge of the sign-up sheet or to follow up with phone calls to those wishing to volunteer. After a protracted awkward moment, one man agreed to take the sheet.

The Rendell Park watch group began its patrols about two weeks after the organizational meeting of the Rendell Park Advisory Committee, and the group continued patrolling throughout the summer of 1994 and sporadically thereafter until early 1995. Of the dozen or so people who had signed up to patrol, few did so with regularity. The group attempted to raise money for its cause by having a concert fund-raiser in Rendell Park.

The watch group did raise some money at the festival, mainly by going door-to-door and soliciting donations, but it never got to use the money that was raised at the festival because the funds reverted to the local park district. After the summer months of 1994, the Rendell Park watch group patrols were intermittent during the fall and winter of 1994–1995, when they finally folded ignominiously. Thereafter, the control of the park reverted to haphazard informal work by volunteers and park district staff and intermittent visits by the newly assigned beat officers for the area.[4] Neely Martin, the Rendell Park supervisor at the time, explained the demise of the watch group as something that was inevitable. She explained,

> I think they all started fighting with each other. I knew that was coming. They took it so serious and they had kids hangin' round with them, all they were doing is chasing kids who aggravated their kids. They were sitting out there thinking they all had this power and they were gonna make a big deal out of it. I think it went to everybody's head.

In sum, the Rendell Park watch group spent the best part of seven to nine months patrolling. The group succumbed to personality conflicts and the lack of a coherent organizing structure. The patrol was formed in the wake of the Thompson shooting but failed to capitalize on the intense emotion and activity that the incident stimulated. The Rendell Park watch group was the first effort at informal social control in the wake of the Thompson shooting. The second neighborhood response, the foundation of the SON group, was unfolding simultaneously.

Save Our Neighborhood

Brenda Belinski and Maria Causio used the sign-up sheet that they had passed around at the end of the stormy LSC meeting in April to notify people of a meeting to be held on the first Sunday in May in the United Methodist Church in Beltway, located just a few blocks away from the Gerald School, west of Columbia Avenue. The organizers also invited Sharon Allen, of the nearby Mountain Ridge Patrol, described by the local newspaper as "a grass-roots organization designed to help community members combat gang activity in the Mountain Ridge community," and John Black, of the Carver Heights neighborhood watch group.

About 150 people attended the first SON meeting, and the assembly was loosely described as a "crime-fighting group" in the newspaper report of the meeting. Once again the meeting itself was an unruly affair, and, at times, the atmosphere closely resembled that at the LSC meeting at the Gerald School. A number of people reiterated that the gang problem had mushroomed in the neighborhood, and most people agreed that something had to be done to combat gang violence. Maria Causio attempted to steer the meeting to talking about possible solutions for the perceived gang problem. To this end, John Black spoke about the Carver Heights patrol, which operates in a neighborhood adjacent to Beltway. Black told the meeting,

> We have had problems with gangs down in Carver, and it's not just kids from [outside] that's comin' in. It's the gangbangers in our own neighborhood. But we organized and went out on patrol. We report what we see to the police. We have a set of bylaws, and everybody that comes on patrol with us has to be on probation for the first six months. I tell you, though, the gangbangers know that we are out there patrolling, and they know better than to do anything out in Carver.

Brenda Belinski also addressed the meeting and stressed the need for the group to keep the neighborhood safe:

> I want this neighborhood to be safe like when I was growing up here. People need to get out of their houses and talk to each other. What we should do is create phone trees, so when one person sees something goin' on, they can call the next person in the tree and then all the people can call the police. It's more powerful when thirty people call than if just one calls.

Other speakers at the meeting underscored the themes of safety and neighborhood responsibility. Maria Causio told the crowd that the SON group planned to have pictures taken of the gang graffiti in the area and have them analyzed by gang specialists from the local police district. She stressed that it was important both that people know what the graffiti meant and that they painted over it as soon as possible. The discussion at the meeting then turned to the dimensions of the gang problem in the neighborhood. A number of people testified that the gang problem was being imported from other neighborhoods, especially the area around Victory Park.[5] However, one resident pointed out that Thompson was a known gang member and thus that there had to be at least some gang members in Beltway. Maria Causio then told the meeting that the SON group planned to protest the simple battery charge against Frank Smyth for shooting Thompson. Causio passed around a petition that everyone present at the meeting signed, and she stated that she planned to present it to the judge when the case went to trial. She explained: "[A] slap on the wrist is an invitation for more firearm use in our area. We need stiffer penalties to protect our community and the innocent bystanders. The shooting was just a few blocks from the school where our kids go!"

The meeting broke up soon after the petition was signed, and a meeting was set for block captains for later that month. As a result of the decision to organize the petition about the simple battery designation, which is a misdemeanor, the charge was upgraded to aggravated battery, a felony offense. The tactic of going to court to protest had also been employed by the Gerald LSC and concerned neighbors in another case; when Orlando Santos, a local teen, was caught scratching graffiti onto sound-resistant windows of the Gerald School, the group had gone to court.[6] Going to court is an important tactic of informal social control that is utilized to great effect by Beltway residents, probably because it requires only a one- or possibly two-time commitment.[7]

It was notable that the first SON meeting was a strictly adults-only affair. We later learned from Paula Gerber, the pastor of the Beltway United Methodist Church (UMC) at the time, who had been delighted to accommodate SON in her church hall, that young people had actually been prohibited from entering the meeting for fear that they were gang members. Members of the UMC youth group later confirmed this in a conversation with us about the Thompson shooting and subsequent events. The fact that the young people were prohibited from going to the SON meeting is important because it illustrates the high level of distrust between older Beltway residents and young people in the neighborhood. In other interviews, Beltway youth that we spoke with underscored the fact that they have felt left out and persecuted simply because they are young.

It should also be noted that the SON meeting was not the only public forum that has an absence of youth. Young people were rarely present at LSC meetings, community policing meetings, or civic league meetings. The absence of youth at these venues is hardly surprising, but it did contribute to sort of intergenerational closure, where there was limited contact between members of different generations in the community. More generally, relations between adults and youth were strained.[8]

The second SON meeting was held more than two months after the first one, in July 1994, again at the Beltway United Methodist Church. The guest speaker at the meeting was a Cook County gang intervention officer named Peter Rooney. He addressed the meeting, telling those present that neighborhood crime fighting groups should work together to reduce the threat of gangs in their neighborhoods. After this July 1994 meeting, SON never really met again as a group, apart from a loose amalgam of block captains, all of whom knew each other before the SON group was organized. As a result of the efforts of SON, a number of block clubs in the Rendell Park area were founded, and some are still in existence, mainly as a conduit for organizing annual block parties held during the summer months. The block clubs that were started tended to be in blocks where founder members of SON, such as Maria Causio, Brenda Belinski, and Monica Medina, resided at the time. These block clubs were the only tangible results of the SON meetings, and the group never mounted a fully operational neighborhood watch.

The Rendell Park watch group and SON never coordinated their efforts to keep the neighborhood safe. Maria Causio at one point asked the Rendell Park supervisor, Neely Martin, about the park watch group. Apparently, Causio had read about the group in the local paper, and she had been shocked to see that this group was patrolling the park and the neighborhood and had had no involvement or contact with SON. Neely told Causio that she wasn't sure what the Rendell Park watch group did and that she, too, had been surprised to hear that they patrolled the neighborhood. She said, "I'm not sure what they do because I don't see them do anything but stand around at the front gate." Causio told Neely that SON was taking a cautious approach, and when Neely described the Rendell Park group, which was more aggressive about approaching kids, Causio shook her head in dismay and said, "That's exactly kind of stuff we don't want to do."

Like the Rendell Park watch group, SON had a brief period of activism and then ceased to exist as an organization. There is a great deal of research on grassroots organizations that come to life to combat internal threats, whether from gangs or other sources, that documents just this kind of trajectory.[9] In many cases, the organizations fold because the threat that brought them into existence diminishes or disappears. However, this was not the case in Beltway. The threat from youth gangs did not diminish in 1994; if anything, the problems in the neighborhood increased at that time. There are several possible reasons for the failure of SON and the Rendell Park watch group to get off the ground. Unlike the examples of successful civic activism in the previous chapter, neither group effectively tapped in to the resources available in the neighborhood. For example, the BCL was not exhorted to really help with either group. John Belinski did address a BCL meeting on behalf of SON, and Ron Zalinsky, the president of the BCL, attended a SON meeting, but there was never a direct appeal by either SON or the Rendell Park watch group to the BCL for help. A second possible explanation is that neither group built quickly enough on the initial interest among residents. SON had more than 150 people at its first meeting, but the number of people who attended the next meeting declined, mainly because there was no real follow-up or agreed-upon plan of action. The signs were more ominous for the Rendell Park watch group when, at its first real organizational meeting, no one really wanted to take charge of the sign-up sheet. Thus, neither SON nor the Rendell Park watch group could sustain the initial levels of interest they had generated. For SON, the main emphasis was setting up block clubs instead of organizing a more general neighborhood watch group, which seemed to have been its original stated intent. The Rendell Park watch group did actually patrol but did so in a haphazard and borderline vigilante fashion, which probably scared off more potential recruits than it did gang members. Finally, neither group raised funds that could have helped sustain them. One of the most straightforward means of sustaining a group is raising funds, and neither group really managed to do that. The case of SON is summed up by Ron Zalinsky, who commented that the group "tried their best but they couldn't get anywhere with it. They had some big meetings, but it just didn't pan out."

The SON organizers remained active in the Gerald/Frederick LSC (Maria Causio was elected to the LSC in April 1996) and were also regular attendees at community policing meetings throughout our time in Beltway. John Belinski, in his capacity as a member of the Gerald/Frederick LSC, arranged for one of the local CAPS beat meetings to be sponsored annually by the Gerald/Frederick LSC. The community policing beat meeting provided a forum for former SON activists to report problems they encountered in their area and to receive information about crime in Beltway, which may also help to explain why SON failed to build upon its initial momentum. However, there has been no push on the part of either the local residents or community policing officials to organize another neighborhood watch in the area around Rendell Park.[10] While the SON group and the Rendell Park watch group have been consigned to history in Beltway, a third initiative that was conceived in the wake of the Thompson shooting lasted beyond a few months—the Rendell Park boxing program.

The Rendell Park Boxing Program

Perhaps the most unusual response to the Thompson shooting was the one proposed by Sean O'Rourke and Fred Reilly. O'Rourke is the Chicago firefighter who spoke up at the Gerald LSC meeting and challenged people to get involved. Fred Reilly, a good friend of O'Rourke, is another local man who shared the dismay of other Beltway residents at the events in the neighborhood at the time. When I spoke with O'Rourke and Reilly, I got the impression that they never engage in anything they are not 100 percent committed to, nor are they likely to ever back down in the face of a difficult task. It may be a peculiarly Irish trait, but I sensed in them kindred spirits who actually enjoy something more when the odds are stacked against them. When Sean O'Rourke challenged the people at the Gerald LSC meeting to do something positive for the neighborhood and to get involved, it was not an empty exhortation. He was also prepared to volunteer his time and money to benefit the neighborhood.

The question for O'Rourke and Reilly was what particular contribution they could make; in this regard, they decided to play to their strengths. O'Rourke had been an amateur boxer, and, while Reilly had never boxed, he had coached youth football and baseball. So, instead of channeling their energies into patrolling (O'Rourke never patrolled with the Rendell Park watch group), they chose instead to begin a boxing program in Rendell Park in the fall of 1994 that they hoped would provide an alternative to gangs for area youth (at least the young men). Reilly explained that he got involved because he was concerned about the incidents around the park at the time; he felt that at the root of the problem was the fact that most kids had nothing to do. O'Rourke and Reilly began the boxing program from scratch, and they spent a great deal of their own money getting the program off the ground. They began modifying the Rendell Park fieldhouse in September 1994, installing a makeshift sparring ring, some speed bags, a heavy bag, and sparring mitts, and the program started soon after.

The boxing program proved to be an immediate success among young men and their parents. In the initial month, about twenty youth signed up for the program. However, the initial achievement was tempered by a number of organizational hurdles O'Rourke and Reilly had to overcome, the largest of which was the difficulty of securing adequate funding. The crux of the funding issue was the fact that the park district allocated funds in a discretionary manner. O'Rourke explained:

> The funding ability of the Park [District] really stinks. Tryin' to get money allocated to us over there, it took us over a year to get that little ring we had. Fred and I bought all the equipment that's over there. It's silly because people think that in a middle-class neighborhood that there is no gang problems. [We] don't need the money over here because it's a working community, so nobody bothers with [us]. But they don't realize that these kids [here] are the same as other kids throughout the inner city.

Reilly reiterates that one of the reasons that Rendell Park was overlooked is that the park district assumed it was a privileged area. In sum, they felt that, in comparison to other areas of the city, Rendell Park did not receive its fair share of resources. They maintained that some of the kids that Rendell Park was supposed to serve are underprivileged, but, because they are white, they were not thought of that way by the city and the park district. In the end, Rendell Park did receive some new equipment after Reilly and others wrote "numerous letters" and solicited the help of Anthony Gaudio, the new area alderman, who replaced James Belak in November 1994.[11]

The boxing program sputtered along, and, while the number of young men involved fluctuated, at its high point the program boasted twenty-five members. However, the lack of space and adequate facilities made it difficult to enroll a large number of kids in the program. In spite of these obstacles, O'Rourke and Reilly were quick to point out that the boxing program itself had some success, and the overall effort of getting residents involved and showing young people that there are alternatives to gangs was very successful. Reilly talked about the program's impact:

> We had no idea of the success and the impact that it would have. In a matter of a few months, these gangs went somewhere else to hang out. Rival gangs went this way and that way, and there was no graffiti, no problems. The kids were back in the park, the parents were thrilled, the neighbors were thrilled.

While Reilly may be overstating the connection between the boxing program and the reduction in gang activity in the area, perhaps more important is the symbolic nature of the venture.[12] This was an intervention that sought to involve and stimulate area youth (albeit only boys) and that did not focus solely on controlling and monitoring what young people were doing. Also significant for both Reilly and O'Rourke was the opportunity to have meaningful and potentially transformative interactions with young people who might turn to youth gangs. For example, O'Rourke recounts the apocryphal story of how he met John Murphy. O'Rourke was sitting on his stoop when Murphy walked by smoking a cigarette. At the time, Murphy was a scrawny eleven-year-old, and O'Rourke bellowed at him to "get up on the porch." O'Rourke asked him his name, and, while Murphy may have been expecting a lecture on smoking, O'Rourke simply told him to come to the park the following week for the boxing program. Murphy was known locally as a troublemaker at the time, and O'Rourke was surprised when in fact he did show up at the program. Murphy stayed in the program for more than a year and a half and became, in O'Rourke's words, "pretty good." Even after several years, Murphy still stays in contact with O'Rourke, and, for the most part, Murphy has managed to stay out of trouble. The individual successes that O'Rourke and Reilly had with some young men in the neighborhood gave them the encouragement they needed to persevere. However, they are not naïve, and they know that individual successes are not enough.

More important, Sean and Fred realized that the problem of youth gangs is not one that they alone can solve because there are a number of root causes that are outside their control. For example, they cite parents who "do not know where their kids are" and the ravages of drug addiction, which can, in their words, "deteriorate a neighborhood," as root causes of youth gangs. Another problem that O'Rourke and Reilly think exacerbates the youth gang phenomenon is that young people are not fully aware of the benefits of education. The realization that their boxing program was merely a stopgap led them to think about moving to a larger space and fashioning a more comprehensive youth organization that would have a boxing gym, but also a job referral service, personal computer training, and other facilities. The object of the exercise was to use boxing to "get to the kids" and then to equip them with the tools they need to get an education and a job. While these ideas are not new by any standards, the proposed program was unique in Beltway. O'Rourke and Reilly did not labor under the illusion that they will achieve overnight success, and they maintained that they were in for the long haul.

The Rendell Park boxing program is an extremely interesting example for two reasons. First, it lasted for almost three years. Second, the boxing program utilized a different approach to informal social control because it attempted to prevent gangs, rather than react to their presence. Gang prevention is a notion completely absent from the discourse surrounding neighborhood safety in the wake of the Thompson shooting. However, the boxing program and the expanded focus on education and employment by the proposed youth foundation were primarily about providing an alternative to gangs. The program was intended to provide a means for youth to exit gangs and to prevent youth from joining gangs in the first place.

Discussion

The Thompson shooting and the reaction to it provide the first evidence of a serious gang problem in Beltway and the first case studies of informal social control in action. The Rendell Park watch group, SON, and the boxing program all owe their origins to the Thompson shooting, and each response tells a different story in terms of the strategies of self-regulation. In stark contrast to the case studies of the previous chapter, in which the campaigns waged by Beltway residents were ultimately successful, the Rendell Park watch group and SON, in particular, did not achieve much in the way of their stated goals. The watch group did patrol for a while, but the patrols were neither systematic in what they did nor sustainable beyond a few months. Whether the watch group met its goal of keeping Rendell Park safe is unclear, but it is apparent that internal disagreements and a lack of organization eventually scuttled the group.

SON started out with a great deal of popular support, but its goals were never fully articulated, and, consequently, the organization collapsed after a short period of time. The boxing program also encountered a number of practical obstacles but managed to endure longer. The boxing program differed from the park watch group and SON not simply in terms of its longevity but also, and more fundamentally, in its articulation of its central goals and the goals themselves. The boxing program had a clearly stated goal: to provide an alternative to gangs. Similarly, whereas the Rendell Park watch group and SON were primarily reactive responses to the problem of youth gangs and the crime associated with them, the boxing program was proactive and aimed at gang prevention. The boxing program also had a wider focus in terms of its stated objectives, underscored by the fact that O'Rourke and Reilly wanted to expand their operation to include training and job referral.

The present case studies illustrate just how difficult it can be for a neighborhood to informally control crime and disorder. The Rendell Park watch group and SON attempted to re-energize informal social control in the eastern part of Beltway. The watch group especially was redolent of what I call traditional parochial control, that is, a paradigm in which the wider community monitors local youth and intervenes when trouble occurs. In fact, the Rendell Park group was almost too gung-ho in its activities, to a point where the group aroused concern among other community activists, Maria Causio, for example. SON began in the same vein of traditional parochial control in which the wider community seeks to augment control strategies. At the outset, SON contemplated starting a watch group, but this aspiration never came to fruition. In terms of the concept of the new parochialism, then, the case studies of the Rendell Park watch group and SON illustrate how traditional parochial control at that time was difficult to enact in Beltway. The fact that there was gang activity in the first place seems to indicate a diminution of neighborhood control, and attempts to re-establish those controls at the neighborhood or parochial level foundered.

The Rendell Park boxing program is an atypical response in terms of informal social control because it took a preventive approach, aiming to divert young men from gangs by offering alternative outlets for youthful endeavors. However, the theory that involving youth in wholesome activities means there is less opportunity to get into trouble has received limited support in the research to date.[13] Not all delinquent youth who play sports or engage in other prosocial activities desist from their errant ways, though there is a case to be made that structured leisure acts as a protective factor that inhibits delinquency.

Another important point to note at this stage is the lack of concern about youth gangs among and involvement of other Beltway organizations. The members of the BCL, for example, were aware of the problems in the Rendell Park area and had actually had a police officer come to one of their monthly meetings in 1994 to talk about gangs in the area.[14] However, the BCL did not officially get involved with any of the efforts described here, though some SON members attended the BCL from time to time. Similarly, there is no real evidence that either the Rendell Park watch group or SON made connections with other community groups or with the alderman's office to solicit aid for their campaigns. Indeed, it is worth reiterating that the two groups did not even coordinate with each other, even though they had overlapping interests and coexisted in the same physical space. Why, then, were the watch group and SON seemingly so disconnected with neighborhood resources?

In previous work on Beltway, I have illustrated that for many Beltway residents, the area around Rendell Park is scarcely recognized as part of the neighborhood.[15] Historically, the area, known locally as "the Village," was built to house migrant workers from Appalachia who came to work in the nearby factories during the Second World War, and the housing around the park was constructed using cheap materials. The western part of Beltway was built up primarily in the 1950s and 1960s, and the internal division between it and the Village means that, for many residents, the problems that culminated in the Thompson shooting were not really a concern. These problems could be explained as in keeping with the reputation of the Village. Lydia Donovan refers to the division as that between what she terms "Beltway A and Beltway B," and she speculates that part of the reason community initiatives centered in the Village failed is that there was no widespread community support for them. However, it is too simplistic to say that internal neighborhood divisions alone brought down the watch group and SON. Particularly in the case of SON, the initial meetings attracted many so-called Beltway A residents. I suggest that there are two general explanations that can account for the failure of the groups to endure and fulfill their stated goals. These explanations derive from two disparate strands of literature, namely research on resource mobilization and the study of moral panics.

Resource Mobilization

The first possible explanation for the groups' failure stems from the literature on how activist groups mobilize resources. Although the concept is normally applied to wider social movements,[16] recently there has been a focus on how resources are mobilized at the local level.[17] For example, John McCarthy and Mark Wolfson argue that there are three features of mobilization efforts that can explain how local groups mobilize resources. The first element is *agency,* which they define as the "sheer amount of effort activists invest in collective action."[18] Second, they assert that the role of *strategy* is crucial to a local organization. Typically, organizations pursue a mix of three general types of strategy: public education, direct service to people affected by the condition the group wishes to change, and structural change. The third factor that McCarthy and Wolfson examine is the *organization* of group activities, which may produce variable levels of mobilization. Organization is measured by items such as the number and type of meetings and the establishment of committees to accomplish specific tasks. McCarthy and Wolfson also state that the age of an organization can be crucial with respect to procuring resources. In particular, they speak of the "liability of newness"[19] and state that the longer a group is in existence, the better it should be at mobilizing resources. In order to assess how relevant the resource mobilization model is to the current case studies of the Rendell Park watch group, SON, and the boxing program, it remains for us to revisit the strategies in terms of the three elements just outlined, as represented in table 4.1.

The Rendell Park watch group does not score very high in terms of agency. Few people in the group invested a great deal of effort to ensure its success, a point underscored at the first organization meeting when no one wanted to take charge of the volunteer list. While some group members were enthusiastic about the patrols, there was no sustained effort in terms of keeping the organization active beyond weekend patrols. In terms of the second element, strategy, the watch group did not engage in any form of public education, nor did it attempt structural change. It did,

TABLE 4.1

Resource Mobilization in Beltway after the Thompson Shooting

	Rendell Park Patrol	*SON*	*Boxing Program*
Agency	Low	Mixed	High
Collective Action	No	Yes	Yes
Strategy	Low/mixed	Mixed	Mixed
Public education	No	Yes	Yes
Structural change	No	No	No
Direct service	Yes	No	Yes
Organization	Low	Mixed	Low
#/Type meetings	No	Yes	No
Task committees	No	No	No

Adapted from John D. McCarthy and Mark Wolfson, "Resource Mobilization by Local Social Movement Organizations: Agency, Strategy, and Organization in the Movement against Drinking and Driving," *American Sociological Review* 61 (1996): 1070–1088.

however, provide a direct service in terms of the intended effect of the patrols, keeping the park safe. Finally, the watch group did not score high on the organization front. It did not schedule regular meetings. In fact, after the first organizational meeting in May, there were few formally organized meetings, and the group existed on an ad hoc basis. Certainly, there were no task committees, as evidenced by the manner in which the concert fundraiser was hastily assembled. Facing the liability of newness, the Rendell Park watch group demonstrated only partial success on one element.

The SON group fares somewhat better in terms of the three features of mobilization efforts. SON exhibited a higher degree of agency in terms of collective action. Several SON members expended a great deal of effort convening meetings, handing out fliers, and, eventually, organizing block clubs. In terms of strategy, SON did make an effort at public education via using fliers and garnering publicity in the local press, which published reports of the first two meetings. SON did not really provide any direct service in terms of action to control gangs and crime in Beltway, nor did it advocate for structural change.[20] Finally, with regard to organization, SON started off well by scheduling two well-publicized and well-attended meetings, but it faltered thereafter. While there was certainly a core group that was in effect the central committee, it did not establish task committees beyond the evolution into block clubs, which were autonomous from the main group.

The Rendell Park boxing program is the only one of the three initiatives that scores unequivocally high in terms of agency. Even though it was essentially a two-man show, the two expended an enormous amount of effort starting and maintaining the program. The boxing program also had limited success in terms of strategy. O'Rourke and Reilly strove to incorporate education as part of the program, though, by their own admission, the education aspect of the boxing program could have been better. The boxing program also provided a direct service, though it was limited to the number of participants it could accommodate and also limited by gender.[21] Last, in terms of strategy, there was no attempt to bring about wider structural change. In terms of organization, the boxing program did not have regularly scheduled meetings, nor were there task committees. There was an aspiration to transform the group into a youth foundation that would have a board of directors, but no such structure actually existed.

To summarize, in terms of the features of mobilization outlined by McCarthy and Wolfson, none of the three strategies born in Beltway after the Thompson shooting was consistently successful. Of the three, the boxing program fared the best, and it also lasted the longest. However, the main point to note from this is that none of the groups could mobilize sufficient resources to overcome the liability of newness and to sustain its efforts. Perhaps we could speculate that if the groups had followed the example of the case studies in the previous chapter and tapped into the BCL or the ward organization, they could have mobilized resources on the strength of these longstanding and well-connected groups. Certainly, there is a fair degree of plausibility to this argument. I suggest that we be mindful of the question posed by Robert Sampson and reiterated in the previous chapter—organized for what? The groups that appeared after the Thompson shooting were reacting to the first signs of serious gang activity in Beltway; as such, there is another possible explanation for their rise and fall. Beyond the failure of these groups to adequately mobilize resources, I think another process can shed light on events in Beltway after the Thompson shooting. Specifically, I invoke the nature of the reaction to the Thompson shooting. I argue that it sparked a mini moral panic and that it is this reaction that helps explain why the groups failed.

Panic on the Streets of Beltway

What exactly is a moral panic, and how did it play out in Beltway at this time? The term "moral panic" was first used by Jock Young,[22] and it was brought to prominence by Stanley Cohen in his seminal study of Mods and Rockers in 1960s England.[23] Cohen explains the concept:

> Societies appear to be subject, every now and then, to periods of moral panic. A condition, episode, person or group of persons emerges to become identified as a threat to societal values and interests; its nature is presented in a stylized and stereotypical fashion by the mass media . . . sometimes the panic passes over and is forgotten, except in folklore and collective memory; at other times it has more serious and long-lasting repercussions and might produce such changes in legal and social policy or even in the way the society conceives itself.[24]

For Cohen, a moral panic occurs at the level of society as a whole, and the mass media play an important role in bringing about the panic. With respect to the Thompson shooting, the media did have a role in that there was a general discourse about gangs and gang violence at the time, which received a great deal of coverage in newspapers and on local television in Chicago. These stories provided part of the available store of knowledge from which Beltway residents interpreted the shooting. Locally, the shooting was covered in the local newspaper, which helped amplify the reaction, although word-of-mouth among residents probably did more to spread the news about the event.

Ben Goode and Nachman Ben-Yehuda elaborate Cohen's formulations and refine the concept of moral panic: "Panic [is] not simply the product of the overactive imagination of a number of unconnected individuals. . . . Rather . . . the fear and concern [have] a social foundation, a dynamic that reveal[s] the inner workings of the society in which it takes place."[25] Goode and Ben-Yehuda go on to elaborate the connection between moral panics and social control, which helps situate the present argument about Beltway. They state,

> The moral panic, then, is characterized by the feeling, held by a substantial number of the members of a given society, that evildoers pose a threat to the society and moral order as a consequence of their behavior and, therefore "something should be done" about them and their behav-

ior. A major focus of that "something" typically entails strengthening the social control apparatus of the society.[26]

In Beltway, the evildoers were the gang members who shot at one another, and the public's general feeling was that something should be done to control them.

Because the concept of moral panic is normally applied to a unit larger than a neighborhood, the question remains whether the events of 1994 truly constituted a moral panic in Beltway. There are five indicators of a moral panic. First, there has to be a heightened level of *concern* over the behavior of certain groups (in the present case, the groups that caused concern were youth gangs, and there was significant concern over the criminal activities associated with them). Second, there must be an increased level of *hostility* toward the group. Third, there should be widespread *consensus* that the threat posed by the group is serious. Agreement that a problem exists can grip residents of a community or neighborhood area. Fourth, the criterion of *disproportionality* should be met; that is, the people who engage in the panic must feel that there are more people involved in the feared behavior than there are in actuality. The fifth criterion is *volatility*; moral panics can erupt suddenly and, just as suddenly, disappear. Some moral panics can become institutionalized, such as when a social movement organization is formed in response. Cohen and Goode and Ben-Yehuda invoke the idea of folk devils, which are personifications of evil and which are evoked in a moral panic to embody the trouble.

Armed with this checklist of indicators, we can determine whether there was a moral panic about gang-associated crime in Beltway in 1994. I would argue that Chicago in general, and Beltway in particular, at times during the 1990s experienced a moral panic concerning youth gang crime (see table 4.2). Concerns over the proliferation of street gangs, over teenage violence, and over the condition of youth generally propelled the residents around Rendell Park into a moral panic when Thompson was shot.[27] Youth generally, and gang youth in particular, were the "folk devils" that fueled the moral panic. During the course of my fieldwork, Beltway residents, especially those around Rendell Park, became increasingly concerned about the perceived encroachment of street gangs into the neighborhood. Empirically, there were five street gangs said to have a presence in Beltway, two of which were said to be active in the Rendell Park area.[28] Despite the increased presence of gangs, there was no major

TABLE 4.2
Presence of Goode and Ben-Yehuda Indicators of Moral Panic in Beltway after the Thompson Shooting

Criterion	*Presence*	*Level*
Concern	Yes	High
Hostility	Yes	High
Consensus	Somewhat	Low
Disproportionality	Yes	High
Volatility	Yes	High

increase in gang-related crime in 1993 and 1994. Official police data for the period for the area around Rendell Park indicate very low levels of violent crime. From 1993 through the end of 1995, the Village had no homicides and very few aggravated assaults and robberies. So, in terms of violent gang crime, the Rendell Park area could not be said to have a sustained problem. However, the gangs in and around the Village and Rendell Park were said to be engaged in a "turf war" with each other at the time, which usually manifested itself through graffiti, rival groups making their claim to an area by tagging walls, businesses, and garage doors.[29] The gangs in Beltway in 1994 offered a contrast to the corporate gangs that were the focus of much of the scholarly literature at the time.[30] The Beltway gangs were not as organized as the so-called supergangs that reputedly were running much of the drug trade in Chicago. Nor did they seem to be organized solely for profit, the distinguishing feature of the corporate gangs. There is no doubt that gangs were active around Rendell Park, but gang activity was not constantly visible. The most visible cues were the gang graffiti that were painted on walls, and this became a node through which the moral panic in Beltway was initiated.

Beltway residents view graffiti as a harbinger of change, an indication that gangs are trying to take over their community. When a local boy, Orlando Santos, scratched a tag onto one of the special soundproof windows of the Gerald School and was caught by a local resident, a group of people, made up of concerned parents, residents, and the principal of the Gerald School, went to every court case to show their concern. Certainly the act of vandalism at the school was an affront to many residents, but it was compounded by the fear that the tagging was gang-related and symptomatic of a wider problem. In fact, the tag on the Gerald School was simply a moniker for the tagger and not gang-related, but it sowed the seeds for the panic that was to follow the Thompson shooting. The Santos tagging happened in late 1993, and the court case was heard in the early months of 1994. The timing of the Santos incident and the reaction of the residents illustrate how a moral panic can take root.

In terms of the constituents of a moral panic, there was a high degree of concern among Beltwayites about graffiti and the possible connections to youth gangs, and there was definite hostility toward the perpetrators. Moreover, there was a consensus that the threat posed was serious and that something had to be done about it. There was precious little that the public, at the LSC meeting after the Thompson shooting, agreed on, but the one thing that emerged was that people felt that the problem in their neighborhood was serious and that something should be done about it. There was a divergence of opinion on what should be done and who should do it, and thus the consensus was partial and transitory. The evidence of disproportionality is that the panic about the gang problem seemed to be excessive given the crime statistics for the area at the time. This is not to say that there were no gangs there, but the reaction was disproportional to the actual problem. Finally, the moral panic in Beltway was certainly volatile. The attention focused on the Thompson shooting led to a number of well-attended meetings, but the number of participants soon dwindled, as did some of the initiatives sparked by the Rendell Park shooting.

The Thompson shooting and the furor that characterized the reaction to it suggest that perhaps there was a mini moral panic in the Village. This moral panic seems to have played a major role in inciting the flurry of activity that took place in the six weeks following the shooting. It was also instrumental in enabling the strategies of informal social control that were initiated at the time in the area. The concept of moral panic, along with the resource mobilization literature, also helps explain the sudden rise and fall of the park patrol and SON.

The Rendell Park patrol and SON both built on the initial panic after the Thompson shooting in terms of assembling their organizations, but they could not sustain themselves because of their inability to mobilize the resources they needed to succeed. Part of their failure to mobilize resources can be said to be due to the volatile nature of the moral panic, which compounded the liability of the groups' newness. As the moral panic erupted and then died down, the trajectory of the watch group and SON seemed to mirror this rise and fall. The boxing program did last longer, partly because it was not conceived totally in the wake of the

Thompson shooting and partly because its organizers were more successful at procuring resources.

Conclusion

The cases studies in this chapter illustrate the first real skirmishes between Beltway residents and gangs. The Thompson shooting and a handful of other incidents at the time seemed to indicate that there was a youth gang problem in the area, and the response to the problem provides us with our first case studies of informal social control in Beltway. Neither the Rendell Park watch group nor SON was able to parlay initial public interest into a sustainable effort to control crime and disorder. The boxing program lasted longer but was only indirectly about informal social control.

I suggest that the rise and fall of the groups can be explained in terms of a failure to mobilize resources and as a consequence of the mini moral panic that flared up in the area in the wake of the Thompson shooting. I also suggest that part of the reason for the failure of SON and the Rendell Park watch group is what locals constructed as the cause of gang problems. Sean O'Rourke's view, for example, is that the gangs were a result of outsiders moving in to the neighborhood. He said:

> [We have] new people we got coming in from other areas that was gang infested. I know a lot of 'em that are moving in here, the Spanish, are from the Little Village area where there's a high concentration of gangs. They're not from around here. So it's people that are moving from other communities moving in here and bringing the shit with them. Their parents are probably trying to move them out of the neighborhood to do a good thing for 'em, but they bring it with them. Instead of choking the problem themselves, they move away from it. All of a sudden [the kids] are hanging at Rendell Park and they're talkin' gang stuff.

The second thread in the discourse about what caused the growth of gangs in Rendell Park places the blame for gangs at the door of lackadaisical parents. At various public meetings before and after the Thompson shooting, the refrain about the need to hold parents responsible for the actions of their children was heard repeatedly. Fred Reilly summed it up: "You can have activities and a lot [of people] will come in there but where are the parents? Without the parents you can't [make] it safe for kids to go to and from school. Who's terrorizing the kids? Other people's kids."

The construction of the gang problem as something that was generated by outside forces moving into Rendell Park seems to miss the point. The racially inflected discourse had it that Hispanics moving to Beltway were bringing the gangs with them; the fact that both Thompson and his attacker were white and from the area was obfuscated.[31]

The perceived lack of parental involvement and diminished supervision is more pertinent to the present story. In terms of the Hunter typology of spheres of social control outlined in chapter 1, some Beltway residents were acutely aware of the lax nature of informal social control at the private level. Many young people are left to their own devices, and parents are not active in controlling their children. Neither was Rendell Park at the time of the Thompson shooting an area where there was strong parochial control. It was only after the mini moral panic occasioned by the Thompson shooting that there was a concerted effort to invigorate neighborhood controls. The Rendell Park watch group and SON were both short-lived, but they signaled the community's interest in trying to establish some form of neighborhood-level controls.

In terms of the notion of the new parochialism, the case studies outlined in this chapter illustrate the difficulty of establishing effective ongoing parochial control in the traditional sense. There was clearly a need for a communitywide effort to curb the growing gang problem, but the efforts that were made withered on the vine. A crucial point is that the watch group and SON began before the implementation of the CAPS program in Beltway, and so there was no readily available institutional help from formal social control agencies or from public agencies of social order. This lack of assistance from the public agencies of control, coupled with the basic inability to effectively mobilize resources, caused the groups to founder within a year of their formation.

The case studies in the following chapters illustrate how, under different circumstances, the new parochialism becomes a viable approach when private and traditionally parochial controls have diminished in a neighborhood but some residents are willing to take collective responsibility for neighborhood problems. In 1994, in the area around Rendell Park, all of the pieces that make new parochial strategies possible were not in place.

Beltway from the close of 1994 through much of 1995 continued to have a nagging and increasing local gang problem, but there were no ongoing local efforts, except for the boxing program, to address this issue. For many residents in the western part of the neighborhood, the trouble was confined to Rendell Park and was therefore out of sight and very much out of mind. Vicious youth gangs were outside the neighborhood; they sometimes visited and caused trouble. The complacency that many Beltway residents felt about youth crime was about to be shaken to its core.

5

Gang Violence Can Happen Here

The Hastings Murders and Their Aftermath

Introduction

Thursday, December 14, 1995, was a typical day in Beltway. The weather was warm enough for that time of year that a few residents who were around during the day took the opportunity to festoon their houses with ever more elaborate holiday decorations. The sun set early, and while the cool of the evening was not the biting cold that can sweep over the plains at that time of the year, it was enough to send people inside to seek the warmth of their houses. Many other residents who had spent the day at work and those who worked the regular shift or who commuted to white- and pink-collar jobs downtown returned home just as darkness engulfed the neighborhood. People switched on their lawn decorations and Christmas lights, and, though school was still in session, many people's thoughts might have turned to the upcoming holidays.

Just after 6:30 P.M., as people finished up dinner or planned an evening holiday shopping trip to the local mall, the cold quiet outside the empty Hastings School was punctuated by a series of five pops. The noise, which sounded to some residents like small fireworks going off, did not attract immediate attention from the neighbors of the school. Some passed it off as a harmless prank, some kid using the last of the July fireworks in the lead-up to Christmas. Neither did the sound of five youths running away from the school elicit any response. The only thing that might have seemed out of place was the squealing of tires as an early-model Plymouth Voyager sped from the scene. Still, nobody came out to look or paid any attention. It would later turn out that what had transpired at the corner of First Street and Midvale Avenue was that five local youths had strode up to the parked Voyager and one, fifteen-year-old Richard Lindstrom, had taken a .38-caliber service revolver out of his jacket pocket. Lindstrom, who, along with two of his companions, had stolen the gun and one other weapon from a police officer's house in Beltway earlier in the day, aimed the gun at the passenger side of the van and opened fire, shooting five bullets. As Lindstrom shot, the other four youths banged on the van with baseball bats and bricks. When the shooting stopped, thirteen-year-old Teresa Powell, who had been sitting in the passenger seat, and her friend Melissa Harvey, also thirteen, who was seated right behind Powell, had been hit in the head. The youth driving the van, eighteen-year-old Dave Arnold, panicked after he heard the first shot and drove off. By the time Arnold and the two other passengers in the van sought medical help, Powell and Harvey were dead. Both young women had died almost instantly from the shots to their heads.

The circumstances surrounding the shooting underscore the tragically random nature of many such violent events. The two young women were in the van because Powell had been dating Arnold, and they had been listening to music on the van's stereo. Arnold and the other two youth in the van, seventeen-year-old Chad Howard and sixteen-year-old Erica Wendell, were from Lessing Park, a neighborhood several miles north of Beltway. Arnold and Howard had fashioned themselves into a gang and had taken the moniker Regal Vikings.[1] They had also apparently been recruiting in the Beltway area for several weeks before the shooting, and their activities and their van had become known to members of the local white gang, the Black Knights. At the behest of two older leaders of the Knights, gang members had formed a makeshift plan to frighten off the Vikings.[2] According to the prosecutors who later tried the case, Lindstrom, the son of a Chicago police officer, and John Wiseman, another member of the Black Knights, had stolen the two guns earlier in the day from the house of a local police officer, after which they had test-fired the .38 in Wiseman's basement, with the intention of using it against the Vikings. When the shooting stopped, Beltway had its first recorded gang-related homicide, and the victims were from the same streets and went to the same schools as their killer.

The Powell-Harvey murders captured the attention of a city inured to gang violence for a number of reasons: the race of the victims and the gang members; the socioeconomic backgrounds of the murderers; the fact that the shooter was the son of a Chicago police officer; and the location of the murders. The several media stories on the killings repeatedly described the murderers as members of a "white gang." Without a doubt, the race of the victims and the killers transfixed Chicagoans, who, at the time, were accustomed to seeing African American and Latino youths fall prey to gangs and gang violence but were surprised and troubled by white youngsters' involvement in gangs. Many Beltway residents were angered by the tone of the coverage of the murders: they felt that the neighborhood was being portrayed as going "down the toilet," as one resident remarked.

The murders sent shock waves through the community, and there was a flurry of activity in the aftermath of the killings, similar to what happened after John Thompson was shot a year and a half earlier. There were a number of public meetings, the Hastings School held a gang awareness workshop, and a great deal of attention was focused on the neighborhood.[3] The murders of the young girls in Beltway and the reaction to them constitute a pivotal series of moments in the story of crime and social control in Beltway; as residents searched for meaning in the aftermath of the killings, the events illustrate how strategies of informal social control take shape. The homicides signaled that the neighborhood was not immune from the most severe form of gang violence, even though the events were unexpected and unprecedented.

The response to the crime cohered initially into one of two discourses that residents used to make sense of the killings. I label these discourses *denial* and *accountability,* and they pre-existed the murders, defining, for example, the reaction to the Thompson shooting described in chapter 4. Beltway residents who were in denial that there was a gang problem in the neighborhood did not become active in efforts to exert social control; thus, denial had a negative effect on the formation of informal social control strategies. While a number of people who articulated the discourse of denial attended the public meetings in the aftermath of the murders, that was the extent of their activism. In the second discourse, accountability, residents seek to hold someone accountable for the murders. Once again, the aftermath of the Thompson shooting illustrates an earlier evocation of this discourse. Residents who demanded that parents, police officers, and school officials be somehow held accountable for the murders enacted the discourse of accountability; it also leads largely to inaction because residents abrogate collective responsibility by finding scapegoats to blame. The case of the Powell-Harvey murders eventually spawned a third discourse, community responsibility, which led to community action and ultimately bolstered informal social control.

Community responsibility does not follow easily from denial and accountability, but, crucially in the Beltway case, the development of this discourse was aided and abetted by formal social control actors. This latter resource was absent in the aftermath of the Thompson shooting; residents were left to their own devices, and the informal social control strategies that they initiated, SON and the Rendell Park watch group, for example, flourished briefly, faltered, and eventually died. The circumstances after the Powell-Harvey murders enabled a coherent response because of several key interventions.

In the first place, local police officers encouraged people to get involved with the CAPS program. Second, the Joint Community Police Training (JCPT), a police-community problem-solving initiative, began in Beltway in March 1996, three months ahead of the originally scheduled date. The actions of formal actors served to reinforce the discourse of community responsibility by giving shape to what I call "the new parochialism." The case study of the Powell-Harvey murders and their aftermath illustrates how the new parochialism develops; while it takes an extraordinary event to spur residents into action, I suggest that the new parochialism can also develop in nonemergency situations. On a basic level, perhaps the most important thing about the murders was that it brought home to many Beltway residents that youth gangs, and the violence associated with them, were not someone else's problem.

Gangs in Beltway: Masking the Symptoms

As I have shown in previous chapters, the presence of youth gangs in Beltway is not a recent phenomenon. Older residents spoke of gangs that were active in Beltway fifteen and twenty years ago. More recently, there was the shooting near Rendell Park and other incidents that foretold future dangers. However, most residents who lived in the area near the Hastings School chose to ignore what was going on less than a mile to the east. As I noted earlier, many Beltway residents conveniently omit the area around Rendell Park from their cognitive map of the neighborhood, and so the shootings and the subsequent formation of the Rendell Park watch group and SON did not really penetrate the consciousness of many residents who lived in the western part of the neighborhood.

For those residents who were aware of gangs in their part of Beltway, there was an uneasy realization that these gangs bore no resemblance to the gangs of two decades ago, particularly with respect to the violence associated with them. Carla Wiesniski, a thirty-three-year-old city worker who moved into one of the condominiums on the southern edge of the neighborhood, explained how she sees the difference between new and old gangs: "I think [gangs today] are more violent. They don't care about their lives so you can't expect them to care about anybody else's." Other residents spoke about how they had generally become more wary and concerned specifically with youth gangs.

Whether or not residents in the western part of Beltway were aware of gangs seemed beside the point in the immediate aftermath of the Powell-Harvey murders; everyone had to face the fact that these events had happened in their own backyard. Until the murders, there was no consistent public discourse in this part of Beltway about local gangs and the crime that is associated with them. Gangs were assumed to be someone else's problem; if they were operating over at Rendell Park, then that was as far as they had come. The assumption of many residents was that the children of the slightly better-off residents near Hastings Park could never be involved with gangs.[4] However, the murders exploded this myth in no uncertain terms.

At the time of the murders, I was aware that there were youth gangs in all parts of Beltway. When my research began, there was one identifiable youth gang in the neighborhood; at the zenith of gang activity, from 1995 until early 1997, there were allegedly five gangs vying with one another for control of various parts of Beltway turf.[5] Teachers at local elementary schools acknowledged that some of their seventh- and eight-graders were involved with gangs, and interviews I conducted with local youth had bolstered this claim. While local police officers stated that there were not very many young people in gangs at the time, some residents disputed this contention. Whatever the actual levels of gang activity at the time, there were some unmistakable signs. Graffiti, much of it gang graffiti, were among the most common offenses in Beltway for the period 1993–1995.[6] However, many of the graffiti were quickly removed or painted over in the western part of the neighborhood, mainly through a combination of vigilance and the ability to quickly mobilize city services. Swift graffiti removal, allied with the way Beltwayites talked about crime, conspired to mask the symptoms of local gang activity.

Before the Powell-Harvey killings, most people in Beltway explained gang crime as an exogenous phenomenon caused by nonwhite and poor young people.[7] This racially inflected and class-based explanation of crime prevented residents from acknowledging the existence of a local, white, nonpoor gang presence. Beltwayites viewed crime and gangs as invaders that periodically infiltrated their peaceful oasis of beautifully manicured lawns and brick bungalows. Indeed, residents' concerns about crime and disorder were tightly bound up with race- and class-based stereotypes, and people assumed that the community's gang problems were the result of "spillover" from Mountain Ridge, a predominantly Hispanic suburb of Chicago, or from lower-income Hispanic and African American city neighborhoods to the east of Beltway. For many people, gangs were a continuation of the problems they had experienced before they fled to Beltway from formerly ethnic white strongholds. Now the gangs were coming to Beltway and terrorizing these residents in their new homes.

An indication of Beltwayites' view of crime as an exogenous problem that threatened the neighborhood was a controversy that surrounded students who waited for the school bus at Carver Heights High School, located just north of Beltway. Residents often grumbled about African American and Hispanic teenagers from the school who would loiter along the intersection of Third Avenue and Ridge Street in Beltway while waiting for buses after school. There were so many complaints from residents and business owners about the teenagers and the potential for gang violence that Beltway's former alderman John Puchinski arranged for extra Chicago Transit Authority (CTA) buses to run after school in order to prevent the high school students from "hanging out" in the neighborhood. This example underscores the predominant strand of the discourse about gang crime prior to the murders, one that was still very much in evidence after the murders: that gang crime is caused by minority kids coming into Beltway from outside. Indeed, this notion was also prominent in the public discourse after the Thompson shooting. It stands to reason, then, that many residents believed that efforts to control the gang problem should take the form of moving the offending gang members out of the neighborhood, which could be a simple matter of adding buses after school.

However, youth going to and from school was not the only problem to contend with in Beltway. As I have stated, the presence of graffiti was among the most common problems in Beltway over the course of my fieldwork there. To deal with the graffiti problem, the city of Chicago commissioned special "Graffiti Blaster" trucks that were dispatched every day to clean up graffiti trouble spots.[8] In addition to the city service, the local ward offices that serve Beltway made graffiti-removing cleaner and paint available for anyone who wished to remove or paint over graffiti. The ward office also coordinated the use of the Graffiti Blaster trucks, and Beltway, because of its political clout, managed to get the Graffiti Blaster trucks almost on an as-needed basis. Thus, graffiti were dealt with very quickly in Beltway. It was the efficiency and speed with which Beltway residents and civic leaders dealt with graffiti that ironically served to mask the symptoms of the local gang problem. For example, on one occasion, in February 1995, I witnessed the Graffiti Blaster truck remove graffiti from a brick wall near St. Martin's church at 8:45 A.M. This is not particularly noteworthy, but, given the fact that the graffiti had been daubed on the wall a mere five hours earlier, it speaks volumes about the speed of mobilization of city services in the neighborhood.[9] However, paradoxically, this efficacy masked a deeper malady, as out-of-sight certainly put the gang problem out of mind for many residents. People in the western part of Beltway were confident in the knowledge that gang violence and crime "could not happen here" because they literally did not see the writing on the wall; if they did, the prevailing wisdom held that the gangs were from other neighborhoods, anyway.

The symptoms of an internal gang problem were readily apparent throughout the neighborhood long before the shootings. Anyone skilled in gang graffiti cryptography and/or fortunate enough to see some of the graffiti before they were removed would have recognized the gang "tags" that claimed the neighborhood as BK or Black Knights territory. Large Black Knights tags marked the gang's territory along the bus route that brought students to and from Carver Heights High School so that students attending the school would know what gang claimed to control Beltway and neighboring Carver Heights. The no-man's-land out by the factories in the northwestern part of the neighborhood was also covered with gang graffiti.

In the winter of 1993, more than two years before the Powell-Harvey shootings, the principal of the Hastings School hosted a gang awareness workshop for parents on how to recognize that one's child was involved with gangs. At that time, the principal was aware of the Knights' activity in the school and in the neighborhood. Like the community policing meeting before the murders,[10] which had a very low turnout, the gang workshop was attended by a handful of residents and parents. As I mentioned in chapter 4, the Beltway Civic League invited a Chicago neighborhood beat officer, Paul Otis, to speak at the group's monthly meeting in May 1994, and the reaction to his presentation illustrates how little some residents knew or understood about youth gangs at the time.

A police gang expert who was quoted in the newspaper coverage after the Powell-Harvey murders said he was not surprised by the public's naiveté about gangs. Indeed, he underscored the notion that Beltwayites' fastidious and efficient removal of graffiti masked the symptoms of the neighborhood's increasing gang presence from residents. He was quoted as saying: "The Black Knights and the Regal Vikings have been in the neighborhood for some time. They've been throwing up gang graffiti for a long time, and people have been taking it down as fast as it goes up. Some people don't want to believe that there are gangs in their neighborhood." However, that complacency was, in the words of one newspaper article, "rocked" by the murders. What happened in the wake of the murders charts how this shattered complacency eventually reassembled into a proactive community response.

What Happened Next?

The day after the murders, students at the Hastings School wandered around in a daze. Youngsters cried and embraced one another. A friend of one of the girls drew a picture of two headstones with Teresa's and Melissa's names on them. In the drawing, the two headstones are surrounded by flowers. On the top of the picture are the words "We miss you and we love you." The boy brought the picture to Lydia Donovan, the head librarian of the Beltway branch of the Chicago Public Library, and she solemnly displayed the drawing on the front door of the building. Maria Kefalas described the scene outside the school: "Not far from where Powell and Harvey were shot, on the crumbling back steps of the Hastings School, students and neighborhood residents left flowers, cards, and toys, erecting a makeshift shrine."[11]

As the initial shock and outrage subsided, a number of community meetings were held to address the issue of local gangs. The meetings were well-attended but stormy affairs as residents publicly came to terms with the tragic deaths of the two young women. People attempted to make sense of the killings, which was difficult given the way in which the efficient graffiti removal and the prevailing discourse about gangs and crime had masked the underlying youth gang problem. The bulk of the public reaction cohered initially around the two distinct discourses, *denial* and *accountability,* mentioned earlier in the chapter, both of which have implications for how informal social control is practiced in the neighborhood.

Denial

It is easy to see how Beltway residents could be in denial about the gang problem. Despite the presence of gang graffiti in the neighborhood and perhaps because of the graffiti's quick removal, most Beltwayites were blissfully unaware of the existence of the Black Knights. If residents were slow to believe there was a gang problem in the neighborhood, "they could have been lulled to sleep by their solidly [working-class] surroundings of sturdy brick homes, well-kept lawns, and blocks filled with police officers and firefighters."[12] Carla Wiesniski explained that, before the murders, she was naïve about the problems in the neighborhood:

> Before [the murders] I was pretty naïve, I thought it was, I still think it is, a really good place to live, but I didn't know all the things that go on around here. I have a friend that I walk with in the evening, and she [still] doesn't want me to tell her anything that happens because she wants to stay naïve. She wants to think this is a really nice neighborhood, a good place to live [and] to raise kids.

Even after the murders, some residents continued to deny the existence of the gangs. On three separate occasions—at the community meeting for residents, at the gang information workshop held for parents and community members at the Hastings school, and at a CAPS beat meeting held shortly after the shootings—there were residents who said that, despite the killings, they did not believe that Beltway had a gang problem. Pam Preston, a mother of three children and the owner of a local business on Third Avenue, acknowledged that gangs were a growing problem in the neighborhood. Pam's eight-year-old son, Jimmy, had witnessed a gang beating in an alley not far from the family's home. She tried to warn others, but, according to Pam, "You get a lot of anger, disbelief, denial, parents in complete denial. I feel it's a big problem. I feel it's going to get worse unless we as parents can do something."[13]

Thus, while the community reeled from the news of the murders, in public settings Beltwayites avoided describing the girls' deaths as murders or discussing the neighborhood's gang problem. For example, at the memorial service for the two girls, held at St. Martin's Catholic Church, the teachers, parents, and clergy who addressed the audience never mentioned the violent nature of the girls' deaths.[14] It was almost as if the girls were killed as a result of some random natural phenomenon. There was no mention of guns, gang violence, or young people. At the community meetings held throughout the neighborhood in the following weeks, residents, when possible, avoided talking about any details of the murders.[15] In fact, even the police only cryptically referred to the "recent incident in the neighborhood." To this day, some people still refer euphemistically to the murders as the "incident at the school." More striking was the fact that some residents continued to deny the existence of gangs or any type of gang problem. Laura McCreesh, the principal of the Hastings School, when asked whether awareness of gangs had changed since the murders, described some residents' inability to process the significance of the shootings:

McCreesh: Yes! Oh yes! They were shocked. I think that a lot of people were naïve in this neighborhood, not believing that this exists within their community. Even at the community forum we had people come up and say that "No, we don't have gangs in this area." Everybody went, "Whoa, how can you say that!" when an incident like that happened. So we still have [some] people who don't want to believe it.

Interviewer: Why do you think it is so hard for people to believe?

McCreesh: I don't know. I think that maybe because people aren't aware of what is around them. They aren't aware of what to look for. They don't know what they are seeing. If they see a bunch of guys walking down the street with baseball bats, they don't know if they are looking at a Little League baseball team or a group of gangbangers.

Consider Beltway resident Tina Kaiser's reaction to the killings and the neighborhood's gang problem:

Now, I am a little more concerned? [Yes] it heightens my awareness. But I am more concerned about the kids from Carver Heights High School

> [who walk through the neighborhood on their way to the bus]. I know these kids [involved in the Black Knights]. Is that a gang? What everyone around here perceives as a gang and what I see on TV, with the blacks and the Mexican gangs killing each other, these gangs out here are ka-ka, pee-pee gangs.

Like Tina Kaiser, many residents insisted that the murders were a freak occurrence and that the gang problem was not that serious.

Despite a number of community meetings in the weeks after the killings and the involvement of the local aldermen, school administrators, police, and other neighborhood activists, there was no immediate collective neighborhood-level response to the gangs. No neighborhood watches were organized. No parents came together to call for more afterschool activities for local teenagers. There were no marches or candlelight vigils calling for an end to gang violence or better gun control. Beltway is a community with a long history of local activism and civic engagement, a community where residents complained if street signs were crooked or graffiti were not removed quickly. However, despite vigorous prompting from Beltway's leaders, activists and nonactivists alike failed to respond quickly in any meaningful way to the Powell-Harvey murders. Part of the reason for the lack of an immediate response was the presence and strength of the discourse of denial.

As Jim Pratt, an active Beltway resident and a member of the Hastings LSC, remarked at the time: "A lot of people out here have what I call the ostrich syndrome. They think that if they bury their heads then the problem will go away. Well, it won't go away. It's here just the same as it is everywhere. We have gang problems, but some people don't wanna face that." The denial discourse has a number of implications for the story of informal social control in the neighborhood. Denial by Beltway residents that there was a gang problem, even in the face of the graphic evidence of the killings, inhibited communal action to invigorate informal social control. If there is no problem to begin with, then there is no need to get involved in efforts to control local youth. Denial is one of the major reasons for lax social controls in the first place; it is a discourse that predates the murders. However, the persistence of denial as a resonant set of beliefs impeded informal social control in the aftermath of the Powell-Harvey murders. Informal social control was invigorated only when formal social control agencies, in the form of the police force and problem-solving groups, officially got involved in the neighborhood. To the extent that denial held sway, nothing new was put in place to deal with the problems of gangs.

While some residents remained in a fog of denial about the existence of gangs, a second community level discourse about gang crime emerged alongside that of denial. The second discourse sought to explain the murders, accommodate residents' view of Beltway as a safe and secure neighborhood, and also create a scapegoat for gang violence. This discourse about crime and gangs focused on accountability.

Accountability

Accountability differs from denial in one fundamental aspect: residents seek to find out who is responsible for the murders. Accountability in the Powell-Harvey murders went further than the arrest of the five gang members involved in the shooting and, in September 1996, the additional arrests of Knights leaders Jamie Pelzer and Roger Krijt; residents sought to find out who or what was responsible so that such an event could take place. After the shock and denial of the days immediately after the murders subsided for some Beltway residents, they began to try to apportion blame for the killings.

The discourses of denial and accountability were complementary and competing. They were complementary in the sense that for some Beltway residents, denial gave way to accountability in the aftermath of the murders, similar to the stages of grieving, where denial leads to accountability and ultimately to closure. However, at the same time, denial and accountability were competing discourses; some Beltway residents remained in denial, while others sought to make someone accountable for the murders.

Accountability was also not a simple byproduct of the murders. As with denial, the discourse had been evident before the murders in various forms at community meetings, especially those related to crime in Beltway. In the years and months before the Powell-Harvey murders, residents had sought to make three sets of people accountable for trouble in Beltway: parents of deviant and delinquent kids, school officials, and the police and the courts. For example, when the Gerald Elementary School had its windows tagged by a local teen, Orlando Santos, a number of parents with children at the school called for his parents to be held jointly responsible for his actions. The commander of the local police district, Henry Rusnak, when asked how he thought Beltway residents were responding to the CAPS program and to crime prevention generally, also placed the blame for miscreants squarely on parents:

> Well, let me tell you what many of them are not asking themselves, [and this is] where the problem is coming from. It is [coming] from inside the neighborhood. I blame the parents, if you don't know what your kids are up to, or what they are doing. I mean we cannot raise children, and they are at school eight hours of the day.

Specifically, after the murders, many Beltway residents expressed the opinion that parents should have more control over their kids. For example, Jane Pratt, who was actively involved in community groups and in her daughter's life, stated: "These children belong to somebody. They're not aliens. Somebody didn't drop 'em off on a bus. They're in your area, so who do they belong to, and how do you get to their parents?"

At the CAPS beat meeting, three months after the murders, in March 1996, there was a lengthy debate about who should be held accountable for the murders. Many felt that the parents of gang kids were responsible for the problem. Pam Preston, a mother of three who had been interviewed by the *Chicago Tribune* after the Powell-Harvey murders, echoed the sentiment, saying, "I think that if a kid vandalizes a garage, then the taxpayers shouldn't have to pay for that. It should be the parents and the kids who clean up the garages." At another community policing meeting in Beltway, in May 1996, the discourse of parental accountability was again in evidence. Brenda Smith, who had lived in Beltway for more than twenty years and who had raised three children there, told the meeting that "it all comes back to the parents. The parents are responsible for their kids, right? Well, then, I think that the parents should have to go to court along with their kids when anything happens." Brenda's comment was greeted by a chorus of approval.

The notion of parental responsibility and obligation is the most consistent element in the discourse of accountability. Not only was it present before the murders, but it also endured long after the murders and continues to be a theme in neighborhood discourse. For example, a number of Beltway residents blamed parents of local youth who join gangs. Carla

Wiesniski felt that it is a combination of parental responsibility and peer pressure that causes gangs, and she went on to describe the extent of the problem in Beltway:

> Peer pressure, something they're not getting from home, something they want from their parents that they're not getting—respect. Their parents are not home, unfortunately. When I was growing up, my mom was always home, and right when I got out of grade school, that's when everybody's mother started going back to work, and I think that's a big thing to do with it. One parent should be home, but unfortunately people can't afford it. . . . When Kitty and I go out on the watch, she's always very suspicious of any kid we go across, and I'm always like "they're not doing anything, are they breaking windows? No. They're walking down the street, leave them alone." I'd like to think that, but since I have been walking in the evening exercising, my neighbor is a police officer, and we go walking by Hastings and she's like picking them out, "gang member, gang member, gang member." I'm like: "Dolores! They're not doing anything, they're sitting on a swing, how do you know." She says you can tell by their clothes. [But] they're on a swing just playing. I don't think they know how to be kids any more. I still want to be naïve about this, I think. I don't want to believe that all of them are [gang members], I don't think all of them are, but it's growing, some of it has to do with peer pressure, I suppose, but parents don't wanna believe that their kids are in gangs, they're the first to say "No! not my child." And for whatever reason they probably want to deny it like I do. In one respect you can't blame them. But somebody has to open their eyes before something happens again like these two girls [that] got shot.

Other strands in the discourse of accountability were less frequently advanced but resonated all the same. After the murders, Beltway residents also sought to hold the police, the courts, and the schools accountable for the tragedy.

The collective desire on the part of residents for police and judicial accountability was not restricted to the Powell-Harvey murders. People in Beltway had consistently argued that they should have more police coverage and that the courts had failed to mete out sufficient justice; such petitions were renewed with greater force in the wake of the murders. The ironic twist to the narrative is that Richard Lindstrom, the trigger-man in the killings, is the son of a local police officer, one of the many city workers who populate the neighborhood. At the gang awareness workshop convened shortly after the murders, Joe Toal, a local resident, who had two children at Hastings Elementary at the time, addressed the meeting, stating: "According to the newspaper reports, some of the gang members are the sons of police officers. If the police officers can't identify gang members in their own families, how can we?" The railing against the police and courts continued at the community policing beat meeting in January 1996. Jane Pratt asked Commander Rusnak whether more officers were going to be deployed in Beltway. Rusnak replied:

> I don't think we need any extra officers; we just all need to do our job [murmurs of disagreement with his statement]. Of course, it would be great to have an officer on each corner, but we can't have that. You can't put it all on the Board of Ed. and the police department. You can't say that for eight hours of the day the Board of Ed. is responsible, and the police department for the other sixteen. It has to start with the parents. It's no use sayin' that all these kids had no one to talk to, and that's why they are joining gangs. I don't buy that. You have to talk with your kids, find out what they're up to. You wouldn't believe all the parents that come into the station when we pick up their kids. "Oh, no, it couldn't be my kid that's in a gang." And I ask them: "Do you see what your kid is bringing home?" All of my kids went to school, and that was one thing I always did: I checked what they were bringing home. So the kids that we arrest now, I ask to see their school books, and there on the inside cover, there's a pitchfork upside down or a five-pointed crown [common gang symbols]. And it's not because they are suddenly artistic that they are doin' that.

As residents argued that the police should be accountable, police officers, in this case the local commander, deflected this criticism by turning accountability back to the parents. There are a number of points worth noting here. First, the mechanism of community policing makes much of this public discourse about police accountability possible. Second, while the finger-pointing that accompanies the discourse of accountability oscillates among police, schools, and parents, the discourse of denial is also visible, particularly with respect to the parents of suspected gang members.

The last strand of the accountability discourse concerns the schools. A number of Beltway residents felt that the schools, in particular Hastings Elementary School, should be held somehow accountable for the Powell-Harvey murders and claimed, for example, that the schools foster gangs.[16] Fred Reilly spoke of the prevalence of gangs in schools. According to Reilly, teachers at one of the local high schools estimated that about four-fifths of the students there were in gangs. Moreover, the gangs were becoming so violent that students were compelled to join because, in Reilly's words, "even bein' neutral is considered bein' the enemy." However, teachers and administrators were quick to point out the difficulties they faced in trying to cope with a problem that was essentially beyond their purview. The principal of Hastings, Laura McCreesh, had this response to the notion of school accountability:

> The question I would ask is: is it the school's responsibility to determine who is a gang member and who is not? I think our primary responsibility is to educate. I think in recognizing whether or not they are gang members, that is something that should be up to their parents and the community. We see the kids for [only] six hours a day. And the parents have them for the rest of the day and on the weekends. We can only be aware of so much. Parents really need to be aware of what their kids are into and what their kids are doing. You need to look at your kids and [ask], "What is he wearing? Is he wearing black and white or is he wearing blue and black all the time? What does that symbolize?" You have to do this for your child just like you would protect your child from a stranger on the street or being hit by a car.

Overall, the discourse of accountability was more varied than that of denial. While both discourses were evident before the killings, it was the spectacular event of the murders that brought them to the fore. Denial and accountability provide us with an easy way to analyze the reaction to the murders and their implications for informal social control. Denial prohibited the formation of strategies of informal social control because there was no acknowledgment that there was a problem, while the search for accountability caused people to seek an answer to the problem of youth gangs in Beltway.

The Search for a Solution: Losing Innocence and Gaining Activists

The key to rebuilding informal social control in the wake of the murders in Beltway was tapping into the pool of local activists. The community response to the murders was not immediate, and the discourses of denial and accountability played a large part in that delay. However, even more fundamental to the absence of a coherent response was the fact that many of the people who might have been instrumental in helping the neighborhood rid itself of gangs were otherwise engaged in the first four months of 1996. The issue that siphoned off many of the local activists was the control and direction of the Hastings Local School Council. In chapter 3 I described how the Barker faction's despotic reign was successfully brought to an end by the PFH, whose alliance with the local political machine and the Board of Education cemented a landslide victory in the April 1996 election. Many of the people who would later become active in the efforts to rebuild informal social control were members of the PFH. Thus, the upshot of the travails of the LSC was that a crucial core of Beltway's activists was engaged in the struggle to oust the Barker faction. This fact, coupled with the strength of the discourses of denial and accountability, meant that a measured response in the form of reconstituted informal social control was delayed. However, once the LSC elections were over, a number of people turned their attention to the problem of youth gangs in the neighborhood.

While many people in Beltway were in denial about the presence of gangs and still more felt that parents, police, and teachers should be held accountable, a substantial number of people realized that the murders were a wakeup call. Carla Wiesniski asserted that the murders were a turning point for the neighborhood and the stimulus for her own activism:

> The shooting at Hastings—that was the catalyst for me [to get involved]. I just find it unbelievable that this neighborhood, with the second-most police in the city living here, that something like this would happen, you would wanna think that their kids are the best behaved. I know my neighbor [female police officer] keeps hammering on her son she never wants to see him at the [precinct] where she has to pick him up cause he's screwin' around. But you can't watch 'em every minute of the day. I never knew that something like [the murders] would happen out

> here. I think *that's when the neighborhood lost its innocence* [emphasis added].

In a conversation shortly after the murders, Arthur Straub pointed to his chest, saying, "Everyone out here is pointing their finger; it is time that people started to point the finger here." The process by which the discourses of accountability and denial were transformed into meaningful action is complex. There were a number of meetings at which police officers and community activists spoke passionately for a neighborhood response to the murders. For example, at a meeting at Hastings School, in January 1996, Jim Pratt asked Officer Gentile, a Joint Community Police Training Officer who lives in Beltway, how serious the officer thought the gang problem was in Beltway. Gentile replied, "The problem is in infantile stages. With good community involvement you can fight it. Other neighborhoods have worse problems, [but] I'm not saying there's no problem." Also, at a CAPS beat meeting just over a week later, Sergeant Henderson, from Neighborhood Relations, addressed the meeting and said,

> I can see that this incident has polarized people. There's two ways people can react in a situation like this. One of them is fear, and that's no good. I think that something like this can make us all afraid, and what we have to do is get involved and do something. I'm involved with the neighborhood watches in the area. I live in this beat so I'm concerned about all of this. But there's ways that we can fight back. Neighborhood watch is one of those ways, and it's part of the problem-solving training. A number of local neighborhood watches have been very successful. You all know Victory Park? It's near here. Well, they had problems that are much worse than here with the gangs. The folks over there got together and formed a neighborhood watch, and the crime has gone down over there.

Exhortations to form neighborhood watch and problem-solving groups were heard at a number of meetings in the months after the killings. It is notable that no such groups were active in Beltway at that time. The Rendell Park patrol and SON had already disbanded, and, in the Hastings Park area, there had been no groups of this sort in the first place. Interestingly, it was formal agents of social control that were instrumental in stimulating the informal social control apparatus in Beltway. The Joint

Community Police Training (JCPT) run jointly by the Chicago Police Department and the Chicago Alliance for Neighborhood Safety (CANS) began in Beltway in March 1996, and a neighborhood watch group was formed in September from the core members of the problem-solving group.[17] The fact that public agents of social control acted as the link between the watershed event of the Powell-Harvey murders and the formation of problem-solving and neighborhood watch groups was not lost on Jane Pratt, a founder member of both organizations, who said at the time,

> I liked what the [problem-solving group] brought in, and it seemed like exactly what we need in our area; to me like they were like a wakeup call. And that's what most people seem to need before they get involved, a wakeup call, and the timing about everything was right, it was after the shooting.

The arrival of the JCPT and the subsequent formation of the neighborhood watch in Beltway mark the beginning of a new way of viewing crime and disorder in the neighborhood. The discourses of denial and accountability were still present, but a more prominent discourse took shape, that of community responsibility. It was this latter discourse that enabled residents to exercise informal social control in Beltway. When people started to point their finger at themselves, in Arthur Straub's parlance, and decided to become involved in trying to find a solution to the problem of youth gangs in Beltway, the work of reasserting informal social control began. For example, Jim Pratt spoke of his own effort to encourage others to be like him and become involved:

> I figure that even if I do one little thing to make the neighborhood better, I figure it's like the spark that lights the fire under everybody else. If nobody takes initiative in something, nobody's gonna want to do it. Even if I can play a little part, it's better than nothing at all. I like to complain or criticize, so I can't do that unless I take part to change things.

Andrea Malone described how the murders affected her and how she was moved to get involved in efforts to prevent gang crime:

> Well, when that incident happened in December, I have known the one boy accused as the shooter since he was seven years old, and I can't believe that he could do it. He would babysit for kids in the neighborhood;

> he was just a caring child, would never hurt anybody. So that hurts, that Richard could change so much from involvement in the gangs. Then, what's even worse is since I moved here I got to know the brother and the little sister of one of the victims, Melissa Harvey. [So] I knew both sides, I cared about both sides. That whole tragedy ruined seven, eight families in the neighborhood, completely destroyed [them]. It's like I really do not want to know another child that is hurt by gang violence and that is really what does it for me. There's gotta be some way we can stop it, keep the kids away from the gangs, the gangs away from our kids.

Kitty Kelly also cited the Hastings murders as the catalyst for her personal involvement with efforts at informal social control:

> I was very incensed when the two girls were shot over at Hastings Park because those two girls were victims and they never had a chance to enjoy the life that I had when I was growing up, and that's not fair. Everybody should be given a good life. Children should be able to play in the park, and I should be able to walk my dog at nine o'clock at night without having to worry about somebody shooting me cause I got the wrong color on, or I was sitting in the wrong car in the wrong place at the wrong time. If people don't start fighting for their neighborhood and their safety and their protection, they're gonna lose [them].

The murders were a watershed event not just in their immediate consequences but in the manner in which they forced people to take stock. The shock that caused Beltway to lose its innocence also stimulated activism, which was enabled by the efforts of formal agents of social control—the local beat officers and, more important, the JCPT trainers. The JCPT group built on the interest created by the murders by emphasizing community responsibility and collective accountability. While the problem-solving group focused primarily on problems of disorder, the training officers advanced a discourse of community responsibility that resonated with, and was adopted by, a core group of activists.

More important, the discourse of community responsibility was translated into action. Attendance at community meetings declined after the immediate shock of the murders wore off, but the people who remained constituted a core group of activists. This group was made up primarily of women, and some men, who had school-age children; most also had experience being involved in local volunteer groups, especially the PFH. The primary concern of these women was making Beltway a better safer place. They espoused a set of values that resonated with the discourse of community responsibility: taking responsibility for events in the community, helping one's neighbors, and, most important, saving young people from gangs.

Chapter 6 details the formation and growth of the neighborhood watch and problem-solving groups and the issues that they chose to concentrate on. For the purpose of this chapter, however, there are two major points that the Powell-Harvey murders underscored: first, that informal social control in Beltway was insufficient to prevent the tragedy from happening in the first place; second, that the murders were a turning point for the neighborhood in the attempt to rebuild informal social control.

Discussion

The Powell-Harvey murders were a pivotal moment in the story of informal social control in Beltway. The way that residents fashioned a response, specifically the manner in which they talked about and interpreted the murders, provides useful insights into the travails of a neighborhood struggling with crime and disorder. Clearly, Beltway residents were not prepared in any way, shape, or form for the killing of Melissa Harvey and Teresa Powell. Even the residents, activists, and teachers in the local schools, who had been aware of the increasing threat posed by youth gangs, professed shock and dismay at the events. It is also noteworthy that the same Beltwayites who were so skillful at removing the Barker leadership group at the LSC were initially at sea when it came to the local gang problem. Part of the reason that even seasoned activists were scratching their heads in the aftermath of the killings was the proliferation and resilience of the denial and accountability discourses and the fact that the LSC conflict was a primary concern for many people at the time. The first issue to sort out for many residents was what led to the murders in the first place.

Who's in Charge? Diminished Supervision as the Precursor to Gang Activity

The Powell-Harvey murders signified that informal social control was not effective in Beltway. The fact that five local teens, and the adult gang members who encouraged them, could steal a weapon, test-fire it in one of the teen's basement, and then set off to use it illustrated a glaring gap in supervision. Moreover, the fact that there was gang activity in the neighborhood when the majority of residents did not want the gangs there seems to underscore the point that Beltwayites were not fully in control of their neighborhood. But why was this the case? The answer for many residents seemed to lie in the lack of effective collective supervision. I noted earlier that supervision was not comprehensive and was confined mostly to familial and personal social networks. Moreover, the age-graded nature of supervision meant that many teens were left to their own devices, which aided and abetted the murders in a direct way. Put simply, the lack of effective supervision occasioned the lapses in informal social control. For example, Mary Galicio believed that the local gang problem stemmed primarily from a lack of supervision: "I don't think the [kids] have enough to do, I don't think they have enough adult supervision. When we were kids, parks always had stuff goin' on during the summer. We always went to day camp whether we liked it or not." Similarly, Jim Pratt underscored how the lack of supervision caused by parents' working hours can lead to trouble:

> The problem is that if you have a lot of kids who are unsupervised, they're gonna eventually get into trouble. Both of the parents are always workin', and here's teens home alone and they start hanging out with their friends. The gangs are a bigger part of society now than they ever were 'cause people are looking for a family, and their own family is not there for them, and they turn to the gangs.

Carla Wiesniski gave some perspective on the declining role of collective supervision:

> I think everybody used to watch out for everybody else's kid, and nowadays you can't do that. People get very defensive if you yell at a kid

> who's running in the store. And they get so defensive 'cause they know they're not doing their job, and if I happen to say something to some kid in the store it has nothing to do with how I feel about their parents or their parents aren't watching over them. I know you can't do it every second. But you shouldn't get upset when someone else tries to watch out for the child. You need to have an authority figure around the corner. [When I was young] you couldn't do anything. Somebody would be there to break up a fight. Now the kids are on their own, and I think they have too much freedom, too much time on their hands, and they make too many decisions on their own. That's another problem. How do you have one parent stay home when you have two car payments and a mortgage?

Wiesniski's comments touch on one of the core elements of the informal social control dilemma. There has been a decline in collective supervision in Beltway, to the point where some people are reluctant to discipline other people's children. Moreover, the preponderance of families in which both parents work and of single-parent families suggests that there are fewer people available to supervise children in the first place. The time crunch described by many residents with whom I spoke goes some way toward explaining the lack of supervision of youth, especially teens, in Beltway. For example, Bernadette Boniek remarked,

> I think parents today, [families with] two parents; both parents have to work today just to exist in a halfway decent life. I think children have too much time on their own, too much time to fantasize and dream up things to do. They don't have that guidance of a mother at home with the cookies, the warm bread. That was me; I was a stay-at-home mom. [I] was always there. Nothing took place in my house because [I] didn't go anywhere. But I think the fact that both parents have to work, and when they come home, they're tired, and it's just like "go on out, will you, I need to rest, I'm exhausted." Parents don't do enough activities with their children.

More important than the fact that parents are not always present to supervise their children is that fact that this slack is not being picked up by other residents. Carla Wiesniski's comment about the reluctance of nonkin to intervene illustrates the weakness of the wider parochial network of control in Beltway. The lack of consistent, collective, all-age supervision opens the door for gang involvement.

I discuss the developments that circumscribe the changes in collective supervision in more detail in chapter 6. What is clear from the story so far is that youth gangs gained a tenuous foothold in the neighborhood in the early 1990s, and for many residents the main cause of this phenomenon was a dearth of quality supervision. It is important to underscore that this interpretation of the local gang problem is grounded in the testimony of Beltway residents, both those who have lived in the neighborhood for several decades and those who, while they are more recent arrivals, have lived in neighborhoods similar to Beltway. In the in-depth interviews, more than 90 percent of the residents and activists stated that there has been a significant change in terms of what people do to control crime and disorder in the neighborhood. Residents expressed this change in terms of a discourse that emphasized that in the past people were available and willing to intervene if someone, especially a local youth, misbehaved. The type of intervention that many residents say was commonplace no longer takes place. For longtime residents such as Brendan Sheridan, part of the reason is that parents are defensive about the misdeeds of their children, and this leads to a reluctance to intervene because there is no agreement on how social control should be exercised. He stated:

> In days gone by, if you got in trouble in school and then when you got home, you get in trouble for getting in trouble in school. It would be double trouble. [It is] the same way with the neighborhood. If Mrs. Jones down the block or Mr. Jones down the block caught you doing something, he'd kick your butt and send you home. Then he'd tell your dad, and your dad would kick your butt. Now, both in the neighborhood and in the schools, if the teacher complains about you or the neighbor complains about you and tells your dad, your dad goes and complains to the teacher and tells the neighbor to mind his own business, that "my little Johnny isn't like that."

Sheridan's comment alludes to what he perceives as a change in the ground rules of collective supervision and intervention. It is not simply that people don't engage in informal social control; it is there is no longer a set of uncontested norms that govern behavior. Other residents, such as

Jane Schubert, a lifelong Beltway resident, contextualized the change in informal social control practice in terms of general diminution of quality supervision of children:

> A lot of these kids today are left home alone or they're left with sitters that don't care or that are actually doing things that they shouldn't be doing with them. So, how can you control that when people are trying to work two jobs, both parents are trying to work and the kids are not getting the guidance that they need? How do you change that, how does society change it and go back to having people at home with their kids that really care about them?

Whatever the reason given by the residents—defensive or absent parents—there is a sense that there is much less supervision and intervention in Beltway now than there was when adult residents themselves were growing up. The frequency and consistency with which the discourse of diminished supervision and intervention was expressed seems to go beyond residents' simply viewing the past through rose-tinted spectacles.

Supervision is one element of informal social control. Another crucial component is collective responsibility for neighborhood problems. I have shown in the narrative of the story about the murders that, in the aftermath of the killing of Melissa Harvey and Teresa Powell, the predominant discourses were of denial and accountability, neither of which emphasized collective neighborhood responsibility. It was only after a time lag, and with the key intervention of formal agents of social control, that the theme of community responsibility became a prominent discourse in the narrative about gangs and crime in Beltway.

In many ways, the atmosphere in Beltway after the Powell-Harvey murders was similar to that after the Thompson shooting. There was a similar mood of panic, but whether it qualified as a mini moral panic is open to interpretation. In fact, one could argue that many of the worst fears of the previous panic, which centered around the Rendell Park area, had come to fruition when Richard Lindstrom opened fire on that fateful night. However, it is important to illuminate the subtle differences between the aftermath of the Thompson shooting and that of the Powell-Harvey homicides.

After the Thompson shooting, two groups were formed almost immediately to combat gang crime and disorder in the Rendell Park area, while there was no immediate response in terms of group formation after the Powell-Harvey murders. As we see in chapter 6, the delay may not have been an altogether negative development, because of the extracommunity resources that eventually became available for the groups that formed in the wake of the Powell-Harvey murders. In the case of SON and the Rendell Park watch group, there was a conspicuous lack of resources available; neither group was able to procure resources on its own behalf, which proved to be both groups' eventual undoing.

A second major difference between the two instances is the available pool of activists and social capital they brought to the table. I mentioned the internal divisions in Beltway earlier and noted that the Rendell Park area is seen by many Beltwayites as not really being part of the neighborhood. Generally, the main ongoing civic engagement in the neighborhood, typified by the BCL, was centered in the area around the Hastings School, where the bulk of those involved with neighborhood groups resided. In addition, the newer neighborhood activists around the Hastings School were cutting their teeth at this time on the local school council issue, and this experience would prepare them well for subsequent efforts to bolster informal social control in Beltway.

Perhaps the most important difference between the landscape after the Thompson shooting and that after the Powell-Harvey murders is the presence of the community policing apparatus. Despite the fact that CAPS beat meetings in Beltway were not particularly well attended before December 1995, the fact was that there was a mechanism in place at that time that enabled residents to tap into police and judicial resources. In stark contrast, a mere eighteen months earlier, when John Thompson was shot in the Rendell Park area, there was no community policing structure to access. The CAPS program would play a pivotal role in the formation of problem-solving and neighborhood watch groups in Beltway in the wake of the Powell-Harvey murders.

The contrast in the reaction to the two incidents notwithstanding, what is apparent is that the process by which a community reacts to crime and disorder is complex and fraught with difficulties. In Beltway, the extraordinary events of December 1995 brought into sharp relief the fact that there were serious internal problems in the neighborhood that required immediate attention. However, the prevailing manner in which residents constructed gangs and crime prevented the quick development of a discourse of collective responsibility that would enable citizens to solve communal problems and, in this case, to reinvigorate informal social control. This is not to say that the discourses of denial and accountability disappear—vestiges of them remained—but, to paraphrase Arthur Straub again, a number of people pointed the finger at themselves.

Three things facilitated the development of the discourse of community responsibility in Beltway. First, the number of people who attended meetings declined as shock and interest waned, leaving mostly neighborhood activists for whom the notion of community responsibility resonates. Second, the diversion of the Hastings Local School Council ended with the annihilation of the Barker faction at the polls in April 1996. Third, and perhaps most important, the agencies of formal social control in the guise of the JCPT and CAPS programs began problem-solving training in Beltway in the spring of 1996.

The confluence of circumstances that led a critical mass of Beltway residents to assume collective responsibility for neighborhood problems provided the backdrop for the new parochialism. What had gone wrong in Beltway was that most people had ignored the burgeoning local gang problem. Even when the problem resulted in the tragic deaths of Teresa Powell and Melissa Harvey, it was still possible to ignore it or to look elsewhere for the source of blame. The lack of a coherent response indicates that traditional parochial control, that is, collective supervision and intervention in disputes, had broken down in Beltway. The community was not able to regulate the behavior of its youth, and people were unaware and unwilling or unable to do anything about youth in gangs. Beltway residents could be unaware because of the virulent prevailing wisdom that defined gangs as an external phenomenon or, at the very least, confined to the Rendell Park area. Even for those residents who were aware that teens were unsupervised and that the incidence of gang graffiti had increased dramatically, many were not willing to get involved because they did not want to interfere with other people's children or were simply afraid to challenge youth with guns. Other residents may simply have felt unable to do anything about a problem that they could not fully comprehend. Crucial for Beltway residents who desired to keep their neighborhood free from crime was the need to be able to do so in a secure fashion.

Consistently, Beltway residents pointed to a lack of supervision, especially by parents, as one of the contributory factors to the youth gang problem. Parents and community members simply were not around to provide the quality supervision needed to keep young people out of trouble. The time crunch that helped diminish traditional parochial controls also interfered with efforts to remedy the malady. Even if people endorsed the notion of collective responsibility, they still had to find time to act on their inclinations.

The issues of security and time pressures are practical considerations that are addressed by the strategies that form what I call the new parochialism. In chapter 6 I examine in greater detail how informal social control strategies evolved in Beltway after December 1995, specifically the JCPT and the neighborhood watch patrol.

Conclusion

After the Powell-Harvey murders, one of the Chicago newspapers ran a story about the tragedy with the headline "Point of No Return." While there is an element of sensationalism in the phrasing for the headline, in some ways it conveys Beltway's position in terms of its ability to control crime and disorder. Something had gone horribly wrong, and clearly there had to be a response. Residents like Carla Wiesniski and Kitty Kelly did not want to see a repeat of the awful, wrenching scenes that characterized the last two weeks of 1995. Yet, the road to a coherent and effective response was littered with obstacles, not least of which was the prevailing manner of viewing crime and disorder as exogenous problems, caused by racial and ethnic others or as someone else's fault. As strong as the discourses of denial and accountability were in the aftermath of the murders, there was a countervailing way of seeing the world that a core group of residents embraced. Acknowledgment of collective responsibility was possible in part because there was a precedent for this type of activism in the neighborhood. Residents had successfully fought zoning issues and a despotic local school council regime. Allied with the weight of precedent was the fact that there were important sources of social capital in Beltway that these same activists were becoming quite skilled at accessing.

The stage was set for a response to the internal problems that Beltway was experiencing at the time. The initial furor that the murders elicited had subsided, and significant outside help, in the form of the CAPS program and its problem-solving training, was on its way. This intervention was not available for the Rendell Park patrol or for SON in 1994, and, in many ways, it tipped the scales for the Beltway residents who were keen to shoulder responsibility for neighborhood problems and to work to eradicate them.

night out

6

Coming Together

Problem Solving and the Neighborhood Watch

Introduction

It is just after 10:30 P.M. on a bitterly cold February night in 1997, and I have been riding shotgun in Jane Pratt's immaculately clean white Buick Regal. We have been out patrolling for the neighborhood watch group for the past two and a half hours, and we decide to take a short break at the 7-Eleven on the corner of Third and Ridge Avenues. I stow the logbook that has been perched on my lap and scurry out of the warm car into the icy cold of the parking lot. The local beat car is also parked in the lot, and Officer Simpson and his partner for the evening are inside chatting with the owner of the store. Once inside the warmth of the store, Jane and I exchange pleasantries with the officers, and Jane asks Simpson if there is anything to which we should pay particular attention on our patrol. Simpson shakes his head and tells Pratt that everything is pretty quiet. There had been a rumor that some kid was selling drugs out of the 7-Eleven parking lot, and Simpson shows Pratt a business card embossed with a marijuana leaf and a beeper number that he had confiscated from a teen earlier in the week. On this night, the numbing cold is the most effective deterrent to any illegal activity in the parking lot. Reinforced by beakers of freshly brewed coffee, we go back out to the Buick, and, as the car heats up, we plan what we are going to do for the remainder of our shift.

We had concentrated our efforts in the first part of the evening on the myriad alleyways behind the houses in the western part of the neighborhood. We have a system for our shift. As Jane drives slowly through each alleyway, we search for graffiti on garage doors, on walls, even on dumpsters. When we spot a graffito, Jane idles the car, and I log the address, the type of graffito, and the surface on which it is displayed. Occasionally, a crooked street sign or a missing stop sign breaks the monotony. For these we call home base on our two-way radio, and the responder relays the information to the city services twenty-four-hour hotline. The request for service will then be filled in due course from downtown. During the warmer months, there is usually some activity in the alleys, some underage youth sneaking a few cans of beer, or, after 11:00 P.M., the promise of curfew violators at one of the many local parks. On this night, we do the drudgework of logging each single incident of graffiti; at the halfway point in our shift, we have already filled about eight pages of the logbook, by my count more than fifty individual incidences of graffito. We decide to spend time by the factories in the northern part of the neighborhood, because Jane says that no one has recently spent time logging graffiti in this area. For the next hour and a half, until midnight, which is the usual quitting time for the patrol, we try to make good on our resolution, though the sheer volume of graffiti in the end defeats us. Jane decides to tell the next evening's patrol to start at the factories and finish what we started. We go back to Ruth Breslau's house, which is home base for the evening, and, after Jane gathers up the logs, radios, and other paperwork, we call it a night.

This account reflects my third night on the Beltway Night Patrol neighborhood watch. At that time scarcely fourteen months had passed since the Powell-Harvey murders, yet the account of the night on patrol betrays all the hallmarks of a well-worn routine. There was a clear pattern to what we did each Friday and Saturday night (the BNP patrols only two nights a week), one that had been established by Jane Pratt, Kitty Kelly, Carla Wiesniski, Lydia Donovan, and the other volunteers on the BNP. This chapter tells the story of how some of the citizens of Beltway eventually responded to the Powell-Harvey murders. I chronicle the events that led up to the formation of the BNP, specifically the arrival of JCPT trainers in the neighborhood in March 1996 and the subsequent issues that residents chose to tackle.

In essence, this chapter illustrates the new parochialism in action. The following account illustrates how strategies of informal social control that were formed and deployed by Beltway residents owed their existence and their efficacy to partnerships with formal agents of social control. The case studies I describe—the problem-solving group, the BNP, and court advocacy—constitute a "new" parochialism because they differ from the "traditional" parochial controls of collective supervision and intervention in disputes but are established for the same purpose—controlling criminal and deviant behavior in the neighborhood.

Problem Solving in Beltway

In chapter 5, I detailed the reaction to the Hastings murders and how, after a period of time, the discourses of denial and accountability were supplanted by a discourse of community responsibility, which meant that some local residents began taking steps to regain control of their neighborhood. By far the most important intervention in this process of forming and reinforcing community responsibility was the entry of the Chicago Alliance for Neighborhood Safety (CANS) and its organizers into Beltway in March 1996.[1] CANS had been contracted by the Chicago Police Department to run Joint Community Police Training (JCPT) workshops in each of the 279 police beats in the city. The contract, which was worth several million dollars, mandated that CANS work with specially allocated Chicago police officers to train community residents in techniques that would enable them to solve local problems. In the JCPT training, a number of organizers, trainers, and police officers would come into a designated CAPS beat area, train residents in problem solving, and, over the course of four meetings, attempt to identify and solve a problem in the neighborhood. Having done that, the CANS organizers and Chicago police officers would then withdraw from the neighborhood, leaving, it was hoped, a functioning and intact problem-solving group to carry on the work.

The first JCPT meeting in Beltway was held on March 20, 1996. Melanie Jones, a CANS organizer, had publicized the meeting by writing to people who had signed up at the January CAPS beat meeting for the Beltway area. In her letter, Jones invited people to the planning meeting on March 20; in all, about two dozen people attended. The CANS organizers knew the enormity of their task, which essentially was to equip a wide variety of neighborhoods with the basic skills to solve their own problems. One of the most crucial aspects of their job is to give residents realistic expectations of the types of problem they can solve, the basic idea being that the simpler and more manageable the problem, the easier it is to solve. Even given these limitations, Jones and her partner in Beltway, Maeve Reilly, approached each community with a combination of energy and vigor in the hope that it would prove contagious.

At the first planning meeting, the JCPT organizers conducted a training session in the rudiments of problem solving with those present. Jones and Reilly selected fifteen volunteers to act as community liaisons who would publicize and help run a problem-solving orientation meeting to be held on April 3, 1996, at the Beltway Public Library. At that first meeting, Melanie Jones sounded out people on what they thought were the most pressing concerns in the neighborhood. Pam Preston, a local business owner, who had been very vocal after the Powell-Harvey murders, said that some of the bars near her house, located on Third Avenue, were causing a number of problems. Preston explained that the patrons of two bars in particular were often drunk in the street and that there was a makeshift "beer garden" at the rear of one of the bars, called the Corner Tavern. In addition, patrons of the bars were urinating and defecating in the streets, and major noise and parking problems were associated with the taverns. Melanie Jones thought that this was a problem that could be addressed at the first orientation meeting, and she urged Pam Preston and her husband, Paul, to attend the meeting and to voice their concerns about the bars. Jones and Reilly then allotted tasks to the people present, which ranged from handing out fliers on each person's block to publicizing the meeting through the schools and the local churches.

Volunteers distributed fliers advertising the April 3 meeting, and the publicity had the desired effect of generating a good deal of interest among Beltway residents. In all, sixty-four people attended the orientation meeting. The basic idea of JCPT is a variation of what the criminologists Fred DuBow and David Emmons call the "community hypothesis"[2] and what Dennis Rosenbaum labels the "implant hypothesis,"[3] in which local residents are organized to combat crime and disorder. Strategies are "implanted" into a neighborhood by professional organizers.

At the first meeting, the CANS organizers were joined by a CAPS officer. Officer Mary Murphy is a CAPS trainer whose job it was to brief the group on the five-step problem-solving model. In her presentation, Murphy carefully built a rapport with her audience by emphasizing their shared experience. Murphy began:

> I live in the neighborhood out here, and I sure as hell don't wanna move. Like Melanie says, there are problems, but we can work together to solve them. It's no use sayin' that we can't do it, or letting someone else do the work. The police department can't do it all. We have to have you help us. That is what this training is all about, us all working together to solve the problems out here.

As Murphy spoke, people nodded their agreement. Confident that she had their undivided attention, Murphy outlined the five steps of the problem-solving model. She told the group that the first task is to identify and prioritize a problem to solve within the neighborhood area. Once the problem is selected, the next step is to analyze the problem. Third, the group designs strategies to solve the problem. In the fourth stage, the group implements the strategies it has designed. Finally, the problem-solving team evaluates what it has done and acknowledges success. Murphy outlined each step in the process in an easy-to-understand manner, and, at each stage, she offered common-sense examples. Having outlined the problem-solving process, Murphy asked the people present what they thought were the major problems in the neighborhood.

A number of people at the meeting said that they thought that gangs were the biggest problem in the neighborhood. Murphy told the meeting that gangs were not a problem that they could deal with within the context of problem solving. Murphy explained that if the causes of the problem were not easy to fix, "then it's not a CAPS problem. We have to focus on things we can work on here, okay? We can't solve the lack of jobs here. That's not what we're about." The organizers were intent on concentrating on the rogue tavern problem, as it was certainly a CAPS problem.

To further illustrate the problem-solving process, Murphy and Jones then outlined the "Crime Triangle." The organizers explained that the crime triangle allows a problem-solving group to examine a problem from several different perspectives. The triangle consists of three elements—the offender, the victim, and the location of the crime. The triangle is depicted in figure 6.1. Murphy explained to the group that, instead of devoting most of the attention and resources to the offender, which was part of the bad old police ways that were now undergoing change because of CAPS, the crime triangle gives equal attention to the location of the crime and to the victim. In the same way, then, problems of crime and disorder can be viewed through the lens of the triangle. Jones then asked people to focus on the problem of the bars that had been suggested. After dividing people into three working groups, Jones gave the group leaders, all of whom had attended the planning meeting, the task of focusing on either the crime, the location, or the victim.

After about twenty minutes of group discussion, the meeting was reconvened, and each group leader gave a summary report of what had been discussed in his or her group. The summaries were collated into a crime triangle "action plan." The crime part of the triangle summarized the offenses that area residents associated with the bars, namely the illegal "beer garden" at the Corner Tavern, public intoxication, urination

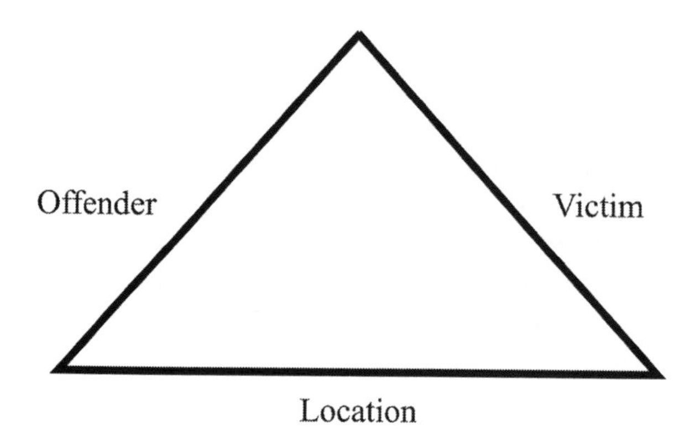

Figure 6.1. Crime Triangle.

and defecation, panhandling, public order violations, and possible drug dealing, especially at the Corner Tavern. The victims were listed as the people living in the immediate environs of the bars, the businesses on the street and, to a lesser extent, everyone else in the community, since people felt that all community residents were affected by the shenanigans at the bars. The location report centered on where the bars are positioned and the surrounding areas. After the reports were delivered, Jones and Reilly called the meeting to a close. A follow-up meeting was scheduled for April 24 at the library, at which time the group was to develop an action plan for dealing with the problem of the bars.

Problem Solving in Action: Bringing the Taverns to Task

The meeting on April 24 was well attended, although, with forty-two people present, there was a decline from the April 3 meeting. Maeve Reilly had replaced Melanie Jones as the CANS trainer for the Beltway group, and she and Officer Murphy cochaired the meeting. Once again the organizers privileged the rogue tavern issue, although there was some dissension from the residents present.

After getting the group to agree to focus on the taverns, Reilly outlined the next stage in the problem-solving process—developing an action plan. Officer Murphy asked the rhetorical question "If we are having a problem with someone, what do you think you should do about it?" Jim Pratt replied, "Let him know!" Murphy responded, "Exactly! There's no point in trying to solve the problem unless you let someone know that you are having one. So the first thing we should do is to invite the owners of the taverns here for our next meeting." It was agreed that Jane Pratt, in consultation with Reilly, would write to the owners of the Corner Tavern and the Liberty Bar to invite them to the next meeting, scheduled for May 14. Paul and Pam Preston, Denise Pawlikowski, Dagmar Braun, and Bud and Bernadette Boniek all volunteered to talk with business owners on the same block as the bars to find out what problems, if any, they were having with the taverns, and Rachel Stein, a local resident, who worked as an assistant attorney general for Cook County, volunteered to get the license information for both bars. After Stein found out the name and address of each license holder, she passed on the information to Jane Pratt. The letter Jane Pratt drafted explained that the community had a number of "concerns" about their premises and would like to "work with them towards a solution to these problems."

Working Together? JCPT Meets the Corner Tavern

The meeting on May 14 proved to be a turning point in the problem-solving initiative in Beltway. The meeting, which was also attended by the beat officers assigned to the neighborhood, opened with a report from the volunteers to whom various tasks had been assigned. Maeve Reilly then reported that the group had invited Jeff Moore, licensee of the Corner Tavern, and Pauline Hartley, of the Liberty Bar, to come to the meeting and noted that they would have a chance later in the meeting to address some of the issues that the community had brought up. Jeff Moore was present, along with one of his bar staff, and Pauline Hartley, owner of the Liberty Bar, was also there with the doorman, John Jurkynas.

Maeve Reilly was the first to speak, and she outlined the concerns of the community to Jeff Moore and Pauline Hartley.

Reilly: I'm pleased to welcome Jeff and Pauline here tonight. At our last meeting, a number of community residents expressed that they felt that there are some problems with some of the customers that frequent the Corner Tavern and the Liberty Bar. Specifically, people complained that people are drinking outside the Corner Tavern, that some people are panhandling, that they are urinating and defecating in the street, and that they are generally drunk and out of control. Jeff, what we'd like to do is work with you to help solve these problems.

Moore: [cutting in and raising his voice] What problems? I never heard nothin' about no problems. Who has problems with my place? This is the first I heard about it. I got a letter sayin' come to this meeting and no one ever came and said they had problems with me or how I run my business. Who has problems with me? Tell me face to face.

Reilly: Jeff, the community has decided that they do have problems with some of your customers, and we're trying to work with you to solve these problems.

Moore: Prohibition didn't work, did it? You can't stop people from drinking. It ain't against the law. What are you gonna do? I'm just tryin' to make a livin'. I have three kids at home.

Officer Murphy: Yes, but, Jeff, what about the complaints that the community residents are making? Can't you tell your customers not to urinate in the street? Can't you stop serving people when they have too much to drink?

Moore: [voice getting louder] Prohibition didn't work! They tried that. All these things, this is the first I heard of it! This is a disgrace. All I'm doin' is tryin' to run my business.

Reilly: Are you just gonna get mad, Jeff, or are you gonna try and work with us?

Moore: I pay my taxes, and I'm a widower. My wife died of cancer, and I'm tryin' to feed three kids, I don't have to sit and take this abuse. If you have a problem with me, then come and tell me about it. Don't send me these letters.

At this point, Jeff Moore abruptly left the meeting. There was quite literally a gasp of astonishment as he exited. Maeve Reilly and Officer Murphy had bemused looks on their faces, and Reilly quipped, "Well, it doesn't seem as if Jeff wants to work with us now, does he?" She turned to Hartley and Jurkynas and asked, "Do you want to walk out, too?" Jurkynas responded,

No. [laughing] We think we'll stay. We have listened to the complaints that the community has, and we would like to assure you that we will do

> our best to work with you to solve the problems. We know some of the people that have been causing the trouble, and we do not let them in. I'm on the door most nights and always on the weekends, and I make sure that these guys don't get in.

Officer Naseem Ahmed, who had been observing the interactions intently, interjected that he and his partner didn't really have any problems with the Liberty Bar. He added: "Jeff's bar is the problem. There's a lot of scum that hangs out there. We'll be keeping an extra eye on him from now on." Maeve Reilly urged the residents at the meeting to likewise keep an eye on the Corner Tavern and to report anything untoward to the police.

With respect to what to do next about the Corner Tavern, Reilly and Murphy explained that, since Jeff Moore did not seem to want to work with the community, the group should write to the liquor commissioner and invite him to a meeting.[4] Jane Pratt volunteered to write the letter to the liquor commissioner to inform him of the community's concerns and to invite him to the next meeting.

Operation Corner Tavern

Jane Pratt wrote to the liquor license commissioner in a letter dated May 23, 1996, in which she detailed some of the residents' complaints. Pratt wrote,

> Community residents involved in CANS under the CAPS problem-solving workshops met recently to discuss some of the ongoing problems in our area. One business in particular, "The Corner Tavern," owner Jeff Moore, was cited by the community residents and businesses as an establishment that is creating an unfavorable situation.
>
> Some of the complaints are:
>
> Operating a beer garden without a license—drinking customers are usually loud, disturbing the community.
>
> The residents feel unsafe because some of the clients are urinating and defecating in their doorways. Children are scared by their drunkenness and cannot play in front of their houses. Customers from the bar are harassing the community by panhandling for food and money. Customers are seen drinking outside of the bar, on the sidewalk. After leav-

> ing the bar, they are seen walking along 3rd Street and end up leaving their empty bottles in front of business and houses. One local business, Bill's Florist Store, blocked off their parking lot because of some of the above problems and had one of their windows busted. Afraid of further retaliation, they removed the chains from the entrances and deal with the littering and nuisances.
>
> Mr. Moore, the owner of "The Corner Tavern," was invited to and came to a CANS workshop on May 14. He listened to the community's complaints, became defensive and left without offering a resolution. The community feels there will be no cooperation from Mr. Moore.
>
> We would like to meet with the director of the Liquor License Commission, along with Mr. Moore, to resolve our community's concerns.

Jane Pratt received a reply, dated May 24, from the director of the Liquor License Commission, asking her to appear at the offices of the commission on June 5 at 10:00 A.M. to air citizen complaints regarding the Corner Tavern.[5]

Several members of the Beltway group attended the meeting on June 5, along with representatives from CANS and the tavern owner, Jeff Moore. The liquor commissioner asked Moore to respond to the concerns of the community and to initiate measures to control the disorder in and around his tavern. Moore protested that he was being treated unfairly and that his was not the only bar in the area that was causing problems. The commissioner directed Moore to comply with the wishes of the community residents and said that he would notify both parties of the next meeting at the commission.

The Beltway delegation was pleased with how the first meeting with the Liquor Commission had gone, and it reported back to the next meeting of the problem-solving group, held on June 19. Jeff Moore did not attend this meeting. There was also a discussion about some of the specific offenders who hung out at the bars. Officer Simpson explained to the group,

> The thing about Jeff's place is that it's the same few people all the time who seem to be causin' most of the problems. And we've been picking them up as often as we can. I'd say we visit Jeff's place once or twice a week [Officer Ahmed nods in agreement], and we let 'em know that we're watching them. The problem is really Billy Lundy and Sarah Craven. Those two are the worst. He's not homeless; at least when we pick him up he gives an address. I think his mother lives somewhere

> around here. Now Sarah, she's homeless. She sleeps rough most of the time. We're always picking her up, too.

The next meeting with the liquor commissioner took place on June 26, 1996, and the liquor commissioner asked Jeff Moore whether he had complied with the wishes of the community. Moore replied that he had, but the Beltway delegation at the meeting disputed Jeff's version. The liquor commissioner told Moore at this meeting that he should take the problems of the community seriously and admonished him by saying,

> Holding a liquor license is a big responsibility, and you need to start taking this more seriously than you are. We appreciate that you are starting to recognize [the problems] and trying to work with the community, but you . . . need to do more, be more compliant.

The Beltway Problem-Solving Group Graduates

The problem-solving meeting on July 8 saw the control of the Beltway problem-solving group devolve from the CANS organizers to the residents of Beltway. Jane Pratt, along with Bernadette and Bud Boniek, were the cofacilitators of the problem-solving group, and Jane was responsible for chairing the first meeting not under the direction of JCPT organizers. Maeve Reilly and Officer Murphy did attend the meeting, and Reilly delivered a short speech at the beginning of the meeting in which she thanked the group for its efforts and wished it luck in its problem-solving projects.

Jane Pratt started the meeting proper with an update on "Operation Corner Tavern." Pratt exhorted the members of the group present to monitor that "what is supposed to be done is being done." One of Jeff Moore's bar staff, Kathleen Quinn, was at the meeting, and she requested that the group not close the bar down. She stated: "We are doin' our best, but some of these people that come in . . . well, what do you do when a customer walks in fine, has one drink, goes to the bathroom, and comes out toasted?" Jane Pratt asked Quinn to clarify whether she was you talking about customers using illegal drugs. Quinn replied that she was and asked how was she supposed to be able to control such behavior? Pratt replied that it was certainly a problem if Quinn was aware that some of the customers might be doing drugs and had not done anything about it.

Quinn was quickly losing her composure and began to exclaim in a shrill voice, "That's easy for you to say—you're not the one being threatened by some of these people. I just don't think it's fair that you keep singling us out." The bizarre exchange between Quinn and Pratt had made matters worse for the Corner Tavern; Quinn had admitted that people were using drugs in the bar.

One final act in what was fast becoming a farce occurred when Sarah Craven, one of the tavern patrons who was the focus of many of the complaints and who appeared to be intoxicated or high, lurched to the front of the room and shouted: "If anyone has a problem with me, then tell me to my face and don't be goin' around talkin' behind my back." Jeff Moore stood and applauded Sarah, presumably out of appreciation for her continued patronage, while the beat officers kept a watchful eye from the back of the room. Jane was nonplussed by this unscripted performance and thanked Sarah for her "intervention."

Down on the Corner: Beltway Gets Tough on Bars

After the July 8 meeting at which Kathleen Quinn, the bartender at the Corner Tavern, had admitted that there was drug use in the bar, Jane Pratt wrote to the liquor commissioner to inform him of Quinn's admission, saying,

> [Quinn] also stated that the bartenders are being threatened by customers who do drugs. This is contradictory to Mr. Moore and his bartenders' previous statements that there isn't any drug activity in their bar that they are aware of.
>
> Also, Mr. Moore said that he was going to have a professional security guard as of Friday, July 12. I haven't seen anyone with an identifiable type of uniform.

At this time, Anthony Gaudio, the alderman for the ward in which the Corner Tavern and the Liberty Bar are located, became involved with the Beltway problem-solving group. Gaudio had sent one of his precinct captains, John Mackey, to the previous Liquor Commission meeting after repeated entreaties from Pam Preston and Jane Pratt to get involved with the issue. Gaudio had told the problem-solving group that he felt strongly about the problems associated with the bars and that he would provide as much assistance as the group needed. Gaudio placed several calls to the Liquor Commission on behalf of the group, urging the commissioner to take action.

The liquor commissioner convened a meeting on August 2, and he mentioned to the Beltway group the possibility of having a referendum in the precinct on prohibiting the sale of liquor at the Corner Tavern.[6] The commissioner also related to Moore that he had one last chance to accede to the wishes of the community.

The Beltway problem-solving group did not think that the Corner Tavern would comply with the liquor commissioner's directives, and it decided to pursue the option of placing a question on the ballot on whether to prohibit the sale of liquor at the Corner Tavern. There are two possible courses of action in such referenda. One is to have a dry precinct; the other is to have a dry address. The problem-solving group opted for the dry address and followed the guidelines for putting the question on the ballot. The guidelines are:

1. To place on the ballot the question of prohibiting the sale of liquor at a particular street address, you must get signatures of at least 40 percent of the registered voters in the precinct.
2. The circulator of the petition has to be a registered voter in the precinct.
3. Only registered voters of the precinct can sign the petition.
4. The signer should sign their [*sic*] name as it appears on the poll sheets.[7]

Pam Preston volunteered to organize the petition and set about visiting all the houses in the precinct during the month of August. She collected more than 200 signatures from the 487 registered voters and brought the petitions to the ward office. Alderman Gaudio then ensured that the question would be placed on the ballot for the November election.

There was a final meeting at the Liquor Commission on August 14, and the Beltway problem-solving group reported that there had been little change at the Corner Tavern. Alderman Gaudio was present at this meeting, and he informed the commissioner of the plan to put the issue on the ballot for the November election. The commissioner agreed that mediation had not succeeded in this case and that perhaps it was time to let the voters of the precinct decide. Jeff Moore protested that he was being unfairly treated, but the commissioner said that it was now up to the community to decide the fate of the Corner Tavern.

The Campaign and the Vote

The Beltway problem-solving group campaigned for a yes vote in the November 5 referendum. A small but committed group canvassed the precinct to ask people to vote yes to the question: "Shall the sale of liquor be prohibited at the following address: [the address of the Corner Tavern]." The problem-solving group drafted a flier that it distributed to all homes in the precinct, and Pam Preston personally handed out palm cards on the day of the election. Jeff Moore did mount a halfhearted countercampaign to keep the bar open, which consisted of handing out fliers on the day of the election. The flier exhorted people to keep the bar open and played on Moore's status as a widower and father of three. In the November 5 election, 333 of the 487 registered voters in the precinct cast ballots, and they voted 240–93 in favor of prohibiting the sale of liquor at the Corner Tavern. The problem-solving group had solved its first problem.

While Moore had the right to appeal the decision, there was no realistic hope that he would have his license renewed after such an overwhelming vote. There was a thirty-day period after the election in which Moore had the opportunity to file a petition. On December 11, 1996, the City of Chicago clerk's office stated that the deadline had passed and Moore had not filed an appeal. The Chicago Police District served papers to close the Corner Tavern on December 12, 1996.

Eyes and Ears: Neighborhood Watch in Beltway

In August 1996, the Beltway problem-solving group decided to form a neighborhood watch group, and it convened a meeting for that purpose. It collected information from the local police district concerning guidelines for a neighborhood watch and invited members of the Carver Heights Patrol, one of the more successful and longstanding local neighborhood watch groups.

The neighborhood watch informational meeting was held on August 14, 1996, and about eighteen people attended. John Black and Geraldine Olsen, of the Carver Heights Patrol, were there to address the Beltway group, as were the local beat officers and Sergeant Cleeves, from Neighborhood Relations. John Black and Geraldine Olsen addressed the meeting. Black recounted how the patrol was formed and how it had been maintained over time. He began,

> Back before we started the group, Carver Heights was overrun with gangs. We had gangbangers on every block, graffiti all over the neighborhood. People were afraid to go out at night on the streets. A few of us said that we did not want to see the neighborhood going down, so we decided that we were going to patrol the neighborhood. I went to talk with Commander Rusnak and said: "How do we go about it?" I have to say that the district has been great; they helped us start up the group and have been very supportive. We started out in 1989, and there were only about five of us, and we have been patrolling seven days a week ever since. If we see anything that looks suspicious, we report it. We never get out of our cars. We never chase anyone or get involved. Right now we have thirty-four volunteers who go out on patrol. We have a set of bylaws that each member must abide by, and there is a six-month probation period for people on patrol. There is almost no gang activity in our neighborhood. I know the gangbangers and they know me, and they know not to do anything in Carver Heights.

The Beltway group assembled draft bylaws by the early part of September 1996, and an inaugural meeting was set for the Beltway watch group on October 2.

The Beltway Night Patrol Is Born

In all, about eighteen people attended the inaugural meeting of the Beltway neighborhood watch group on October 2. At this meeting, the group decided to adopt the name Beltway Night Patrol (BNP), and it drafted bylaws for the group. The BNP decided to patrol on weekend nights and to try to have two cars patrolling on each night, dividing the territory of the beat in half. The group also elected its first slate of officers, and Jane Pratt was unanimously approved as president. The BNP decided to organize a Candlelight Bowl to raise money. By the close of the meeting, the Beltway Night Patrol had agreed on a set of bylaws, elected a group of officers, and begun to think about patrolling the neighborhood. The stated purpose of the Night Patrol is: "(a) to promote neighborhood safety by patrolling the community and contacting police and proper authorities when action is required. (b) to assess community problems through the use of problem-solving techniques."[8]

Working on the Night Patrol: Neighborhood Watch in Action

The Night Patrol began patrolling in mid-October 1996. The group could not afford to buy two-way radios at the time, so it borrowed them from Angelo Bonanno, one of the members of the group. At first, there were about ten members of the Night Patrol who went on patrol, and about three additional residents that regularly volunteered to be home base.

My first night out on patrol was in January 1997. As a new member, I had to go out with more experienced Night Patrol volunteers as part of my probation. I went with Kitty Kelly, who had been patrolling twice a month since the BNP began in October. The evening we went out, we were the only car patrolling, and, consequently, we had to cover the entire area of the police beat, from Columbia Avenue in the east to the city limits in the west, and from 5th Street in the south to the railway tracks in the north. Evelyn Fontina served as the designated home base, with help from Mary Galicio, the Night Patrol team leader.

Kitty drove, while I took charge of the radio and the logbook. The logbook is used to note each incidence of graffiti that the patrol encounters. After each weekend, the Night Patrol president, Jane Pratt, calls in each incidence. The local ward office sends out the Graffiti Blaster truck to remove graffiti on residences and businesses;[9] for graffiti on dumpsters in alleyways, Pratt calls the companies responsible for the dumpsters, which take care of the problem. Similarly, the U.S. Postal Service removes mailboxes that have graffiti on them and repaints them at a USPS facility. The logbook is also used to note situations that require city services.

At first, we drove around the neighborhood to see whether there was any activity worth noting. There were a few people on the streets that night, since the weather was not particularly cold for January. We began our patrol in the alleyways behind the neat rows of Chicago bungalows that make up the majority of the neighborhood. Most of the graffiti we encountered were in the form of general tags, which are not gang affiliated. Later, we chanced upon some gang tags on our tour through the alleyways in the area between 3rd and 5th Streets between Columbia and Ridge Avenues, territory that was claimed by one of the gangs active in the neighborhood at the time. We did observe one group of teens near the location of the graffiti, and after a while they went their separate ways. Kitty joked that the kids knew that the "moms were on patrol," and consequently they were behaving themselves.

The remainder of the patrol consisted of logging graffiti and areas that required city services. By the finish of our shift at midnight, we had almost five pages of graffiti incidences logged, about thirty-five in all. Most of them were small tags on dumpsters and stop signs, but there were a few larger gang tags. There were four items for city services, one set of streetlights that was out, and three stop signs that had been turned around or removed. All in all, it was not a bad tally for a first evening on patrol.

The BNP's First Year

The BNP gathered momentum of sorts in the late months of 1996 and into 1997. There were a number of central goals that characterized the activity of the group in its first year of existence, namely the need to achieve financial self-sufficiency, the need to reduce disorder in the neighborhood, and the need to ensure that every home address in the area was easily identifiable. The first goal was to raise funds.

The BNP set financial self-sufficiency as one of its top priorities and set about achieving it with characteristic vigor and determination. It had a number of successful fundraisers and managed to become financially self-supporting within its first six months. It also raised enough money to purchase two-way radios.

The second goal of the BNP was less specific than the first. I stated earlier that the objective of the problem-solving group was to solve problems that could be addressed with relative ease; the issue that came to prominence was the disorder created by rogue taverns. The notion of reducing disorder as a precursor to lowering crime rates has been a central part of crime-fighting strategy for about two decades, since the criminologists James Q. Wilson and George Kelling first advanced the "broken windows" thesis. Wilson and Kelling argue that if disorder is eradicated, then more serious crime can be prevented.[10] Further, they argue that communities will be nicer, fear of crime will diminish, and informal social control will increase. These ideas have been developed and translated into practical applications, and the "broken windows" logic underscores many of the recent community policing initiatives, especially in Chicago.[11]

At the time, BNP members spent the majority of each patrol logging cases of graffiti to be removed. At each BNP monthly meeting, there was a report on new graffiti in the area, and a number of BNP members became skilled at "reading" graffiti and could tell what gang messages, if any, were being communicated. Graffiti removal in Beltway was swift; most incidences were up less than a week before they were taken down. Jane Pratt also took it upon herself to remove small scraps of graffiti on garage doors, on stop signs, and on dumpsters. She estimated that in her crusade she had removed more than two hundred pieces of graffiti. In addition, in its first year of operation, from October 1996 through October 1997, the BNP called in 698 separate graffiti incidences. There was a decline in the number of incidences of graffiti from the end of 1996 through the summer of 1998, when I ceased patrolling with the group.[12] It would be fair to say that at least some of this decrease can be attributed to the activities of the BNP. Clearly, the fact that the graffiti were reported quickly and efficiently and that the Graffiti Blaster truck visited Beltway regularly played a role. Additionally, there was evidence that graffiti were not being thrown up as frequently as they had been.

The third goal of the BNP in the first year was to aid the local beat officers in identifying house numbers, especially in the myriad alleyways that crisscross the neighborhood. The police officers explained that if they were called to an emergency or a burglary in progress at a certain address and they had to waste valuable time trying to locate the address, it interfered with their efforts to help victims or to apprehend a suspect.[13] The BNP estimated that only about one in ten garages had any identification on it, and it encouraged residents to paint or stencil house numbers on their garage doors. The BNP offered to stencil numbers on garage doors and garbage cans for a $5 fee, and scores of residents took advantage of this service.

All told, the BNP made some headway on its first three goals. However, its fourth goal—to increase membership—did not fare as well.

Maintaining Momentum: The Usual Suspects

A number of studies of neighborhood watch groups, citizen patrols, and community participation in crime prevention strategies have documented the difficulties that such groups have in maintaining momentum and interest over time.[14] These studies have illustrated that unless neighborhood watch groups become multi-issue organizations and expand their focus to concerns other than crime, their life span can be quite short. The BNP in its first year recognized the need to expand its membership, while at the same time maintaining the interest level of its members. To accomplish this, the BNP issued a newsletter in the spring of 1997, sold raffle tickets outside the local 7-Eleven, and had an information booth at the St. Martin's summer festival, all of which was designed to publicize the group within the neighborhood and to galvanize a membership drive. These efforts, however, did not immediately translate into an increase in the number of new members.

At the time, the active member roll numbered in the low thirties, but the core group of people who took on the majority of the tasks in the BNP was about half that size. Some of these core members complained that the group needed new blood. For example, Kitty Kelly commented on the dearth of new members: "I wish we had more than just thirty people in there. When you think about it, we're supposed to have 4,000 families out here and we got thirty people, it's not enough, we need one person from each block. [It] gets to be tiresome and frustrating." In spite of the difficulties the BNP experienced recruiting large numbers of volunteers early on, it survived and thrived, though the core membership changed over its almost seven years of existence to date. When I interviewed her in 1997, Carla Wiesniski replied that the group had outlasted her expectations even at that time. Carla remarked, "Well, I think it's gone a lot longer than I thought it would. It's lasted over a year now. I think it will go on."

Overall, the feeling of the many group members that I interviewed from 1997 through the summer of 1999 was that the BNP would continue but that it had to bring in new members in order to do so. The members have been rewarded for their faith and prescience. Over the eight or so years at the time this was written that the group has been active, there have been a number of personality conflicts, and key officers have come and gone, but the BNP is still patrolling the streets and alleyways of the community. The changing cast notwithstanding, a determined and predominantly female core has been the backbone of the group and has kept it operational. The BNP has defied the odds against a single-issue organization and has maintained its focus on crime and disorder. Perhaps the greatest success of the group has been the fact that the local gang problem that culminated in the Powell-Harvey murders has, over time, faded away. It is also fair to say that the aggressive prosecution of seven members of the Black Knights also put a severe dent in the local gang problem. But disorder has largely been kept in check, thanks in no small part to the vigilance of the BNP and to the swift and efficient manner in which it mobilizes city services.

Even after its first year, then BNP president Jane Pratt felt that the group had already had an impact on the community. When I interviewed her in October 1997, Pratt declared,

> When I drive through the neighborhood, there's almost no graffiti. Some of the businesses have said that they have noticed a difference in the area. Some of the businesses that have added to our problems are no longer here. Last week, when I went to clean up graffiti, there was very little for me to clean. Most of what I turned in to the ward offices were street signs that needed to be repaired. The graffiti is almost gone.

While many of the members of the BNP are confident that they have made a positive contribution to life in Beltway, there are some who fear an increase in crime, specifically gang crime, and who do not want people to get complacent. Events such as National Night Out help reaffirm the BNP and remind members why they patrol, even if the routine has become mundane. It is this commitment of the "moms on patrol" that guards against complacency, sustains the BNP, and ensures its survival.

Along with logging graffiti and requesting city services, the BNP also coordinates local representatives for the Court Advocacy Program, which is a part of CAPS. In the Court Advocacy Program, volunteers attend court hearings involving offenders who have committed crimes of particular interest to neighborhood residents.

Letting the Judge Know That the Community Cares: Court Activism and the Court Advocacy Program

The tactic of getting a group of people to go to court to "let the judge know that the community cares" is one that historically has been used to great effect in Beltway and actually predates the Court Advocacy program. The case involving Orlando Santos, who was apprehended while scrawling graffiti on the Gerald School, was concluded successfully after three hearings that were attended by an average of a dozen local residents.

The CAPS initiative introduced the Court Advocacy Program in 1996 to coordinate community action in the courts. The following description of the program comes from a police department brochure. It states:

> Each of the 25 police districts has a Court Advocacy Subcommittee. With input gathered at beat meetings or from other members of the community, the Court Advocacy Subcommittees, working with the Police Department, identify and track cases of interest to the community. Cases can range from violent crimes, such as murder or rape, to "quality of life" cases, such as drug dealing and public drinking, abandoned buildings and negligent landlords, and problem liquor establishments. Volunteers then attend court dates associated with those cases. Court Advocacy Subcommittees play an important role in advancing the goals of making our neighborhoods safer. First, volunteers provide support for victims and witnesses who may be hesitant to testify in court. The presence of Court Advocacy volunteers from their community can make the difference in whether a victim or witness decides to appear in court. Second, the presence of Court Advocacy volunteers sends a strong message to the defendant, the judge and all other interested parties in the criminal justice system: *the community cares about the outcome of these cases and is willing to devote its time and energies to monitoring the workings of the judicial system* [emphasis added].

The Court Advocacy Program organized a delegation from Beltway when the cases of the gang members accused of killing Teresa Powell and Melissa Harvey came to trial in July and August of 1997. Kitty Kelly, the BNP team leader at the time, coordinated with the District Court Advocacy Subcommittee and distributed buttons with "Court Advocate" printed on them. The buttons are worn in court to identify "concerned members of the community" and also to ensure anonymity.

For the most part, court advocate volunteers tend to be retirees, who, in the words of Marcia Moran, a BNP member, "just have more time to go to court, day in and day out. I would love to go to all of the cases about local issues but I cannot take all that many days off work." In certain instances, Beltway residents take off work to go to court. In the Santos case, four of the Beltway delegation took days off or swapped shifts with coworkers to attend the hearings. Court advocates, like the Beltway problem-solving group, engage in informal social control in a bounded and secure setting. There is no real direct contact between advocates and delinquents or criminals. The whole point is that the advocate is a general representative of the community, the embodiment of the popular will. In this regard, the court advocate is one careful step removed from the front line.

However, on occasion, being a court advocate or part of a neighborhood watch group is not without its risks. In 2003, a court advocate from the police district that includes Beltway was threatened by a defendant in a drug case. The man who issued the threat was charged with a felony, and CAPS organizers from around the city appealed for volunteers to attend the case in order to show solidarity with their fellow volunteer. In all, five busloads of volunteers attended the indictment hearing. The statute under which the accused man was prosecuted is known as the Arnold Mireles law, named for a CAPS and community volunteer who was murdered in December 1997 in his South Chicago neighborhood. Mireles had been a CANS organizer for several years and had been instrumental in fighting gangs and bringing slum landlords to task in his neighborhood. One particular landlord, whom Mireles had brought to court several times, hired two teens, who shot and killed Mireles as he walked home one evening. Despite these incidents, court advocates and CAPS volunteers rarely face intimidation and physical danger, and the secure and bounded nature of these activities is part of the attraction for many residents who wish to participate in efforts to control crime and disorder in their neighborhoods.

There are other strategies that Beltway residents utilize to informally control their neighborhood. These strategies include using phone trees for calling 911 and utilizing the local zoning board to fight unwanted buildings or licensed premises, as the Chestnut Courts example detailed (in chapter 3) demonstrates. These strategies, along with the case studies of the problem-solving group, the BNP, and the Court Advocacy program, are all examples of the new parochialism in action.

These case studies illustrate the interdependence of the parochial and the public levels of control in Beltway. The examples are neither wholly parochial nor wholly public forms of control. The neighborhood groups such as the BNP and the problem-solving group are community groups, but, in order for the informal social control strategies they engage in to be effective, they link up with public agents of control—beat officers, the liquor commissioner, judges, or aldermen—to procure goods and services from the public arena. Indeed, public agents of control help establish and enable some of the neighborhood groups in the first place, as in the case of the JCPT. Taken together, the activities that I have described in this chapter constitute what I call the new parochialism, a new parochial order of control that demonstrates the diminishing significance of private and traditionally parochial forms of control and the increasing interdependence of parochial and public forms of control. In the remaining sections, I situate the new parochialism, explain why it is new, and assess the theoretical and empirical implications of the Beltway case.

The practices of informal social control in Beltway now revolve mainly around problem solving, neighborhood watch, court advocacy, and phone trees. These strategies are examples of informal social control in that the residents of Beltway enact them to engage in self-regulation, but they are coproductions of Beltway residents and actors from formal agencies, such as police officers, problem-solving trainers, aldermen, and city bureaucrats. The new type of parochial control is certainly more formal than the hand-to-hand immediacy of collective supervision and intervention. Beltway residents now have a buffer between themselves and disruptive teens. They can call 911 to report miscreant teens, they can monitor local wrongdoers through court advocacy, and they can contact the liquor commissioner when they have a problem with a local tavern. The new parochialism thus allows for a more formalized and, for some residents, a more secure type of activism.

Discussion

Why, in essence, is this a new parochialism? It is certainly accurate to say that residents in neighborhoods that resemble Beltway, especially white ethnic neighborhoods in Chicago, have always used ties to the public sphere to solve their problems. However, the partnerships in Beltway between parochial and public agents of control that were described in the case studies are formed specifically to enable Beltwayites to engage in self-regulation, a process that by its very nature has always been internal to the neighborhood. Beltway residents have not outsourced the control of crime and disorder; rather, a new hybrid organization for self-regulation has arisen in response to local, citywide, and national changes.

The argument that the Beltway case study presents a new, hybrid form of informal social control necessitates an examination of the assumption that there was a great deal of traditional informal social control in the past both in Beltway and, generally, in places similar to Beltway. In his book *The Social Order of the Slum,* the sociologist Gerald Suttles describes a Chicago neighborhood in the 1960s and alludes to what he calls a "segmented social order."[15] Suttles illustrates the strength of localized control, while identifying the limitations faced by neighborhoods that lack strong political ties.[16] More important for the current argument is the testimony of Beltway residents, both those who have lived in the neighborhood for several decades and those who, while they are more recent arrivals, have lived in neighborhoods similar to Beltway. In the in-depth interviews more than 90 percent of the residents and activists stated that there has been a significant change in terms of what people do to control crime and disorder in the neighborhood. Residents emphasized that in the past people were available and willing to intervene if someone, especially a local youth, was misbehaving. The type of intervention that many residents say was commonplace no longer takes place. The quotations earlier by Brendan Sheridan, Jane Schubert, and Carla Wiesniski all highlight this discourse. At this point, we should examine the changes that seem to give rise to new parochial forms of control.

Historical Context of the New Parochialism

The historical context in which the new parochialism has been forged is crucial to understanding its existence. In particular, a number of national trends have set the stage for the new parochialism. First, increasing numbers of women have joined the labor force, either because they wished to supplement or maintain family income (particularly among working- and middle-class women) or because they were coming off welfare rolls (particularly poor women), and this trend affected every neighborhood. The 1999 *Report on the American Workforce* states that the labor force participation of "women has risen sharply from 41.6% in 1968 to 59.8% in 1998."[17] Moreover, married women and women with children are working or looking for work in greater numbers. The proportion of women with children under three in the labor force rose from 23 percent in 1969 to 63 percent in 1998,[18] and the percentage of married women working full-time doubled between 1969 and 1998. While the average weekly hours worked for women has remained steady over time, the average for married couples as a unit increased by about fourteen hours per week from 1969 to 1998.[19] This latter increase occurred among married couples both with and without children; couples with children under six experienced the largest increase. Put simply, for many parents there has been a change in what Cohen and Felson call routine activities[20] that has taken them from the household to the workplace, leaving less time for home-based activities.[21] The implication of these trends is that parents have less time to devote to basic parental responsibilities, let alone volunteer activities. This dramatic change in routine activities impacts many important neighborhood processes, including the maintenance of informal social control. In more two-parent families, both parents are working and putting in longer hours on the job,[22] and for many there is simply not enough time to collectively supervise and socialize neighborhood youth.[23]

In Beltway, it is not simply the fact that more women are working that has changed the social fabric. Labor force participation among Beltway women has steadily increased, from a little over 40 percent in 1960 to close to 60 percent in 1990. But what is telling is that mothers of children under eighteen years in the neighborhood have increasingly joined the labor force. For example, labor force participation for married women with children under six doubled from one-fifth to two-fifths between 1970 and 1980; by 1990, more than half of children under six living with both parents had both parents in the labor force. The labor force participation of married women with a husband present also increased between 1970 and 1980; in 1990, more than two-thirds of children in Beltway ages six to seventeen years who lived with both parents had both parents in the labor force. The large proportion of dual-earner families with children under eighteen has considerable implications for informal social control. For example, Ruth Breslau, a lifelong resident, explains how she views the impact of dual-earner families on youth gang formation:

> The reason why the gang activity has kind of exploded. [is] that both parents are not home. Mom is working now, which has taken [an] adult [away]. It used to be when I was a young girl there was moms home on the block. God forbid you did something wrong, you were gonna hear it not only from that mom who caught you doing it, but she would tell your mother.

The economic imperatives that compel increased labor force participation do not affect only two-parent households; one can speculate that the need to work is even greater for single parents. However, the net effect in terms of supervision of youth is, to use Cohen and Felson's phrase, "the absence of capable guardians."[24]

A second national trend that has impacted Beltway and made the new parochialism possible is the rising rate of juvenile crime, especially violent crime, that occurred in the latter half of the 1980s and continued into the early 1990s, peaking in 1993.[25] Much of the violence was associated with youth gangs and the illicit drug trade. By the mid-1990s, Chicago was reputed to have about 130 youth gangs with an estimated 36,000 members.[26] More important, Wesley G. Skogan, a political scientist and a longtime evaluator of the CAPS program, and his colleagues report that the Chicagoans they surveyed in 1996 said that crime was by far the city's most important problem.[27] While in Beltway the gang problem was not as severe as in other parts of the city, the perception among Beltwayites in the mid-1990s was that if the problem was left unchecked, gang crime could get significantly worse. One of the specific elements of this discourse in Beltway was an avowed fear of youth with guns. The concerns and fears of residents in response to the rising rates of youth crime and the possibility that teens were carrying guns also affected the tenor of internal community controls.

The increasing participation of women (especially mothers of children under eighteen) in the workforce and trends in youth crime were also evident at the national and the metropolitan levels. In Chicago, a larger proportion of women, especially those with children, were in the labor force in the 1990s[28] than at any time since World War II, and youth violence and gang violence in particular peaked nationally and locally in the early to mid-1990s.[29] Changes internal to the city were also reshaping Chicago.

The Latino population in Chicago increased during the 1990s from 19 percent to 26 percent of the total population; in real terms, more than three-quarters of a million Chicago residents are Latinos. As the Latino population, which is predominantly Mexican in origin, increased in many neighborhoods, especially on Chicago's south and southwest sides, Latinos began to displace not only whites but also African Americans. Latinos were increasingly populating Beltway, too, where they went from constituting one-tenth of the population in 1990 to accounting for one-fifth in 2000. The arrival of large numbers of Latinos was a cause of concern for some Beltway residents.[30] However, the Latinos who settled in Beltway were primarily middle-class second- and third-generation Mexican Americans and Puerto Ricans for whom Beltway was a stepup neighborhood and who owned their own homes and shared many of the values and practices of their white neighbors.[31] Latinos in Beltway in the 1990s participated in civic groups, and many volunteered their time for the neighborhood watch and problem-solving groups. However, the ethnic turnover and increasing heterogeneity of Beltway did have implications for the strength of local social ties. Residential mobility alone can weaken social ties; if people are constantly moving in and out, it is hard to get to know your neighbors, and when this process is combined with ethnic heterogeneity, the potential for what we have traditionally thought of as informal social control is diminished.

The advent of the CAPS program in Chicago, as I have demonstrated, is perhaps the development that most directly impacted the new parochialism. CAPS and its problem-solving component were instituted in the 1990s as a response to rising crime rates and as an attempt to allay citizens' fears and to enable them to become involved in controlling crime and disorder in their neighborhoods. The fact that the CAPS program focused on changing the whole policing model in Chicago over time and was not an experiment carried out in only one or two districts underscores its potential as a transforming agent. The CAPS focus on stimulating local problem-solving efforts and on encouraging citizen participation represented a formal avenue for action in communities concerned with regulating crime and disorder.

Implications of the New Parochialism

The story of crime and its control in Beltway can tell us a great deal about informal social control. The prevailing wisdom about the process has held that strong social ties are necessary for successful informal social control.[32] In fact, close social ties are not a prerequisite for successful informal social control. In concrete terms, the practices of informal social control in Beltway exist in spite of the diminished role of private and traditionally parochial forms of control, both of which are dependent on close ties. Beltway residents who are involved with problem solving or neighborhood watch bemoan the fact that not everybody gets involved or knows other people in the neighborhood.[33] Moreover, they attest to the fact that many parents simply do not have the time to supervise children.

The rise of dual-earner families and the unwillingness of residents, in particular seniors, to "deal with teens" have created a situation where the usual patterns of informal social control—supervision and intervention—have been supplanted and replaced by a set of more structured and formalized practices. For example, older residents in Beltway may be unwilling to supervise young people or confront them when they witness wrongdoing, but they do get involved with the Court Advocacy Program. Lydia Donovan explains why she thinks seniors don't pick up the slack with regard to informal social control:

> They don't want to be bothered in the sense that either (a) they think they've done their community efforts and they're tired of that, or (b) they could be physically afraid of the situation that they see overwhelming them. And, I mean, whether it's a gang situation or theft or drugs or any of that, if they feel physically intimidated about it, they are not going to get involved. Actually, it's the mental intimidation even more than a physical intimidation.

Loose ties can be efficacious, but effective control may depend on the strength of local institutions or the ease with which partnerships can be formed between parochial and public levels of control. Some of the recent studies of collective efficacy and social capital offer insights as to how we may go beyond the systemic model.[34] Neighborhoods that are not characterized by dense social ties may be capable of exercising effective control over crime and disorder because of the ease with which they can access political and institutional resources outside the neighborhood. For example, neighborhoods that can use ties with politicians, police, judiciary, and the city bureaucracy to help keep their area free from crime and disorder should have an easier time exercising effective social control. The new parochialism in Beltway suggests the central importance of partnerships between parochial and public actors for effective social control. Areas that can access resources such as the JCPT and that engage in problem-solving efforts to control crime and disorder should be able to exercise effective informal social control regardless of the density of social ties within the neighborhood.[35] In terms of Al Hunter's typology of the private, parochial, and public spheres of control,[36] effective control can occur where there is not a perfect articulation among the three levels. An effective partnership between the parochial and the public spheres, for example, can offset deficiencies at the private level.

The Beltway case also speaks to more general issues of civic engagement. It has not been my intent to weigh in on the debate about civic engagement and whether it is declining.[37] However, the Beltway data do showcase civic engagement in action and, as such, tell us a little about the phenomenon in the late 1990s. The restrictions on time for volunteering that Putnam talks about in his most recent work, and the diminishing capacity of middle-class women (long the stalwart volunteers) to allocate time to civic engagement because of their increased involvement in the labor force may go some way toward explaining the new parochialism in Beltway.[38] For example, about three-quarters of the local residents involved in the problem-solving group and the BNP are women, and almost all of these women either work in full-time or part-time employment. Their time is precious; consequently, their activism must be focused and have identifiable outcomes. The strategies of the new parochialism, then, may take root because they are coproduced by local residents and by actors from the public sphere; local activists are not wholly responsible for their initiation and implementation. Moreover, time is used efficiently when tasks are laid out in advance and there is a definite division of labor. Even those residents who are pressed for time can volunteer when there is a framework that facilitates efficient involvement.

Of course, the people who volunteer are still in the minority, and among those who do give up their time, a core group undertakes a disproportionate amount of the work. However, the new parochialism is attractive in part because it can fit into the hectic schedule of women such as Lydia Donovan, Carla Wiesniski, and Kitty Kelly, all of whom remarked that, even though they work full-time, allocating five or six hours a month to volunteer with the BNP is not a hardship. The bounded nature of the new parochialism compared to the traditional parochial activity of ongoing supervision, for example, makes it an attractive option for many residents. One of the central theses of Putnam's recent work is that, while traditional forms of civic engagement may indeed be declining, other alternative avenues of volunteerism and civic participation may be opening up.[39] Certainly, the new parochialism in Beltway seems to mirror that particular finding.

The new parochialism also has implications for community policing initiatives. The main strategies of the new parochialism in Beltway were created at the behest of the CAPS program. On a purely practical basis, the strategies and campaigns of the problem-solving group and the BNP have yielded some positive results, including the closing of the disorderly tavern and the reduction of graffiti in the neighborhood. Some of the other initiatives have had less tangible outcomes. For example, it is not altogether clear what effect, if any, the Court Advocacy Program or the painting of house numbers on garage doors have had on crime and disorder.[40] However, the fact that actors from the public sphere of control have facilitated the initiatives that Beltway residents have undertaken provides evidence for the possible success of new parochialism partnerships within a community policing model.[41] The new parochialism is not about applying the same strategy to solve the same problems in every neighborhood. The approach of equipping interested citizens with the wherewithal to solve problems for themselves is adaptable across neighborhood context precisely because the problem-solving skills can be molded to suit the exigencies of each particular situation. Given the flexibility of the approach, it is important to note that neighborhoods that have less access than Beltway to public sphere goods and services, or whose citizens lack experience in procuring such amenities, may have a harder time achieving success. However, even for residents in impoverished and high-crime neighborhoods, the new parochialism, with its brand of specific, secure, and bounded activism, may be a model for the initiation of meaningful community-police partnerships.[42] While it would be naïve not to recognize the historically privileged position of whites, especially middle-class whites, with respect to the ability to secure public goods for themselves and their communities, I contend that the current sociopolitical climate in Chicago dilutes this position of privilege somewhat, especially with respect to the new parochialism. There is no longer a white hegemony in the City Council, and Mayor Richard M. Daley's power base is maintained by coalitions he has formed with African American and Latino politicians and ward organizations. And, perhaps more important, the CAPS program and the problem-solving initiatives are active in all city neighborhoods.

Building on the latter point, a final implication of the new parochialism relates to policy on community control of crime. The new parochialism demonstrates how successful partnerships to combat crime and disorder are forged between parochial and public agents of control. The semiformal organization of initiatives such as the problem-solving group and the BNP suggests a possible blueprint for future community policing and crime prevention initiatives. At the very least, the Beltway case study illustrates what works in terms of the CAPS program for that neighborhood.[43] Perhaps similar strategies can be employed in other cities to good effect. Further, the existence of the new parochialism provides firsthand evidence of civic engagement in action and at the microlevel bears out Robert Putnam's argument that it is not simply that civic engagement is on the wane. For many Americans, the nature of engagement itself may be changing, and future policies aimed at stimulating civic engagement should take into account the fact that many people have limited time to devote to volunteerism and may opt for engagement that is structured, organized, and, in the case of informal social control, secure.

BELTWAY NIGHT PATROL
Your
NEIGHBORHOOD
WATCH GROUP

7

Conclusion

Civic Activism and the New Parochialism

What is the relevance of the Beltway story to what we know about the control of crime and disorder in American society? Certainly, taken in isolation, it is a cautionary tale about a neighborhood where youth gangs had quietly taken root in a seemingly unlikely place. The events that culminated in the deaths of Melissa Harvey and Teresa Powell illustrate how easily order can be undone in a place that many would call a paragon of neighborhood stability. The response to the murders, which unfolded gradually and eventually cohered in the form of the BNP and problem-solving efforts, illustrates how difficult it can be for communities to restore order and control crime. The Beltway response took a great deal of time and effort, and it had to be jump-started by community organizers and police officers. Outside forces played a crucial role in stimulating the practice of informal social control internally in the neighborhood, which marked a departure in terms of community control of crime. The Beltway story thus illustrates the changes in what people do to keep their communities free from crime and disorder. Specifically, the Beltway case study makes it clear that control at the local level is no longer accomplished solely through traditional practices of collective supervision of neighborhood youth and intervention in disputes. Many of the Beltway residents I spoke with alluded to the fact that their neighbors don't supervise or intervene any more because they are afraid or unwilling to get involved in that way. Indeed, I think it is fair to say that the problems that beset the neighborhood in the first place with respect to teens joining gangs were enabled by these changes in patterns of control. The traditional forms of local control have been supplanted in Beltway by variants of control that are more secure and that are coproduced by actors from the formal control sphere. The problem-solving initiative in Beltway, the neighborhood watch group formed from the initial problem-solving cadre, and the court advocacy program all offer Beltway residents an outlet through which they can contribute to the collective goal of keeping their neighborhood safe and crimefree. However, the activism entailed by these commitments is specific, bounded, and secure. So, while the actions of Beltway residents are certainly deployed at the parochial or community level, they represent a new brand of parochialism that has implications for how we think and talk about what ordinary citizens do to control crime and disorder in their communities.

The Beltway experience has wider applicability in terms of the manner in which informal social control is practiced and also with respect to the actual activities performed by residents. In the first place, the new parochialism seems to codify the external linkages that the criminologist Tim Hope argues are so crucial for successful community crime prevention.[1] External linkages are "nonlocal centers of resources and expertise,"[2] and it is apparent in the Beltway example that access to such resources is crucial in helping initially structure the response to the crime problems in the neighborhood. So, too, thereafter, the links to outside resources continue to be important and instrumental in solving community problems. The case studies in chapter 3 demonstrate that the practice of residents tapping in to resources beyond the community is not new, but doing so routinely to help control crime and disorder is new. The new parochialism that emerges to deal with insurgent crime and disorder problems is brought about by a number of distinct but interrelated local, regional, and national trends. The increasing number of women who have joined the workforce, the peaks in juvenile violent crime in the early 1990s, the introduction of community policing initiatives in many municipalities, and the increasing diversity of many of America's cities combine to create the conditions under which the new parochialism emerges. It remains to assess the relevance of Beltway for wider discussions about citizen activism and engagement and about community policing, and to articulate how the case studies described in this book provide hope for neighborhoods across America that are experiencing similar problems.

What Can Communities Do? Evidence from Other Contexts

The data from Beltway call to mind the great conundrum that is community-led action to control crime and disorder. As citizens have less time to devote to day-to-day informal social control work, much less to more generalized local activism, the need for, and, in some places, the opportunities to engage in these activities have increased. Few would doubt the need for community involvement in maintaining internal controls, or the broadly shared aspiration of residents to live in an area free from crime. However, questions remain about what shape community control of crime can take when residents face numerous competing demands on their time. Even more important is the question of how success can be achieved through such activism.

One way of categorizing the Beltway experience is to see it as part of the tradition described by Warren Friedman and Michael Clark as "people taking responsibility and launching their own efforts against crime." The authors go on to say that "side by side with the development of new problem-solving methodologies by law enforcement and new theories of community policing, there has arisen a deeper and broader grassroots tradition of active community anticrime work."[3] However, the one crucial distinction is that what happens in Beltway cannot be characterized solely as a grassroots insurgency. In fact, grassroots insurgencies like the Rendell Park watch group and SON are short-lived, unable to either sustain themselves or make any real impact on local crime and disorder problems. The successful initiatives occur when the aspirations of Beltway residents to do something to control crime and disorder are organized, structured, and enabled by professional organizers. Such an approach illustrates how a partnership between citizens and organizers emerges, and this knowledge can be applied in other contexts. Indeed, other communities have entered into similar new parochial arrangements to combat internal crime and disorder problems.

Beltway is not alone in its efforts to control crime and disorder. All across America, especially in the past decade and a half, communities have mobilized to meet the nascent threat of crime and disorder. There are many examples of the new parochialism in action in various towns and cities. For instance, Alexander Von Hoffman details examples of urban revitalization that have occurred in some of the most disadvantaged and blighted inner-city areas in the United States.[4] Von Hoffman reports on the bootstrap efforts of citizens in cities as distinct as New York, Boston, Chicago, Los Angeles, and Atlanta, and he demonstrates how community activists have reclaimed once-derelict areas. Although he does not focus solely on efforts aimed at reducing crime and disorder, some of the examples Von Hoffman showcases clearly indicate how the actions of residents to reclaim their communities have crime control as their centerpiece. Moreover, what is more important for the ongoing discussion is the contention that the successes in each context are possible because of the partnerships that are formed between citizens operating at the grassroots level and local government and other extracommunity resources.

There are other examples that center on community control of crime and disorder. For example, Recheal Stewart-Brown, a licensed social worker and community organizer in San Diego, describes how the City Heights neighborhood in that city, a diverse area of some 60,000 residents where the rate of violent crime is more than double the citywide average, mustered the resources to combat crime and disorder.[5] The process by which the City Heights Neighborhood Alliance worked with local law enforcement and community organizers to identify problems and implement solutions is remarkably similar to that employed in Beltway. However, the neighborhood differs markedly from Beltway in that it is more ethnically, racially, and culturally diverse, and more than 30 percent of City Heights residents are poor. More salient than the contrasting profiles of Beltway and City Heights is what unites residents across these social contexts, namely their desire to rid their neighborhood of crime and disorder. To achieve this goal, ordinary citizens in both neighborhoods collaborate with police officers and community organizers to tackle local problems. In the case of City Heights, the problems that were seen as most pressing were an apartment complex that was host to drug dealing, prostitution, and the cause of daily 911 calls and a local market that was also a center for drug dealing, prostitution and panhandling. In City Heights, as in Beltway, the core group of active residents was quite small, between fifteen and twenty-four people, and they met twice monthly to plan strategies and get progress reports. The end result of the activism of the City Heights Neighborhood Alliance was what Stewart-Brown calls "a wrap-around problem solving approach where police and community members work in a true partnership to solve crime and quality-of-life issues."[6]

The City Heights example provides a useful comparison to Beltway because, despite the contrast in neighborhood characteristics, the actions undertaken by residents and the support for the actions from police and community organizers are remarkably similar. Scores of other community policing programs seek to actively involve community residents in solving local crime and disorder problems. For example, Mike Powers used the phrase "the hidden strength of communities" to describe the Oakland, California, experience written about by Lloyd Street.[7] Street details how residents of some of Oakland's most disadvantaged neighborhoods came together and formed coalitions to petition the city and county government to step up their efforts to eliminate drug dealing in their communities.

While the policing strategies that make use of community partners have a variety of monikers, the overall approach that forms the bedrock upon which the new parochialism flourishes is usually referred to by the acronym CAMPS, which, according to David Bayley, stands for Consultation with citizens, Adaptation through flexible resource allocation, Mobilization of citizens to share policing and public safety tasks, and Problem Solving to address local issues.[8] The case studies from Beltway stand solidly in the CAMPS tradition and illustrate what can be accomplished when citizens are afforded the opportunity to initiate, develop, and implement strategies of informal social control. However, implementing a CAMPS model is far from being a straightforward proposition. In the first place, there has to be the political will to seek out long-term as opposed to short-term solutions to crime and disorder problems because, as several authors have pointed out, CAMPS requires that constituencies be established in urban neighborhoods.[9] A number of commentators have indicated that getting municipalities to take a long-term view of crime and disorder is a challenge that many politicians are simply unable or unwilling to face.[10] More fundamental even than persuading local government to focus on capacity building and long-term solutions is the task of providing opportunities for neighborhoods that do not have access to a large supply of political and social resources or that are having difficulty mobilizing citizens to solve common problems. The great danger with a CAMPS approach is that strong, healthy neighborhoods that have an available set of local institutions and strong connections to outside resources—in other words, an available stock of social capital—are primed to be the ones that can most effectively control crime and disorder. Thus, any discussion about this approach or implementation of a CAMPS program must pay explicit attention to the potential for inequality that exists in terms of how the initiative takes shape in a neighborhood or the results that are realized. Neighborhoods where residents have had a checkered history of police relations, or where citizens have not had the same access to public goods as their counterparts in better-off neighborhoods, are especially likely to encounter difficulty in initiating successful new parochial strategies. However, the dispatches from City Heights and Oakland offer more than a glimmer of hope on this front. Additionally, there is some evidence from the various social research projects in Chicago[11] to suggest that even in neighborhoods where legal cynicism is high,[12] there is a good chance that collaborative problem solving can work.[13]

There are other variants of community policing, many of which stand in contrast to CAMPS approaches. Some jurisdictions implement community policing in a manner that advances the rhetoric of the approach but that focuses more on the police agenda than on that of the community.[14] Other police departments use problem-solving strategies that do not actively involve the citizenry in the process. For example, in the small town of Pittstown, Pennsylvania, a local park had become the center of vandalism and drug dealing, and police there employed what is known as the SARA technique (the acronym stands for Scanning, Analysis, Response, and Assessment). The upshot was that crime was reduced in this area, but the citizenry were not actively involved in the process. It is not just small towns that don't involve the citizenry in problem-solving and community control of crime. The spectacular success of New York City in reducing serious crime in the 1990s had little to do with involving citizens and a lot to do with the advancement of aggressive policing tactics.[15]

Even though some jurisdictions have no intention of actually partnering with the public, a great many of the current experiments in community policing have some form of citizen involvement built in. For instance, Mark Correia reports on the Community Action Support Team (CAST) program in Sioux City, Iowa, where policing has changed in response to citizen concerns about quality-of-life issues.[16] In his examination of the Sioux City program, Correia investigates what motivates citizens to get involved in community policing initiatives. He contends that for community policing to be effective, it should spawn collective action, which he defines as "activities which produce collective goods."[17] The difficulty is finding a way to stimulate this action on the part of citizens. The results from Sioux City indicate that it is important for citizens to feel that they can trust local officials and that they have access to public agencies and goods before they will engage in collective activity. The success of citizen initiatives to control crime and disorder depends on how easy it is first to stimulate engagement and then to procure the resources needed for change.

When we observe the ways in which people combat crime and disorder, as in the current example of Beltway, the central question is how to best stimulate sustained and involved collective action that contributes to informal control. The burgeoning field of study of civic engagement can help focus this discussion. This is where the rubber meets the road in terms of what the Beltway case study can tell us about American civic engagement early in the twenty-first century. Something has changed with respect to what people do in terms of informal social control and, more generally, of civic activism. Put simply, people in Beltway have changed what they do and how they do it. In order to build upon these efforts, it is imperative to understand and contextualize the Beltway experience. The first step toward learning what we can from Beltway is to assess what is generally known about citizen activism at the local level.

The Changing Nature of Citizen Involvement: What Beltway Tells Us about Civic Engagement in Modern America

The Beltway story provides fodder for national debates on community policing, civic activism, and the nature of community in early-twenty-first-century society. A great deal of attention has been focused on civic participation and engagement in modern America, specifically whether people are now more or less civic-minded and involved than they used to be. The political scientist Robert Putnam lit the fuse on this debate in the mid-1990s when he advanced the thesis that many Americans no longer participated in civic activities the way that previous generations had done. The metaphor of "bowling alone" sparked a vigorous debate about what kinds of civic activities ordinary citizens engage in and to what extent. Putnam argued not that no one was bowling anymore but that bowling in organized leagues had declined precipitously over the past thirty years, and he maintained that this change was indicative of a wider trend; in general, people were not joining local civic groups or volunteering with local church groups as much as previous generations had.[18] Symptomatic also of the changes in civic activity was the fact that VFW posts all over America were closing their doors. What was important for Putnam is that these trends erode social capital, which Putnam defines as "features of social organization such as networks, norms and social trust that facilitate coordination and cooperation for mutual benefit."[19] Putnam's original thesis provoked a number of responses.

For example, Frances Lappe and Paul DuBois take issue with Putnam's assertions and argue that it is not simply that social capital is diminishing but that the capacity of people to solve problems is on the wane.[20] Lappe and DuBois say that social capital is rooted in people's capacity to realize their interests, and, to be truly useful, the concept should incorporate a notion of agency. They point out that opportunities for civic activism are actually expanding, not contracting, and they allude to prospects for activism in schools and community organizations, some of which have been formed to deal with crime and disorder. Central to Lappe and DuBois's critique of Putnam is the assertion that it is not only voluntary activity that generates social capital but also workplace and school-based activism.

The point that activism generates social capital calls to mind the question of whether there is a distinction between volunteering and social activism. John Wilson, in his summary essay on volunteering, points out that social activism and volunteering are often seen as separate because activists are "oriented to social change while volunteers focus more on the amelioration of social problems."[21] However, in practice there is a great deal of overlap in the two practices, and the circumstances of the particular situation should dictate how the roles associated with each activity relate to one another. More important for the current discussion is that Wilson reports that the data on voluntary activity illustrate that Americans volunteer as much now as they have in the past, even though the focus of their volunteer work may have changed and societal developments may have affected their choices and decisions regarding voluntary activism.[22] In terms of the opportunities to volunteer, there are new types of grassroots organizations that expand the range of available options. In addition, even though a greater proportion of women are in the workforce now than four decades ago, they are as likely to volunteer as before. On this latter point, Wilson states that "women have simply changed what they volunteer for as they take up paid employment; and a 'third age' population of healthy elderly is volunteering at higher rates than ever before."[23] Certainly, the evidence from Beltway supports the finding that there are new avenues for volunteer activism and that working women and the healthy elderly are key participants in groups such as the BNP and the Court Advocacy program. What matters most for these groups of volunteers in Beltway is the structured nature of their involvement and practical issues related to time use and safety.

Putnam himself addresses the debate that his original thesis generated in his expansive tome *Bowling Alone: The Collapse and Revival of Amer-*

ican Community.[24] Putnam amasses a dizzying array of data on trends in voting behavior, political involvement, and participation in voluntary activity, and he asserts that, while he stands by his earlier contention about the waning of traditional civic participation, at the same time there seems to be a burgeoning slew of opportunities to become civically engaged in other ways. Putnam maintains that Americans are less involved now in the social and political life of their communities and that people have "invented new ways of expressing our demands that demand less of us."[25] For Putnam, place-based social capital is being replaced by function-based social capital as local grassroots groups are replaced by interest groups led by professional organizers. The new parochialism seems to fit into the trend that Putnam describes in that it is emblematic of the decline in traditional means of civic activism and the new interest in more directed and focused ways of doing things. Some of the trends that I suggested make the new parochialism possible overlap with those that Putnam argues have occasioned the decline in civic engagement, particularly the pressures of time and money that have translated into the larger proportion of women in the workforce. However, in another, more profound way, the Beltway case study bucks the trend of the unraveling of community life. The central thrust of what Beltway residents do is to work to keep their community free from crime and disorder; as such, the activities of residents are place-based and are dependent on social capital for their sustenance. Overall, the evidence from Beltway seems to suggest that there is still some considerable life in local civic engagement, even if the way it happens has changed.

Making Something Happen: Loose Connections and a Little Help from New Friends

Informal social control matters for overall civic well-being.[26] The key is to uncover how successful civic activism happens and how efforts to invigorate informal social control can take their cue from other successful campaigns. The theme of what citizens do to contribute to their communities and enrich civic life is taken up by the sociologist Robert Wuthnow, who uses the term "loose connections" to describe how civic activism becomes possible in a socially fragmented world.[27] The impetus for fragmentation can be the increasing demands on time faced by working- and middle-class wage earners, or the result of living in a hostile environment and suffering the effects of what William Julius Wilson calls "social isolation."[28] Every neighborhood faces a distinct set of challenges when it comes to procuring public goods, one of which is the maintenance of order. Perhaps the most pressing challenge is making even loose connections efficacious.

Wuthnow discusses how the nature of civic involvement has changed for many people, in terms of both the type of involvement that most people favor and the roles enacted by them. In the 1950s, in America, three roles personified how people were engaged—the organization man, the club woman, and the good neighbor. The organization man was an amateur who could function "with good intentions, common sense and a little help from his friends."[29] He belonged to clubs such as the Rotary or Kiwanis and tried to promote the common good of the community whenever possible. The female counterpart to the organization man was the club woman, who epitomized "practical knowledge, sociability and service."[30] Finally, the good neighbor was someone who extended the notion of service to all those around him and who performed "routine acts of kindness and hospitality."[31] Wuthnow charts the changes each of these roles has undergone, the ways that the nature of civic engagement has been transformed by the type of problems people have had to contend with in their communities, and forces that have led people to realize that, in many cases, they would need professional help. Wuthnow summarizes the changes:

> The meaning of involvement has changed as people have come to see the problems facing their communities or the larger society as extremely serious. To the organization man, the club woman, and the good neighbor, the challenges of community life generally seemed tractable. . . . In contrast, the problems on which many of the people in the 1990s focus seem to pervade the entire society or have defied the best efforts of several generations.[32]

As a result of citizens' perceiving problems as difficult to solve, there is a new role for the professional volunteer from the nonprofit sector, who is viewed as the person most capable of solving these problems. For example, the BNP case study illustrates how CANS and CAPS organizers focused the efforts of the Beltway group, and, in so doing, made it possible for community members to build a viable and successful community organization. Wuthnow explains that, for many citizens, involvement is less about being part of an organization and more about how effective their involvement can be, and what they can achieve.

The contribution of Wuthnow's study is that he contextualizes the changing roles of activists not simply in terms of the categories of their activity, which is Putnam's main concern, but in terms of the problems with which they have to deal. Cast in these terms, it is understandable that patterns of civic activism have changed: what is the point of being an upstanding Rotarian if your neighborhood is beset by crime and disorder? Loose connections are both a cause and a consequence of some of the more pressing problems that face many neighborhoods, but what is heartening is that these loose ties can translate into effective action that helps secure public goods.[33] Crucial to the process of moving from loose neighborhood ties to efficacious activity is the ability to mobilize resources.

The Beltway case studies demonstrate the importance of resource mobilization. For example, one of the reasons the Rendell Park patrol and SON initiatives failed was their inability to mobilize the required resources. The contrast between these groups and the BNP is striking.[34] In terms of the three criteria for resource mobilization, the BNP score high in terms of agency, strategy, and organization.[35] Specifically, BNP members showed a great deal of agency; they invested a great deal of effort in collective action, evidenced by the work on problem solving, the ongoing patrols, and the actions of court advocates. The BNP also scored high on strategy; it performed a direct service through problem solving and patrols and tried to educate the public in their campaign to have people paint their house numbers on garage doors. The only element of strategy on which it did not score high was structural change, though it could be argued that it was part of a wider movement in the community control of crime. Finally, the BNP scored high on the organization front; it scheduled regular meetings and displayed a high degree of organization in terms of how it allocated tasks to specific committees. Table 7.1 details the comparison of the three initiatives centered on the Rendell Park area that I described in chapter 4. I add a fourth variable—that of intervening help, which seems to be the crucial difference between the experiences of SON, for example, and the BNP. It is through the intervention of nonlocal organizers that the BNP was able to tap into the ini-

TABLE 7.1
Resource Mobilization in Beltway before and after the Powell-Harvey Murders

	Rendell Park Patrol	*SON*	*Boxing Program*	*BNP*
Agency	Low	Mixed	High	High
Collective Action	No	Yes	Yes	Yes
Strategy	Low/mixed	Mixed	Mixed	High
Public education	No	Yes	Yes	Yes
Structural change	No	No	No	Mixed
Direct service	Yes	No	Yes	Yes
Organization	Low	Mixed	Low	High
#/Type meetings	No	Yes	No	Yes
Task committees	No	No	No	Yes
Intervening help	No	No	No	Yes

Adapted from John D. McCarthy and Mark Wolfson, "Resource Mobilization by Local Social Movement Organizations: Agency, Strategy, and Organization in the Movement against Drinking and Driving," *American Sociological Review* 61 (1996): 1070–1088.

tial linkages that helped it engage in successful campaigns. The pivotal role that successful resource mobilization plays in promoting informal social control is borne out by the contrasting outcomes for the initiatives in Beltway.

Effective Activism: The Beltway Experience as a Blueprint for Fighting Crime and Reducing Disorder

Marshaling the threads of the analysis, the Beltway case study offers a timely look at civic engagement that is designed specifically to control crime and disorder. The configuration of strategies in Beltway was forged in the fashion of problem-oriented community policing; it shares common ground with programs in other cities and jurisdictions. Moreover, the opportunities afforded by new variants of policing are occurring at a time when the nature of citizen involvement in civic affairs has changed and many people find it difficult to allocate time to volunteer work.[36] These seemingly paradoxical tendencies are further complicated by an increasing reluctance of people to socialize collectively or intervene in situations when they encounter youth misbehaving. Many citizens are unwilling to engage in what I call traditional informal control because they fear reprisals by youth or they do not feel closely tied to their neighbors.

In spite of loose ties and the diminution of traditional forms of community or parochial control, it is still possible to have effective activism. The key ingredient seems to be the new parochial partners that help jump-start the initiatives to combat crime and disorder. How, then, does Beltway force us to rethink what we know about informal social control, and does this give us a blueprint for activity that can be undertaken elsewhere?

In the first place, the Beltway story calls for a rethinking of what we normally consider informal social control.[37] The story of what happened in Beltway as youth gangs became active there in the early 1990s illustrates the diminution of the role of private and traditional parochial forms of control. The response to the Powell-Harvey murders showcases a new form of parochial control, characterized by a strong interplay between the parochial and the public spheres. The partnership between the parochial and the public levels of control gave rise to the strategies that I dub the new parochialism—in essence, a set of semiformal practices coproduced by neighborhood residents and formal control agents. The new parochialism is grounded in the context of Beltway but speaks to wider trends and developments. It is new in the sense that it is a new form of organization that is there specifically to deal with informal social control because the traditional forms of parochial control are no longer widely practiced in Beltway. It would be a mistake to assume that the new parochialism does not have a degree of continuity with other forms of community organization. Certainly, the tradition of the ward system in Chicago, and the practices associated with it, give residents a repertoire for getting things done.[38] However, the ward organization and its ties to agencies outside the neighborhood have rarely been used for self-regulation, except in extreme circumstances and then only as a conduit to ask for stronger formal control. More important is the fact that the new parochialism is a set of strategies of ongoing informal social control, enabled by community policing initiatives, that arise in response to the confluence of trends in labor force participation, youth crime, and neighborhood change that render traditional forms of parochial control more difficult to undertake.

The Beltway case study, then, compels us to reconstruct existing theory about informal social control because the developments underpinning the new parochialism are not limited to neighborhoods that share Beltway's profile. Specifically, the central tenet of what is known as the systemic model of control—that strong social ties are crucial to engaging in effective neighborhood control—is called into question.[39] Beltway residents engage in effective informal social control, as evidenced by the successful campaigns to close down the tavern and to reduce graffiti in the neighborhood, but the neighborhood is not characterized by dense social ties. Indeed, it is the dearth of dense social ties that contributes in part to the diminished role of private and traditionally parochial forms of control. The central insight of the social disorganization approach—that neighborhoods have differential capacities for controlling crime and disorder—remains pertinent, but the mechanisms that contribute to effective control are changing. Instead of private, parochial, and public forms of control acting in concert to maintain effective neighborhood controls, in the Beltway case we see that, when private and traditionally parochial forms of control are weak but there is a strong interplay between the parochial and the public levels of control, effective control can be exercised.

Second, whether the new parochialism is a blueprint that can operate in neighborhoods with different levels of crime and different class and racial profiles remains to be seen.[40] Some of the evidence from similar models in places as diverse as San Diego and Sioux City suggest that there is potential for the application of this approach in different contexts. In sum, I believe that neighborhoods that have crime and disorder problems may find that the new parochialism is an appealing and often effective way to control crime. Indeed, with fear of teens and crime at high levels, the new parochialism may be increasingly the most prevalent form of informal social control in many urban neighborhoods. In particular, the new parochialism may be particularly relevant for suburban neighborhoods. Some suburban neighborhoods have seen crime rates increase recently,[41] even as crime rates drop in many urban areas, and perhaps in many suburban areas that are newly established, where dual-earner families are common, or where there are residentially transient populations, there is also a paucity of private and traditional parochial forms of control.[42] In such a situation, the interplay between parochial and public forms of control may increasingly be adopted. With respect to urban initiatives to fight crime and disorder, some community policing and neighborhood organizing programs have emphasized the notion of partnerships between parochial and public groups to achieve desirable outcomes.[43] There is institutional support for the new parochialism, and in Beltway it seems to resonate with neighborhood activists. The general approach of equipping interested citizens with the wherewithal to solve problems of crime and disorder is feasible in the short term and tenable over time. It is important to bear in mind that the efforts of citizens to control crime and disorder should be sustained and consolidated. As Friedman and Clark point out, "the capacity to sustain efforts must be embodied in ongoing community-based organizations that do not have to be reorganized to deal with every new crisis."[44]

In Beltway, the BNP is still active after seven years, though the gang activity that forced it into being has long since dissipated. The members still patrol and assiduously remove any trace of graffiti in the neighborhood; if a problem arises, they have the institutional resources and experience to know what to do. In many ways, then, the experience of Beltway residents can form a blueprint that other neighborhoods can employ. The new parochial strategies are flexible and applicable to different contexts and to different problems, and they have the potential to have a speedy impact on local problems.

Prospects for the New Parochialism

What are the prospects for the new parochialism? The data from Beltway suggest that the problem solving in general and the CAPS initiative in particular have produced some beneficial results for the neighborhood, though others have pointed out some of the negative outcomes associated with CAPS and programs of its ilk.[45] The Beltway problem-solving group and the BNP owe part of their success to CAPS, and it will be interesting to see whether similar initiatives in other neighborhoods and cities have similar outcomes.

If Beltway's efforts were efficacious because of its strong political ties, then efforts should be made to provide neighborhoods that are not well connected with the means for achieving effective social control. If everybody wants to live in an area free of crime, then it is imperative that they be provided with the means to achieve this goal, and in a way that empowers those who are cynical or alienated from the legal system and those who have been denied access to the requisite political and social resources increasingly needed for successful self-regulation.

Simply put, the new parochialism has the potential to provide citizens with a set of tools with which they can begin to tackle crime and disorder problems in their neighborhoods. Its great advantages are its adaptability across contexts, and the fact that, given the changes that have occurred in American society, the new parochial strategies I have described here may increasingly be the way that informal social control is practiced.

Appendix

Getting In and Out of Beltway

It is something of a tradition in ethnographic studies to have a methods appendix in which the author expounds on his or her field experiences. While I am keeping up the tradition, perhaps we should take these stories a little more seriously and not practically hide them away in an appendix. That said, I am hardly blazing the trail for change, though I consider the recounting of the field experience to be of the utmost importance. In the following pages I elaborate on how Maria Kefalas and I began our research and how my fieldwork evolved over time. I do this in order to more fully explicate how I completed the research and to provide examples of field methods in action.

Getting In

I came to meet up with the Beltwayites with whom I spent five years studying informal social control as the result of a number of happy coincidences. After Beltway was chosen as one of the sites for the Comparative Neighborhood Study, it was up to Maria Kefalas and me to make our way in the neighborhood and to get to know some of the key individuals: a simple task, or so it seemed. We had spent a good deal of time roaming the neighborhood, getting a feel for the place, and we decided that perhaps the best way to make a first contact would be to identify a key resident and ask to speak with him or her. While browsing through the local weekly paper, I noticed that there was a column on Beltway, with a smiling picture and a contact number for the scribe, Mary Winchester. I called Mary and told her about the CNS and my interest in the neighborhood, and I asked if she wouldn't mind meeting with Maria and me to talk generally about the area. To my dismay, Mary was very reluctant to talk to me, and she told me that she didn't feel qualified to talk knowledgeably about Beltway. This was not going very well for a first contact. I assured her that whatever she knew was a great deal more than my own knowledge, yet she insisted that she would not be the best person with whom to talk. I was feeling a little mystified that someone who looked out so benevolently from her column should know so little about the very place she writes about each week, but I put it down to a prudent caution about researchers who call up out of the blue asking to meet with people. I tried to reassure her that the project was only in its initial stages and that I just wanted to talk in vague generalities about Beltway. Finally, she said that she would call Ron Zalinsky, the president of the Beltway Civic League, and ask him to call me. She wanted us to meet Ron because, in Mary's words, "he just knows so much more about Beltway than I do, and he's better at talking about it." I hung up the phone and waited for Ron to call, which he did after ten anxious minutes, and we set up a meeting for the next day at Mary's house. I hung up, grateful that I had not botched my very first official contact.

Maria and I set off for our first meeting, and we pulled up at the appointed time outside the Winchesters' home, a beautifully maintained Chicago bungalow on Fifth Avenue, the main thoroughfare through the neighborhood. Mary's house is bordered by a small lot that has lush green grass and an assortment of flowers blooming along its neatly trimmed edges. We rang the front door bell and were greeted by Mary, who had seen us arrive. Ron also arrived just as we had alighted from our car, and we went in together. The front door of the house led directly into a bright and beautifully appointed living room. Later we learned that people usually enter Beltway houses through the back door, and only formal guests are received through the front door. Mary ushered us in warmly, and she seemed to be relieved that we seemed normal. Her husband, Fred, joined us shortly after we sat down. Fred describes himself as a retired blue-collar worker who likes to stay active in the neighborhood. Ron is a thin, wiry man in his midsixties who is full of nervous energy. He has a booming voice that increases in volume when he speaks about issues that rankle him, of which there are many. Ron has been president of the Beltway Civic League for more than a dozen years, and he runs the organization on the sheer strength of his will and on the boundless energy he seems to possess. Everyone in Beltway knows Ron, and whether one's opinion of him is favorable, unfavorable, or indifferent, everyone respects him as someone who works tirelessly for the neighborhood. In the spring of

2003, Ron and his wife, Margaret, were honored for their contribution to the community by having a street in the neighborhood renamed for them.

Our first meeting went very well. We chatted with Mary, Fred, and Ron for a couple of hours, and they brought us up to date on some of the more pressing local issues. Ron explained that he viewed the Beltway Civic League as a watchdog for the community and that his own role was to "holler when I see something wrong. That way people know you're out there." More important, they recommended a number of people with whom we should speak, and they invited us to attend the civic league meetings. This method of building contacts from initial contacts is called snowball sampling, and we were fortunate to speak with Mary, Fred, and Ron because, with their wide range of contacts, we had, in essence, gained entry to Beltway.

Key Informants

Far and away the best suggestion we received at our first meeting was to speak with Lydia Donovan, the head librarian at the Beltway Public Library. As a scholar, I have long been aware of the benefits of being friendly with librarians, but it was not until Maria and I met Lydia that I realized the benefits of knowing one while doing field research. Lydia describes herself modestly as an activist librarian, one who is not content merely working and living in a neighborhood but who wants to make her neighborhood a better place. Maybe Lydia is not the first activist librarian ever, but her voluminous volunteer résumé and her indefatigable appetite for public service give new meaning to the term. When we walked into the cramped storefront library in the summer of 1993 and told her about our project, she immediately smiled and told us that there would be enough material in Beltway for six or seven volumes. Since then, Lydia has helped us with archival research; she has introduced Maria and me to numerous key players in Beltway and generally helped in more ways that it is possible to recount in a few sentences. The term "key informant" is used to describe someone central to the kind of ethnographic research we undertook in Beltway. The researcher builds contacts from a key informant and stays informed of important events; by associating with the key informant, the researcher gains a wider acceptance in the neighborhood. The term hardly does justice to the breadth and range of what Lydia did for us, but for now it will have to suffice.

Fieldwork of the kind that Maria and I completed in Beltway can be a series of fortunate occurrences. Many ethnographers would agree that there is a certain degree of luck needed to do the work we do, and any research that spans five years requires that you ride your luck when you can. So it was when we met Jane Pratt, who became my other great key informant. Maria and I first met Jane at a local school council meeting at the Hastings Elementary School. Earlier that same day, we had attended a local school council meeting at the Gerald School, located about a dozen blocks south east of Hastings. At the time, we had been following events at the Gerald School and were regular attendees at the local school council meetings there. We knew vaguely that Hastings had some issues at the time; while at the meeting at Gerald, we decided to leave early and try to catch the meeting at Hastings. The brisk, businesslike tone and general consensus that were the hallmarks of Gerald Local School Council meetings stood in stark contrast to the divisive bickering and finger-pointing that characterized the first Hastings LSC meeting we attended. We had in essence walked into the middle of an LSC that was about to implode.

Jane Pratt, whose husband, John, was a parent representative on the LSC who consistently voted against the self-appointed oligarchy, was one of the many parents at Hastings who found herself ignored and left out of many of the decisions taken by the council. As the groundswell of parents who opposed the tactics of the oligarchy on the council grew, Jane became one of the de facto leaders of the campaign to impeach and replace the six members of the council. It was in this capacity that Maria first approached Jane after our first Hastings LSC meeting. Jane was initially wary of us, as the climate at Hastings was one where suspicion was rife, but she soon warmed to the task of telling us her side of the events. Jane is another Beltwayite with a seemingly unquenchable appetite for volunteer work. As my project developed and my focus became informal social control, Jane proved to be a constant source of information, and I am eternally grateful for her meticulous record keeping and willingness to answer my seemingly endless questions.

It is perhaps unfair to single out a few individuals when so many Beltway residents took the time to talk with me about their views on crime, disorder, and their role in reducing them. There are scores of others who welcomed us into their houses and invited us to block parties, fundraisers, birthday, and graduation celebrations.

Field Roles

In the course of the five years I spent doing research in Beltway, I occupied a fairly wide range of roles. At various times I was a soccer coach, a volunteer on political campaigns, an active patrolling member of the BNP, a court advocate, and a volunteer with a youth group. The diversity of the role set enabled me to tap into a variety of networks in the neighborhood and to get to know residents of the neighborhood in several ways. Some of the roles, such as my participation on the neighborhood watch and in the court advocacy program, were crucial to my research on informal social control, while others, notably the soccer coaching, were undertaken out of an altruistic wish to use my skills for the benefit of the community. Even with the variety of roles, the constant was that I was always the researcher, the student who was writing about the neighborhood. All of my roles were overt, and I was careful to inform people about the research project. I think that the disparate roles I undertook helped to normalize my presence for many Beltway residents, and the fact that I helped out whenever I could was also appreciated.

Getting Out

As difficult as getting into a neighborhood can be, getting out or finishing the research can be just as difficult. Even the most objective fieldworker builds up affective ties over time, and I was no different. In my five years in Beltway, I befriended many people. I worked alongside them on political campaigns, I rode shotgun on the neighborhood watch, and I attended court with them. I also had the great fortune to just get to hang out at block parties or graduations or go bowling or gambling. About a third of the people who came to my thirtieth birthday party were from Beltway.

Getting out is not simply about loosening affective ties. It is about withdrawing from a neighborhood or place that has become a part of your life. There is also the nagging feeling that if you stay a little longer there might be another revelation around the corner. There probably will be more things of note, and this kind of research is a procrastinator's dream. However, it is important to exit, and perhaps what I learned in Beltway is that it is best to prepare one's exit. I also learned that is too easy to go back, which I did so a year after officially finishing the fieldwork to complete more interviews. I am glad I did those interviews because some were extraordinarily thoughtful and appropriate. But, in truth, instead of reinforcing to me that I had done just about all I could do, my return visit sowed seeds of doubt that perhaps I could do yet more work. There is no ideal length for an ethnographic project. I spent five years in Beltway, but it could have been three or six or two. It is important to continually assess the state of the research, to review notes and transcripts, and to analyze data as they emerge. Such practical steps can ensure that however long is spent in the field is the right amount of time.

In the end, as I said earlier, the advice that Gerry Suttles gave his students is the best. It is only by knowing what you have, which is sometimes difficult when you are in the moment, that you will know when to stop.

Conclusion

This study is meant to contribute to the canon of Chicago style ethnographies. I do not think that my fieldwork experiences have forged a new path, but I do think that the reportage from the field can be of some use to others contemplating this kind of research. Ethnography is important. It can document living process, generate and test theory, and force us to rethink taken for granted assumptions. I am personally gratified that so much quality ethnographic work is being done currently, and I hope that people read, engage, and critique this work.

Notes

NOTES TO CHAPTER 1

1. National Night Out is an annual event, begun in 1982, sponsored by the National Association of Town Watch (NATW). National Night Out is designed to "heighten crime and drug prevention awareness; generate support for, and participation in, local anticrime programs; strengthen neighborhood spirit and police community partnerships; and send a message to criminals letting them know that neighborhoods are organized and fighting back." Available at the NATW Web site, http://www.natw.org.

2. There have been a number of studies of police officers' commitment to community policing. The research has focused on officers' perception of their role and the differences between a community police officer and a traditional or professional officer. The key study in the present case is the one reported in Arthur J. Lurigio and Wesley G. Skogan, "Winning the Hearts and Minds of Police Officers: An Assessment of Staff Perceptions of Community Policing in Chicago," *Crime and Delinquency* 40(3) (1994): 315–30. Lurigio and Skogan illustrate the ambivalence of Chicago police officers as they transition to the CAPS program. Officers are positively disposed toward some of the changes but resent others, and they are generally pessimistic about the prospects for reducing crime. There are other studies that do not pertain specifically to Chicago. See, for example, Richard E. Adams, William M. Rohe, and Thomas A. Arcury, "Implementing Community-Oriented Policing: Organization Change and Street Officer Attitudes," *Crime and Delinquency* 48(3) (2002): 399–430; Kevin Ford, Daniel A. Weissbein, and Kevin E. Plamondon, "Distinguishing Organizational from Strategy Commitment: Linking Officers' Commitment to Community Policing to Job Behaviors and Satisfaction," *Justice Quarterly* 20(1) (2003): 159–85; E. J. Williams, "Officer Attitude Surveys in Community Policing Organizations: What Are They Really Telling Management?" *Policing and Society* 12(1) (2002): 37–52.

Adams et al. (2002) find support for community-oriented policing (COP) among COP and traditional officers, with the former group more favorable. Ford et al. (2003) make the point that there is a crucial distinction between commitment to the police organization as a whole and commitment to the actual strategy of community policing. Commitment to the organization is related to job satisfaction, while commitment to community policing is related to the frequency of engaging in community-policing behaviors. Williams (2002) questions the role of the attitude survey in the assessment of police officers' perception of role transition to community policing, and he argues that the use of these surveys is based on an outdated bureaucratic model.

3. The motto of the Beltway Civic League is "For Country and Home," and this general and populist phrase underpins the wide-ranging aims of that organization. The BCL is equally at home combating the building of incinerators in the area and dispensing gardening tips in its monthly newsletter. The range of issues tackled by the group over its four decades of existence belies a preoccupation with the preservation of community from vague and ill-defined threats. By contrast, the BNP mobilized to face the specific and well-defined threat of gang violence in the neighborhood.

4. Research on crime-fighting community groups, for example, has shown that many groups face organizational problems, which makes it difficult for them to endure over time. See Gary Marx and Dane Archer, "Citizen Involvement in the Law Enforcement Process: The Case of Community Police Patrols," *American Behavioral Scientist* 15 (1971): 52–72; James Garofalo and Maureen McLeod, "The Structure and Operations of Neighborhood Watch Programs in the United States," *Crime and Delinquency* 27 (1987): 326–44. Other studies question whether neighborhood watch programs have any effect on crime rates. See P. Cirel, P. Evans, D. McGillis, and D. Whitcomb, *Community Crime Prevention Program: Seattle, Washington* (Washington, DC: National Institute of Justice, 1977); Dennis P. Rosenbaum, Dan A. Lewis, et al., *The Impact of Community Crime Prevention Programs in Chicago: Can Neighborhood Organizations Make a Difference?* (Evanston, IL: Northwestern University Center for Urban Affairs and Policy Research, 1985); Trevor Bennett, *An Evaluation of Two Neighbourhood Watch Schemes* (Cambridge: Cambridge Institute of Criminology, 1987); Anthony M. Pate, Marlys McPherson, and Glenn Silloway, *The Minneapolis Community Crime Prevention Experiment* (Washington, DC: Police Foundation, 1987).

5. See Robert D. Putnam, *Bowling Alone: The Collapse and Revival of American Community* (New York: Simon and Schuster, 2000). Putnam discusses trends in civic engagement and some of the possible reasons for the recent decline.

6. See Robert J. Bursik Jr. and Harold Grasmick, *Neighborhoods and Crime: The Dimensions of Effective Control* (New York: Lexington Books, 1993). See also Robert J. Sampson, "What 'Community' Supplies," in *Urban Problems and Community Development*, ed. Ronald F. Ferguson and William T. Dickins (Washington, DC: Brookings Institution, 1999), 241–92. While some may argue that it is not possible to have any desire that is shared universally and that some

people may want to live in a crime-ridden area, this particular desire does have an almost universal appeal.

7. See Stanley Cohen, *Folk Devils and Moral Panics: The Creation of the Mods and the Rockers* (Oxford: Basil Blackwell, 1980). Cohen coined the term "folk devil" to describe how certain groups come to personify evil or danger in the public mind. At the time, there was a large amount of gang-related violence in Chicago, much of it centered about two miles east of Beltway. For an excellent account of some of the circumstances surrounding the high levels of gang violence at the beginning of the 1990s in Chicago, see Sudhir Venkatesh, *American Project: The Rise and Fall of a Modern Ghetto* (Cambridge, MA: Harvard University Press, 2000).

8. See Clive Emsley, *The English Police: A Political and Social History* (London: Longman, 1996).

9. See Michael E. Cavanaugh, *Policing within a Professional Framework* (New York: Prentice Hall, 2003).

10. George L. Kelling and Catherine M. Coles, *Fixing Broken Windows: Restoring Order and Reducing Crime in Our Communities* (New York: Simon and Schuster, 1996).

11. See, for example, Wesley G. Skogan and Susan Hartnett, *Community Policing: Chicago Style* (New York: Oxford University Press, 1997).

12. Several evaluations of community policing initiatives have illustrated that one of the major difficulties in implementing these programs is the reluctance of police officers to buy into the new policing philosophies. Some commentators have explained this as being caused by an adherence to the professional model of policing, which holds that the police are trained to be professional crime fighters and that citizens should not get involved. See Skogan and Hartnett (1997) and Lurigio and Skogan (1994) for more detail on this argument.

13. See Putnam (2000). Putnam's "Bowling Alone" thesis originally appeared as "Bowling Alone: America's Declining Social Capital," *Journal of Democracy* 6(1) (1995): 65–78.

14. Morris Janowitz, "Sociological Theory and Social Control," *American Journal of Sociology* 81 (1975): 82–108.

15. See Robert J. Sampson, Steven Raudenbush, and Felton Earls Jr., "Neighborhoods and Violent Crime: A Multilevel Study of Collective Efficacy," *Science* 277 (1997): 918–24.

16. See, for example, David Simon and Edward Burns, *The Corner: A Year in the Life of an Inner-City Neighborhood* (New York: Broadway Books, 1997). In this book, Simon and Burns depict the reality of the drug trade in a West Baltimore neighborhood, and they illustrate how the drug trade itself has changed, particularly with the wider use and availability of cocaine and crack, and the effect that this has had on some urban neighborhoods. Informal social control in these neighborhoods is almost nonexistent in the usual sense of the

term. To be sure, drug dealers exercise a certain variant of control over their personnel, often using violence to ensure that their turf is protected and their profits are maximized, but in the sense of control of community crime and disorder in its environs, informal social control does not exist in areas like West Baltimore.

17. Mark Cooney, "The Dark Side of Community: Moralistic Homicide and Social Ties," *Sociological Focus* 35(2) (1998): 135–53.

18. U.S. Department of Labor, *Report on the American Workforce* (Washington, DC: U.S. Department of Labor, 1999). The *Report on the American Workforce,* for example, illustrates that people are working longer hours and that more women are in the workforce than in previous decades; in many two-parent families, both parents are working.

19. Michael Burawoy, "The Extended Case Method," in *Ethnography Unbound: Power and Resistance in the Modern Metropolis,* ed. Michael Burawoy (Berkley: University of California Press, 1991), 271–90.

20. Mercer Sullivan, "Integrating Qualitative and Quantitative Methods in the Study of Developmental Psychopathology in Context," *Development and Psychopathology* 10 (1998): 380.

21. Albert Hunter, "Private, Parochial and Public Social Orders: The Problem of Crime and Incivility in Urban Communities," in *The Challenge of Social Control,* ed. Gerald D. Suttles and Meyer Zald (Norwood, NJ: Ablex, 1985).

22. For a more complete explication of Hunter's typology, see Bursik and Grasmick (1993: 16–17).

23. For example, for the period 1994–1995, Beltway ranked in the lowest decile of community areas in Chicago in terms of overall violent crime rate.

24. See Wesley G. Skogan, *Disorder and Decline* (New York: Free Press, 1990), for a more complete discussion of how residents adapt to a fearful environment

25. This finding is echoed by Robert J. Bursik, "The Informal Control of Crime through Neighborhood Networks," *Sociological Focus* 32(1) (1999): 85–97.

26. It is worth noting that most informal control is aimed at controlling young people, and there is real intergenerational conflict at the heart of most of what goes on under the guise of crime control.

27. Local school councils, or LSCs, are the product of an Illinois school reform bill, passed in 1988, that attempted to shift control of local schools from a central bureaucracy and into the hands of teachers, parents, and local community representatives working together as a team. The law made provision for the election of LSCs, which consist of eleven members: the principal of the school, who is automatically elected; six parent and two community representatives, who are chosen by an electorate of parents of children at the school and all community members over eighteen years of age who live in school's catchment area;

and two teacher representatives, who are chosen by the teachers at the school. The eleven-member LSC is charged with responsibility for approving the school budget and the School Improvement Plan and for hiring and firing principals. Additional duties that fall within the purview of the LSC center on general matters pertaining to educational policy and school development, except for the day-to-day running of the school, which is the responsibility of the permanent teaching staff. The term of office for LSC members is two years, and being the parent of a child currently registered at the school or being from the community area are the only criteria for membership on the council.

NOTES TO CHAPTER 2

1. Perhaps the most rapid change in Chicago over the past decade has been the expansion of the Latino population, the majority of whom are Mexican. One of the most visible portents of this change is the opening of *carnicerias,* which are Mexican corner stores.

2. The Beltway of this book was one-tenth Latino in 1990, and this proportion increased during the 1990s to a little more than one-fifth of the area's population in 2000.

3. Much of the expansion was fueled by the passing of the GI Bill, or "Servicemen's Readjustment Act of 1944," which initially provided for six major benefits for veterans of World War II. The first three benefits, which provided funds for education and training, loan guarantees for the purchase of a home, farm or business, and unemployment assistance for up to one year, had a profound impact on the postwar landscape. The GI Bill made it possible for millions of veterans to receive an education and to buy a house after demobilization; in the peak year of 1947, veterans accounted for just under half of college enrollment. The World War II GI Bill ended in 1956, but there have been subsequent GI Bills for veterans of the Korean conflict and of the war in Vietnam. The GI Bill initiated great changes in higher education, and the mortgage subsidies for home purchase led to an increase in demand for housing. It is estimated that one-fifth of all single-family homes built in the two decades after World War II were financed by GI Bill loans (*West's Encyclopedia of American Law*).

4. Chicago Fact Book Consortium, *Local Community Fact Book Chicago Metropolitan Area* (Chicago: Academy Chicago Publishers, 1995).

5. Thomas Lee Philpott, *The Slum and the Ghetto* (New York: Oxford University Press, 1978). Philpott discusses how the so-called Black Belt came into being in the early part of the twentieth century as white ethnics, many of whom had been immigrants themselves and had lived in the sprawling tenements in and around the stockyards and factories in Chicago, sought to segregate the growing population of African American migrants. See also Jeffrey Morenoff and Robert J. Sampson, "Violent Crime and the Spatial Dynamics of Neighborhood Transi-

tion," *Social Forces* 76 (1997): 31–64. This article contains several maps that illustrate population shifts in Chicago over the course of several decades.

6. For a more thorough discussion of white attachment to place in Beltway, as well as the historical significance of changes in Chicago, see Maria J. Kefalas, *Working-Class Heroes: Protecting Home, Community in a Chicago Neighborhood* (Berkeley: University of California Press, 2003).

7. The designation "very well" derives from the question asked in the Census about native language.

8. Latinos in Beltway are involved in both Catholic parishes. Also, there are Latino members of the local school councils, and, importantly for the present discussion, Latinos volunteer for the neighborhood watch and are involved in the community policing initiatives.

9. In keeping with the tradition of other excellent sociological ethnographies, I explain my methods and field experiences in an appendix.

10. The CNS tried to study neighborhoods that were comparable over a range of general indicators, among them income. However, it was impossible to find a majority Latino neighborhood that had income levels that corresponded to working- or lower-middle-class status. The majority Latino neighborhoods in Chicago are mixed-income neighborhoods, where working-class residents live alongside poor and working poor residents. However, given the rate of internal migration in Chicago, it is only a matter of time before some neighborhoods are stable working-class- or lower-middle-class-majority Latino areas. Of the four CNS neighborhoods, Archer Park has a median income level well below that of the other three neighborhoods.

11. Under the direction of Robert Park, chair of the Department of Sociology at the University of Chicago, students were sent into the city of Chicago and reported back about hobos, taxi-dance halls, upscale neighborhoods, and slums. The breath and depth of the ethnographies is astounding and contributed to a keen understanding of process, according to Andrew Abbott, "Of Time and Space: The Contemporary Relevance of the Chicago School," *Social Forces* 75 (1997): 1149–82. It is this concern with process that I hope to replicate here, specifically by describing how informal social control as a process works over time in Beltway.

12. Fred Matthews, *Quest for an American Sociology: Robert E. Park and the Chicago School* (Montreal: McGill-Queen's University Press, 1977).

13. See Kefalas (2003).

14. Bunco is a gambling dice game popular among working-class women in Chicago. The game is played with three dice, and the object is to roll three of each number in a sequence. As it is played in Beltway, bunco is more of a social occasion than an opportunity to gamble.

NOTES TO CHAPTER 3

1. The position of committeeman is one of the most important in the ward organization. The committeeman is responsible for picking and choosing who will serve as the Committee's nominee for alderman and who will serve as precinct captain. Unlike the alderman, the committeeman is not elected by the people; the ward committee selects him. Democratic committeemen in Chicago are very powerful as they directly influence the makeup of the ward organization.

2. Sampson (1999: 241–92).

3. The name that Murphy gave the development was Chestnut Courts.

4. Not all condominiums are owned by the people who live in them. In some cases people purchase condos to let them out to tenants.

5. For a more complete discussion of the meaning of home ownership in Beltway, see Kefalas (2003).

6. We did attempt to speak with members of the ruling faction on the LSC, but we were warned off, and thus the account is somewhat one-sided. However, the weight of the opinion not only of local people but of school administration professionals was overwhelmingly on the side of the proreform group.

7. Bill Romanoski had taken over from John Puchinski as the alderman for the ward when Puchinski decided to run for a citywide office. Romanoski had the backing of the committeeman and won the election, despite a spirited campaign from a number of other local candidates.

8. The acronym is for Partnership of parents/community/staff; Reform; Involvement; Diversity; and Education.

9. See Thomas M. Guterbock, *Machine Politics in Transition* (Chicago: University of Chicago Press, 1971).

10. For example, John D. McCarthy and Mayer N. Zald, "Resource Mobilization and Social Movements: A Partial Theory," *American Journal of Sociology* 82(6) (1977): 1212–41. See also Craig J. Jenkins, "Resource Mobilization Theory and the Study of Social Movements," *Annual Review of Sociology* 9 (1983): 527–53. While the action described in this chapter could hardly be characterized as a social movement, the usage of the resource mobilization model is pertinent in this case study, as it describes how grassroots groups leverage support and mobilize resources to advance their cause.

11. See Glen Loury, "A Dynamic Theory of Racial Income Differences," in *Women, Minorities and Unemployment Discrimination,* ed. P. A. Wallace and A. L. Mund (Lexington, MA: Lexington Books, 1977), 153–86; James S. Coleman, "Social Capital in the Creation of Human Capital," *American Journal of Sociology* 94 (Supplement) (1988): S95–S120; James S. Coleman, *Foundations of Social Theory* (Cambridge, MA: Harvard Belknap Press, 1990).

The term "social capital" was coined by Loury (1977), who used it to explain racial inequality, and the notion was brought to prominence by Coleman (Coleman 1988; Coleman 1990). Coleman defines it: "Social capital is defined by its function. It is not a single entity but a variety of different entities having two characteristics in common. They all consist of some aspect of social structure and they facilitate certain actions of individuals who are within that structure . . . social capital inheres in the structure of relations between persons and among persons. . . . Social organization constitutes social capital, facilitating the achievement of goals that could not be achieved in its absence" (Coleman 1990: 302–4). Social capital, then, exists in the relations between people, and it can be activated to help people achieve goals that they could not have in its absence.

12. For a more complete discussion of patterns of volunteering, see Putnam (2000), especially chapter 7. See also John Wilson and Marc Musick, "Attachment to Volunteering," *Sociological Forum* 14 (1999): 243–72.

13. No data on volunteering are available from the Current Population Survey after 1989.

14. See Putnam (1995: 70).

15. In interviews and conversations, several Beltway residents commented on the fact that fewer people sit on their porches than in the past, especially during the summer months. Residents blame air conditioning for this change and lament the fact that people seemed to be more community-centered in the past.

16. For example, Putnam (2000: 25) talks about how the sense of a "waning" community is shared by ordinary Americans. More than half of baby boomers interviewed in 1987, for example, felt that their parents' generation was better in terms of "being a concerned citizen, involved in helping others in the community." More than three-quarters of respondents in the same survey said that the nation was worse off because there is "less involvement in community activities." Putnam also reports that several 1999 surveys found that more than two-thirds of respondents said that America's civic life had weakened in recent years.

17. The point mirrors the work of Lawrence E. Cohen and Marcus Felson, "Social Change and Crime Rate Trends: A Routine Activity Approach," *American Sociological Review* 44 (1979): 588–608, who posit that crime rates are related to societal changes in the routine activities of citizens. For a crime to happen, there must be a coincidence in time and space of a motivated offender and a suitable target in the absence of capable guardians. Such an occurrence becomes more likely as people's routine activities take them away from the safety and security of their homes. The post–World War II movement of women into the labor force and the increase in leisure activities outside the home are some of the changes in routine activities that increase the chances for victimization. Following the same logic, then, the idea here is that it is not simply that routine activities take people away from the home but also the fact that these routine activities

are more numerous and time consuming, forcing people to prioritize what they will do at any one time.

18. Robert J. Sampson and William J. Wilson, "Toward a Theory of Race, Crime and Urban Inequality," in *Crime and Inequality,* ed. John Hagan and Ruth D. Peterson (Stanford: Stanford University Press, 1993), 37–54.

19. Ibid., 39.

20. See Clifford R. Shaw and Henry D. McKay, *Juvenile Delinquency in Urban Areas* (Chicago: University of Chicago Press, 1942; rev. ed., 1969); Ruth Rosner Kornhauser, *Social Sources of Delinquency* (Chicago: University of Chicago Press, 1978). The argument by Shaw and McKay was not a strict-control model of crime and delinquency. For example, Kornhauser argues that, in addition to the control theory that lies at the heart of social disorganization theory, there is a subcultural model in which Shaw and McKay posit that there is an intergenerational cultural transmission of deviant values, which creates a subculture of delinquency in disorganized areas. Kornhauser further asserts that such a "mixed model" obfuscates the strength of Shaw and McKay's theory.

21. Shaw and McKay (1942) relied on three types of official data: records from delinquency petitions brought before Juvenile Court in Chicago; information on delinquents committed by Juvenile Court to correctional institutions; and records of alleged delinquents dealt with by probation officers with or without a court appearance.

22. For example, Christen Jonassen, "A Re-Evaluation and Critique of the Logic and Some of the Methods of Shaw and McKay," *American Sociological Review* 14 (1949): 608–14. See also Clifford R. Shaw and Henry D. McKay, "Rejoinder," *American Sociological Review* 14 (1949): 614–17. Jonassen argues that Shaw and McKay's theory is flawed on a number of counts. In the first place, it does not account for all groups that lived in so-called disorganized areas. Jonassen cites Asians in the Chinatown section of Chicago as a group that lived in a disorganized neighborhood but that had low levels of delinquency. Jonassen criticizes Shaw and McKay for not paying attention to cultural variation among the different immigrant groups that could explain different outcomes in disorganized areas, and he also maintains that their theory seems to ignore differences between blacks and whites in terms of rates of delinquency. In their rejoinder to Jonassen, Shaw and McKay reply that they did not gloss over important cultural differences between the different immigrant communities that resided in high-crime neighborhoods over time. Rather, they emphasized the fact that the rates of delinquency on an aggregate level exhibited a remarkable stability over time, regardless of what group lived in the neighborhood. Certainly, within their framework there is room for cultural variation. Second, Shaw and McKay respond that the difference in rates of delinquency between blacks and whites are the result of the fact that it is impossible to reproduce in the white communities the circumstances under which black children live.

23. Robert J. Bursik Jr., "Social Disorganization and Theories of Crime and Delinquency: Problems and Prospects," *Criminology* 26 (1988): 519–42.

24. Sampson (1999).

25. John Kasarda and Morris Janowitz, "Community Attachment in Mass Society," *American Sociological Review* 39 (1974): 328–39.

26. Janowitz (1975).

27. See Bursik and Grasmick (1993).

28. See Bursik (1999).

29. See Sampson (1999).

30. Mary Pattillo-McCoy, *Black Picket Fences: Privilege and Peril among the Black Middle Class* (Chicago: University of Chicago Press, 1999); Venkatesh (2000).

31. See also Mary Pattillo, "Sweet Mothers and Gangbangers: Managing Crime in a Middle-Class Black Neighborhood," *Social Forces* 76 (1998): 747–74

32. Sampson (1999: 13).

33. See Guterbock (1971).

34. Kefalas (2003) describes Beltway as one of the last garden spots in Chicago.

NOTES TO CHAPTER 4

1. The account of Thompson's shooting is based on the report that was published in a local newspaper on April 21, 1994 (name of newspaper not given to preserve anonymity).

2. By the mid-1990s, Chicago was reputed to have about 130 youth gangs with an estimated 36,000 members. See Carolyn R. Block et al., *Street Gangs and Crime: Patterns and Trends in Chicago* (Chicago: Illinois Criminal Justice Information Authority, 1996); Carolyn R. Block and Richard Block, "Street Gang Crime in Chicago," *Research in Brief* (Washington, DC: National Institute of Justice, 1993); Wesley G. Skogan et al., *On the Beat: Police and Community Problem Solving* (Boulder, CO: Westview, 1999). More important, Skogan and his colleagues report that the Chicagoans they surveyed in 1996 said that crime was by far the city's most important problem.

3. A number of the people that I interviewed did not grow up in the neighborhood. These residents moved to Beltway from other neighborhoods in Chicago and said that one of their reasons for moving was to get away from areas where violent street gangs operated.

4. The Chicago Alternative Policing Strategy (CAPS) started in Beltway late in 1994. The Rendell Park area was part of a larger beat that covered the adjacent neighborhood of Greendale, which is east of Beltway. The remainder of Beltway comprises one stand-alone beat area.

5. The Victory Park area, which is located about a dozen blocks to the north of Beltway, had a great deal of gang activity in the early 1990s. There were a number of blocks near the park that were notorious for being open-air drug markets and havens for prostitutes. However, a number of citizens in the Victory Park area formed an active neighborhood watch/problem-solving group and, with the assistance of the police department, have decreased the amount of gang activity in the neighborhood. At one meeting, Jane Petoski, a prominent member of the Victory Park Neighborhood Watch, joked that the residents had exported their problems to nearby neighborhoods. It is difficult to gauge the veracity of her statement. However, there was, and still is, a belief among some Beltway residents that the gang problem in the neighborhood is chiefly the result of gang-bangers from surrounding areas coming in to the neighborhood to cause trouble.

6. There is a complete discussion of the Orlando Santos case in Patrick J. Carr and Maria J. Kefalas, "Sometimes It's More Than Class and Race: The Orlando Santos Case and Place in Beltway," unpublished manuscript, Saint Joseph's University. Also see Kefalas (2003).

7. This practice was later formalized in the Court Advocacy program that is currently an integral part of the CAPS program.

8. See James S. Coleman, *Adolescent Society* (New York: Free Press, 1971). The fact that youth are left to their own devices in many ways is not an entirely new phenomenon. Coleman notes that American teens have always enjoyed a modicum of freedom. However, there is a crucial distinction between enabling young people to be independent and excluding them from public forums.

See also Pierre Dasen, "Rapid Social Change and the Turmoil of Adolescence: A Cross-Cultural Perspective," *International Journal of Group Tensions* 29(1–2) (2000): 17–49; Anne C. Peterson, "Presidential Address: Creating Adolescents: The Role of Context and Process in Developmental Trajectories," *Journal of Research on Adolescence* 3(1) (1993): 1–18; Stuart Traub and Richard A. Dodder, "Intergenerational Conflict of Values and Norms: A Theoretical Model," *Adolescence* 23 (1988): 975–89.

Traub and Dodder argue that youths and adults do not accept the same values and that, moreover, there is normative dissensus between youth and adults. Other authors, such as Dasen (2000) and Peterson (1993), have argued that adolescence is not necessarily a period of storm and stress. The so-called generation gap is in fact situationally and culturally produced. Dasen argues that problematic aspects of adolescence are linked to periods of rapid social change and acculturation.

9. See Trevor Bennett, "Factors Related to Participation in Neighbourhood Watch Schemes," *British Journal of Criminology* 29(3) (1989): 207–18; Bennett (1987); P. Cirel et al. (1977); Fred DuBow and David Emmons, "The Community Hypothesis," in *Reactions to Crime,* ed. Dan Lewis (Beverly Hills, CA: Sage, 1981), 167–81; Fred DuBow and Aaron Podolefsky, "Citizen Participation in

Community Crime Prevention," *Human Organization* 41 (1982): 307–14; Garofalo and McLeod (1989); Kevin Hourihan, "Local Community Involvement and Participation in Neighbourhood Watch: A Case Study in Cork, Ireland," *Urban Studies* 24(2) (1987): 129–36; Gary T. Marx and Dane Archer, "Community Self-Defence," *Society* 13(3) (1976): 38–43; Marx and Archer (1971); Pate, McPherson, and Silloway (1987); Dennis P. Rosenbaum, "The Theory and Research behind Neighborhood Watch: Is It a Sound Fear and Crime Reduction Strategy?" *Crime and Delinquency* 33 (1987): 103–34; Dennis P. Rosenbaum, "Community Crime Prevention: A Review and Synthesis of the Literature," *Justice Quarterly* 5(3) (1988): 323–95; Wesley G. Skogan and Michael Maxfield, *Coping with Crime* (Beverly Hills, CA: Sage, 1981); Richard Yarwood and Bill Edwards, "Voluntary Action in Rural Areas: The Case of Neighbourhood Watch," *Journal of Rural Studies* 11(4) (1995): 447–59.

For example, the finding that the neighborhood watch/patrol groups falter after an initial period of intense activity has been replicated widely throughout the literature on community crime prevention. A number of authors have noted the organizational problems that face community patrols and neighborhood watch groups, ranging from group survival to the maintenance of legitimacy (Marx and Archer 1971; Marx and Archer 1976; Hourihan 1987; Bennett 1989; Garofalo and McLeod 1989). Others have argued that community crime prevention programs have difficulty building lasting organizations because crime is not a salient issue for building membership (DuBow and Emmons 1981; DuBow and Podolefsky 1982; Rosenbaum 1988). Skogan and Maxfield (1981) indicated that quality-of-life issues, and not simply crime, are what motivate people to get involved in community organizations. Other studies on neighborhood watch groups have found that they have little effect on crime (Cirel, Evans et al. 1977; Rosenbaum, Lewis et al. 1985; Bennett 1987; Pate, McPherson et al. 1987) and only moderate effects on residents' fear of crime (Bennett 1989; Yarwood and Edwards 1995). With respect to informal social control, Rosenbaum (1987) argues that there seems to be no evidence that watch meetings cause local residents to engage in behaviors necessary for the invigoration of informal social control. DuBow and Emmons (1981) state that for social control to work, there must be agreement on values, willingness on residents' part to intervene when violations occur, and sufficient opportunities to monitor behavior. They make the point that strong community and effective informal social control are not necessarily linked, and they doubt that a community crime prevention program can alter the pattern of informal social control, a finding echoed with respect to neighborhood watch by Garofalo and McLeod (1989).

10. In the early months of 1998, a number of residents in Beltway began to work with local beat officers, and they tried to set up a neighborhood watch group. Roberto Ochoa, a six-year resident, was one of the chief organizers of the venture.

11. James Belak retired from his post of alderman to take a post as Director for Special Events. In 1996, Belak was accused of misusing funds in a ghost payroll scam. The appointment of Gaudio was an internal affair. There was no election at the time, and Gaudio then ran unopposed for the aldermanic seat in March 1995.

12. The neighborhood as a whole actually saw increased gang activity in the months following the start of the boxing program, even if there was less activity actually centered around Rendell Park.

13. See Travis Hirschi, *Causes of Delinquency* (Berkeley: University of California Press, 1969). Instead of asking why people commit crime, Hirschi begins with the question of why people conform. The central assumption of control theory is that people whose bond to society is weak or broken are more likely to engage in delinquent acts. Hirschi outlines four elements of the social bond that, when working, ensure an individual's commitment to conformity.

The first element of the bond is *attachment* of the individual to others. When attachment is strong, people stay out of trouble because they care about the wishes and expectations of others. *Commitment* is the second element of the social bond; it refers to how invested an individual is in conventional behavior. Put simply, the more a person is committed to law-abiding behavior, the less likely she is to jeopardize her standing by engaging in delinquent or criminal behavior that might incur heavy costs. *Involvement,* the third element of the bond, is the individual's level of conventional activities; the more one has to do, the less time he has available for deviant acts. The final element of the social bond, *belief,* is the extent to which a person believes in the moral validity of norms and laws.

Perhaps one of the most striking things about Hirschi's theory is that he has tested it empirically. He found that attachment, commitment, and belief are important in predicting delinquent behavior but that involvement can actually be related to delinquency.

14. Officer Otis caused quite a stir at the meeting when he informed the mostly senior crowd that the gangs were infiltrating the neighborhood and that it was impossible for people to know who was in a gang. The confusion that Otis caused was evident later at the same meeting when Arthur Straub, a BCL member, introduced an eleven-year-old Boy Scout, Tom Gillen, who was involved in a program to clean up the neighborhood. Several members of the BCL were under the mistaken impression that Gillen was a gang member, and they rebuked and reprimanded him before Straub could correct them.

15. Patrick J. Carr, *Keeping up Appearances: Informal Social Control in a White Working-Class Neighborhood in Chicago.* Ph.D. dissertation, University of Chicago, Department of Sociology, 1998.

16. For example, see the work by Doug McAdam, especially *Political Process and the Development of Black Insurgency* (Chicago: University of Chicago Press, 1982). Also pertinent is the general discussion of social movements by

Doug McAdam, John McCarthy, and Meyer Zald, "Social Movements," in *The Handbook of Sociology,* ed. Neil J. Smelser (Beverly Hills, CA: Sage, 1988), 695–737. Finally, a pertinent summary of the theory can be found in Jenkins (1983).

17. John D. McCarthy and Mark Wolfson, "Resource Mobilization by Local Social Movement Organizations: Agency, Strategy, and Organization in the Movement against Drinking and Driving," *American Sociological Review* 61 (1996): 1070–88.

18. Ibid., 1071.

19. Ibid., 1072.

20. It could be argued here that the protest and petition to have the charge upgraded in the Thompson shooting qualifies as activity for structural change, but the action was limited to one case and there was no sustained advocacy for tougher penalties.

21. Though women have increasingly taken up boxing, there were no young women in the Rendell Park program.

22. Jock Young, "The Role of the Police as Amplifiers of Deviance: Negotiators of Drug Control as Seen in Notting Hill," in *Images of Deviance,* ed. Stanley Cohen (Harmondsworth: Penguin, 1971).

23. Cohen (1980).

24. Ibid., 9.

25. Eric Goode and Nachman Ben-Yehuda, *Moral Panics: The Social Construction of Deviance* (Oxford: Basil Blackwell, 1994), 11.

26. Ibid., 31.

27. See Block et al. (1996); Block and Block (1993); Skogan et al. (1999).

28. The five gangs were the 49ers and the Yellowjackets in the Rendell Park area and the Black Knights, the Ridge Boys, and the Regal Vikings in the western part of Beltway (although the 49ers also operated west of Middle Avenue). During the course of my fieldwork, other gangs were mentioned, such as the Latin Kings and the Satan Disciples, but they do not seem to have had a strong presence in the neighborhood. The data on the gangs come from police officers, school officials, and residents including area youth.

29. For an excellent discussion of gang graffiti and the inherent meaning of tags and tagging see Susan Phillips, *Wallbangin': Graffiti and Gangs in L.A.* (Chicago: University of Chicago Press, 1999). See also Ray Hutchinson, "Blazon Nouveau: Gang Graffiti in the Barrios of Los Angeles and Chicago," in *Gangs: The Origin and Impact of Contemporary Youth Gangs in the United States,* ed. Scott Cummings and Daniel Monti (Albany: SUNY Press, 1993), 137–71.

30. Examples of this literature are Scott Decker and Barrik Van Winkle, *Life in the Gang* (Cambridge: Cambridge University Press, 1996); John Hagedorn, *People and Folks: Gangs, Crime and the Underclass in a Rustbelt City* (Chicago:

Lake View Press, 1988); Martin Sanchez Jankowski, *Islands in the Street: Gangs and American Urban Society* (Berkeley: University of California Press, 1991); Felix Padilla, *The Gang as an American Enterprise* (New Brunswick, NJ: Rutgers University Press, 1992).

31. There were Latino gang members in the Rendell Park area of Beltway, but it was a mistake to assume, as many residents did, that *all* gang members were Hispanic and originally from other neighborhoods.

NOTES TO CHAPTER 5

1. Several gang officers at the time said that the Regal Vikings had at one time been a gang on the north side of Chicago, but, according to the information they had at the time, the gang had not been active in well over a decade.

2. The two leaders, Jamie Pelzer, who was eighteen at the time of the killings, and Roger Krijt, then twenty-three, were later charged with ordering the murders.

3. Both of the metropolitan Chicago daily newspapers ran stories on the murders, which were also covered by the television news stations. The local daily and weekly papers continued to run stories for weeks after the shootings.

4. I have mentioned how Beltway residents stratify their neighborhood. Those who live in the bungalows around Hastings see themselves as better off than people who live in the World War II–era housing around Rendell Park. Census income data confirm that the difference is in fact slight; the median family income for residents in the Rendell Park area is approximately $1,000 less than that of residents around Hastings Park. However, this minimal difference on paper is reified by residents so that, in the words of Lydia Donovan, they see things in terms of Beltway A and Beltway B.

5. The information on local gangs was obtained from the local police department's gang officers, the local beat officers, and young people in the neighborhood. There are, of course, different types of gangs and, indeed, different levels of involvement. For the present purposes, all gangs referred to have at least five active members in the neighborhood who engage in illegal gang activities, such as violence or drug dealing. Gangs also have identifiable names and colors associated with them and have engaged in some form of gang tagging (the spray-painting of graffiti) in Beltway. There are two main types of tagging—general tagging, in which the tagger or graffiti artist "throws up" his specific tag or moniker, and gang tagging, in which members of a gang paint slogans to mark their territory or to communicate messages to other gang members. Typically, gang tagging has specific letters and symbols that represent the particular gang throwing up the graffiti.

6. Note that the proxy measure for graffiti is criminal damage to property,

which is an imperfect measure. Police officers estimate that about 65 percent of criminal damage to property offenses are graffiti offenses. Since late 1996, graffiti has been coded separately, but the data represented here run only through December 1995.

7. This interpretation of gangs and crime is quite common in white working- and middle-class neighborhoods. For example, see Theodore Sasson and Margaret K. Nelson, "Danger, Community and the Meaning of Crime Watch," *Journal of Contemporary Ethnography* 25(2) (1996): 171–200.

8. Graffiti are removed from public areas as a matter of course. The removal of graffiti from private residences and business requires a waiver. Many businesses sign a blanket waiver. For other businesses and for private residences, the local ward office will sometimes facilitate the signing of waivers.

9. It should be noted that this example is perhaps not typical because the graffiti had been thrown up the night before an election; perhaps part of the reason for its lightning-fast removal was that the alderman, who was up for re-election and was facing a tough fight, wanted to illustrate to people, literally, as they walked to the polls, that he could get things done quickly.

10. Community policing meetings in Beltway were among the city's worst attended. Despite advertisements in the local newspaper, on average only twelve people attended the monthly meetings. Ironically, the December 1995 beat meeting, held just days before the murders, had a record low attendance; only nine residents were present. The Neighborhood Relations Officer actually joked that there were more police officers than community residents at the meeting.

11. Kefalas (2003: 89).

12. The quotation is from Phil Jurik, "Point of No Return," *Daily Southtown,* December 24, 1995, A1.

13. Ibid.

14. The account of the memorial service is based on fieldnotes by Jennifer Pashup and Erin Augis, two colleagues from the Comparative Neighborhood Study. We are indebted to them for going out of their way to attend the service, since Maria and I were in Boston when the funerals took place.

15. Kefalas (2003: 89–90).

16. In chapter 3 I illustrated how the Barker faction used the issue of the homicides to discredit the administration at the school in the run-up to the LSC election. The more generalized desire to hold the schools accountable was not prompted by Barker's actions. Rather, it came from a pervasive sense among a number of residents that somehow the school had failed the community.

17. The original starting date for the JCPT in Beltway was August or September 1996. However, after successful lobbying by local police officers, the starting date was brought forward to March.

NOTES TO CHAPTER 6

1. The Chicago Alliance for Neighborhood Safety (CANS) was formed in 1981 to provide "training, technical assistance, research, and education to community organizations to help them create safer, friendlier neighborhoods." In its first years of existence, CANS "assisted in the organization of more than 1,500 block watches and school safety zones." CANS advocated for proactive and problem-oriented policing, and, after the introduction of the CAPS program, CANS was tapped to administer the JCPT. While the initial hope was that each of the 279 police beats in the city would receive problem-solving training, the funding for the project ran out before all of the beats could be trained.

2. See DuBow and Emmons (1981: 167–81).

For DuBow and Emmons, the basic assumptions are that:

1. Neighborhood residents can be mobilized by community organizations to participate in collective crime prevention projects.

2. Involvement creates a stronger community because people will take greater responsibility for their own protection and local problems.

3. Stronger sense of community and increased interaction imply more effective informal social control.

4. Aside from the direct effects of strong community involvement in reducing crime and fear, the rebuilding of social control can also by itself help reduce crime and fear.

3. Rosenbaum (1987). Rosenbaum states that neighborhood watch is attractive, but there are a number of questions about theoretical and empirical foundation of the approach. There have been no real tests of implant hypothesis, and there have been well-documented implementation difficulties and theory failure. For example, there is little evidence that meetings cause local residents to engage in neighborhood surveillance, interaction, and intervention, which are the behaviors necessary for invigorating informal social control. One issue that Rosenbaum raises is whether proponents should try harder in high-crime areas where getting adequate participation is more difficult or take a more skeptical view that program may be inappropriate for such neighborhoods.

4. The liquor commissioner is part of the Mayor's License Commission and Local Liquor Control Commission. The commissioner oversees the license application procedure and also hears complaints about establishments serving liquor.

5. The City of Chicago Mayor's License Commission and Local Liquor Control Commission facilitates what they call "community meetings." The commission "assists local community members and licensees to resolve these problems together by facilitating community meetings. Community meetings are prompted at the request of neighboring residents, local Alderman, or local police district commanders. At these meetings, the Commission's Director encourages the establishment's licensee, police officers from the local police district, local Alder-

man and concerned citizens to discuss and identify problems. Strategies and ideas are shared in attempt to pro-actively resolve the identified concerns. Progress is monitored by the Commission with follow-up community meetings."

The community also has the potential for input into the issuing of liquor licenses. Anyone living within a 250-foot radius of an establishment applying for a license is notified of the application and can object. The Chicago Liquor Control Commission says that between 1990 and 2002, it has denied more than 460 license requests because of opposition from the community.

6. There is an ordinance in the City of Chicago that allows voters in a precinct, which is a subdivision of a ward, to place a public question on the ballot. Whether voters want to prohibit the sale of liquor at a street address is an example of a public question.

7. Memo from Alderman Gaudio's office, August 1, 1996.

8. Beltway Night Patrol bylaws, October 1996.

9. The Graffiti Blaster program was created in 1993, and in its first five years the program cleaned graffiti at more than 300,000 sites. The Graffiti Blaster uses ordinary "baking soda sprayed under high water pressure to removed painted graffiti, a process environmentally friendly compared to sandblasting or chemical solvents." In addition, the City of Chicago provides "anti-graffiti paint free to block clubs and other community groups to cover up graffiti on wood or painted surfaces."

10. James Q. Wilson and George L. Kelling, "Broken Windows," *Atlantic Monthly* 249(3) (1982): 29–38.

11. See for example George Kelling, "Acquiring a Taste for Order: The Community and the Police," *Crime and Delinquency* 33 (1987): 90–102; Kelling and Coles (1996); Skogan (1990); Skogan and Hartnett (1997).

12. In a June 2003 conversation, Lydia Donovan said that the graffiti in Beltway are "almost nonexistent." Lydia continues to patrol each month and the group has managed to reduce the incidence of graffiti dramatically over the past eight years.

13. The first newsletter that the BNP produced stated: "Addresses should be visible on both your garage and garbage can to identify exact locations for reporting crime and emergency services. This request comes from the CPD Officers in [our local beat] and the Beltway Night Patrol. Time is critical when an emergency vehicle is responding to a call from the fire or police department." Beltway Night Patrol Newsletter, 1(1): 2.

14. See for example Trevor Bennett, *Evaluating the Neighbourhood Watch* (Aldershot, UK: Gower, 1990); Bennett (1987; 1989); Cindy Davids, "Understanding the Significance and Persistence of Neighborhood Watch in Victoria," *Law in Context* 13(1) (1995): 57–80: DuBow and Podolefsky (1982); Randolph Grinc, "Angels in Marble: Problems in Stimulating Community Involvement in Community Policing," *Crime and Delinquency* 40(3) (1994): 437–68.

Tim Hope, "Support for Neighbourhood Watch: A British Crime Survey Analysis," in *Communities and Crime Prevention,* ed. T. Hope and M. Shaw (London: H.M.S.O, 1988), 146–63; Hourihan (1987); Paul Lavrakas and Elicia J. Herz, "Citizen Participation in Neighborhood Crime Prevention," *Criminology* 20 (1982): 479–98; Marx and Archer (1971); Rosenbaum (1987; 1988); Yingyi Situ and Weizheng Liu, "Restoring the Neighborhood, Fighting against Crime: A Case Study in Guangzhou City, People's Republic Of China," *International Criminal Justice Review* 6 (1996): 89–102; Yarwood and Edwards (1995).

15. Gerald D. Suttles, *The Social Order of the Slum* (Chicago: University of Chicago Press, 1968).

16. The case study that Suttles describes concerns the proposed expansion of the University of Illinois at Chicago's campus and the failed attempts at opposing it.

17. U.S. Department of Labor, *Report on the American Workforce* (Washington, DC: Department of Labor, 1999), 41.

18. Ibid., 96.

19. Ibid., 100.

20. Lawrence E. Cohen and Marcus Felson, "Social Change and Crime Rate Trends: A Routine Activity Approach," *American Sociological Review* 44 (1979): 588–608.

21. It should be noted that during this time, an increasing number of people began to work from home or telecommute. However, the proportion was sufficiently small that it did not detract from the overall argument that more time spent working means less time available for parenting, volunteering, and informal social control.

22. Perhaps the major reason that there are more dual-earner couples in Beltway and that people are working longer hours is that, in real terms, income has declined for most Beltway residents. When we adjust median household income to 1996 dollars, we can see that median household income declined from almost $50,000 in 1970 to just over $40,000 in 1990. Put simply, Beltway residents have had to work more and for longer to maintain their income levels.

23. See Toby L. Parcel and Elizabeth G. Menaghan, *Parents' Jobs: Children's Lives* (New York: Aldine De Gruyter, 1994) for a more complete discussion of the effects that parents' jobs have on children.

24. Cohen and Felson (1979).

25. For a good discussion of these trends in juvenile crime see Phillip J. Cook and John H. Laub, "The Unprecedented Epidemic in Youth Violence," in *Youth Violence,* ed. Michael Tonry and Mark H. Moore (Chicago: University of Chicago Press, 1998), 27–64; Phillip J. Cook and John H. Laub, "After the Epidemic: Recent Trends in Youth Violence in the United States," in *Crime and Justice: A Review of Research,* ed. Michael Tonry (Chicago: University of Chicago

Press 2002), 1–37; James A. Fox, *Trends in Juvenile Violence* (Washington, DC: U.S. Department of Justice, Bureau of Justice Statistics, 1996).

26. See Block et al. (1996); Block and Block (1993); Skogan et al. (1999).

27. Skogan et al. (1999).

28. In 1996, 55.6 percent of adult women in Chicago were in the civilian labor force. See *Geographic Profile of Employment and Unemployment* (Washington, DC: Bureau of Labor Statistics 1998).

29. Cook and Laub (1998; 2002).

30. For example, a common discourse centering on Latinos in Beltway was that "they were bringing the gangs with them from the old neighborhood." This was used to explain the increase in gang activity that occurred in the neighborhood in the early 1990s. In reality, while there were some Latino gang members, the vast majority of local gang members were white.

31. The vast majority of the Latinos in Beltway are Catholic, and many take an active role in both neighborhood parishes.

32. However, a number of scholars have recently called this assumption into question. See, for example, Barbara Warner and Pamela Wilcox Rountree, "Local Social Ties in a Community and Crime Model: Questioning the Systemic Nature of Informal Social Control," *Social Problems* 44 (1997): 520–46.

33. In the extended interviews, the themes of lack of involvement in neighborhood groups and lack of parental supervision were addressed by 77 percent and 87 percent of those interviewed, respectively.

34. For example, Jeffrey D., Morenoff, Stephen W. Raudenbush, and Robert J. Sampson, "Neighborhood Inequality, Collective Efficacy and the Spatial Dynamics of Urban Violence," *Criminology* 39(3) (2001): 517–60; Robert J. Sampson, Jeffrey D. Morenoff, and Felton Earls, "Spatial Dynamics of Collective Efficacy for Children," *American Sociological Review* 64(5) (1999): 633–60; Sampson, Raudenbush, and Earls (August 15, 1997).

35. For a more detailed discussion of how different types of neighborhood engage problem solving under CAPS see Skogan et al. (1999).

36. See Hunter (1985).

37. See Putnam (1995); Frances M. Lappe and Paul DuBois, "Building Social Capital without Looking Backward," *National Civic Review* 86(2) (1997): 119–28; Pippa Norris, "Does Television Erode Social Capital? A Reply to Putnam," *Political Science and Politics* 28 (1996): 474–80.

Much of the debate focused specifically on social capital, defined by Putnam (1995: 67) as features of social organization, such as networks, norms, and social trust, that facilitate coordination and cooperation for mutual benefit. For example, Norris (1996) takes issue with Putnam's assertion that television is one of the causes of declining civic engagement and political participation. Lappe and Du Bois (1997) argue that Putnam's focus on voluntary activity alone ignores arenas of participation in the workplace and in schools and that increasingly there are many possible sources for activism.

38. Putnam (2000).

39. Ibid.

40. Of course, not every action has the result of reducing crime. It may well be important for people to feel involved, as in the Court Advocacy Program, or they may feel more secure when they paint house numbers on their garage doors. Such intangible benefits are vitally important for individual and civic well-being.

41. See Nigel Fielding, *Community Policing* (Oxford: Clarendon Press, 1995); Skogan and Hartnett (1997). The concept of community policing used here includes all policing approaches that seek to involve the citizenry in some way in the overall goal of maintaining order (see Fielding 1995 for a more thorough discussion). The variants of community policing are as plentiful as the departments that employ it, either wholly or in part, but, in general, it stands opposed to the professional model of policing. The professional model holds that police are the only people who should deal with crime and disorder. Even as concepts of community policing differ, so too does the willingness of officers to put the ideals into practice (see Skogan and Hartnett 1997).

42. Venkatesh (2000); Robert J. Sampson and Dawn Jeglum Bartusch, "Legal Cynicism and (Subcultural?) Tolerance of Deviance: The Neighborhood Context of Racial Differences," *Law and Society Review* 32(4) (1998): 777–804; Skogan and Hartnett (1997).

Skogan and Hartnett (1997) report that beat meetings were well attended in African American beats, even areas with high crime rates, but attendance in Latino beats was not as high. While Venkatesh (2000) does not talk about beat meetings or the CAPS program, it is apparent that many residents of the Robert Taylor homes wanted to have more control over the youth gangs in the area but feared for their personal safety. I suggest that the new parochialism might be especially attractive in such circumstances. However, the crucial caveat is that any stimulation of local action and any partnerships between parochial and formal control agents must be able to take account of and overcome what Sampson and Bartusch (1998) call legal cynicism on the part of many residents in disadvantaged and minority neighborhoods.

43. See Skogan et al. (1999) for a more detailed discussion of police and community problem solving in other Chicago neighborhoods.

NOTES TO CHAPTER 7

1. Tim Hope, "Community Crime Prevention," in *Building a Safer Society*, ed. Michael Tonry and David Farrington (Chicago: University of Chicago Press, 1995), 21–90.

2. David E. Duffee, Reginald Fluellen, and Thomas Roscoe, "Constituency Building and Urban Community Policing," in *Measuring What Matters: Proceedings from the Policing Research Institute Meetings,* ed. Robert H. Langworthy (Washington, DC: National Institute of Justice, 1999), 102.

3. Warren Friedman and Michael Clark, "Community Policing: What Is the Community and What Can It Do?" in Langworthy (1995: 121–31).

4. Alexander Von Hoffman, *House by House, Block by Block: The Rebirth of America's Urban Neighborhoods* (New York: Oxford University Press, 2003).

5. Recheal Stewart-Brown, "Community Mobilization: The Foundation for Community Policing," *FBI Law Enforcement Bulletin* (June 2001): 9–17.

6. Ibid., 17.

7. Mike Powers, "The Hidden Strength of Communities," *Human Ecology* 23(3) (1995): 13.

8. David H. Bayley, *Policing for the Future* (New York: Oxford University Press, 1994).

9. Duffee, Fluellen, and Roscoe (1999)

10. For instance, Mary Ann Wycoff and Wesley G. Skogan, *Community Policing in Madison: Quality from the Inside Out* (Washington, DC: National Institute of Justice, 1993). Wycoff and Skogan point out that few politicians are willing to take a long-term approach to crime, focusing instead on what quick fixes can be applied.

11. I am here referring to two distinct yet vast research projects that are ongoing in Chicago. The first is the Project on Human Development in Chicago Neighborhoods (PHDCN), which has been collecting data on a wide variety of topics since the mid-1990s. The PHDCN utilizes an accelerated longitudinal design to capture the experiences of youth at a variety of life stages, and thus far the principal investigators have conducted community surveys, individual surveys about criminal and violent behavior and exposure to violent events, and systematic social observation of public spaces. The data have formed the basis of several important articles about collective efficacy, exposure to violence, and the relationship between disorder and crime.

The second major ongoing Chicago study that I refer to comprises the various components of the evaluation of the CAPS program, which in turn has informed a number of influential publications on community policing and problem solving.

While the two studies are separate, they nevertheless inhabit the cityscape of Chicago, and I suggest that they have a great deal to say to one another.

12. See Sampson and Jeglum-Bartusch (1998).

13. Jill DuBois and Susan Hartnett, "Making the Community Side of Community Policing Work," in *Policing and Community Partnerships,* ed. Dennis J. Stevens (Upper Saddle River, NJ: Pearson, 2002), 1–16. DuBois and Hartnett outline problem solving in Chicago under the CAPS program and point to the

success that it has had in African American neighborhoods, where previously the police have not been well liked or trusted. However, two important caveats should be noted. First, the program had more success among middle-class African Americans. Second, CAPS was not as successful among Latinos, especially those for whom English is not a first language, so many Latinos were not receiving any real benefits from the program.

14. See Wilson Edward Reed, *The Politics of Community Policing: The Case of Seattle* (New York: Garland, 1999). Reed discusses how the community policing model in Seattle during the late 1980s and early 1990s was primarily designed to co-opt lower-class populations into supporting the police while at the same time addressing the serious crime problem in the city. Reed argues that internal and external political pressure shaped the peculiar form of community policing in Seattle. The end result was a compromised version of community policing.

15. For example, see William Bratton and Edward Knobler, *Turnaround: How America's Top Cop Reversed the Crime Epidemic* (New York: Random House, 1998). Bratton was the police commissioner who was responsible for many of the reforms that led to a precipitous drop in serious crime in New York. Also, Kelling and Coles (1996) report on the etiology of the New York policing strategy, how many of the strategies that Bratton had utilized when he oversaw the New York City subways were later employed by the NYPD, and how aggressive order maintenance brought down levels of not only disorder but also serious crime. There is a flip side to the New York strategy. For example, David Gonzalez (1999), a staff writer for the *New York Times,* has reported that aggressive police tactics have alienated many city residents, especially minority males who feel unfairly targeted. So, too, the cases of Amadou Diallo, who was gunned down by police in the lobby of his apartment building, and of Abner Louima, who was physically abused while in custody, illustrate that the New York approach can have deleterious effects. Aside from the more spectacular cases of egregious police wrongdoing, the New York policing approach stands in stark contrast to the programs that seek to involve citizens in crime reduction and order maintenance.

16. Mark E. Correia, "Social Capital, Collective Action and Community Policing: A Case Study in Sioux City, Iowa," in *The Move to Community Policing: Making Change Happen,* ed. Merry Morash and J. Kevin Ford (Thousand Oaks, CA: Sage, 2002), 223–40.

17. Ibid., 227. Here Correia is using Pamela Oliver's definition of collective action. See Pamela Oliver, "If You Don't Do It, Nobody Will: Active and Token Contributors to Local Collective Action," *American Sociological Review* 49 (1984): 601–10.

18. In fact, Putnam points out that in the previous year more American than ever went bowling, but fewer than ever did so in leagues.

19. Putnam (1995: 67).

20. Lappe and DuBois (1997).

21. John Wilson, "Volunteering," *Annual Review of Sociology* 26 (2000): 216.

22. Ibid., 216.

23. Ibid., 217.

24. Putnam (2000).

25. Ibid., 183.

26. The PHDCN research reported by Sampson Raudenbush and Earls (1997) finds that mutual trust and altruism among neighbors, combined with a willingness to intervene in situations where youth are misbehaving, are associated with reduced levels of neighborhood violence. Informal social control is here operationalized as a willingness to intervene, which is in turn reinforced by cohesion between neighbors. I suggest that even where the willingness to directly intervene is lacking, which seems to be the case in Beltway, there is scope for effective informal social control.

27. Robert Wuthnow, *Loose Connections: Joining Together in America's Fragmented Communities* (Cambridge, MA: Harvard University Press, 1998).

28. William Julius Wilson, *The Truly Disadvantaged: The Inner City, the Underclass and Public Policy.* (Chicago: University of Chicago Press, 1987).

29. Wuthnow (1998: 32).

30. Ibid., 37.

31. Ibid., 37.

32. Ibid., 46.

33. See Mark Granovetter, "The Strength of Weak Ties," *American Journal of Sociology* 78 (1973): 1360–80; Paul Bellair, "Social Interaction and Community Crime: Examining the Importance of Neighbor Networks," *Criminology* 35 (1997): 677–703; Barbara Warner and Pamela Wilcox Rountree, "Local Social Ties in a Community and Crime Model: Questioning the Systemic Nature of Informal Social Control," *Social Problems* 44 (1997): 520–46. The finding that loose connections of weak ties can be efficacious is not new. For example, Granovetter (1973) postulated that weak ties can be important for a range of social action, even the control of crime. So, too, the recent research by Bellair (1997) and Warner and Rountree (1997) underscores the fact that dense social ties are not necessary for crime control.

34. I am using the BNP here to refer both to the patrol and to the problem-solving group that preceded it. The acronym in this instance stands for all of the activism that residents engaged in from the inception of the problem-solving group.

35. McCarthy and Wolfson (1996).

36. Putnam (2000). For example, Putnam illustrates that women are working more because they have to and that women who are working full-time be-

cause they have to have the lowest rates of community involvement (2000: 198–200).

37. Patrick J. Carr, "The New Parochialism: The Implications of the Beltway Case for Arguments Concerning Informal Social Control," *American Journal of Sociology* 108 (6) (2003): 1249–91; Burawoy (1991); Sullivan (1998); Jaap Van Velsen, "The Extended-Case Method and Situational Analysis," in *The Craft of Social Anthropology*, ed. Alvin L. Epstein (London: Tavistock, 1967), 129–49.

For example, I have argued elsewhere (Carr 2003) that the Beltway case study forces us to reconstruct existing theory of informal social control and addresses the issue of generalization by using what Burawoy (1991: 280) calls a "genetic" explanation of particular outcomes. Burawoy argues that the extended case method, which I have employed here, can derive generalizations by reconstructing existing theory, which it does by investigating the implications of the case study for society, thereby uncovering how the microsituation is affected by wider societal processes. Crucially, the extended case method (see also Sullivan 1998; Van Velsen 1967) tests and refines theory by working "outward and upward to identify the contexts relevant to understanding that case" (Sullivan 1998: 389).

38. See Thomas M. Guterbock (1980).

39. See Kasarda and Janowitz (1974), who argue that the structure of relational networks, or the density of social ties, determines the extent to which a neighborhood can engage in self-regulation or practice informal social control.

40. See Pattillo (1998) and Pattillo-McCoy (1999), who note that the overlapping of licit and illicit networks in the African American neighborhood of Groveland can work against partnerships between residents and formal agents of control. Such a situation is certainly one that could compromise a new parochial order, and it would make for an interesting empirical test.

41. In the first half of 2002, the FBI reported a 3.6 percent increase in serious crime in suburban counties generally across the United States (Federal Bureau of Investigation 2002). This increase was addressed by the U.S. Senate Judiciary Committee on December 16, 2002. Senator Patrick Leahy (D.-Vermont) spoke about "the new trend showing an unprecedented rise in suburban crime. Nearly every type of crime is up in suburban counties, with murders rising a staggering 11.5 percent and forcible rapes up 3 percent."

42. For example, the *Frontline* documentary "The Lost Children of Rockdale County" details the troubled lives of affluent teens in the middle-class suburb of Conyers, Georgia. One of the recurring themes in the documentary is the ubiquitousness of working parents and, consequently, the lack of supervision and how this can lead to self-destructive, deviant, and, in some cases, criminal behavior.

43. See, for example, Jenny Berrien and Christopher Winship, "Lessons Learned from Boston's Police-Community Partnership," *Federal Probation* 63(2) (1999): 25–32; Anthony A. Braga, David M. Kennedy, Elin J. Waring, and Anne M. Piehl, "Problem-Oriented Policing, Deterrence and Youth Violence: An Eval-

uation of Boston's Operation Ceasefire," *Journal of Research in Crime and Delinquency* 38(3) (2001): 195–225.

44. Friedman and Clark (1995: 127–28).

45. Eric Klinenberg, "Bowling Alone, Policing Together," *Social Justice* 28(3) (2001): 75–80. Klinenberg argues that while the CAPS program may improve relations between citizens and police, among the negative outcomes of CAPS are a reduction in social programs and neglect of community support tasks.

References

Abbott, Andrew. "Of Time and Space: The Contemporary Relevance of the Chicago School." *Social Forces* 75(4) (1997): 1149–82.

Adams, Richard E., William M. Rohe, and Thomas A. Arcury. "Implementing Community-Oriented Policing: Organization Change and Street Officer Attitudes." *Crime and Delinquency* 48(3) (2002): 399–430.

Bayley, David H. *Policing for the Future.* New York: Oxford University Press, 1994.

Bellair, Paul E. "Social Interaction and Community Crime: Examining the Importance of Neighbor Networks." *Criminology* 35 (1997): 677–703.

Bennett, Susan F., and Paul J. Lavrakas. "Community-Based Crime Prevention: An Assessment of the Eisenhower Foundation's Neighborhood Program." *Crime and Delinquency* 35(3) (1989): 345–64.

Bennett, Trevor. *An Evaluation of Two Neighbourhood Watch Schemes in London.* Cambridge: Cambridge University Institute of Criminology, 1987.

———. "Factors Related to Participation in Neighbourhood Watch Schemes." *British Journal of Criminology* 29(3) (1989): 207–18.

———. *Evaluating Neighbourhood Watch.* Aldershot, UK: Gower, 1990.

Berrien, Jenny, and Christopher Winship. "Lessons Learned from Boston's Police-Community Partnership." *Federal Probation* 63(2) (1999): 25–32.

Block, Carolyn R., and Richard Block. "Street Gang Crime in Chicago." *Research in Brief.* Washington, DC: National Institute of Justice, 1993.

Block, Carolyn R., Antigone Christakos, Ayed Jacob, and Roger Pryzbylski. *Street Gangs and Crime: Patterns and Trends in Chicago.* Chicago: Illinois Criminal Justice Information Authority, 1996.

Braga, Anthony A., David M. Kennedy, Elin J. Waring, and Anne M Piehl. "Problem-Oriented Policing, Deterrence and Youth Violence: An Evaluation of Boston's Operation Ceasefire." *Journal of Research in Crime and Delinquency* 38(3) (2001): 195–225.

Bratton, William, and Edward Knobler. *Turnaround: How America's Top Cop Reversed the Crime Epidemic.* New York: Random House, 1998.

Burawoy, Michael. "The Extended Case Method." In *Ethnography Unbound: Power and Resistance in the Modern Metropolis*. Edited by Michael Burawoy. Berkeley: University of California Press, 1991.

Bursik, Robert J., Jr. "Social Disorganization and Theories of Crime and Delinquency: Problems and Prospects." *Criminology* 26 (1988): 519–22.

———. "The Informal Control of Crime through Neighborhood Networks." *Sociological Focus* 32(1) (1999): 85–97.

Bursik, Robert J., Jr., and Harold Grasmick. *Neighborhoods and Crime: The Dimensions of Effective Community Control*. New York: Lexington Books, 1993.

Carr, Patrick J. *Keeping up Appearances: Informal Social Control in a White Working-Class Neighborhood in Chicago*. Ph.D. dissertation, University of Chicago, Department of Sociology, 1998.

———. "The New Parochialism: The Implications of the Beltway Case for Arguments Concerning Informal Social Control." *American Journal of Sociology* 108(6) (2003): 1249–91.

Carr, Patrick J., and Maria J. Kefalas. "Sometimes It's More than Class and Race: The Orlando Santos Case and Place in Beltway." Unpublished manuscript, Saint Joseph's University, 2003.

Cavanaugh, Michael E. *Policing within a Professional Framework*. New York: Prentice Hall, 2003.

Chicago Fact Book Consortium. *Local Community Fact Book Chicago Metropolitan Area*. Chicago: Academy Chicago Publishers, 1995.

Cirel, P., P. Evans, D. McGillis, and D. Whitcomb. *Community Crime Prevention Program: Seattle Washington*. Washington, DC: National Institute of Justice, 1977.

Cohen, Lawrence E., and Marcus Felson. "Social Change and Crime Rate Trends: A Routine Activity Approach." *American Sociological Review* 44 (1979): 588–608.

Cohen, Stanley. *Folk Devils and Moral Panics: The Creation of the Mods and the Rockers*. Oxford: Basil Blackwell, 1980.

Coleman, James S. *Adolescent Society*. New York: Free Press, 1971.

———. "Social Capital in the Creation of Human Capital." *American Journal of Sociology* 94 (1988): S95–S120.

———. *Foundations of Social Theory*. Cambridge, MA: Harvard Belknap Press, 1990.

Cook, Phillip J., and John H. Laub. "The Unprecedented Epidemic in Youth Violence." In *Youth Violence*. Edited by Michael Tonry and Mark H. Moore. Chicago: University of Chicago Press, 1998.

———. "After the Epidemic: Recent Trends in Youth Violence in the United States." In *Crime and Justice: A Review of Research*. Edited by Michael Tonry. Chicago: University of Chicago Press, 2002.

Cooney, Mark. "The Dark Side of Community: Moralistic Homicide and Social Ties." *Sociological Focus* 35(2) (1998): 135–53.

Correia, Mark E. "Social Capital, Collective Action and Community Policing: A Case Study in Sioux City Iowa." In *The Move to Community Policing: Making Change Happen.* Edited by Merry Morash and J. Kevin Ford. Thousand Oaks, CA: Sage, 2002.

Dasen, Pierre. "Rapid Social Change and the Turmoil of Adolescence: A Cross-Cultural Perspective." *International Journal of Group Tensions* 29(1–2) (2000): 17–49.

Davids, Cindy. "Understanding the Significance and Persistence of Neighborhood Watch in Victoria," *Law in Context* 13(1) (1995): 57–80.

Decker, Scott, and Barrik Van Winkle. *Life in the Gang.* Cambridge: Cambridge University Press, 1996.

DuBois, Jill, and Susan Hartnett. "Making the Community Side of Community Policing Work." In *Policing and Community Partnerships.* Edited by Dennis J. Stevens. Upper Saddle River, NJ: Pearson, 2002.

DuBow, Fred, and David Emmons. "The Community Hypothesis." In *Reactions to Crime.* Edited by Dan Lewis. Beverly Hills, CA: Sage, 1981.

DuBow, Fred, and Aaron Podolefsky. "Citizen Participation in Community Crime Prevention." *Human Organization* 41 (1982): 307–14.

Duffee, David E., Reginald Fluellen, and Thomas Roscoe. "Constituency Building and Urban Community Policing." In *Measuring What Matters: Proceedings from the Policing Research Institute Meetings.* Edited by Robert H. Langworthy. Washington, DC: National Institute of Justice, 1999.

Emsley, Clive. *The English Police: A Political and Social History.* London: Longman, 1996.

Federal Bureau of Investigation (FBI). Uniform Crime Reports. Washington, DC, 2002.

Fielding, Nigel. *Community Policing.* Oxford: Clarendon Press, 1995.

Ford, Kevin, Daniel A. Weissbein, and Kevin E. Plamondon. "Distinguishing Organizational from Strategy Commitment: Linking Officers' Commitment to Community Policing to Job Behaviors and Satisfaction." *Justice Quarterly* 20(1) (2003): 159–85.

Fox, James A. *Trends in Juvenile Violence.* Washington, DC: U.S. Department of Justice, Bureau of Justice Statistics, 1996.

Friedman, Warren, and Michael Clark. "Community Policing: What Is the Community and What Can It Do?" In *Measuring What Matters: Proceedings from the Policing Research Institute Meetings.* Edited by Robert H. Langworthy. Washington, DC: National Institute of Justice, 1995.

Garofalo, James, and Maureen McLeod. "The Structure and Operations of Neighborhood Watch Programs in the United States." *Crime and Delinquency* 27 (1989): 326–44.

Gonzalez, David. "Where Police Are Eroding Self-Respect." *New York Times*, February 10, 1999: B1.

Goode, Eric, and Nachman Ben-Yehuda. *Moral Panics: The Social Construction of Deviance.* Oxford: Basil Blackwell, 1994.

Granovetter, Mark. "The Strength of Weak Ties." *American Journal of Sociology* 78 (1973): 1360–80.

Grinc, Randolph. "Angels in Marble: Problems in Stimulating Community Involvement in Community Policing." *Crime and Delinquency* 40(3) (1994): 437–68.

Guterbock, Thomas M. *Machine Politics in Transition.* Chicago: University of Chicago Press, 1980.

Hagedorn, John. *People and Folks: Gangs, Crime and the Underclass in a Rustbelt City.* Chicago: Lake View Press, 1988.

Hirschi, Travis. *Causes of Delinquency.* Berkeley: University of California Press, 1969.

Hope, Tim. "Support for Neighbourhood Watch: A British Crime Survey Analysis." In *Communities and Crime Prevention.* Edited by T. Hope and M. Shaw. London: H.M.S.O, 1988.

———. "Community Crime Prevention." In *Building a Safer Society.* Edited by Michael Tonry and David Farrington. Chicago: University of Chicago Press, 1995.

Hourihan, Kevin. "Local Community Involvement and Participation in Neighbourhood Watch: A Case Study in Cork, Ireland." *Urban Studies* 24(2) (1987): 129–36.

Hunter, Albert. "Private, Parochial and Public Social Orders: The Problem of Crime and Incivility in Urban Communities." In *The Challenge of Social Control.* Edited by Gerald D. Suttles and Meyer Zald. Norwood, NJ: Ablex, 1985.

Hutchinson, Ray. "Blazon Nouveau: Gang Graffiti in the Barrios of Los Angeles and Chicago." In *Gangs: The Origin and Impact of Contemporary Youth Gangs in the United States.* Edited by Scott Cummings and Daniel Monti. Albany: SUNY Press, 1993.

Jacobs, Jane. *The Death and Life of Great American Cities.* New York: Vintage, 1962.

Jankowski, Martin Sanchez. *Islands in the Street: Gangs and American Urban Society.* Berkeley: University of California Press, 1991.

Janowitz, Morris. "Sociological Theory and Social Control." *American Journal of Sociology* 81 (1975): 82–108.

Jenkins, Craig J. "Resource Mobilization Theory and the Study of Social Movements." *Annual Review of Sociology* 9 (1983): 527–53.

Jonassen, Christen. "A Re-evaluation and Critique of the Logic and Some of the

Methods of Shaw and McKay." *American Sociological Review* 14 (1949): 608–14.

Jurik, Phil. "Point of No Return." *Daily Southtown,* December 24, 1995: A1.

Kasarda, John, and Morris Janowitz. "Community Attachment in Mass Society." *American Sociological Review* 39 (1974): 328–39.

Kefalas, Maria J. *Working-Class Heroes: Protecting Home, Community and Nation in a Chicago Neighborhood.* Berkeley: University of California Press, 2003.

Kelling, George. "Acquiring a Taste for Order: The Community and the Police." *Crime and Delinquency* 33 (1987): 90–102.

Kelling, George, and Catherine Coles. *Fixing Broken Windows: Restoring Order and Reducing Crime in Our Communities.* New York: Simon and Schuster, 1996.

Klinenberg, Eric. "Bowling Alone, Policing Together." *Social Justice* 28(3) (2001): 75–80.

Kornhauser, Ruth Rosner. *Social Sources of Delinquency.* Chicago: University of Chicago Press, 1978.

Lappe, Frances M., and Paul Du Bois. "Building Social Capital without Looking Backward." *National Civic Review* 86(2) (1997): 119–28.

Lavrakas, Paul J., and Elicia J. Herz. "Citizen Participation in Neighborhood Crime Prevention." *Criminology* 20 (1982): 479–98.

Loury, Glen. "A Dynamic Theory of Racial Income Differences." In *Women, Minorities and Unemployment Discrimination.* Edited by P. A. Wallace and A. L. Mund. Lexington, MA: Lexington Books, 1977.

Lurigio, Arthur J., and Wesley G. Skogan. "Winning the Hearts and Minds of Police Officers: An Assessment of Staff Perceptions of Community Policing in Chicago." *Crime and Delinquency* 40(3) (1994): 315–30.

Marx, Gary, and Dane Archer. "Citizen Involvement in the Law Enforcement Process: The Case of Community Police Patrols." *American Behavioral Scientist* 15 (1971): 52–72.

———. "Community Self-Defence." *Society* 13(3) (1976): 38–43.

Matthews, Fred. *Quest for an American Sociology: Robert E. Park and the Chicago School.* Montreal: McGill-Queen's University Press, 1977.

McAdam, Doug. *Political Process and the Development of Black Insurgency.* Chicago: University of Chicago Press, 1982.

McAdam, Doug, John McCarthy, and Meyer Zald. "Social Movements." In *The Handbook of Sociology.* Edited by Neil J. Smelser. Beverly Hills, CA: Sage, 1988.

McCarthy, John D., and Mark Wolfson. "Resource Mobilization by Local Social Movement Organizations: Agency, Strategy, and Organization in the Movement against Drinking and Driving." *American Sociological Review* 61 (1996): 1070–88.

McCarthy, John D., and Meyer N. Zald. "Resource Mobilization and Social Movements: A Partial Theory." *American Journal of Sociology* 82(6) (1977): 1212–41.

Morenoff, Jeffrey D., and Robert J. Sampson. "Violent Crime and the Spatial Dynamics of Neighborhood Transition." *Social Forces* 76 (1997): 31–64.

Morenoff, Jeffrey D., Stephen W. Raudenbush, and Robert J. Sampson. "Neighborhood Inequality, Collective Efficacy and the Spatial Dynamics of Urban Violence." *Criminology* 39 (2001): 517–560.

Norris, Pippa. "Does Television Erode Social Capital? A Reply to Putnam." *Political Science and Politics* 28 (1996): 474–80.

Oliver, Pamela. "If You Don't Do It, Nobody Will: Active and Token Contributors to Local Collective Action." *American Sociological Review* 49 (1984): 601–10.

Padilla, Felix. *The Gang as an American Enterprise.* New Brunswick, NJ: Rutgers University Press, 1992.

Parcel, Toby L., and Elizabeth G. Menaghan. *Parents' Jobs and Children's Lives.* New York: Aldine De Gruyter, 1994.

Pate, Anthony M., Marlys McPherson, and Glenn Silloway. *The Minneapolis Community Crime Prevention Experiment.* Washington, DC: Police Foundation, 1987.

Pattillo, Mary. "Sweet Mothers and Gangbangers: Managing Crime in a Middle-Class Black Neighborhood." *Social Forces* 76 (1998): 747–74.

———. *Black Picket Fences: Privilege and Peril among the Black Middle Class.* Chicago: University of Chicago Press, 1999.

Peterson, Anne C. "Presidential Address: Creating Adolescents: The Role of Context and Process in Developmental Trajectories." *Journal of Research on Adolescence* 3(1) (1993): 1–18.

Phillips, Susan. *Wallbangin': Graffiti and Gangs in L.A.* Chicago: University of Chicago Press, 1999.

Philpott, Thomas Lee. *The Slum and the Ghetto.* New York: Oxford University Press, 1978.

Powers, Mike. "The Hidden Strength of Communities." *Human Ecology* 23(3) (1995): 13.

Putnam, Robert D. "Bowling Alone: America's Declining Social Capital." *Journal of Democracy* 6(1) (1995): 65–78.

———. *Bowling Alone: The Collapse and Revival of American Community.* New York: Simon and Schuster, 2000.

Reed, Wilson Edward. *The Politics of Community Policing: The Case of Seattle.* New York: Garland, 1999.

Reiss, Albert J. "Why Are Communities Important in Understanding Crime?" In *Communities and Crime.* Edited by Albert J. Reiss and Michael Tonry. Chicago: University of Chicago Press, 1986.

Rosenbaum, Dennis P. "The Theory and Research behind Neighborhood

Watch: Is It a Sound Fear and Crime Reduction Strategy?" *Crime and Delinquency* 33 (1987): 103–34.

———. "Community Crime Prevention: A Review and Synthesis of the Literature." *Justice Quarterly* 5(3) (1988): 323–95.

Rosenbaum, Dennis P., et al., *The Impact of Community Crime Prevention Programs in Chicago: Can Neighborhood Organizations Make a Difference?* Evanston, IL: Northwestern University Center for Urban Affairs and Policy Research, 1985.

Sampson, Robert J. "What 'Community' Supplies." In *Urban Problems and Community Development.* Edited by Ronald F. Ferguson and William T. Dickins. Washington, DC: Brookings Institution, 1999.

Sampson, Robert J., and Dawn Jeglum Bartusch. "Legal Cynicism and (Subcultural?) Tolerance of Deviance: The Neighborhood Context of Racial Differences." *Law and Society Review* 32(4) (1998): 777–804.

Sampson, Robert J., Stephen W. Raudenbush, and Felton Earls. "Neighborhoods and Violent Crime: A Multilevel Study of Collective Efficacy." *Science* 277 (August 15, 1997): 918–24.

Sampson, Robert J., and William J. Wilson. "Toward a Theory of Race, Crime and Urban Inequality." In *Crime and Inequality.* Edited by John Hagan and Ruth D. Peterson. Stanford: Stanford University Press, 1995. 37–54.

Sasson, Theodore, and Margaret K. Nelson. "Danger, Community and the Meaning of Crime Watch." *Journal of Contemporary Ethnography* 25(2) (1996): 171–200.

Shaw, Clifford R., and Henry D. McKay. *Juvenile Delinquency in Urban Areas.* Chicago: University of Chicago Press, 1942.

———. "Rejoinder." *American Sociological Review* 14 (1949): 614–17.

Simon, David, and Edward Burns. *The Corner: A Year in the Life of an Inner-City Neighborhood.* New York: Broadway Books, 1997.

Situ, Yingyi, and Weizheng Liu, "Restoring the Neighborhood, Fighting against Crime: A Case Study in Guangzhou City, People's Republic of China." *International Criminal Justice Review* 6 (1996): 89–102.

Skogan, Wesley G. *Disorder and Decline.* New York: Free Press, 1990.

Skogan, Wesley G., and Susan M. Hartnett. *Community Policing, Chicago Style.* New York: Oxford University Press, 1997.

Skogan, Wesley G., with Susan M. Hartnett, Jill DuBois, Jennifer T. Comey, Marianne Kaiser, and Justine H. Lovig. *On The Beat: Police and Community Problem Solving.* Boulder, CO: Westview, 1999.

Skogan, Wesley G., and Michael Maxfield. *Coping with Crime.* Beverly Hills, CA: Sage, 1981.

Stewart-Brown, Recheal. "Community Mobilization: The Foundation for Community Policing." *FBI Law Enforcement Bulletin* (June 2001): 9–17.

Sullivan, Mercer. *Getting Paid*: Youth Crime and Joblessness. Ithaca, NY: Cornell University Press, 1989.

———. "Integrating Qualitative and Quantitative Methods in the Study of Developmental Psychopathology in Context." *Development and Psychopathology* 10 (1998): 377–93.

Suttles, Gerald D. *The Social Order of the Slum.* Chicago: University of Chicago Press, 1968.

Traub, Stuart, and Richard A. Dodder. "Intergenerational Conflict of Values and Norms: A Theoretical Model." *Adolescence* 23 (1988): 975–89.

U.S. Department of Labor. *Report on the American Workforce.* Washington, DC: U.S. Department of Labor, 1999.

Van Velsen, Jaap. "The Extended-Case Method and Situational Analysis." In *The Craft of Social Anthropology.* Edited by Alvin L. Epstein. London: Tavistock, 1967.

Venkatesh, Sudhir A. *American Project: The Rise and Fall of a Modern Ghetto.* Cambridge, MA: Harvard University Press, 2000.

Von Hoffman, Alexander. *House by House, Block by Block: The Rebirth of America's Urban Neighborhoods.* New York: Oxford University Press, 2003.

Warner, Barbara D., and Pamela Wilcox Rountree. "Local Social Ties in a Community and Crime Model: Questioning the Systemic Nature of Informal Social Control." *Social Problems* 44 (1997): 520–46.

Williams, E. J. "Officer Attitude Surveys in Community Policing organizations: What Are They Really Telling Management?" *Policing and Society* 12(1) (2002): 37–52.

Wilson, James Q., and George L. Kelling. "Broken Windows." *Atlantic Monthly* 249(3) (1982): 29–38.

Wilson, John. "Volunteering." *Annual Review of Sociology* 26 (2000): 215–40.

Wilson, John, and Marc Musick. "Attachment to Volunteering." *Sociological Forum* 14 (1999): 243–72.

Wilson, William Julius. *The Truly Disadvantaged: The Inner City, the Underclass and Public Policy.* Chicago: University of Chicago Press, 1987.

Wuthnow, Robert. *Loose Connections: Joining Together in America's Fragmented Communities.* Cambridge, MA: Harvard University Press, 1998.

Wycoff, Mary Ann, and Wesley G. Skogan. *Community Policing in Madison: Quality from the Inside Out.* Washington, DC: National Institute of Justice, 1993.

Yarwood, Richard, and Bill Edwards. "Voluntary Action in Rural Areas: The Case of Neighbourhood Watch." *Journal of Rural Studies* 11(4) (1995): 447–59.

Young, Jock. "The Role of the Police as Amplifiers of Deviance: Negotiators of Drug Control as Seen in Notting Hill." In *Images of Deviance.* Edited by Stanley Cohen. Harmondsworth, UK: Penguin, 1971.

Index

About the Author

Patrick J. Carr is Assistant Professor of Sociology at Rutgers University.

Power and Resistance

THE COLONIAL HERITAGE
IN LATIN AMERICA

Power and Resistance

THE COLONIAL HERITAGE IN LATIN AMERICA

Sakari Sariola

CORNELL UNIVERSITY PRESS

ITHACA AND LONDON

First published 1972 by Cornell University Press.
Published in the United Kingdom by Cornell University Press Ltd.,
2-4 Brook Street, London W1Y 1AA.

International Standard Book Number 0-8014-0741-9
Library of Congress Catalog Card Number 72-4387

Printed in the United States of America by Vail-Ballou Press, Inc.

Librarians: Library of Congress cataloging information
appears on the last page of the book.

To Karin and Taina

Contents

Figures

Table

Power and Resistance

THE COLONIAL HERITAGE
IN LATIN AMERICA

Quien desea no puede,
y quien puede no desea.

I

Introduction

From the Conquest to the present, Latin American history offers a wealth of data on success and failure in large-scale planning of communities, on regulation of thought and daily activities, on attempts to induce innovation and to manipulate motivation. The student is awakened to the realization of bygone attempts at ideological guidance, induced social change, and the maintenance of stability by force. With the rise of neomilitarism, these processes are today focused with a new fervor in Latin America. The teachings of history are of increasing relevance now, at a time when Latin America is facing pressures for change and Latin Americans are searching for ideas and agreement on policy to guide their national development.

Clichés like "the teachings of history," "historical patterns," and "heritage of the past," however, are suspect. For historians who abstain from historicism, the explanation of any phenomenon will be essentially unique. Explanation involves subjectivism, inherent difficulties in its techniques, unpredictability, and other qualities that make it an art rather than a science. The historians' argument can be carried to the extreme, and sociology, for instance, may then be envisaged as even inimical to history. With its flair for synthesis and its demand for generalization, sociology is merely, as historian Allan Nevins has said, "that age-old siren, the philosophy of history." [1]

The historian in this tradition ventures no predictions, or his predictions are exercises in studied modesty. He draws a line between the dwelling in the research of the past and the finding of answers to the controversial problems of to-day's modernity; he rarely acclaims the utility of his scholar-ship beyond pointing out that planned action should be sensitive to history; and he prefers to study his subjects in boxes neatly organized to correspond to subdivisions of locality and periods of historical time.

On the other extreme, there is the social scientist. He generalizes and looks down on those who "only" describe; he is systematic in his use of the operational principle in research and in hypothesis formulation; and he is wary of the hu-manistic elasticity of the historian's method. He holds it a virtue to be parsimonious in explanation, to tell history without names and dates, to use technical language, to com-pare, to control his independent and dependent factors, to classify, to build typologies and factor clusters, and to mea-sure. He finds lack of scientific sophistication in the maxim "every historian should be his own historicist." [2] Rather than accept the position that history is a "hard" subject of con-crete consequences, or the position that history should be considered a "virulent factor in political and social conflicts and a basic substance in the structure of personalities," [3] the social scientist may shun historical exploration altogether, either because he considers history to be unamenable to controlled observation or because the past, he believes, can be adequately assessed by studying how and why individuals act *now*. The totality of past experiences of individuals and groups, in the latter view, is reflected in their recorded ac-tion at the moment it is being observed.

I contend that these disciplinary prejudices and differences of opinion result from perspectives that have now become obsolete; that the relationship between the historical approach and the social-scientific approach needs further examination; that the discrepancy believed to exist between the two approaches is particularly harmful in studies of such politically explosive entities as Latin America, where the lack of political participation among vast sectors of the people may be traced back to their having been powerfully deprived of their opportunity to engage fully and share equally in the determination, historical development, and direction of the national system; and where the oppressive effect of the Conquest warrants consideration of the area as a single dependent entity, despite the ethnic, social, and ideological idiosyncrasies relating to the debatable issue of Latin American "common destiny." I also contend that new explanatory perspectives make it possible to state the relationship between history and the social sciences in less conflictive terms than have been used up to now, and that the combining of historical description with social scientific explanation makes interdisciplinary emphasis possible in both history and the social sciences.

Much of the controversy between the historians and the social scientists focuses on the theoretical and methodological principles involved in the so-called functionalist approach that the latter are likely to use. Functionalism in the social sciences is the outlook that concentrates on the end-oriented meaningful quality of social action, seeking to find out how individuals as ultimate microsocial units of analysis act in order to obtain something of value; and on the already existing, primordial oneness or integration of the rationale that is taken for granted as underlying the sociopolitical order on every level. It attempts to explain observed action and observed events in terms of goal orientation, need satisfaction, value orientation, purpose, the individual's "definition of the situation," meaningfulness, and rationality.* The explanatory frame of reference is thus subtly teleological, it is oriented toward the future, ahistorical, agenetic, and motivational. Individuals are seen to move to action not as a result of being powerfully guided by others, not in dependence, but for the sake of promoting independently some future states that they all individually hold in esteem and that are seen to be operative in their present action; in order to participate in the operations of the societal subsystems that fulfill service functions geared to the maintenance of the total society and that safeguard its overall "system prerequisites," such as its survival and stability. Present voluntaristic action on the lower levels of the society is explained as a projection of "needed" adaptive action on the level of the societal whole, rather than as what the establishment or the polity commands, offers, promises, prohibits, or makes available. The shared meaningfulness and rationality of social change is thus emphasized, and it is seen to flow at all times from the verifiable consent of the people or from a minimum of consensus. The incompatibility and conflicts of interest of different societal subgroups are deemphasized, and so too is the role of unintended, built-in obstacles to change, including the limiting and disruptive circumstances carried over from the past. Functionalism represents an attempt to explain social change without providing understanding of the impact of public action and the latent collective counteraction that will arise in its shadow. The roles of official programming, established ideology, induced change, arbitration, administration, counseling, education, legislation, social control, censorship, and "enclosure" from

* This excludes human ecology and other branches of social science that do not use values or other subjective or motivational explanatory devices.

the polity sector are deemphasized. The existing social structure is analyzed in an atomistic fashion as it may be extracted from the values individuals profess, from the informal normative pattern and, in the extreme scientistic tradition of behaviorism, from the attitudes and platitudes that interviewees as a sample may express verbally, or from their observed action in a laboratory setting, or from simulated action.

Society, thus, does not "happen," according to the functionalist; it is created and gradually modified by "man" in abstraction, in relative societal consensus extending throughout the entire system. Latent tendencies, value disagreements, conflicts, tensions, and dysfunctional aspects of social and institutional arrangements admittedly exist; their study, in fact, is recognized as perhaps the most delicate duty of the social scientist; but these aspects are studied as consequences, concomitants, or dependent factors of existing institutional practices rather than discrete and explosive elements of historical change. The role of power and policy making as both the source and wrecker of inequality is ignored. In the functionalist view, a man is rarely studied in his dependence on another man; rather, men are studied in their mutual, equilibrated interaction. Built-in inequalities, parasitism, and exploitation do not fit the man-centered functionalist conception; the polarizing range of privileges and the eventual breakdown of the castelike pattern ensuing are equally overlooked. "In sociology so far," as Amitai Etzioni puts it, "by and large the question . . . what guides differentiation, has not been raised. The patterns of societal differentiation and its consequences are frequently studied, but not its guidance mechanism." [4]

The present book thus reflects the notion that the discussion on functionalism is not yet closed. To those who may argue that there is no built-in teleological or ahistoric bias in functionalism,* I would like to point out that functionalism itself can be explained either functionally or anti-functionally, in either a friendly or a hostile manner. Functionally, it may be explained as a meaningful, generally agreed-upon, objective, and fairly consistent endeavor to acquire knowledge about social change, whose rationale rests upon its capacity to fulfill the needs of "the society." Anti-functionally, it may be explained as an unintended outcome of research styles in natural science and of the ambition of social scientists to make their models agree with principles derived from an individualistic empiricism. The functionalists make their generalizations on social processes appear similar to the formulations developed in the natural sciences, whereas the data needed to support these generalizations are commonly taken not from history but from isolated and static settings involving experimental design, the questionnaire method, the control of factors, simulation, and mea-

* An example: Sociologists in the functionalist orientation study the issue of the American blacks in the synchronic framework of discrimination, scapegoating, and other attitudinal frames, but rarely as a historical continuity of legal slavery, plantation structure, and other agrarian structures in the South. For a similar point, see Roy Simon Bryce-Laporte, "The American Slave Plantation and Our Heritage of Communal Deprivation," *The American Behavioral Scientist*, 12 (March–April, 1969), 2ff. The black Americans, Bryce-Laporte points out, have had no efficient participation in deciding for themselves if, where, and how they wanted to settle and what would be the prevailing patterns and policies of the larger community in which they settled. Martin Luther King, Jr., writing from a Birmingham jail in 1967, made the same point when he referred to "the superficial social analyst who looks merely at effects, and does not grapple with underlying causes." Martin Luther King, Jr., "Letter from Birmingham City Jail," in *Civil Disobedience: Theory and Practice*, ed. Hugo Adam Bedau (New York, Pegasus, 1969), p. 73.

surement. When one natural-science approach, the Darwinian organic approach, proved inapplicable to human systems, it was replaced. The present approach starts analytically from the assumption of a finite set of individuals in a "group," and it is considered irrelevant whether this "group" be politically organized or not. In their affiliation to the "group" the individuals are thought to be equally capable of initiating contacts or interacting with one another. The approach exploits the free-floating mobility of individuals, the reciprocity of any interactive situation, the absence of structural bottlenecks, the unbound capacity for need fulfillment on all system levels, adjustment, and rational predictability of change in terms of "more of the same." The relative difficulty of quantifying historical data, the ease with which questionnaire data can be quantified, the short-term explanatory and predictive power of the functionalist approach in the study of relatively small and closed groups have contributed to the functionalist trend. This trend consequently now "happens" to be the main stream within the social sciences and is ritualistically perpetuated by a power-bound body of professional sociologists who do not sense the need for martyrdom that may be involved, academically, in proposing macrosociological or interdisciplinary perspectives. Within the social sciences, moreover, the departmentalization in college organization happens to correspond to the pattern of functional differentiation; thus a totalizing view is made inaccessible to the powerless students, who are kept busy in the exacting task of quantification.

The choice, in the present essay, is not between the art of the historian and the methodological formalism of the social scientist, but between the overly integrative, individualistic, and rational functionalist model of social processes and some novel, untried alternatives, less ahistorical and less insensitive to the legally and ideologically transmitted cleavages that divide the sociopolitical system in a manner that encourages the emergence of serious splits and breakaway movements.

One way to solve the dilemmas of polity versus society, government versus people, the acted-upon versus acting aspects of man, and guided "development" versus spontaneous "growth" is to regard the reactive and active modes of change as occurring, so to speak, hand in hand, or in a manner of dynamic interplay between intentional guidance from outside and spontaneous responses to it from the target. Yet, unless this approach is fully explicated, it will remain just another opaque verbalization that may prove both rhetorical and misleading. It may suggest some kind of automatic equilibrium emerging from the interplay of output (public policy) and the input (responses to policy) and thus to ignore the diversity of qualities that the interplay may assume.

By accepting the simple input-output model of political control, the possibility is left out that social change may become understandable not from popular consensus regarding the relationship between government and the people but from dependence which has become a programmed feature introduced in Latin America, for instance, by the act of conquest; and that dependence may be perpetuated, in the sociopolitical system, through the imposition of inequality-maintaining mechanisms of an ideological nature similar to those of conquest. The contrary, of course, may occur: liberation from a previous power affiliation may be obtained, or it may be attempted. If this be the case, the important issue of finding a new justification for sovereignty must be faced and solved in order to "save" the new kind of oneness attempted. The general point I wish to make here is that interaction and voluntarism alone cannot adequately account for the permanency, certainty, credibility, coerciveness, the building up of security and solidarity, and the image of legitimate oneness, which distinguish officially established sociopolitical systems of power from systems that are informal or normative. The officially established, institutional aspects of life that make up the public sector of social life are based not on mutual benefit or on immediate experiential evidence but on commitment and on publicly reinforced faith, spiritual, patriotic, political, or speculative, on a set of promises and beliefs that holds together the diverse aspects of life. Faith, just like commitment to public principles in general, entails at one time at least an integrating quality; splits on issues of ideological commitment may later introduce the disintegrating experience of a credibility gap and a difficulty in reconciling ideals with reality. Public ideologies signify a transition from the pluralistic world of basic human uniqueness toward legitimate enforcement of uniformities and shared responsibilities. Yet, confronted with the increasing degree of deviance, any ideology will eventually be made open to question, and counterideologies will challenge its earlier monopoly.

The problem of how to obtain a reconciliation of ideals and realities bears upon the further problem of legitimacy. Max Weber has persuaded many social scientists into accepting a view of society in which verifiable competence will be increasingly recognized as the basis of social order, and the emotional and traditional tenets, along with personal power, will eventually disappear. Legitimacy will then be gained gradually through purposeful and rational processes. The social scientist in the Weberian school does not consider the possibility of personal power becoming fully legitimized, too, just as ideologically mature and "competent" political philosophies may become legitimized. Yet, the social scientist sensitive to the issue of power will contend, the order-creating action of a Napoleon or a Latin American *caudillo* (strong man) may become legitimized far beyond the anachronistic and ineffectual "routinization of charisma" that Max Weber contemplated.

Further problems for the social scientist are involved here. In the Weberian view, whereas the natural sciences are concerned with identifying regularities and are consequently "nomothetic" in nature, the social sciences are concerned with explaining unique events and are consequently "idiographic." The social historian, Weber says, will deal with a multiplicity of causal circumstances, which he will find pragmatically "operative" within the actor.[5] The "rationally understandable togetherness of different events" must be laid open in the process of explanation. Weber's "understanding sociology" thus consists of the artful technique of imputing existing practices (such as capitalism and Protestantism) to "ideal types" of historical men and tracing these practices back to their affinity in the realm of ideas. Weber does *not* teach, it is true, Marxism, "turned upside down." He does not claim that Protestantism, for instance, would be the causal key to the understanding of capitalism. What he does is to impute to Protestantism and capitalism similar values and mental attitudes. The mind (or the "spirit"), with Weber, again, must be considered as essentially "free," although the subject may voluntarily associate with an authoritarian organization.[6] The individual "joins," in a voluntaristic fashion, any power system: he joins the Church as well as he will "join" the State. The misleading conclusion may then follow that the individual would become free from these allegiances in the same voluntaristic fashion. Contrary to man-centered atomistic views, if power is emphasized in explanation, the overwhelming *unfreedom* and the ties of commitment and responsibility affecting the popular sectors must be stressed, not their freedom of choice. From the creative freedom of ideology makers one should not deduce that the same freedoms would apply to the dependent civil sectors.

A new way to look at the issue of polity versus society is offered by the so-called modern systems theory, better named the gubernatorial theory of social change.[7] We shall summarize some of the propositions that in the historical context seem to follow from the gubernatorial theory.

The alleged alternative between explanations derived from sources external to the actor on the one hand and those from conscious, man-generated action on the other is wrongly phrased and must be abandoned. Goal-oriented, willful guidance and planning by the holders of power, or the ruling elite, induce action that always blends with unplanned resistance, deviance, or other kind of reactive and factious dissent. The reactive forces arising from the field, thus, are instrumental in provoking an innovative or rejuvenating kind of command-action that can no longer be explained by any set of a priori principles nor by any single set of projected end-states. There is the continuously emerging dialectical (self-critical) corrective process that explains social change. The notion of immanent evolutionary mechanisms operating in law-like fashion through universal and determinate steps or stages is as difficult to defend as the notion of totally man-made and man-controlled social change.

A distinction must be made, analytically, between the officially established and "staffed" component of the system and the unplanned, informal, spontaneous, or civil component of the system. The former may be called the polity, government, rulership, establishment, or administration. The latter includes "the people," the citizens, the subjects, or, in the Latin American colonial context, the vassals. On the national level, "State" refers to the totalizing idea-system comprising both the government and the people. A Nation-State is assumed to be vested with sovereignty in relation to other Nation-States. In fact, sovereignty may be questioned, since international relations between Nation-States may be equally power-bound. The totalizing effect of the State should be distinguished from the custodial effect of "total" systems such as slavery, the armed forces, the hospital, or the prison, and from the oppressive-expansive effect of "totalitarian" systems, such as dictatorships.

Policy making on the level of the polity has a binding quality. By this we mean that it has legitimacy for the whole system. This quality of command cannot exist unless the totalizing power system remains *one*. In this respect polity differs from all civil systems, which are merely normative and pluralistic. Arguments within the establishment must be fought out before a decision will be reached, often in secrecy, and from there on all factions of administration must abide by the new policy.

Despite the ethos of oneness, there are compounding "misguided," unanticipated and deviant impulses arising from the civil sector that will, in the long run at least, make it necessary to modify policy making. Thus, there always develop an emergent informal network and fractions of mutual interaction, expectations, norms, and standards that, although not binding, will make it increasingly difficult for the policy makers to fully explain and control a situation, and to be fully prepared for major trouble. The polity is then made to keep its "ear to the ground" in order to know what may be brewing. At times, a split may occur within the establishment between those who want "more of the same" and those who call for ideological and programmatic innovation that would regulate the "errors" introduced. Splits in the top level of the State may add to the power of certain segments. These may gain strength from a power vacuum, from socially inherited caste privileges, or from concessions by the holders of power. Counterideologies may arise as against the earlier justification of oneness.

Social change occurs through a process of collective goal-seeking, whereby the polity will establish and legitimize certain explainable and desired common objectives and the public means by which they may be obtained. The resulting gubernatorial action produces effects upon both the civil sector and the acting entity. The overall consequence is the necessity for those who make a bid for power to refute at times some of the important core items in the initial principle and, once in power, to publicly amend them. Yet, it will be necessary to create a bureaucracy, to delegate power, to exert controls, to educate, and to handle latent tensions *as if* all these measures would flow from a single unrefutable set of lasting principles. Guidance, education, and communication are instituted in order to create continuity of high-level systems despite the obvious change. The ability to maintain unity is thus the ultimate test and essence of power.

Unlike the consensus model within the functionalist school, the gubernatorial model concentrates on the notion that the diverse goal-seeking actions from the polity and, for instance, from the States within the State are essentially incongruent. The polity, when this is the case, must possess the ability to mobilize the civil sectors, to gain political commitment from them, to compete for power, even to the point of gaining overcommitment by the people. Credibility and legitimacy are obtained by the holders of power who convey to the civil sectors an image or a promise of the benefits to be derived from greater unity, and an image of the dangers involved in losing the previous unity. Lasting sociopolitical arrangements, therefore, always go beyond the immediately verifiable; they involve a transcendental element. Images of a better future, images of security, and pleas to "trust us a little longer" make a part of the ideology of power. Resistance, noncooperation, subversion, lower-level alliances and other reactive movements are dramatized, blown into major proportions, censored, and placed in sharp contrast with the ideology of conservation. The image of internal and external enemies (and their fusion) is created; threat and promise are applied simultaneously, in the manner of "stick and carrot."

Power is delegated within the politically organized system and thereby the goal-seeking action "descends" within it toward strategically important lower levels. Delegated power, as opposed to the self-assumed power of the States within the State, may be called authority. This obtains its legitimacy "from above." Authority consequently involves a degree of dependency and impersonality; it is bound to the letter of the law, so as to make authority holders on the lower levels "more papish than the Pope." Authority must be distinguished from the kind of counterpower that reactive or revolutionary groups may derive from their self-organization and from their militant quasilegitimate ideology arising on the lower levels. In normal circumstances, the "seams" caused in the sociopolitical fabric by counterpower do not open into anything beyond ideological battle. Yet, at times, countermovements may swell from the initial latency into major uprisings and revolutions.

In the gubernatorial approach we do not assume that there would be causal sequences or chains occurring in a repetitive manner, which would, for instance, make every power system ultimately dissolve. The circumstances underlying systemic unity may be bettered or worsened. Yet, there are certain systemic imperatives that must be accomplished for the unity to survive. A major difference lies herein between the functionalist view and the gubernatorial view. Whereas the functionalists focus on goal attainment, adaptation, integration, and pattern maintenance (tension management), in other words, on processes that take it for granted that the ultimate principles on which the group life is founded are sound, the gubernatorial approach involves the necessity of a critical and dialectical reexamination and sorting out of the guiding principles themselves as one more prerequisite of the system's survival. There is, then, a nonfunctionalistic kind of system imperative, which may be called the imperative of yielding. It means that the wielders of power must be prepared not only for partial failure and partial success, but also for major failure relating to some core items of the ideology, and for loss of face. Unless the holders of power are willing to yield, not to overreach, and to overcome their fear of enemy and collapse, the whole system may be confronted with resistance and tension beyond their capacity to integrate and manage.

The kind of policy making tailored to the functionalistic system imperatives (goal attainment, integration, and so forth) flows from basically experimental sources. It is, in other words, derived from an ex post facto process of verification of public action that has proved successful. In contrast, the imperative of yielding flows from an anticipation of necessary reversals. It involves foreknowledge, foresight, and historical memory, but it also includes information from the field and a view of what is going on in the outside world. Anticipation thus may lead to learning, to the capacity to combine these diverse elements in a creative, free, and unmechanistic manner. Policy making cannot be explained by means of selected sociological or social-structural variables measuring progressive trends alone. It not only follows the rationale of "more of the same" but also aims at *undoing* some of those institutions, ideological tenets, and privileges supporting lower-level power systems which may appear to be depriving the marginal sectors of the society of their equal opportunity for development and participation. In this sense, the gubernatorial view would suggest that, for the systemic oneness to last, some of the earlier items must necessarily go, and that the principle of promoting oneness may overweigh the principles of efficiency and linear advancement.

We shall now examine the processes of change in the early Latin American systems, keeping in mind the frame that we have outlined.

The salient feature of the Conquest rests on the rigidity of its rationale as it was derived from Western theories of universal harmony and of natural systems. This involved the notion that the principle of lawfulness made up one single integrated whole, although it could be approached in the seemingly diverse perspectives of eternal truth, revealed truth, the natural law, and the legislated law. The Western notion of universal harmony implied, moreover, that all mankind constitutes a single unity, irrespective of whether it has received the revelation. The New World was to become a part of Catholic Christianity; its inhabitants were to "return," gently and painlessly, to their "natural" and "original" participation in the world-wide communion of men. One of the popular early theories of the origin of the American Indians maintained in fact that these were descendants of Ham, the second oldest son of Noah. Along with the motif of conversion but, as we shall see later, in programmatic conflict with it, there were also the Aristotelian theories of natural superiority and inferiority and of natural servitude, justifying the castelike division of power in society.

As a way of sharing the responsibilities that power implies (Catholic philosophers sometimes call it the principle of subsidiarity), the Pope entrusted the colonial power center, the Court of Spain, through the so-called *patronato real*, with the protection of the Church within the boundaries of imperial Spain within the New World. Again, on a lower level of subsidiarity, the alliance of the Church and the State in the New World was defended and personified in impressive approximation to an "ideal type" by men like Hernán Cortés, the king's "advance man," who on his shield and coat of arms wore the motto: *Judicium Domini apprehendit eos, et fortitudo ejus corroboravit brachium meum* (The judgment of the Lord overtook them, and his strength supported my arms). Oneness of the sociopolitical system was sought in the underlying oneness of the spiritual world system, evidenced by the one eternal law.

The Court maintained a monopoly over the right to make expeditions to the New World and an access to revenue from these undertakings. The king and his Council of the Indies (founded in 1524) exercised a theoretically complete jurisdiction over all commercial, administrative, military, civil, juridical, and spiritual matters, and the supreme power ultimately rested in the juridical person of the king. Through the Inquisition and by other means, the colonies were isolated from the secular influences of the rest of the world. In order to keep its control over the ongoing penetration, the Crown appointed viceroys and colonial officials called *adelantados*, who acted upon authority delegated to them by the Crown but could retain the profits from their own economic enterprises. The secular branch of colonial administration, however, soon became involved in a power struggle with the ecclesiastical authorities and the ecclesiastical branch of justice. Rivalry occurred on all levels, from the offices of viceroys and archbishops to those of the local *corregidores* (minor administrators and judges) and parochial priests; it strengthened the power of the militarily efficient semifeudal landed aristocracy, whose claim to power and landownership was initially derived from their military performance during the Conquest. Furthermore, the feudal aristocracy had access to the use of Indian labor. Local communities were thus absorbed by the emergent system of politically powerful landed estates (*haciendas* or *estancias*). Whereas municipalities in Spain had wrested a degree of autonomy from the rural aristocracy by maintaining an alliance with the Crown, in the colonies such an alliance between local populace and State government did not occur. The municipality in the Colony, in fact, did not evolve at all; it represented at best the ambitions of the Spanish (and later the Creole) landowning elite. The Crown and the colonial governments were drawn into a power struggle with the States within the State —the Church, the military, and the landowning oligarchy.

The case I wish to present is that the *initial* motives and ideologies of those involved in the Conquest were derived from conflictive evidence to justify it and soon ceased to explain the processes going on in the colonial system. The overall picture is one of intrasystemic conflict and administrative overlapping, of side effects such as corruption and increasing resistance to carrying out the Court's wishes; we discover an attitude of "I obey but I do not comply" among the colonial elite and the colonial bureaucracy. Conspicuous ill effects of the colonial ideology hinged on the Indian issue; on the long aftermath of wars; on the "black legend," exploiting the cruelties of the Spaniards; on the regimentation, economic exploitation, semislavery, maltreatment, and institutionalized marginality of the Indians; on the undermining of their self-confidence and self-image; on the Indian liberation movements, aiming at a symbolic oneness of their own, and the consequent reprisals; on the peasant revolts; and on the bourgeoning problems of the *mestizaje* (the blending of the Europeans and Indians).

Marginality within a power system will receive particular attention in this book. The term refers to a state of powerlessness that affects entire sectors of a population not only because the people within these sectors feel powerless but also because they are indeed, by an a priori programmatic societal definition, considered by the established ideologies as outsiders, politically subservient, silent, unprepared, or incapable. If the marginals propose counterideologies of their own, these are promptly denounced as premature, Messianic, or subversive. The establishment will then think and plan *for* the marginals, and it will assume the patronizing and benevolent attitude of knowing all about "our" peasants, "our" poor, "our" humble classes, or "our" Indians.

A second feature of the marginals is the fact that their destinies depend on power constellations, splits, alliances, and superposed layers of power forming "above" the system level in which they immediately participate. Las Casas was the first one in colonial Latin America to point out that Indians were destitute because they were subjected to demands and exploitation by four different masters, the king, the *encomendero* (colonist entitled to Indian labor), the administrator of the latter, and the Indian cacique. The burden upon the Indians was thus multiplied, and a conflict in demand might occur.

Third, marginality breeds latent side effects such as sullen avoidance, quietism, overcommitment, ritualism, and escapism. Given a circumstance in which things are felt to change from bad to worse, the marginals will project their latent hostilities and aggressions outward. From latency, thus, there is a brief, abrupt, and unanticipated step to martyrdom, to techniques of disruption, to militancy, guerrilla action, protest, appeal, self-organization and counterideology. That is why the popular analytic devise of anomie will not be useful in explaining the plight of the Indians and the peasants in Latin America. Anomie entails inability to choose between conflictive standards in a pluralistic society. It reflects the failure of the individual to distinguish between right and wrong in a situation that is torn by normative conflicts. Anomie thus reflects a sociopolitical state in which conflicting pressures from the civil sectors pull the public policy in different directions and the individual participant has difficulties in taking sides in the ideological struggle ensuing. It represents an inner crisis confronting the system, accompanied by the debunking of some earlier principles of legitimacy and the eventual emergence of novel principles. Marginality reflects a sociopolitical state in which the efficient command is unilaterally established and the participant's dilemma consists of his choice's being limited to double standards, escape, or hostility. It reflects a sociopolitical state in which the marginal individual perceives an outside *obstacle* to his liberation. Unlike anomie, marginality implies that the individual denies the ultimate validity of the present official ideology and the present arrangements.*

* Emile Durkheim elaborated the idea of excessive regulation by an outside agent and called this state "fatalism." He applied the concept to slavery but subsequently dropped the device, as he considered it unimportant in modern society. Durkheim's bias against the element of power from above has helped to enhance the atomistic, actor-centered type of analysis that characterizes modern sociology. Karl Marx, in contrast, stressed the power-bound aspects of socio-

Sometimes laws (such as those on vagabondage) prohibit escape from marginality. Sometimes escape can be effected only by a total exodus; thus the Indians' and the peasants' escape from the rigid agrarian power structures toward the city slums in Latin America. Although rural inmigration may enhance the feeling of liberation of the marginal individuals, they must risk arriving in the city unprepared, often unsupported by their families, and must give up the several fringe benefits of the "cushioning" mechanism of the protective hacienda system. This exodus of the marginals to the cities makes up one aspect of the vicious circle of accumulating "deviance" in the city slums, as the public sector defines it, and public-policy makers will tend to treat the displaced marginals as if their presence distorted the initially well planned urban design. Public planning will proceed as if these displaced marginals could be understood within the frame of reference of their present setting. On the part of the marginals themselves, the vicious circle of displacement and unpreparedness will destroy self-confidence and induce an "underdog"mentality.

With the initial ideologies no longer serving as an infallible guide, and with the castles upset, explanatory principles

---

political change. He pointed out that some impersonal processes take hold of the system, which then becomes alienated from itself and acquires the nature of an automaton. The individual's means of life then belong to someone else, his desires are unattainable because someone else possessed the means to realize them, and everything is "something different from itself," to the point that an "inhuman power rules over everything." I consider that both Durkheim's fatalism and Marx's alienation are indispensable elements of any sociopolitical analysis and that they may be combined in the generic concept of marginality. See Emile Durkheim, *Suicide: A Study in Sociology*, transl. John A. Spaulding and George Simpson (London, Routledge & Kegan Paul, 1952), pp. 276f. *Karl Marx, Early Writings*, transl. T. B. Bottomore (London, C. A. Watts, 1963), pp. 177f.

will have to be modified, brought closer to reality, and some of the initial principles will have to be discarded. In Latin America, this has meant, for instance, the replacement of the missionary universalistic and ultramontane principles of Christianization by secular justification of the power and sovereignty of the State. In this essay, *power* is considered as a totalizing tool that the public sector applies in order to accomplish ideological revision without the loss of systemic continuity of existence as an unbroken entity.

Power enables its holders to obtain ideological transformation without inducing severe splits that would become permanent and ramify into political breakaway groups. Consequently, power aims at removing marginality within the sociopolitical system. Marginality thrives on the existence of secondary power holders on a level inferior to the one wherein the supreme power rests, and the curbing of the power of the secondary contenders is often the power purpose of the supreme ruler. Equalization is in the interest of the executive power, and power may then be used for democratic ends. This is of course the essence of the Hispanic notion of benevolent dictatorship.

Power is exercised under circumstances in which its "victims" cannot escape from responding, in a way that they can no longer totally control, to the command. It involves, initially at least, resistance and coercion, or the coercive element is disguised by the "victim's" overly willing enthusiasm, the cult of person, or the fervor of overcommitment. Since the individuals subjected to power have no effective alternative to remaining under command, their self-generated means to prediction and foreknowledge of events are limited. The targets of power will have to assume an attitude of assent, for the power holder acclaims an initiatory role that is essential to the exercise of power. The definitions of justice and injustice, means and ends, and the statements of correspondence between ideals and reality that the victims of power may formulate and verbally express no longer validly describe the social structures, or the larger context, in which they form a part. Thus, the simple model of the reciprocal patterns of expectations and mutually defined roles (about which the standard texts in sociology talk) no longer suffices to explain how a politically organized system will change.

Instead of using the familiar imagery of a continuous network of mutually defined expectations, this book associates social change with the notion of a juridical person, or a body of persons, whose willful public action will always combine and oftentimes clash, with the normative pressures and demands arising from the civil sectors. The juridicial person vested with public power assumes an arbitrating, totalizing, and sanctioning role. The initiatory command by the public sector may be tailored to an ideology of progress, expansion, or increased collective achievement. Or the official (public) ideology may reflect a desire to maintain the traditional values intact; this was the intention in colonial Latin America. Whatever the case may be, official ideologies involve propositions and prophesies about how things "ought to be," rather than statements about how things actually are. These public propositions cannot be extracted from the pluralistic pushes and pulls flowing from the civil sectors. They obtain their cognitive sharpness by creating a visionary superstructure detached from experience and removed from the limitations of time and space. Policy becomes a captive, so to speak, of abstract forces that will eventually become more and more distant from the common man and his immediate necessities.

Public ideologies are produced by relatively known and relatively few individuals, policy makers, writers, social philosophers, and members of officially appointed committees. They are mediated into policy measures by a juridical person that the respective holder of power represents. Thus the decision making underlying public policy cannot be reduced into the informal processes of choice making that go on at the level of civil sectors. As a juridical person, the public sector deals with issues of general order, issues such as legislation, administration, appointments, law enforcement, education (as distinguished from socialization), civil rights, planning, security, peace and war, foreign relations, and other issues of political responsibility. In these areas the public sector sets precedents, demands commitment, assumes the right to sanctioning, imposes taxes and arranges for public financing, and guides, irrespective of whether the particular system in which this occurs be considered totalitarian or democratic.

When the official ideology assumes an overreaching and severe nature, cleavages may occur within the public sector, and resistances from the civil sectors may seriously threaten the legitimacy of the official intentions. The justification for the politics of power may then be sought in its moderating capacity, in its capacity to carry the collectivity through a period of crisis. Imageries of collective danger may help the power holders to mobilize sentiments to guard against collapse. Utilitarian notions of common good may be replaced by defensive ones, and the alarmist cry of collective insecurity may be voiced. In all these instances, intentional policy operates as if it were analytically independent of the trends occurring in an unplanned manner within the civil sectors.

In analyzing power we attempt to explain not only what the particular sociopolitical objectives of the power holders are, how these objectives are implemented and with what success, but also what means the power holders may use in order to face a mounting crisis. We examine the ways in which the power holder may modify the directive principles in order to yield to popular resistance. Many of the circumstances and events that had an impact on public policy in colonial Latin America, such as the French Revolution, occurred outside the boundaries of the Hispanic empire. In this dimension, the public intentions of the colonial policy reflected the power holders' reactions to events that occurred elsewhere in the world. But the modifications of public intentions also reflected the power holders' sensitivity to the necessity for change at a time when the domestic situation was becoming increasingly complex, with the marginal sectors becoming more resistant and the Creoles, as a matter of principle, demanding priority in all official appointments. Thus, public intentions reflect the power holders' mastery over domestic problems and their insight into events occurring on the outside. Power therefore has both its external and its internal nexus and acquires an unbound mandate, which does not flow from any set of determined preconditions. The power principles used to shape the society not only interpret social order, they assert the responsibility that individuals and institutions have in promoting public aims.

A complete study of colonial power in Latin America would require attention to the international role of Spain and Portugal as well as to the influence of international events upon colonial policy. This has not been attempted in the present book. Our concern will be with the internal aspects of power, with ideologies and theories of power, justification of war and dominance, and with the impact these elements had upon the subjects of power. We shall also be concerned with the information feedback from the field, with the unanticipated side effects of the initial ideology, and with the ensuing error-regulating responses the information from the field evoked in those who exercised power. Moreover, we shall be concerned with noncompliance within the establishment itself, which in Latin America eventually evolved into splits and alliances among the power holders of the middle range and which the central power sought to control in a totalizing manner.

II

The Principle of Power: Oneness

Hispanic Christianity

From the early eighth century up to the time of the discovery of the New World, the Spanish people lived in diffuse coexistence with the invading, culturally mobile Moslems. Initially there was a state of profound cultural interpenetration and political accommodation during which the earlier oligarchic rule of the Visigoths was, without much resistance, replaced by a Moslem protectorate. Later, particularly from the eleventh century on, there developed a state of intermittent warfare against the invaders.

Under Moslem domination the nuclei of Spanish Christians, the so-called *mozárabes*, were able to maintain their own autonomous local institutions, their own churches and cloisters, civil authorities, judges, laws, and language.[1] On the other hand, the Spanish people derived definite benefit from association with the progressive Moors: in manufacturing and farming the Moslems were far ahead of the Spaniards; they introduced to the Spanish peninsula such innovations as irrigation, stock-raising, mining, wool and silk industries, and paper making—the last, for example, was practiced in Spain perhaps three centuries before it became known in the rest of Europe. They also introduced several new farm crops. The Moslems were dedicated to science and learning; their scholars were familiar with Greek literature, which was extensively translated into Arabic; and their learning, as well as their arts, embodied most of the elements of the classical civilizations of the Near East, India, and China. Spanish Moslem cities, notably Córdova, flourished during the ninth and tenth centuries in a manner unmatched by the medieval centers in the rest of Europe.

Under these circumstances *la Reconquista,* as the wars against the Moors were called, were only rarely based on the embittered spirit of resistance of a conquered people. Instead they reflected the increasing power of the monarchs over their rivals, the church and nobility, whose earlier dominion had been shattered by the Moorish invaders. The Spanish monarchs were able to assume during the Reconquista the feudal right to dispose of the lands taken from the Moslems and to turn this right into a political asset.

The distribution of lands following the Reconquista was carried out in a manner that emphasized not only the authority of the Crown but also, on the local level, the legalization, under royal patronage, of a new political entity—the municipality. As a matter of general rule, the occupied territories of the *tierras de fuera,* lands that belonged to the Moslems, were annexed to Christian territories by permitting colonizers to settle on them, by having them present their claims for tenure, which could be validated by local authority. In order to defend the new frontier against the Moslems, the colonizers could either seek the protection of a feudal lord (this practice led to a system of vast *latifundios,* large landholdings, common, for example, in Valencia) or could become vassals of the king. In the latter case the pioneer villages and towns created their local militia, or *caballerías.* Also, military and religious orders could gain control over the newly conquered territories. The oldest of these was the Order of Santiago, organized about 1170. Its battle cry,

Santiago y cierre España! (St. James, and close in, Spain!), was soon to represent the nationalistic and religious ethos of the Reconquista.[2]

The Reconquista helped to shape the ideal of the charismatic *hidalguía,* a way of life exulting in adventure, bravery, honor, and dedication to a noble cause. It broke down the rigidly dualistic and ethnically closed class lines of the earlier society, made freedmen of scores of former slaves, and caballeros of scores of townsmen who were wealthy enough to maintain a horse and to equip themselves for war. But it also slackened the effort to progress in nonmilitary performance. "In all feudal Europe the soldier took the first place on the scene of history," Spanish historian Claudio Sánchez-Albornoz says, "but the anguishes and the duration of the 'divine' war of the Reconquista accentuated in the Hispanic Christianity the esteem of *hombría* [manliness], audacity and warlike impetus to such a degree that the tasks which were slowly gaining in value beyond the Pyrenees—literary and scientific creation and the production of wealth—lagged far behind." [3]

Politically, the Reconquista served to reduce regionalism and to create and maintain an ambitious consciousness of Hispanic solidarity—a totalizing religio-nationalistic ethos of morals, opinion, and faith, and a demand for oneness of religious and political sovereignty. The ideal of the political unification of the Spanish people was associated throughout the Middle Ages with the ethos of a sacred obligation to surrender oneself to the authentic, divinely ordered national calling to the Hispanic people in unquestioning, unselfish, and obedient service to promote the cause of the one veritable religion. Spanish Catholic nationalism originated much earlier than either the romantic, tradition-oriented nationalism of the Germans or the secular nationalism of the British, which tended to become associated with the ideals of freedom of conscience and individual liberty. The expression, "to defend the *patria,*" for example, appears in Spanish documentary sources as early as the 1450's, nearly a century before the neologism *patrie* was introduced into French.[4]

As a patriotism infused with Catholicism, the Hispanic missionary spirit was similar to the universalism of Dante. According to Dante, God sponsors and justifies the expansion of the Christian empire on earth. In contrast were the utilitarian monarchical doctrines of Marsiglio of Padua and Machiavelli, in which religion is valued only in its instrumental use. The Spanish commitment to the religious and nationalistic cause was a total form of "vassal religiosity," which entailed an attitude of noble, unquestioning, overcommitted and passionate servitude in the ranks of Christian militants as an unalterable, diffuse "given" and an imperative of undivided faith, passion, and action. The Spanish soil was liberated from the infidels for God *and* the king, public and military functions were inseparable from one's duty as a Christian, jurisprudence was inseparable from theology, and the power of the king was coordinate with the Divine Providence. Ideally at least, personal values were totally absorbed by public demands.

To describe in the language of gubernatorial analysis the Spanish national system that emerged from the war effort results in a tonality not entirely different from what an analytically uncommitted historian might choose to employ. The initially unplanned consequences of the long war effort entailed the emergence of the national-monarchist system from localistic feudal arrangements; this occurred in an alliance between the Castilian Court and local municipalities, an alliance representing a loss of power for the nobility and clergy. As morphogenetic side effects of the new national alliance for power, such practices and organizations as land distribution and caballería were institutionalized. The ideological and public-policy changes derived from these institutions were reflected in a new emphasis on the ownership of land and on military performance; in underestimation of manual work; and in the efficiency, under the Crown's tutelage, of the externally derived local power of the municipality. The alliance between the Nation-State and the Catholic Church created the image of a "divine war" against the infidels, of a common enemy, and of Spain's glorious role of carrying it and similar wars to an inevitable victory. As a side effect, the Crown, accepting Spain's universal role in promoting Catholicism, established innovations in State administration. These included the establishment of a State treasury, the unification of monetary system, and the creation of special councils, committees, and new administrative posts. A mercantile concept of political and economic power balance developed; the goal was to establish the political and economic supremacy of the Kingdom of Castile in its rivalry with other Spanish kingdoms and with other nation-states. Under this concept, the soldiers of fortune willing to serve in the New World were given a rewarding opportunity, subject, however, to the Crown's securing a monopoly on drawing revenue from the fruits of their conquests.

Unilateral Integration: Vitoria

The medieval rationale of universal Catholic solidarity stood in contrast to the rationale of the Renaissance, with its incipient humanism, ethnic pluralism, and dogmatic schisms, and the nascent ascendancy of a number of sovereign nation-states in Europe. By 1492 Spain had advanced toward political, territorial, and spiritual unity; in the course of this year, the last of the Moorish kings of Granada surrendered to Ferdinand and Isabella, and the Jews were expelled from the Spanish peninsula. Yet, power would entail challenge. A new problem had to be faced as a consequence of the discovery of the populated and inhabitable New World, with the failure to "pacify" the Indians. The primary responsibility for solving this problem rested on the monarchy and the theologian-jurists.

One of the first comprehensive theories applicable to the pluralistic, international, post-Colombian society was offered by Fray Francisco de Vitoria (1486?–1546), *prima* professor * of theology at the University of Salamanca. Catholic kings frequently consulted Vitoria, and Emperor Charles V honored him in 1536 by attending one of his lectures.

Vitoria's philosophical starting point was the classical teleological principle derived from Aristotle and modified by Thomas Aquinas. The nature and the necessity of all things, in the classical view, are derived from the purpose for which they have been created. God is the latent, remote first cause of things, and His rule is mediated in different, essentially autonomous realms of things, through a hierarchy of laws: eternal law (*lex aeterna*), representing the sometimes incomprehensible yet never irrational Will of God which ultimately governs the whole universe; natural law (*lex naturalis*), representing the knowable and expressible aspects of eternal law deposited in man as a participating rational being; secular law (*lex positiva humana*), the application of the natural law in enacted legislation; and divine law (*lex divina positiva*), directly revealed and issued by God and elucidated in Holy Scriptures, in edicts of the Popes, and in writings of the Church Fathers.

* A rank recognizing the holder's authority as scholar. It is distinguished from *véspera* chairs. Prima lectures were delivered in the early morning, the vespera lectures in the afternoon. The student body had the right to choose the prima professor from among candidates competing for the position.

To Vitoria all reality was meaningful, pregnant with rationality and guidance whose sole origin was God. Evil was recognized to exist, but the "error" flowing from it would be ultimately governed, it was believed, by God's rule—only the Manicheans argued that evil was no part of the divine design but in every sense separate from it. It was up to man to interpret and to apply, in his particular role and capacity, the generic principles of harmony and rationality in each specific case. This required scholarly investigation of the sources of the divine law, the cultivation of reason in private and public affairs, a sense of responsibility, civic obedience and, for the holders of sovereignty, the just application of the power handed down to them by divine disposition. For Vitoria, the possibility of a contradiction between the different hierarchies of laws was either unthinkable or, if such contradiction existed superficially or by appearance, it was due to error or ignorance on the part of man and should be corrected. Law and authority rule were "necessitated" by man's inherent tendency to "err." Deviation might increase, and a crusading effort to control it might be necessary at a time of crisis.

The State, according to Vitoria, was a "perfect community" in the Aristotelian sense of being self-sufficing and complete in itself. It was not a part of another structure. In their autonomous capacity, all particular states must be considered as equal in principle—not only the more advanced European states, not only the Christian states, but also the less advanced, non-Christian states of the Indies. The Indian aborigines, Vitoria says, "have, according to their kind, the use of reason" and they "have definite marriage and magistrates, overlords, laws and workships, and a system of exchange." They have the modest but sufficient prerequisites of legitimate dominion, political and economic, over their own affairs, and they also have a kind of religion.[5]

By what right, then, did the Spaniards come into dominion of the Indians and their lands? Not because the emperor of Rome is the lord of the world, Vitoria says; nor because the Pope had proclaimed the kings of Spain sovereign over the aborigines—as he actually had done. The emperor is not the lord of the whole world, and the Pope has no authority in secular matters. Not by the right of discovery recognized by the Roman *jus gentium* (this right, under which Columbus had set forth on his first voyage, was nullified by the fact that the New World was found to be inhabited). Not even because the Indians refused to accept the faith of Christ, nor because of their alleged sins against the law of nature—cannibalism and promiscuity. And not because the aborigines had, perhaps voluntarily, transferred the dominion over their affairs and properties to the Spaniards: for a voluntary transaction of this kind to become binding, the choice could not be influenced by fear or ignorance.[6] Power must be justified, Vitoria's position implies, by means other than raw force and capacity to exploit.

The Indians, Vitoria argues, were not bound to accept Christianity as the true religion merely because it was announced to them as such "without miracle or any other proof or persuasion." They need not accept it until it was put before them "with demonstrable and reasonable arguments, and this be accompanied by an upright life . . . and this be done not once only and perfunctorily, but diligently and zealously." Now, Vitoria warns, "I hear of no miracles or signs or religious patterns of life; nay, on the other hand, I hear of many scandals and cruel crimes and acts of impiety. . . . [A]lthough many religious and other ecclesiastics seem both by their lives and example and their diligent preaching to have bestowed sufficient pains and industry in this business [of missionary work], had they not been hindered therein by others who had other matters in their charge." [7] Unless there is something worthy of belief in it, or some evidence in its favor, Christianity has no credibility for the Indians. The weight of probability should be on the side of one of the two religions, the Christian or the pagan, and by applying force the Spaniards only make the Indians feign belief, which is a sacrilege.

But, Vitoria says, the Spaniards did have the right to "natural society and fellowship" with the Indians. This entailed the right to travel in the lands of the Indians and to sojourn there, he continues, "provided they do no harm to the natives, and the natives may not prevent them." They could lawfully carry on trade with the Indians, as long as the terms of trade were just, "by importing thither wares which the natives lack and by exporting thence either gold or silver or other wares of which the natives have abundance." If there were among the Indians any things which "are treated as common both to citizens and to strangers, the Indians may not prevent the Spaniards from a communication and participation in them. . . . If children of any Spaniard be born there and they wish to acquire citizenship, it seems they can not be barred either from citizenship or from the advantages enjoyed by other citizens." [8] In these clauses Vitoria justifies in fact the legitimacy of certain tendencies naturally growing from the civil sectors.

Were the Indians to prevent the Spaniards from enjoying any of these natural rights—all of which Vitoria deduced from the Roman *jus gentium*—Spaniards ought in the first place to use reason and persuasion in order to peacefully perform their duty as ambassadors of Christian peoples. If, after this recourse to reason, the barbarians declined to agree and proposed to use force, the Spaniards could defend themselves and do all that was consistent with their own safety, it being lawful to repel force by force. The "naturalness" of the Spaniards' demands would justify in full the pursuit of their power purpose against militant resistance. By the law of nations, ambassadors enjoy an inviolable status, and the native Indians were bound to give them at least a friendly hearing. But if the Indians prevented the Spaniards from communicating with them, and if they threatened the Spaniards' security, these could open a war for their own protection. If the circumstances pressed the Spaniards further, they could carry the war to the extreme of "seizing [the Indians'] cities and reducing them to subjection," "despoiling them [the Indians] of their goods, reducing them to captivity, deposing their former lords and setting up new ones," and "seizing the provinces and sovereignty of the natives." Moderation and humane understanding, however, were essential: driven by fear, the Indians, at the sight of men strange in garb and armed and much more powerful than themselves, might resort to war and unite their efforts to drive out the Spaniards or even to slay them. "There is no inconsistency, indeed," Vitoria points out, "in holding the war to be a just war on both sides, seeing that on one side there is right and on the other side there is invincible ignorance." [9]

This point deserves amplification. Since God was the sole origin of rationality and justice, all nations—whether or not they possessed the divine law—must be recognized as participating, theoretically at least, in the same source of self-governing sufficiency, that is, the natural law. To non-Christian nations consequently must be extended, as far as their international status is concerned, full juridical rights. On the other hand, it was inconceivable to Vitoria to consider wars inherently and equally "just" from the point of view of both contending nations. "Apart from ignorance the case clearly cannot occur," he declares, "for if the right and justice of each side be certain, it is unlawful to fight against it, either in offense or in defense." And again: "Assuming a demonstrable ignorance either of fact or of law, it may be that on the side where true justice is the war is just of itself while on the other side the war is just in the sense of being excused from sin by reason of good faith, because invincible ignorance is a complete excuse." In other words, war evidenced either willful, wicked departure from the unitary standards of justice or ignorance, on the side of a least one of the parties concerned.

In addition to their right to trade and communicate with the Indians, Vitoria believed, the Spaniards had the right freely and without hindrance to preach the Gospel. If the Indians prevented this, or if they hindered conversion "either by killing or otherwise punishing those who have been converted to Christ or by deterring others by threats and fears," a war would be justified.

Vitoria's reasoning is particularly intriguing here: by preventing Christianization, "an obstacle would be put in the way of the Indians themselves such as their princes have no right to put there." Therefore, the Spaniards can make war, especially "as such vitally important issues are at stake," and especially if "any of the native converts to Christianity be subjected to force or fear by their princes in order to make them return to idolatry." [10] Further, if a large part of the Indians were converted to Christianity, could not the Pope give them a Christian sovereign and depose their unbelieving rulers? Vitoria's answer is in the affirmative.

Vitoria's missionary clause has a political corollary: "Another possible title," he claims, "is founded either on the tyranny of those who bear rule among the aborigines of America or on the tyrannical laws which work wrong to innocent folk there." It was also possible that the Indians, "aware alike of the prudent administration and the humanity of the Spaniards," would accept the king of Spain as their sovereign and that among the Indians waging lawful wars with one another the side which has suffered a wrong might summon the Spaniards "to help and share the rewards of victory with them." In all these cases, Vitoria argued, a war against the Indian communities would possibly be justified.

One further possible legal cause of intervention in the Indians' affairs preoccupied Vitoria: the case for beneficial liberation of the Indians, not from political tyranny, but from their own backwardness. "Although the aborigines in question are . . . not wholly unintelligent, yet they are little short of that condition and so are unfit to found or administer a lawful State up to the standard required by human and civil claims. . . . They have no proper laws or magistrates, and are not even capable of controlling their family affairs; they are without any literature or arts, not only the liberal arts, but the mechanical arts also; they have no careful agriculture and no artisans; and they lack many other conveniences, yea, necessaries of human live." [11]

Should not the sovereign of Spain, in the interest of the Indians themselves, undertake the administration of the primitive native communities?

This point Vitoria left unsettled. If the Indians were wanting in intelligence, intervention would be not only permissible but also highly proper; indeed the Spanish sovereigns would be bound to intervene. This argument, we note in passing, is similar to the one that John Stuart Mill (1806–1873) much later made in favor of intervention in the affairs of the less developed people.* The fact that the barbarians

* "Despotism is a legitimate mode of government in dealing with barbarians, provided the end be their improvement, and the means justified by actually effecting that end. . . . I regard utility as the

appeared to be "slaves by nature" would similarly have favored a possible "charitable" intervention. It seemed to follow from all this discussion, Vitoria pointed out, that the Spaniards were not obliged by any legal principle to discontinue either trade with the Indians or the expropriation of commodities (pearls and precious metals) which the natives treated as ownerless or common. Also it was evident, Vitoria concluded, "now that there are already so many native converts, that it would be neither expedient nor lawful for our sovereign to wash his hands entirely of the administration of the lands in question." [12]

There could be no doubt, in Vitoria's view, concerning the ultimate outcome of the universal strife between the righteous forces representing ignorance and alienation from the Will of God. He shared, without reserve, Thomas Aquinas' conviction that in this God-created world "good is the end of each thing" and the processes of change, within any order of things, are equivalent to the gradual, inevitable progress towards perfection. The rationale of spiritual conquest was still there. Vitoria believed in progress, and by this he meant

---

ultimate appeal on all ethical questions; but it must be utility in the largest sense, grounded on the permanent interests of man as a progressive being." Mill held that liberty "has no application to any state of things anterior to the time when mankind have become capable of being improved by free and equal discussion." John Stuart Mill, *On Liberty* (London, Watts & Co., 1938), pp. 12f. An interesting contrast is offered by the Chilean liberalist José Victorino Lastarría (1817–1888), who held that liberty is "nothing but the right of anyone . . . to develop in all his physical, moral and intellectual faculties." Lastarría condemned Mill's position for justifying equally well despotism and liberty; for being vague, leaving such words as "utility," "permanent interests" and "general good" undefined; and for Mill having unknowingly accepted a Latin aberration—the tendency to identify order with progress. J. V. Lastarría, *La América,* 1 (Madrid, Editorial-América, n.d.), pp. 56ff.

the triumph of Christianity, the abolition of wicked tyranny, the victory of humanitarianism and justice over wrong-doing, and an advance in the general welfare, spiritual and material. As actively and consciously participating social agents, men naturally drift and work toward a fuller realization of these supreme goals. Every man in his particular position has to be alerted against obstacles and conspiracies undermining the universal progress. It did not occur to Vitoria to anticipate, for example, the Indianization of the Spaniards interacting with the aborigines—an inverted process of cultural diffusion which actually has occurred in Mexico and in other Latin American countries where there are large Indian and mestizo populations—nor was he concerned with prescribing safeguards to secure the unhindered diffusion of indigenous cultural or religious elements among the Christians. Moreover, Vitoria was not concerned with the prospect that the "natural" right of the Spaniards to trade with the Indians would result in an imbalance in the terms of trade and benefit the Europeans' mercantile cause.

Vitoria's views on the justification of benevolent wars of liberation and other forms of benevolent intervention were expressed with studied moderation. He consistently speaks of "possible" rights of this kind. But the underlying possibility of warlike one-sided expansion—or escalation—of the "just" European cause and of the divinely ordered, "universal," and "progressive" rationale of the European culture is distinctly there. His is basically a unilateral power model for social processes and social change. It emphasizes the perfective oneness of goals and rationale which exists, and "ought" to exist, among the individuals and groups who make up the single total process of history, yet with the Europeans as its spearhead. Progress is made by converting and convincing, by increasing consensus, by reducing the areas of ignorance and by winning the alienated to the cause of good. An unrestrained, balanced, give-and-take relationship between the enlightened "just" and the "invincibly ignorant" is conceivable in the area of trade relations only; and the possibility of cultural feedback, resulting in fusion, or contamination, of ideological elements—such as might result from the system considered as given to ignorance cannot be thought of as beneficial to the unyielding enlightened system, and there is no need to study it closely; the outgoing traffic of elements from the powerful system is expected to ultimately result in the total conversion of the powerless from paganism to Christianity and to the European ways of life.

If there is no semantic confusion, ignorance, or ill will, according to this point of view there can be no disagreement about what the ultimate goals and values are; and in the long run there can be no incorrigible conflicts over imperialistic goals, for Christianization is assumed to be ultimately beneficial to the Indians, irrespective of whether they could value the divine gift when it is bestowed on them. Although the universal divine disposition might be dimly comprehended and poorly realized for a time, enlightened observation bears witness to its existence and its penetration, throughout history, into the human society, as aided by individual voluntarism. This is a belief in the absolute power of Christianity. It implies little concern with feedback information on errors and deviance produced by Christianization, little preparedness to yield.

Yet Vitoria and the monarch did have "news" from the New World, and Vitoria had reacted to it and learned from it at the same time he wrote his comments. Vitoria had learned that the Indians might have accepted Christianity out of fear of the Spaniards, or disloyalty to their own leaders, or for reasons of opportunistic overcommitment. He knew that the Spaniards were perhaps driven by lust for gold more than by Christian soldiership. He had learned that no miracles had occurred in the New World, that crimes had been committed by the Christians, and that the crusade had frozen into a state full of latent tensions and into a warlike confrontation between the Indians and the Europeans. The validity of at least some of the core items in Christian orthodoxy became questionable as far as the programming of the Conquest was concerned.

Incongruity was thus produced, in Vitoria's mind, between a priori theories and actual facts. This incongruity Vitoria proceeded to reduce by eliminating, one by one, the invalid or unjust tenets of the originally monolithic official ethos of the Conquest, and by specifying, in an articulate manner, the remaining valid tenets: the right to self-defense and the right to preach the gospel. The Spanish jurist was laboring to produce what the modern philosopher of science Karl Popper in the general context of logic has called a new "criterion of demarcation" [13] between what is valid and invalid, just and unjust in terms of the theory of legitimacy, by a refutation of those tenets which no longer validly explained or rightfully justified the ideology of the ongoing Conquest. The point to make here is that the logic of power, in its yielding function, seeks to establish a level of consistency in enforcing a sanctioning system which would be removed from the consideration of whatever is particular, and general enough to serve as the standard of right and wrong, in the name of whatever, or for the sake of whatever, coercion may be legally applied. The natural communion of men that Catholicism represents served for Vitoria as the system level from which the highest principles of the official ideology should be deduced.

The issue is important because of the many different

meanings attached to the evasive term "ideology." Western thought inherited from the Greeks the view that the ideal reality was outside of the empirical world and transcendent to it, and that the empirically operating social order was a function of the ideas or the divinity descending upon it, as mediated through visions by philosopher-kings or spiritual authorities.[14] In modern writing ideology is often seen in the contrary sense as determined by empirical reality, extracted objectively from it in the manner of a summary; or as a common-to-all synthesis, cognitively organizing the agreed-upon world postulates; or, in the Marxian sense, as justifying, deceptively, the existing social order.

Karl Mannheim, in turn, correctly emphasized the *intentional* aspect of ideology (in a partial sense, as he considers it here): "Ideologies are the situationally transcendent ideas which never succeed *de facto* in the realization of their projected contents. Though they often become the good-intentioned motives for the subjective conduct of the individual, when they are actually embodied in practice their meanings are most frequently distorted." [15] Mannheim goes on to explain how the ideological mind, confronted by the discrepancy between ideals and the powerful operating social order, proceeds in different forms. One way of reconciling ideology with reality consists of the politicized subject's being "prevented" by the whole body of axioms present in his thought from becoming aware of the incongruence of his ideals with reality. Another way is the overly committed "cant mentality," the tendency to sacrifice one's awareness of the incongruity to some vital emotional interest. A third way is that of conscious deception; this means the reactive tendency to interpret ideology as a purposeful lie.[16]

In the theory of power elaborated in the present essay, ideology and the production of innovative ideas are viewed, in a manner similar to Mannheim's, as something removed from reality, and in relation to the source of power. Theodor Geiger has suggested four basic types of this relation and consequently four types of relationship between the holders of power and the intelligentsia.[17] First, ideals may be proclaimed to have primacy over power. This is the case of classical idealism in the history of philosophy. Power, in this view, has the function of translating ideal into reality. Second, intelligence may pay respect to power; ideology in this case is the apotheosis of the existing power constellations. Third, intelligence, particularly scientific intelligence, may be in the service of power without risking its claim to objectivity and without sharing responsibility for the political aims of the power holders. Fourth, intelligence may maintain a critical relationship to the power holders. This, Geiger holds, is its most important social function.

The intelligentsia, Geiger points out further, form no social class; they "belong" to all classes and none; they are "socially free-floating" and distant from economic life. As Franz Adler puts it, in this view the intelligentsia have a social mandate. "They are expected to create new cultural values, just as entrepreneurs are expected to create new economic values." [18] They no longer only synthesize; laboring in a "free," unmechanistic fashion, they follow neither inductive nor deductive logic.

This is in essence the nature of a creative sustaining public ideology within a purposive power system. It neither synthesizes nor proceeds rigidly from a priori postulates; in other words, it is neither completely fact oriented nor completely theory oriented. It is derived from neither empirical generalizations nor universally valid lawlike rules. The emergence of principles that obtain the status of official ideologies thus tends to defy scientific prediction. These principles emerge from the decision-making process of a power holder or a body of important insiders, and they obtain legitimacy from declarative statements ex cathedra on crucial matters concerning the course of action to which the public sector will commit itself in matters of general interest. They often involve the official replacing of the old ends-means scheme by new criteria of priority. The recognition of modifications of the ends-means scheme must arise from an act that is duly processed and publicized; otherwise an innovative ideology does not assume a sociopolitical function as a public act of yielding. When the power holders have made public their decisions on matters of ideological modification, they can no longer be in error, in terms of legitimacy, unless by "being in error" we mean the act of publicly revoking some principles held legitimate in the past. It is misleading, therefore, to hold that only the Pope, among the wielders of power, has some sort of unique prerogative to infallibility. No matter how the chief executive's position be filled, his statements on policy, if they are publicly made, are unalterable by definition. They are not immediately responsive to cravings from civil sectors in a one-to-one correspondence between stimulation and response, or passive political reconnaissance, but they flow from an anticipatory totalizing and mobilizing aim which embraces values beyond those expressed in public opinion. At any moment, power speaks in declarative sentences, whereas the ideology makers and "the people" may use the conjectural, wishful, and uncertain mood of the subjunctive. The doctrine of the infallibility of the supreme holder of power, within his jurisdiction, should be no more shocking to the modern man than the imperative that the ruling of a lower court will be binding until an appeal, made to a higher court and approved, reverses the earlier verdict.

Changes in the legitimate ideology thus reflect not only

the "needs" of the society in abstraction but also the need of the power holders to implement a creative response, independent from consensus, to meet the pressures appearing in the field, which otherwise might endanger the continuity and the oneness of the power system. Ideology does not reflect the immediate synchronic pressures from the field. It is in the first place concerned with the relevance these pressures may have on the totalizing effort with which the gubernatorial action is concerned. The intentional nature of an ideology, therefore, should be examined in two different dimensions. In the perspective of the power holders, it appears in its planned capacity to "save" the system as one and to "make it work." In the perspective of the "victims" of power, it appears as the rationale of legitimacy and oneness as this is induced from above through channels of authority. As such, it may be accepted or opposed, hailed or feared, in a feedback response reflecting the counterideologies and fractions it evokes. Most likely, the civil sectors will be split, with some sectors accepting and others opposing the official command, thus creating a polarized response pattern.

Militant Christian Colonialism: Sepúlveda

In the long standing public controversy revolving about the justification of the Conquest, Juan Ginés Sepúlveda (1490?–1573)—historian, hellenist, protégé and official translator (from Greek) of the Pope, and chronicler of the Court of Spain—carried most authority among the "hawks" in favor of warlike action against the Indians.

For Sepúlveda, a just war was nothing but the limiting case in an effort to achieve lasting peace. The law of nature permits anyone to repel force by force, within the limits of just self-defense. On the level of State affairs, the decision to repel injury by war belongs to the monarch, who should use military force in moderation and with good intentions, and only after all other means to achieve justice have been exhausted. The goal of a just war is the same as the goal of all legislation: to enable people to live in enduring, enforced tranquillity.[19]

A war is just when it aims at self-defense, and also when it is undertaken in order to recover property illegally taken or to impose punishment on the party who has committed an offensive act. Still, the war against the Indians is justified on particularistic grounds: the natural state of the Indians is such that they have to obey others and consequently they have to be dominated by force.

Sepúlveda's doctrine of natural superiority and inferiority was derived from Aristotle. Perfection always has dominion over imperfection, strength has dominion over weakness, and virtue has dominion over vice, just as "form" has dominion over matter and soul has dominion over body. It is natural, therefore, for honest men to have dominion over the vicious and depraved, and men of reason over men of appetite.

The weaker party benefits from protection. Although domesticated animals, for example, are superior to wild animals, it is beneficial for them to submit themselves to the imperium of man; similarly, it is beneficial for the weaker, inferior, or less perfect among men to submit themselves to the imperium of the strong, superior, and perfect. Those who are slow in understanding, no matter how strong physically, are better off as servants to their natural masters, for in this position they are exposed to the virtuous, civilizing example and to the discipline of their superiors. According to Sepúlveda, "correcting a son, even though with severity, does not lessen paternal love. Work on him, even against his will and despite suffering, because, even though he does not want it, pain seems to be necessary for his salvation."[20]

In Sepúlveda's best possible State, sovereignty "naturally" belonged to the most prudent and best elements. Deviations from the natural may occur, a bad prince may come to power, just as bad and corrupt humors may gain dominion over the human body. An attempt to brusquely exterminate the bad humors easily leads to the total destruction of health, and it often is advisable to abstain from risky cures. By analogy, bad princes therefore should be tolerated, not because their judgment is natural and just, but in order to avoid rebellions and civil wars. A civil war is worse than an external war, not only because it is not founded on the authority of the prince, but also because it disregards the laws and customs of the past that adhere to the principle of succession of reign within the same family. Whereas civil war runs counter to the laws and institutions of the past generations, resulting in fatal perturbations of the republic, external war involving a Christian state is instead based on the law of nature and is expected to offer to the conquered infidels a good opportunity to learn from Christians the value of human dignity, a chance to practice virtue, and a chance for advice that will eventually lead to their conversion.

But was it not true that the Spaniards were fighting the war against the Indians simply to plunder for loot? Still, whoever accepts the dominion of a prince over his subjects, Sepúlveda answered, does not by necessity approve of the sins possibly committed by his ministers. If certain evil and unjust men have committed crimes against the barbarians, as news from the New World put it, the value of the inherently good cause of the monarch and his honest subjects is not thereby cast into doubt. "We are not now discussing the moderation or cruelty of the soldiers and captains," Sepúlveda said, "but the nature of this war and its relationship with the just King of Spain and his just ministers." [21]

The "logical process" of the war, according to Sepúlveda, is this: first, the war has to be declared and the barbarians admonished to accept peacefully the important benefits proceeding from submission to the Spaniards; and, if they do so, they next have to be instructed in the superior laws and customs of the Spaniards, taught to embrace the veritable religion and to assume citizenship in the Spanish empire. If the natives were to ask for time to deliberate, this should be ceded to them, provided the time granted would not be unreasonably long. In Sepúlveda's intricate reasoning, to explain to them all the fine points of Christianity and civilized life would take an infinitely long time: the advantages and virtues of the Christian life, in fact, could be learned only through experience, by a functioning member of the European community.

The most damning proof of the Indians' natural wickedness and degradation, for Sepúlveda, was their adherence to idolatry and human sacrifice. Their deviations, in this respect, from the law of nature cannot be reduced to mere individual shortcomings. Their deviations are institutionalized, public malpractices by which their society victimizes its virtuous members and are consequently sins not only against man but also against God. This is why the war against the Indians has its sacred quality: to the innocent victim of a misguided society the conqueror appears a good Samaritan. In New Spain (Mexico) alone, Sepúlveda calculated, before the Conquest over 20,000 individuals were sacrificed every year —more than the number of Indians killed in Cortés' war of conquest. The law of virtue consists, Sepúlveda held, not of bearing injustice but repelling it. The right to vengeance, insofar as the crimes committed by societies are concerned, belongs to the "judges of the world," the chiefs of temporal states and bishops.

Did this doctrine, after all, lead to the conclusion that pagans could or should be forced to accept the faith? Sepúlveda did not believe so. Faith calls for free will. Instruction must precede baptism. Although the pagans could be moved by force to live in communities under Spanish rule, they could not be forced to accept baptism. It was a question of limiting the use of force, and to apply it only in order to create circumstances where proselytizing is possible. To proselytize appears to be subsequent to the pacification and coercive legal subjection of the pagans. This also is the safest and, consequently, the most rational way: word has come from the New World about priests being killed by the Indians as soon as the Spanish troops are withdrawn. Those who (like Las Casas) undertake proselytizing missions unarmed are not only foolhardy; they jeopardize the sober, organized Christianizing effort of others. Rigorous laws and their unswerving application are necessary in any society to restrain evil men and to inculcate virtue.

After all, Sepúlveda asked, what do the Indians have to lose in the war against them? Their total loss amounts to the obligation, when necessary, to accept a Christian prince to replace a pagan one and to give up a part of their property—their gold and silver, metals of little value for the Indians. In return they receive from the Spaniards metals of immensely more practical utility, iron and bronze. How much more is it to the benefit of the Indians if we add the wheat, barley, cereals, scores of different vegetables, horses, mules, asses, oxen, sheep, goats, pigs, grapevines and countless numbers of trees, all introduced to them by the Spaniards? Who can assess the value of literacy, of civilization, of excellent laws and institutions, and of the most precious thing of all—the knowledge of God and Christian religion? Those who oppose the war against the Indians do not act in the best interest of the barbarians; they help to deprive them of inestimable advantages.[22]

Why should the task of subjugating the Indians belong to the Spaniards? Why not the French, or the Italians, or any other Christian nation? The Pope had chosen the Spaniards for this task in 1493, Sepúlveda reiterated. Besides, although this matter is somewhat open to debate, very few nations compare with Spain in prudence, justice, and religiosity. *Jus gentium* finally suggests that lands like those in the New World belong to the discoverer, not because they did not already have owners but because those owners did not belong to any Christian nation.

The expropriation of the Indians' lands and the subjection of the Indians, if it was to be legal and just, should be carried out by the State, in an institutional and lawful fashion, according to Sepúlveda. Except for those guilty of atrocious crimes in warfare, perfidy, cruelty, and obstinacy, the Indians should not be reduced to slavery. Their new status should combine the rights and duties of a trusted, tribute-paying, and perhaps wage-earning servant under seignorial rule and those of a minor, subject to paternalistic rule. Their status should be flexible enough to enable them to earn new degrees of liberty in accordance with their attested achievement in civilization and Christianity. Nor should the Indians be pampered with liberties above their "nature and condition," for this might make them want to win back their former primitive status. Nor should they be oppressed with undue hardship to the extent of inciting them to rebellion against the Spaniards. In due time, Sepúlveda ventures, the Indians might gain in maturity and prudence enough to assume minor responsibilities: "It is beneficial to trust the plebeians with posts of minor importance and with offices simultaneously performed by many. For were this not done, the state of the Republic would be disturbed and even its political stability destroyed, a large majority being estranged into opposition."

Of particular interest is Sepúlveda's effort to work out an argument in favor of the forced inclusion of the Indians in the early colonial institution of *encomienda.* This controversial institution emerged during the first years of the Conquest in the Caribbean and in New Spain under Cortés with the hesitant approval of the Crown.* It involved the allocation of pacified Indians (by villages or by specific numbers) among deserving conquistadores who would assign them for work in domestic service, in farm labor, in the building of urban residences, in search for gold or pearls, or in mines. In exchange for the menial labor and services received, the encomendero (the grantee of encomienda) was expected to instruct the Indians in the preliminaries of Christianity.

High-ranking Spaniards with the right to encomienda and with their land grants would, however, rarely take residence on their haciendas in the provinces. It became customary for them to entrust the administration of the Indian affairs to a class of overseers, called *calpixque* by the Indians in New Spain.† These were lower-class Spaniards or Negroes

* Cortés assigned encomiendas to deserving *conquistadores* as soon as they were released from war. A royal order prohibited encomiendas in 1523, but Cortés refused to obey it. He coveted the capital city and the surrounding provinces in the Valley of Mexico, which he apparently wanted to maintain as his private holding. The Crown responded to Cortés' demands by granting him in 1529 the title of *marqués* and the civil and ecclesiastical jurisdiction to numerous towns mostly outside the coveted Valley of Mexico. Charles Gibson, *The Aztecs under Spanish Rule* (Stanford, California, Stanford University Press, 1964), pp. 58ff.

† Properly the name refers to the imperial tribute collectors of the Aztecs. Encomienda, in a decentralized form, replaced the former imperial system of tribute exaction. See Gibson, pp. 34, 182, 194f.

who, as chronicler priest Toribio Motolinia puts it, "had become the real masters of this land, who bore command over its natural principals the way they would over their slaves, . . . like drones who eat up the honey belabored by the poor bees, the Indians." Terrorism was particularly the rule in mining communities. Motolinia describes the mines of Oaxyecac where the air was contaminated with the stench of decaying human flesh and where "half a league around and in many parts of the road one could hardly walk without stepping on corpses or human bones; and so many birds of prey came to devour the dead bodies that they shadowed the sun, and for this many villages and towns were depopulated, the rest of the Indians having escaped to the mountains, abandoning their homes and haciendas." [23] Charles Gibson stated:

> The record of the first encomienda generation, in the Valley [of Mexico] as elsewhere, is one of generalized abuse and particular atrocities. Encomenderos used their Indians in all forms of manual labor, in building, farming, and mining, and for the supply of whatever the country yielded. They overtaxed and overworked them. They jailed them, killed them, beat them, and set dogs on them. They seized their goods, destroyed their agriculture, and took their women. They used them as beasts of burden. They took tribute from them and sold it back under compulsion at exorbitant profits. Coercion and ill-treatment were the daily practices of their overseers, calpixque, and labor bosses. The first encomenderos, without known exception, understood Spanish authority as provision for unlimited personal opportunism.[24]

Even when the European tried to comply with his duty to Christianize and civilize the Indians and to use the humanitarian approach, the results were far from reassuring. In the morning, the Indians were herded in front of an image of the Holy Virgin; they were compelled to attend

Mass on Sundays and taught to parrot the *Ave María, Pater Noster, Credo* and *Salve* (the minimum of formularies for lay worship demanded by the Church), a chore most Indians succeeded in mastering only by memorizing meaningless sequences of homonyms from their own language. Better than anyone else the missionaries, particularly the Dominicans, were uncomfortably aware that lay indoctrination, if associated with the encomienda, was inefficient, or would only alienate the Indians and that terrorism, cruelty, and greed would make the parallel Christian crusade degenerate into a dark scandal.

In Sepúlveda's conception and in the practice adopted by Cortés [25] and other conquistadores, the encomienda was essentially a State-level system of public relationships between the Crown and the conquered people, not a civil arrangement between an employer and an employee. Tribal Indian caciques, consequently, shared with their people the official responsibility for maintaining the system; it was up to them to see that the quotas of *encomendados* (Indians subject to encomienda) set for a particular village were met and that the required number of Indians showed up for work. The Indians working for an encomienda were free from the obligation to pay direct Crown tax, a duty they otherwise were thought to have in their nominal status as "free vassals of the King"—an expression that conveys not only royal protectionism from abuse by the colonists but also dignity and independent status. In contrast to slavery, belonging to encomienda, by Sepúlveda's definition, was supposed to be a transitory arrangement; and it was supposed to imply that the encomendado was not deprived of his property and of his human and legal rights. He had the right to take his complaints to the colonial tribunal of the Crown. There was nothing in the letter of the regulations of the encomienda to make it impossible for the encomendado to retain his lands and thus to obtain partial release from his dependence, hard as this might prove in practice.

Sepúlveda specified that the Indians were to be kept in a condition that would combine the principle of *herile* (the secular, seignorial, and vertical relationship between the master and the servant, which might or might not involve remuneration) and *paterno* (the authoritarian and diffuse principle of familial dependency ties).[26] In theory then, the relationship between the Indians and the Europeans would be a fusion of the master-servant and parent-child relationship of a household; a combination of legal contract and natural tie, underscoring in both senses the submission of the Indian. It was Sepúlveda's intention to defend not a caste society, in the strict sense, but rather a minimally open society where the Indians' bargaining power and mobility, social and physical, were efficiently curtailed; where the Indian was reduced in status to half citizenship; and where his rights and duties, work conditions, and material rewards were unilaterally determined and his self-organization prevented. Eventually these rights were to be revised in the spirit of compassion by the Spaniards, in accordance with the Indian's progress in Faith and Europeanization; any ideological revising, however, would be dictated from above.

Practices of institutionalized marginality were as commonplace in Europe at the time of the Conquest as they had been in the Roman Empire, which was the administrative master model for Sepúlveda and most of his contemporaries. In the feudal agrarian structure inherited from the Romans, nominally free tenants, or *coloni*, had gradually replaced slaves. The *coloni* were commonly bound to dependence on wealthy landowners by the practice of the *precarium*, whereby a small landowner commended himself and his land to a landlord in exchange for protection, a loan, or to escape heavy taxation. He would receive the land back, with the right to exploit it on specified terms of rental and service, in precarious tenure. Under the system of *patrocinium*, again, a landless person could render his services and labor to a landlord in return for protection, aid, and the right to make a living on lands belonging to the *patron*.

European feudalism, including its Spanish version, however, evolved in response to the need for protection against immediate external dangers, wars, robbery, famine, disease, and other hardships of life beyond the individual's capacity to control in a disorderly and hazardous society where centralized political authority was weak and where effectual personal security was derived from local patronage. The subjection of the European peasantry, Marc Bloch points out, occurred during a historical period when the sluggishness of trade and monetary circulation helped to undermine the capacity of the independent small farmer to maintain economic self-sufficiency and when the economic situation and safety of the lordless man could be far from enviable.[27]

In Spanish colonial America, the natives were suddenly burdened with the imposition of the encomienda and with arbitrary demands on their labor harsher and more comprehensive than the ones forced upon them by the earlier indigenous feudalism. In addition, the acceptance of the new work arrangement as "just" and free participation in the supposedly civilizing and disciplinary encomienda would have meant, on their part, an implicit acceptance of a wretched, degrading self-image. The justification of the encomienda, including the cruelties and excesses associated with it, supposedly rested not on the need for protection against external dangers, but on the miserableness of the condition of the Indian himself, on his alleged deep-rooted wickedness, paganism, ignorance, and backwardness. There were, on the one hand, the merciless encomendero and his calpixque pressing the Indian hard into a position of exploitation, debt, and servile dependence; and on the other hand there was the zealous missionary priest denouncing the old religious habits, threatening with a Hell as deep and fiery as the volcanos that the Indians knew, identifying the old Gods with the Devil, leaving no stone unturned in the search for idols to destroy, and suspecting the Indian of being inherently deficient in morals and in spiritual maturity, because an inner disposition made him forever forgetful of what he had been told about the doctrine, and prone to relapse into idolatry and vice. The fusion of these two pressures, on the institutional level, made up the rationale of the encomienda. The Indians, in brief, were forcefully exposed to Christianity through the same instrument that was employed to expose them to vicious economic exploitation. Their regimentation into the system of encomienda was supposedly done for their own ultimate benefit, to save them from being themselves.

The Crown and the theologian-jurists back in Spain were aware of the incompatibility of the exploitative and the evangelizing functions of the Conquest. Already Christopher Columbus had assigned Indians to service among his captains; a few of them were taken to Spain, where they were shown to the Catholic kings. The latter promptly overruled Columbus' action, and the Indians—the first encomendados—were rushed back to America. During the first half of the sixteenth century the position of the Crown on the status of the encomienda was irresolute; numerous, often contradictory amendments to it were promulgated. Sepúlveda's treatise on the justification of the war against the Indians was banned. Though the censoring authorities considered it sound in itself, they nevertheless "did not believe it was suitable for publication." [28] In the early 1550's one more committee of theologian-jurists was appointed by the Council of the Indies to reexamine the issue, and a public debate was arranged between Sepúlveda and Las Casas, the two most conspicuous protagonists in the controversy. This failed however to bring the opposing views any closer to agreement.

The Binding Quality of Power

Sepúlveda's dialogue offers us an opportunity to examine conceptually some of the tenets of the sociological tradition and their derivation from presociological thought in the West. The issues of power, authority, legitimacy, and the conditions of the oneness of the sociopolitical entity are concerned here. We may first examine Max Weber (1863–1920), the German sociologist who made some of the most explicit statements on these issues.

Domination (*Herrschaft*) in society, Weber held, means the chance for influence or command. Domination may rest on a number of motives, personal gain, habit; or upon a belief in the "rightness" of the commands. The latter case was termed "legitimate domination," commonly translated as "authority." Legitimacy, according to Weber, may be based upon purely affectual emotional surrender (charismatic authority), long standing tradition (traditional authority), or formally and rationally established rules (legal or bureaucratic authority).[29]

Although Weber elaborated a typology of authority and a set of analytical guides to exploit its possibilities in the study of sociopolitical change in history, his interest in power (*Macht*) has not altogether vanished. Power, with Weber, however, is defined as a clearly *residual* category. It means the chance to impose personal will on others, even when it meets resistance; yet the specific mechanics of implementing and perpetuating personal power are left out of Weber's argument. Consequently, power is, Weber said, a "sociologically amorphous" concept.[30] Unlike authority-oriented social order, the one based on power is void of internal organization; it is staffless, and it rests on the omnipresent and assumedly arbitrary word of a powerful person. While an authority-oriented social order, and particularly the one based on legally established rules, is explained in terms of increasing organization, bureaucratization, and complexity, a power-oriented social order—it seems to follow from Weber—remains ossified; it entails no morphogenetic processes. Analytically, personal power remains thus a useless "black box" looming large mostly in the depth of history, and best exemplified in the "pure" but extinct case of slavery. Since Weber conceived of power as the ability to rule without the support, consent, understanding or sentiment of loyalty, or without support from any specific mechanisms of reinforcement or further development, it has no true sociological profile; it defies prediction and explanation.

In a manner very similar to Weber's the renowned French sociologist Emile Durkheim (1855–1917), in his attempt to analyze the modes of relationship between the individual and group minds, nearly neglected in his classification the case of personally regulated total, totalitarian and totalizing systems. He did add a footnote, however, to recognize the case of "excessive physical or moral despotism," or "fatalism," which, he thought, had become so rare in history that it would seem "useless to dwell upon it." [31] By slighting the role of guidance and legitimate man-made controls, these lofty figures in Western sociology have distorted our views on the broad issue of social causation.

It is interesting to note, in contrast, that Sepúlveda, with his Aristotelian starting point, solved the problem of legitimate social order by his notion of "legitimate power." There was, in the New World, only *one* society which was full-fledgedly legitimate; this was the European-controlled society with its built-in castelike division. Although the Indians could not be forced to accept the Faith, they nevertheless *could* be legitimately forced to live in regulated communities under Spanish rule; they could be made to accept marginal membership within the colonial society; and to accept, against their will, a situation where the benefits of Christian and Western ways of life would eventually impinge on them. In due time, Sepúlveda anticipated, they will be granted minor responsibilities in society.

Whereas with Weber power was simply "assumed to be there," remaining an impotent feature of sociological nomenclature, of no consequence in the analysis of contemporary processes, with Sepúlveda it was relatively permanent, natural, necessary, explanatory, effective and consequential; and, significantly, it was a "given," independent of the legitimacy principle itself and antedating the acceptance of legitimacy.

We may paraphrase Sepúlveda's notion of programmed power to arrive at a general definition of this concept:

Power as an ordering principle of a system means the precarious ability of an individual, or a ruling group, to maintain control over the action output and movement of other individuals or groups by impeding them, through some reinforcing mechanism felt to be justifiable and derived from an extra-individual preexisting system level which does not "belong" to the holders of power, from spontaneously aligning with other individuals, from "escaping" the interactive system, from "leaving the field," or from finding alternative outlets for their output. Thus, power creates a hierarchy; it prevents self-generated change and imposes control over responsive output. The tension thereby accumulating will lead to increasingly explosive situations that necessitate periodic modification of the power principle to preclude overt rebellion among the subjects of power. Power is justified by the claim that its holder is not an obstacle to the collective tendencies of "the people" and that his function cannot be deduced in an impersonal one-to-one manner from the pressure factors in the field, but is an indispensable synthesizing and moderating one which enables the system to meet the segmental pressures and still remain, in some significant global aspects, one.

To become institutionalized, a power system requires a specific mechanism. *Figure 1* illustrates the restricted circular relationship and the auxiliary devices involved in implementing and perpetuating power. Individual *A* commands here another individual *B*, through initial unilateral rules *k*, in circumstances, however, where a filter mechanism consisting of *P* and *M* is also in operation. The filter mechanism of *P-M* makes it possible to transform *B*'s spontaneous response *a* into restricted and guided output *d*, controllable and exploitable for public purposes by *A*. *P* represents *A*'s self-defense against *B*'s spontaneous attempts to repudiate his individual claim for power, or against *B*'s attempts to simply eliminate *A*. *M* represents the extrasystemic circumstance reinforcing *A*'s ability to thwart *B*'s attempt to "escape." This graph should not lead to notions of misplaced concreteness. *P* and *M* may consist of the *same* items, applied both on the individual level *P* and on the institutional level *M*. In the case of the Conquest, the complex filter mechanism consisted of the Europeans' use of carbines, horses; myths of their "divinity"; the encomienda system, "Laws of the Indians"; rationalizations regarding the Indians' inferiority, and the like. An attempt to single out a given determinant of the institutionalized filter mechanism would lead to, perhaps, a theory of Marxian-type exploitation and economic determinism, or to technological or idealistic determinism, or to some other kind of predisposition to accept the causal primacy of a single factor in any historical circumstances.

Yet, the link between power and the oneness of the system remains to be explained. For Sepúlveda, the Europeans

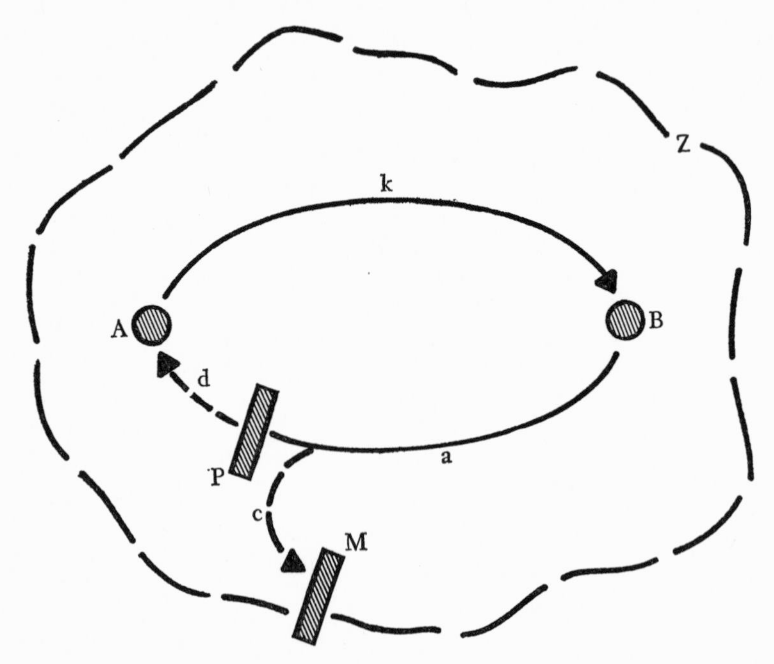

Figure 1. The system of power

had the right to legitimate power over the Indians because they had *foreknowledge* of the Indians' belonging to the same Christian communion. Consequently, since the Indian could not escape from being "one of us," the Spaniards had predictive knowledge about his eventual destiny. This transcendental foreknowledge of spiritual brotherhood, and the implications of vassalage, capacitated the Europeans to pass moral judgments on the Indians; to correct, command, and interpret their behavior; and, in all essence, to know with certainty "what is good for the Indians" in the long run. The same patronizing attitude is reflected today by those Latin American politicians, reformers, educators, and landowners who speak knowledgeably of "our peasants"; who have all the answers for them; and who act "for the peasants' own good," taking their cue not from pressures generated by "the people" but from their own preconceived and education-oriented notions about the situation. When such is the case, the legitimacy of power is derived from the claim of universal, ultimate, and explanatory a priori enclosure of the total situation within the scope of an overall ideological system, represented by Z in *Figure 1*, to which A has a preferential access. Power is exercised within a single global system which, for the purpose of implementing power, must be considered as ultimately unvarying or politically "closed in" by boundaries, and ideologically consistent. It is in this predetermined enclosure alone, which leaves no escape, that command *k* may be considered "binding," final, and all-inclusive.

In the rationale of power, as Sepúlveda saw it, imperfect and varying means are legitimized through the perfect and absolute ends they pursue. Whereas Sepúlveda attached the capacity of natural perfection and ultimate enclosure to the Catholic-Christian system, the modern mind is likely to consider humanity (the past, present, and future generations of mankind) as the ultimate enclosure from which the analytic notion of power flows. Humanity, indeed, is the only power system which cannot be considered a political "enemy" and which does not enable its components to escape, except in death—kill or self-kill. Z, in the modern conception, must be considered as something ultimately derived from continuous humanity—a principle with a totalizing power beyond national and religious ideologies.

Further implications of including power among the social scientist's explanatory apparatus will be discussed more fully in the essay. At this point we may note that the inclusion of power as a tool to interpret morphogenetic processes introduces terms such as avoidance, withdrawal, apathy, fatalism, resistance, martyrdom, and rebellion, some of which concentrate on the prerevolutionary aspects of social change touched upon only marginally in functionalist Western sociology. These hidden or latent precipitants and obstacles of change, in gubernatorial analysis, are treated in their full status regarding their relevance in explanation. On the other hand, the power approach may help explain the power holder's willingness to yield by implementing legitimate changes induced "from above", and to apply his capacity to undo something in order to build up something else, at a time when he is faced with the threat of accumulating latent pressures "from below" and when he is experiencing the fear of total collapse of the unity of the system.

Demilitarized Christian Colonialism: Las Casas

The lifework of the persistent, frustrated Fray Bartolomé de las Casas (1474–1566)—appointed in 1543 Bishop of Chiapas, Guatemala—was to defend and promote a precarious Utopian cause: the liberation of the Indians from their destitute status as semislaves under the Spaniards, their integration within the colonial society, and their Christianizing by means of evangelistic clemency and nonviolence.

Las Casas demanded that the Indians should be conceded "full liberty" (in the restricted sense of making them taxpaying, locally self-governing "vassals of the King"), a status involving, in his definition, the restitution, to a degree, of the sovereignty of the *señores naturales*, the caciques. For the time being, however, he found the idea of mature autonomy "absurd and blasphemous"; therefore he concentrated on the second-best formula of supervised Indian communities —a compromise solution worked out by 1516 by Las Casas, Cardinal-Regent Francisco Ximénez de Císneros and Counsellor of the Court Juan López de Palacios Rubios.

This design [32] called for the establishment of a network of Indian towns of 300 inhabitants each,* located, whenever feasible, near gold mines, and near rivers abundant in fish. Spacious houses would be built in the style of the Indians. There would be an imposing church, streets, a plaza, and a hospital administered by a "conscientious married couple"; and there would be the residence of the cacique, which also would serve as a public meeting place.

The Indians would be convinced of the advantages of living in the settlements; they would be given the opportunity to choose the location for the town. Their movement there, Las Casas anticipated, would be carried out in a voluntary fashion. Power would work without meeting resistance, he implies. The Indians living at a long distance from mines would be brought into agrarian settlements to become farmers and cattlemen. Land would be distributed among all townspeople "according to the quality of the person and the quantity of his family," with the caciques receiving four times more than the rest. Part of the land would be retained in communal ownership to be used as common pasture.

The caciques would administer law and maintain public

* The plan described here was later realized in the so-called *congregaciones*. The Indians, forced to move from their villages to the congregaciones, vacated their former living areas. This indirectly helped the Spaniards to obtain ownership of land and promoted the formation of the hacienda system.

order without being authorized, however, to enforce punishment beyond whipping. Grievous offenses would be handled by either the local priest or the colonial courts. Local officials would be appointed by a council consisting of the cacique, the priest, and the administrator. The last-mentioned official —a Spaniard of uncorrupted conscience—would reside outside the settlement, at a convenient location between two or more towns in his jurisdiction. He would maintain a small militia, either Spaniards or Indians or both.

The administrator and the priest would see that the Indians "wear clothes and sleep in beds and take care of the tools given to them," that "everyone be content with having only one wife," that "women live in chastity," and that the Indians not sell or gamble their possessions "without the permission of the priest or the administrator." The Indians —a wistful afterthought—would be persuaded "not to eat squatting on the ground."

One-half of the administrator's salary would come from community funds, the other half in subsidy from the Crown. The administrator's duties would relate to the work chores of the villagers; the priest would impart religious indoctrination, hold religious services and, among other things, punish in public the villagers not attending classes in religion. There also would be a sacristan, an Indian, to serve in the church and teach school for children up to nine years in age.

One-third of the adult males would be employed in mining, making up teams to work in shifts of two months under Indian supervisors and foremen. Everyone would be obliged to take turns at work on the cacique's lands to a limit of, perhaps, fifteen days a year. The community would collectively possess livestock, and meat would be distributed free. The gold extracted would be divided in equal parts among the

Indian populace, the community, and the royal treasury. A permanent team of prospectors, Spaniards and Indians, would be assigned the task of locating gold fields.

There would be recompense for the lands expropriated from their present owners, the Spanish encomenderos and *hacendados* (large landholders). Some of them might become village administrators; others might operate mines, using either family labor or African slaves; * or there would be some other kind of gratuity to make up for the loss. A high-ranking official would be assigned by the Crown to help enforce the reforms.

Las Casas mapped out an alternative plan to be adopted in case the idea of planned communities did not work. This was essentially a reformist program [33] aimed at the correction of the most noxious abuses of the encomienda such as the employment of women and children in mines, long working hours, forceful relocation of the Indians, inadequate food, low wages, the use of Indians to carry loads over long distances, the cruelties of Spanish foremen, and the prerogative of the Crown's officials to keep large numbers of encomendados. Moreover, Las Casas recommended that laborers and artisans be brought from Spain to work for the Euro-

* Las Casas' plan to replace Indian laborers by Spanish laborers was never realized. In one instance, he managed to recruit workers from southern Spain and ship them to the New World. He was apparently prevented by the colonists and their partisans from boarding the ship; since there was nobody to meet the workers when they arrived at Hispaniola, they soon dispersed among the Spaniards in the colony. The plan to replace Indians with African Negroes was successfully implemented, often against opposition from the colonists. Indian labor, where it was available, was less expensive because of the high price of imported African slaves. For a discussion of the slave trade, see Hubert Herring, *A History of Latin America,* (New York, Alfred A. Knopf, 1956), pp. 100ff.

peans and to train the natives in manual crafts; he also recommended that Negro slaves from Africa rather than Indians be employed in mining.

After 1516 the Crown became directly or indirectly involved in half-hearted attempts to put these schemes into practice, with Las Casas as the passionate driving force in his position of "universal Protector of the Indians." A commission of Hieronymite monks was dispatched to the Caribbean with ample authorization to initiate experiments on the Indians' capacity for self-government. However, the Hieronymites promptly became biased against the emancipation issue; they sent to Spain reports of interviews with influential encomenderos and colonial officers in Hispaniola who had testified that the Indians, if set free, would not only be likely to drift back to idleness and savagery but would also contrive to destroy the colony; that the Indians' lack of ambition and avarice was a proof of their inability in self-government; that vice, drunkenness, lying and stealing were part of their nature; that "they do not pray, not even say *Pater Noster* nor *Ave María* unless they are brought to by force"; and that they should remain encomendados even if many of them die, because "at least their souls are saved." One informant asserted that the Indians should stay in encomiendas because "living a little apart from the Spaniards, the way they do, they can keep their old customs, but were they forced to suddenly change their ways, they would die or kill themselves." One Franciscan friar and colonial administrator favorable to the encomienda ambiguously speculated that the Indians, "if set free only to pay tribute to His Majesty, would multiply in twenty years to five times their present number," whereas in encomiendas they would be decimated in number within the same period of time. There was substantial agreement among the interviewees that to dispense with the labor and services forced from the Indians would bring immediate economic ruin for Hispaniola and for the Crown.[34]

The Hieronymites nevertheless were instrumental in creating in Hispaniola "free" experimental Indian communities administered by Spanish *mayordomos*. New decrees from Spain were later received which aimed at the extension of similar experiments to Puerto Rico and Cuba. All these attempts toward more humane colonial policy eventually failed, both because the opinion of the Spanish colonists was solidly against them and because most of the administrators in charge of the experiments were themselves indifferent or hostile to reform. Most important, the Indians wanted no part in the "different liberty" outlined for them by the colonial experimenters.[35] The slaughtering of the Indians, the high mortality due to mistreatment and overwork, starvation, epidemics (particularly smallpox), and suicide had by now taken such a toll among the Indians that the remnants of the native population in the Caribbean were unable to rise from their state of hopeless dejection.

In the early 1520's Las Casas embarked upon a new missionary plan for the heretofore unpacified regions of the mainland, the Tierra Firme. Under this plan Dominican and Franciscan friars were to establish farming and pearl-fishing settlements, fortressed strongholds manned by the armed "caballeros of the Gilded Stirrup" in the command of the friars, to serve as bases for missionary expeditions. Manual labor in these missions was to be supplied by either Spanish workers or African slaves. The organization was designed to create a frontier situation in which the Gospel would reach the Indians in advance of the soldiers and in which warlike activity would be confined to mere defense. The first attempted settlement of this kind, in Cumaná (Venezuela), was shortly wiped out by hostile Indians.

It was not until 1537 that Las Casas once more ventured a major missionary project, this time with the deliberate intention of not seeking military support of any kind from the Spaniards. A pocket of bellicose Indians in Tezulutlan (Guatemala) had stubbornly resisted Spanish pacification forces, and the province had acquired, among the Spaniards, sinister fame as the unconquerable "Land of War." Las Casas was able to elicit from the governor of Guatemala a concession which authorized a team of missionary padres to evangelize Tezulutlan and to "bring Tezulutlans to the service of the King" as free, tribute-paying subjects, without permitting any lay Spaniards—encomenderos or soldiers—to enter the area during the next five years. This missionary period was later extended to ten years.

Preparations for this mission, according to chronicler-priest Antonio de Remesal's somewhat idealized narrative,[36] were carried out with painstaking care. However, the preparations seemed to depart from the rationally oriented catechistics of scholasticism and from the notion of spontaneous gravitation towards Christianity implicit in Las Casas' earlier schemes. In line with the new humanistic theories of Erasmus of Rotterdam (1466–1536)—in vogue in Spain at the time—Las Casas now seems to have adopted the idea of a "gentle push of the will" toward Christianity[37] as an intrinsically emotional experience instead of a passively repetitive, hortatory drill.

The principal events in the Old and New Testaments were translated into the language of Tezulutlan. Four native traders—converts who knew the area intimately—were taught to chant biblical history to the tune of Spanish *coplas* (popular songs). Once in the Land of War, the merchants, equipped with Spanish-made scissors, knives, mirrors and other attractive gift items, took residence in the house of a cacique and chanted their coplas to the accompaniment of an Indian *teplanastle* until the cacique and his principal men became "warmed in their hearts to the ambassadors of the new Gods." Within a week the Indians had learned the coplas and, anxious to learn more, formally invited the priests to come to their village. The padres enlisted the assistance of the cacique; a mass baptism was held and a church built. The cacique was baptized Juan and later ceremoniously taken on a tour of the capital city, a visit which seems to have left him unimpressed. Elite troops were assigned to the padres to escort them on their expeditions to hostile areas. After several days of discussion with the padre, cacique Juan agreed to the expediency of gathering the dispersed Indian tribes into a compact congregation, an operation which nearly incited some of the clans to take up arms.

Reports on the preliminary success in Vera Paz—the name by which the Dominican concession now was known—aroused rapt enthusiasm among the liberals in Spain.[38] However, from the perspective of the padres, the spiritual and moral status of the Indian neophytes remained doubtful. Underground idolatry persisted, many tacitly gave up the Faith, even the faithful stuck to their "offensive" native garb in which the priests found "very little bolster for morality." The Indians painted their skin as before, wore their hair in unkempt knots, urinated "like dogs and cats" in plain view of each other and, "like eagles," grew their fingernails long and untidy. Animals were secretly sacrificed; baptized infants were taken to hideway places for pagan ceremony, and many other baneful rites were observed. Later, after encomenderos and other Spaniards had wangled their way into the area, the Indians, to the chagrin of the padres, seemed to be adding to their old vices new ones learned from the Europeans.[39] Most damaging of all, the Indians of Lacandón and Puchutla, who were officially a part of the Dominican concession, periodically attacked and burned down the Christian villages of Vera Paz and took prisoners for sacrifice, stubbornly refusing to negotiate peace with the Dominicans or to accept Christianity. After a particularly fiery attack by the rebel tribes in 1555, the hapless Dominicans finally appealed for intervention by the colonial government, thereby officially denouncing the demilitarized missionary policies of Las Casas. A retaliatory war against the unyielding Indians was carried out in 1559, but it was only in 1699 that the conquest of Vera Paz was ultimately achieved.[40]

There are significant ideological and programmatic inconsistencies in the doctrines of Las Casas. He urged recognition of the human rights of the Indians but disregarded those of the Africans. He wanted to restore the authentic rule of the señores naturales; yet (along with practically all of his contemporaries) he took it for granted that, once they were converted, the Indians had to accept tribute and surrender, even in trivial matters, to the pedant *religioso*, or to the colonial administrator turned tutelary benefactor. He believed in the docility of the Indians and in the natural attraction of the Faith in spite of firsthand evidence of the perils his missionaries faced. And he fell into the error of expecting, again along with the dogmatism of his times, that nomadic or seminomadic people, disassociated from their tribes and communities, could be miraculously cast into a mold resembling the Spanish peasant.

The unvarying themes set forth by Las Casas are his disagreement with the practice of the encomienda and his disagreement with conquest by violence. He equated the encomienda with de facto slavery; he was firmly convinced that the secular laws sustaining it are irreconcilable with natural and divine laws. He believed that there is no justification whatsoever for the wars of conquest leading into the enslavement of the Indians and that Christianity in no circumstances justifies killing. He concluded that the Spaniards, consequently, had committed a mortal sin, collectively and individually, and that they could be absolved of it only by paying the Indians reparations for what had been unjustly taken from them. He calculated that some fifteen million Indians were cruelly and needlessly slaughtered in the New World during his stay of over four decades there and that this ruthless genocide, if allowed to continue, would lead to the extermination of the indigenous race.

To those who held the majority opinion favoring the exploitative policies in the colonies, Las Casas' stand came to represent vile betrayal. Calumny against him was spread among his parishioners in Guatemala; pranksters harassed him by discharging firearms outside the windows of his residence and chanting malicious coplas about him on the streets.[41] Even if he could enlist some support in Spain, in the colonies his case was obviously lost.

The New Laws of 1542 did seemingly represent a victory of many of the ideas Las Casas stood for—among others, abolition of the encomiendas of governmental officials, the abolition of hereditary rights to encomienda, and the establishment of the right of the Indians under encomienda to live in villages of their own. But these reforms could not be effectively enforced.*

* *Corregimiento* or the office of corregidor, local magistrate, became the official governing institution to replace encomienda. Royal government was represented in the colonies by viceroy, the *oidores*, and corregidores, in descending order. The last mentioned—also called *jueces*, *justicias*, *alcaldes mayores*, and *subdelegados*—were

Las Casas' efforts to free the Indians bring to focus one of the most controversial and longlasting peculiarities of the Latin American social structure. The plan to "free the Indians," that is, to increase their social mobility and to create a labor force based on cash wages and a free labor market, was strongly opposed by the colonists not only because of their opportunistic self-interest in exploiting Indian labor and their desire to make a fortune, but also because the institutionalized marginality of the Indian and the peasant had become the very basis of the colonial system as a whole. The Crown's efforts to create a free Indian labor force, in the sixteenth century, caused not only economic loss to colonial entrepreneurs in the European upper class but also severe shortages of food in the capital cities.[42] The Indians, if their labor was recompensed in wages and if they were permitted a relatively free choice, tended to withdraw from the European market economy altogether, thus creating a shortage of labor and economic stagnation. Despite their shortcomings, encomienda and *repartimiento* (a system of obligated Indian labor, mostly in urban construction) were the economic backbone of the colonial society and could not be erased without vital risk to the urban centers and, ultimately, to the imperialistic ambitions of the Crown itself.

Implications of Power

In this section, an attempt will be made to transcribe the preceding account of Las Casas' innovative action into terms more closely in agreement with the semantics of gubernatorial analysis. This will involve indulgence in conceptualization and

---

immediately concerned with tribute collection and work assignment. In some areas, encomienda and corregimiento existed in a parallel manner. Charles Gibson, *The Aztecs under Spanish Rule* (Stanford, California, Stanford University Press, 1964), pp. 81ff.

propositions the value of which, at the moment, is heuristic rather than practicable. How does power operate? will be asked here. What are the particular characteristics of personalistic power, as opposed to authority, which denotes impersonality? Under what circumstances do the holders of power move into action in order to delegate power, to modify the manner in which it is implemented, or to seek legitimacy for it?

I propose that the social scientific tradition in the West has absorbed a bias which makes it inadequate in the study of social change and inconsistent with the ethos of objectivity that this atomistic approach professes. This bias arises largely from the social scientists' reluctance to deal with power in its unmechanistic capacity not only to verify and to produce "more of the same" but also to initiate and undo, erect and destroy, institutional practices and large-scale policies and thus to legitimately falsify principles the validity of which in the past has been taken for granted. Only power "from above" has this capacity; authority does not have it. Only power in the gubernatorial sense has the capacity to reduce the recycling of in-system marginality.

The social scientific tradition, following the atomistic approach, in one way or another stresses the point that *the system,* sustained by the participants, impersonally and abstractly on all levels, has the capacity for overall adaptation and equilibrium, and that the system's tendency toward adaptive and equilibrating change, again, can be reduced to the individuals' (all individuals') continuous striving toward efficiency and participation. The individual, then, is dealt with as if he were a free-floating ultimate source of social change, acting rather than being acted upon and determining, in an atomistic fashion, the direction that the systemic change will follow. The benefits from political participation, in this view, are assumed to be equally available to all.

The trouble with this notion lies in its indifference to guidance from the polity, to legislation and law, to administrative controls, to inequalities arising from the past, and to public action that may determine the availability and unavailability of given things and given choices. Planning by the polity creates many institutional structures and consequently channels the individuals' action into a predetermined range. The decision-making processes herein involved, in a large social unit, simply cannot be fully "open" for immediate participation by every individual. The kind of "direct democracy" Rousseau had in mind cannot be practiced in sizable social entities. To phrase it differently, change within a system cannot be understood as being evenly compelled by each and every one of the actors who compose it. To depict change in these terms would be tantamount to forcing it into Rousseau's model of direct democracy, or Spencer's Stateless model, or Marx's "consumers' association." All of these models are Utopian rather than explanatory.

Nor can social change be reduced to "groupism," a chopped-up picture of society in which, as Sheldon S. Wolin puts it, no *general* power component would exist beyond "a series of tight little islands, each evolving toward political self-sufficiency, each striving to absorb the individual members, each without any natural affiliations with a more comprehensive unity." [43]

Political power, instead, can be understood only in terms of a single general order for which, Wolin adds, "no multiplication of fragmentary constituencies will provide a substitute." The political system and the oneness within it will remain in spite of fragmentation in specific areas of function. It is only within the general political order that civic responsibilities and loyalties become meaningful, for there must exist a

reasonably credible way of deducing these from the ge
rationale of the political system.

Historically, it was in reaction to the atomistic fragmer model of the empiricists of the Lockean school that the so-called positivist philosophy arose in France during the 1810's, and this philosophy was widely embraced in Latin America after the 1870's. The task confronting mankind, according to Saint-Simon, Comte, and other positivists, was not to remove the commanding upper structures, not to build up a model "as if" they did not exist and as if the political component was unnecessary. The task was, the positivists argued, one of remaking these upper structures and of inducing in them an ideological change. In other words, the "system," the unifying frame of political order, must be preserved, the positivists warned, for it provides a tenable a priori rationale for the collectivity. Its virtue lies in its capacity to guide and to give structure. A system, as Condillac (1715–1780) already had pointed out, is nothing but "the disposition of the different parties in an art or in a science of the same order to sustain each other mutually, so that the last ones will be explainable through the first ones. Those that explain others are called *principles*, and the fewer the number of principles the more perfect is the system: it is most desirable that they be reduced to one single principle." [44]

It is erroneous to assume, the totalizing positivistic and principle-bound view implies, that the entire unit through all its components at every moment actively participates in building up (or maintaining) social institutions. Most probably, this kind of acephalous society never existed. The polity, moreover, is something beyond a mere crystallization of the prevailing populist currents, and it operates in a manner that cannot be deduced from them. Its base cannot be directly traced back to the shifts occurring in public opinion; in this sense, this view implies, it has a transcendental, directive, and swift-moving quality of its own. The polity will assume a monopoly on public services, and on public expenditure; on the use of naked force and law enforcement, on wars, on foreign relations, and on other public benefits and liabilities of "binding" nature. The power of the polity is binding because it allows no exceptions and it is objectively applied to all elements within its jurisdiction. The kind of monopoly that the polity assumes must be taken into account in explaining social change, not only because the polity has a sanctioning and limiting effect on spontaneous change, but also because developments in it (as opposed to changes in the society) can be effected from the center in an abrupt and planful manner.

Although the problem of the transcendental quality of power from above is extremely broad, its concrete importance in research cannot be enough stressed. The social scientific tradition, to take a few examples, would focus on religious beliefs and attitudes as they have been extracted from a factor analysis of the verbal responses that selected individuals (in a random sample) have given to structured questionnaire items; yet the Church Council might abruptly introduce, in a swift decision-making process involving powerful insiders alone, doctrinal modifications that the researcher of religious systems must be familiar with and that would eventually have an impact upon the beliefs and attitudes of the members. Present beliefs and attitudes must be traced back not only to the synchronic "field" in which they occur, but also to the earlier decision-making processes that have successively shaped the Church dogma.

Similarly, the social scientific school would tell us to study within-culture regularities and between-culture differences as they are reflected in the patterns of response to questionnaire items, yet these patterns may largely depend on the kind of curriculum offered in the schools, and on the kind of ideology the curriculum reflects. Or one may study the Latin-American city plan and its plaza-centered design in its observed consequences alone—this would be the so-called functionalist approach, implying that function is simply some kind of effect of a structure and that this effect is what we should concentrate on explaining. In contrast stands the power-oriented approach, implying that the plaza-centered urban structure came into existence as a response to royal decrees from Spain and that these decrees, again, can be explained only against the ideologies of a Las Casas or a Vasco de Quiroga who, through the Council of the Indies, imposed on the New World their preconceived models for Christian communities.

Must the researcher, then, make his choice between atomistic explanation, which would stress personality variables, and contextual explanation, which would stress the effects of the command as it emanates from the polity? Under the former procedure, change in the system would be held to result from the strivings of the participants toward the maintenance of a minimum of harmony within and among lower-level groups which emerge and develop in a spontaneous way. Under the latter procedure, continuity in change would be explained by public action, by the law, and, in colonial Latin America, by the implementation of Catholic and colonial policy.

The problem is, however, that explanation is complete only if it considers adequately the initiatory public action together with the subsequent reactions to it by the several sectors of the system, including the various forms of reaction by the civil sectors to public programming. Theoretically, each member of the politically organized entity may possess some gubernatorial capacities—to this degree the atomistic notion of a system evenly supported by individual action on all levels is warranted. Yet, these atomistic directive forces of social change will remain latent, concealed by manifestations of collective mood ranging from enthusiasm to fatalism. Some actively resisting elements will eventually, in the name of the people, break off their fatalistic and other primary types of allegiance and, without escaping the system, take up self-organization and overt resistance. Unplanned impulses from the civil sectors force their way into public-policy making by way of open confrontation. Our explanatory task, if one will accept this model of underlying tension between power and civil resistance, consists of an attempt to characterize the mood of resistance as displayed on various levels of the system, and the approaches and alliances the public sector chooses in order to deal with these counterforces whose ultimate aim is in the direction of liberation. The officially established component of the system must be kept analytically separate from the spontaneous, unplanned, or civil components of the system; the polity must be analytically distinguished from the society. The polity (the Crown) is concerned with officially designated goal achievement, programming, legislation, propagation, lawfulness, prohibition, uniformity, order, and ideological manipulation. Yet, policy making must follow fairly closely the spontaneous tendencies flowing from the civil sector. Unless this happens, resistances will intensify and the system's unity will be eventually lost.

In brief outline, the Las Casas episode involved the following:

A legalized learning center (represented in Las Casas' appointment) was established within the colonial system, implying the planners' empathy with the "victims" of power and, structurally, the differentiation of a learning role from a controlling role within the power system.

Selective communication was established between the "field" (including the New World) and the control center (Spanish Court). The Crown, in other words, was no longer satisfied with receiving whatever news might trickle from the colony; it tried to intensify the flow of information and to explore the problems.

This establishment of a communication link indicated, in principle, a willingness on the Crown's part to yield. It meant a step toward "modernization," that is, toward giving more weight in subsequent decision making to feedback from the field as opposed to feedback from official ideology, in other words, from the stock of dogmatic knowledge predominant at the time; including the fourfold laws of Aquinas, the Aristotelian doctrine of natural inferiority, and Roman *jus gentium*.

The learning center specializing in selective learning and communication proceeded with considerable autonomy of action by laying out an experimental set-up to explore the extent of change demanded by the pressures toward modernization.

Information gained from these explorations provided guidelines for "binding" corrective decision making throughout the system.

Decision making thus led to legalized and institutionalized modifications in the predominant ideology. The implementation of power induced changes in the power principle itself. These modifications were endorsed and implemented by the control center, but the error-reducing corrective output was frustrated, to a significant degree, by emergent splits and by resisting mechanisms in the field. These, typically, adhered to the older type of dogmatic ideology.

Once the ideological change was legalized, it assumed the nature of a new "working" ideology which, in comparison with the initial ideology, was more articulate, more up to date, and more sensitive to segmental pressures in the field. Still, the unity of the system was preserved through it.

In a common sociological conceptualization, the official modification of an ideology, such as that accomplished by legislative bodies and governments, comes slowly and is usually an ideological catching up with social actualities.[45] The function of the public sector, in this conceptualization, is seen as an essentially conservative one. This was clearly not the case of colonial Latin America, where the public sector appeared more eager than the intermediate level of colonial administrators to adopt new principles for official programming, and to modernize the colonial institutions. The supreme holders of power labored for very basic change; they were relatively unconcerned with the short-range economic loss that the change would have implied, and relatively more concerned with the long-range ethical and political issues relating to the status of the Indians. The change contemplated was in fact of the kind to work against the vested interests of the localistic power holders; and it would be misleading to assert that the motivations leading to change could somehow be extracted, as the functionalist school implies, from a societal consensus, or that the change ensuing would on all levels reflect the adaptive processes of the total society to its environment. The policy of change, in this instance, was aimed at removing marginality and at institutionalizing practices that would help to remove some of the "errors" of past policy. This is one of the many instances in which the functionalist notion of ideology as the mere crystallization of value preferences of the people proves unrealistic.

Ideology has a directive power of its own, and it operates according to principles that must be analytically dissociated from the tendencies describing individual behavior. As an analytic device, power, linked up with ideology, makes it possible to study social change without resorting to the notion of a consensus prevailing minimally at least throughout the system. In order to remain efficient, power does not require such system-wide support; it can be efficiently applied by playing one sector of the system against another, by pursuing public goals which are in the interest of one sector as against the interest of another sector. Power does not make itself felt by integrating the segmental pressures in an equilibrated way but rather by enforcing, often swiftly, a solution that may hurt the interest of a given sector. Still, it is essential for the holders of power that the system remain whole, that it not lose constituents by either individual or collective disaffiliation, and that it not be infiltrated by elements from rival systems seeking alliance with the dissatisfied "victims" of power. Whenever a power system has lost its capacity to handle dissent or to fend off competition, even the strictest enclosure, rhetorics of unity, "cushioning," or regimentation will fail to prevent the break-up of that system and the emergence of new alliances and new power constellations. Power provides a totalizing solution, always a precarious one involving construction-plus-destruction, to the problems of continuity, which ensue from the formation of new collective movements, interest groups, liberation fronts and other new alignments within the sociopolitical entity. As defined in this essay, power entails the ability of individuals and groups to maintain control over the action output and movement of other individuals and groups by imposing on them restrictions, pushes and pulls, sanctions and attractions, derived not only from individual resources but also from extra-individual societal resources. In changing circumstances, however, power can be maintained only if changes are made in the rhetoric behind the societal action.

Power cannot be considered simply an arbitrary potentiality operating within the reach of the will of the powerful person in the Weberian sense, nor is it only a general "disposition term" as it is used by some other social scientists.[46] It involves in the last instance a disposition of the public sector to yield to political pressure in circumstances where other means of unification have been exhausted and where a threatening image of an impending major "collapse" (loss of unity) on the societal level has been conveyed to the control center, implying a lack of credibility in the established ideology. The disposition to yield entails willingness on the part of the control center to interfere in the field "from above"; this entails the idea of meeting segmental pressures, wherever these emerge, in order to save the oneness of the system. The power holders' creative apprehension of reality relates to their capacity to see, in case major frustrations threaten political unity, that things cannot go on in the usual manner and that a change in the quality of the approach is called for.

The general background for the study of power includes not only the personal benevolence, love, or enlightenment of the control holder, or his lack of these qualities, but also whatever image is projected to him from the field of any pending peril of sufficient scope to threaten the bases of the existing social order. This image involves a notion of the "swelling effect" of the ills; sometimes it involves scapegoatism, a personification of the ills *behind* the isolated ills. "Many" disturbances, incidents, "sins" in theological parlance, disobedience, corruption, and deviance are publicly defined as being vested in an enemy and as creating polarization, latent disloyalty, anarchy, or general disorder of magnitude to threaten the system with total chaos. Over the course of several centuries, the Hebrew notion of "Satan" has undergone such a polarizing cycle of "personifying the enemy." After having had the conceptually clear-cut, system-bound, and power-bound connotation of obstructor in the earliest Hebrew usage, Satan later came to be understood as the adversary and, still later, influenced by the Manichean dualistic model, as the overall Prince of Evil, a counterpart of the Prince of Peace.

At times in such a situation there can be no factual proof for all to see to substantiate the power holders' anticipation of a pending collapse, but the public sector must proceed by issuing prophesies and warnings regarding the public dilemma. The public sector will resort to depicting a dichotomy between things as they ought to be, in the name of collective security, and things as they are, in reality; this dichotomy it uses as a mobilizing device, charging the participants with the responsibility of legitimate commitment to the official goals. In the presence of such a mobilizing device, sensitivity of the participants will increase insofar as the issue of legitimate action is concerned, and hitherto nonpolitical aspects of social life will become politicized. The initiatory ideology therefore has consequences that go far beyond the goals that were contemplated at the outset, and the collective mobilizing devices will gain a self-generating impetus of their own. In the late Colony, the Inquisition anathematized not only heretics but also seditionaries, *judaizantes* (advocates of semitism), separatists, Jacobin egalitarians, Encyclopedists, materialists, atheists, deists, Lutherans, and Calvinists, as if these heterogenous elements constituted one single body inimical to public order and one single source of civil war. In this sense, Finlay, Holsti, and Fagen speak of the "fusion of internal and external enemies," even though the events themselves seldom explain the emergence of political of enmity.[47] Under such circumstances the established leadership labors to dispel feelings of collective insecurity by enhancing the legitimacy principle. Guglielmo Ferrero, in his insightful essay on power, points out how the principle of legitimacy, in an atmosphere of mutual fear between the power holders and the subjects of power, serves to dispel the fear, making it possible to replace force with consent, and how, in fact, the principle of legitimacy emerges from mutual fear.[48]

The image of pending crisis not only heightens the people's awareness of the officially emphasized distinction between legitimate and illegitimate action but is also useful to the power holders as a campaign strategy. Thus Bertram Gross speaks of "crisis creation" as a strategy for justifying the designs of national planners.[49] The notion easily leads to one of conspiracy, implying that the rulers schemingly capitalize on the nation's worst problems in order to build their fame and power upon the ruins of honest politics. Irving Louis Horowitz speaks in a pejorative sense of the "norm of conflict" in modern Latin America; he mentions its capacity to create the perception in its citizens that the State provides a "survival pattern" in response to latent structural sources of instability, such as population explosion, crop failures, transportation and communication breakdowns.[50] In today's Latin America, such great emphasis is placed on the ethos of development that a familiar "survival pattern" is increasingly often found in the ability of a strong government to steer the country away from economic decline. An example may be cited from the speech by Arturo da Costa e Silva, the late president of Brazil, on the third anniversary of his presidency in March 1969. His dictatorial measures, the president claimed, have proved justified as an alternative to the economic, moral, and political chaos into which the country "would have fallen" if the government had not infringed on the rights of the Congress and the State legislatures, if it had not imposed censorship, and if it had not stripped members of the opposition, including three former presidents and about a hundred members of Congress, of their political rights. In 1968, the president asserted, the country had achieved a 6.5 per cent increase in national product, exported $1,890 millions worth of goods, increased electrical power by 8.7 per cent and built more than 1,200 miles of roads. Achievements of this kind, the logic of power implies, are due to the direction by the public sector, and this must be maintained even at the expense of ideals that have been cherished in the past, such as the ideal of the freedom of the individual. The alternative is inevitable collective decline, confusion, or loss of face.

In this case as in general, the power holder claims to have recourse to predictive power irrespective of the evidence immediately available. Guidelines for political action, in the politics of power, are deduced not from comparisons of past records nor from correlating statistical trends which trace development over time. Rather, they are deduced from the presupposed superiority of the ideological design adopted by the power holder, from the certainty that it will ultimately triumph over counterdesigns, and from the monopoly of his design on legitimacy.

The more sensitive the holders of power become to the latent tensions within the system the less tolerant they may prove toward ideological infiltration from the outside. This was probably true of the Spanish colonial government as a whole: it increased restrictions on colonial trade; it prevented the viceroyalties from communicating with the United States and with each other, and imposed other censorship on the communication of ideas; the Inquisition reached the peak of its activities in the late eighteenth century. On the other hand, within the colonial bureaucracy itself there appeared an innovating minority of reformists who were close enough to the center of power to safely embrace bold programs for administrative and ideological change without the risk of appearing to be revolutionaries. In the independent republics toward the end of the nineteenth century the positivists revived the same notion of scientifically induced change sponsored by strong governments. Although the model of scientific management in government became increasingly unpopular among Latin American intellectuals after World War I, subsequent developments suggest a return to the traditional practice of benevolent dictatorship and technocracy, a practice deeply embedded in the Hispanic and Hispanic American political thought.

For these innovators ("learning centers" within the power system) to operate efficiently, that is, to change from a simple conservative-administrative function to a "learning" function, they must share with the control center an awareness of the shortcomings of the existing official set of "ultimates" (ideology) to cover, explain, and control the long-term empirical situation. The inadequacy and costliness of war measures, state-of-siege measures, police-statism, and prohibitions may undermine the people's confidence in their leaders, thus forcing the latter to reexamine the basic tenets of the political credo which in the past were taken for granted. The leaders' dilemma becomes one of *creatively fitting* an empirical situation that is rich in counterevidence and inconsistent, to the traditionally transmitted official frame. Unless the innovators and leaders have an awareness of the contradictions between the existing ideology and the emerging empirical complexity, they cannot give a rational explanation for a deliberate intention to change. This point is similar to the one Karl R. Popper and others have made regarding the general problem of the formation of knowledge.[51] Any situation, one may generalize, will grow out of hand, making the precautionary measures and justifications of order adopted in the past appear inadequate and out of place.

In the sociopolitical setting with a single established ideology, an error-regulating feedback system[52] is introduced by the establishment to "save" oneness despite the changes that are introduced. This error-regulating feedback response may be more articulate and thus less comprehensive in scope than the initial programming. "Target" problems are redefined and narrowed down by the control centers and by the learning centers, the salience of certain key issues is recognized, and the massiveness of the task of saving ideological oneness is reduced to a pragmatic "working" ideology. Types of error-regulating mechanisms may be distinguished, corresponding to the direction the power holder's disposition to yield takes.

We shall examine the main types of error-regulating mechanisms and some of their implications for research, as these mechanisms may be extracted from Las Casas' attempt at fitting ideals to realities (*Figures 2–7*).

"Cushioning" as Corrective Gubernatorial Action. Decision makers sometimes respond to resistance by making the power system appear not merely threatening but also attractive. This they may do by promising to the constituents a better future; by showing responsiveness so as to sustain hope whose validity will be demonstrated in the future; and by enhancing the image of common good, improving security, and increasing other benefits derived from belonging to the system. Power cannot forever rest upon the ability of the stronger to kill; naked power cannot last for long. This is why the "loving" aspect of power is emphasized in

ancient mythologies, for instance, as the softening principle for divine wrath. Thus leaders seek popular support for their power by cushioning it, stressing the efficiency and the utilitarian value of a power-bound system.

One primary type of cushioning simply entails a showy display of impressive symbolism, oratory, and pomposity. The System, the Cause, or the Leader are dramatized as worthy of devotion or cult. In the showy tone, what one says may excite less than how one says it. The Aztec priests, standing in the back of their cave-temples, let their voices ring from behind awe-inspiring masks; their people could hear them but not see them clearly. Jargon and elaborate phraseology obscure the language of the people. Key words are loaded with suggestive power that is derived from their ritualistic usage. The enemy is called by name and this word-label is placed on whatever is not firmly in line with legitimacy. Ultimately, all people become either Christians or enemies of Christianity; the world is reduced to black and white.

Another type of cushioning may entail "charitable" attempts to alleviate, through remedial public action, the ills and abuses existing. Both types of cushioning action are schematically illustrated in *Figure 2*. The command output *k* by the powerful actor A remains unchanged, and so does the supervised output *d* from the powerless actor *B*. The gate-keeping mechanism *P-M* is softened, however, and the softening is expected to lessen the destructiveness of *B*'s spontaneous response *b* and also to lessen *B*'s attempt *c* to escape the power circle. Since the cushioning action is still basically derived from the official ideology Z, it involves no risk to the legitimacy of the principle of continuance, and no fundamental modifications beyond the elaborations involved in "softening" the official command. The system must go on, the rationale of cushioning implies, because by perpetuating the system we will be capable of offering certainty and continuity instead of dissolution. *Trust* becomes the key term. "You will be fully rewarded if you stay with us." By cushioning, the public sector makes an effort to decrease the credibility gap, to publicize and popu-

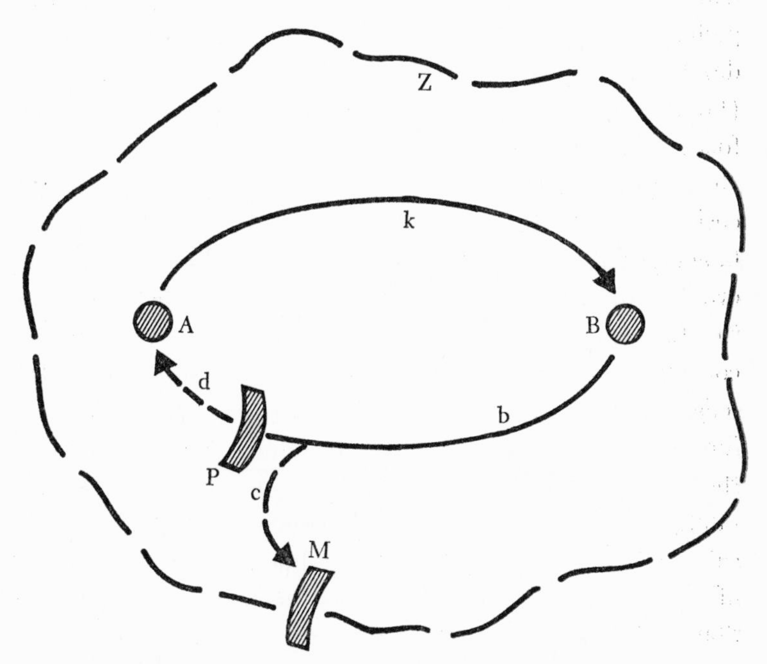

Figure 2. The cushion response in a power system

larize the virtues and benefits of the power system, in order to demand belongingness to it, and to mobilize what Karl Mannheim calls a "cant mentality" among the subjects. Some sort of public relations activity will be initiated.

Examples of a showy response immediately after the Conquest include gift-giving to the Indians, schemed generosity (the hospitality, for instance, cacique Juan was shown during his visit to the capital city), and attention to details of dress and official regalia. In another type of showy action the Spanish Crown invested in luxury projects such as public buildings and monuments, so as to make the capital cities in Latin America ornate showplaces for power. This practice of urban planning has been perpetuated by many latter-day dictator-presidents in Latin America, who prefer monument building to less spectacular projects. The development of charitable institutions in Latin America (hospitals, orphanages, and the like) may be studied by focusing not on their functionality in meeting the overall "needs" of the society in abstraction but rather on the cushion effect these institutions had initially on specific target populations. Latin American hospitals, for instance, evolved from the asylums priests had founded to lodge the thousands of abandoned *mestizo* children collected in country villages and brought to cities in the protection of the religious orders. From these beginnings hospitals developed into self-maintaining institutions; some were relocated in the countryside where they became self-sufficient farm-hospitals, abolished later as a consequence of the anticlerical policy of the independent republics in the second half of the nineteenth century; others were transferred to the State. This illustrates the tendency of a charitable, error-regulating public policy to ramify into institutional and organized welfare development, variously justified by different patronizing power systems.

Symbolism and the performing arts may be used to heighten the impressive effect of showy public action. In the early years of the Colony, the priests in New Spain labored to impress the Indians by staging religious plays, which sometimes depicted the Christians capturing Jerusalem from the infidels. With their colorful banners, the soldiers of Castile and León would march to the town square, carrying their swords and shields. They would be followed by Germans, Romans, and Italians, all of them under the benevolent eye of the Pope, and of the Kings of Spain, France, and Hungary. The Christian soldiers would then receive the Holy Sacrament; they would receive a sign from Santiago, the patron saint of Spain; and they would advance to a crushing victory over the infidels. In general, the showy display of power includes the use of protective symbols, of emblems, titles, protocol, ceremony, flags and rallies; attempts to impress the subjects by slogans, warning of enemy, scapegoating, promises, sayings; and adherence to the rhetoric of God sponsoring the legitimate rulership.

The old regime of the Iberian nations employed the cushioning effect to the extreme. In Latin America, as Francisco Bilbao (1823–1865) and other liberalist writers bitterly pointed out in the mid-nineteenth century, it was the Church which served as the leading advocate of blind belief, tutelage, patronage, myth, symbolism, formality, ceremony, pomposity, obscurantism, and respect for the legitimacy principle. The caudillos, one might add, could put up a similar effect of grandeur through their military accouterments and bravado. The same window-dressing life style marked the hacienda owner and the mine owner. Some documents of the early colonial period tell of owners of mines whose wives "went to church accompanied by a hundred servants, and twenty mistresses and maids," and who kept "their houses open to all who wanted to come to dinner."[53] Against the display of power that the caudillos were capable of furnishing in the independent republics, the European-oriented constitutionalists and political idealists ("*doctores*," as they were often called in contrast to the caudillos) must have seemed colorless. They were unable to mobilize the celebrations, festivities and rituals that the traditionalists could, in order to win over and maintain populist loyalties.

The cushioning of public action involves the idea that permanent political organization is based not on coercion alone or on voluntarism alone but on an appropriate blending of the two elements of political control. Machiavelli, among the first, elaborated guidelines for the planful mobilization of the people for the purposes of power by producing a cushioning effect. The Prince, he said, should combine the wisdom of a fox with the strength of a lion. He should be merciful; yet, he should not mind severity whenever it induces unity and loyalty. It would be better for the principality if the Prince were feared rather than loved. "For instance," Machiavelli proposed, "a prince should seem to be merciful, faithful, humane, religious, and upright, and should even be so in reality; but he should have his mind so trained that, when occasion requires it, he may know how to change to the opposite." [54]

In Spain and Portugal, however, the apologists of monarchy were always careful to keep away from the Machiavellian principles. Benevolent despotism was the official ideology after the days of the Hispanic Enlightenment. By this was meant, to follow Gaspar Melchor Jovellanos (1744–1811), minister of justice under Court favorite Manuel Godoy, that man has always lived in society (a principle that endorses the Aristotelian notion of man as a "political animal" and contradicts Rousseau's notion of a willful social contract); that man is essentially weak and ignorant; and that the ruler's task is the necessary one of communicating the "light" of learning and science from the creative intelligentsia to the best of his subjects, so as to apply from above the ultimate principles upon which the welfare of the people must be built.

In this view, the cushioning action of the power holders is justified, not because it is derived from the populist sentiment or from the consent of the governed, but because the power holders *claim* that it will be charitable, just, and righteous in the long run. Power in itself is a necessary principle, the traditional Hispanic theory of statesmanship declares. In its insistence on power, this theory is diametrically opposed to the Anglo-Saxon one that the government is best which intervenes least. In the Hispanic view, the State must impose its power upon individual wills, in order to serve as the mobilizing force within a responsible, obedient, and at times passive people. These ideas inspired the Spanish and the Portuguese politicians in the late eighteenth century; at this time the French "ideologists" were laboring to establish a view of society based on individual energies in agglomeration, and the British were laboring to establish an economy of free enterprise along the individualistic principle of *ubi bene ibi patria* (wherever it is good, there is my fatherland). People, the corporate, power-oriented Iberian principle of statesmanship implies, before they are given their full political freedoms, should first understand fully the duties that freedom implies. Otherwise freedom will turn into anarchical license. State power must be forever bolstered, fortified, consolidated, and window-dressed. Public power in itself is for the common benefit, for there exists a natural bond between the ruler and the subject, deriving from the very lawfulness of Nature and integrating the subject tighter into the protective body politic into which he is born. The fact that coups d'état are characteristic of the Hispanic American political systems does not reflect the Latin Americans' disregard for the political bond itself, but rather it reflects their fractionalism, familism, and personalism in politics, and the readiness for their military to step in as a moderating force.

In contrast to the power-oriented Hispanic tradition, the French revolutionary philosophy introduced a view suspicious of power. Rousseau gravely cautioned against the evils of power, particularly if it was exercised by a monarch. Perhaps it is true, he conceded, that there is no government which possesses more vigor than monarchy, with all responding to the same mover, and all the springs of the machine being regulated by the same hand. Yet, in no other government does the private will (as opposed to general will) have greater influence than it has in the monarchist one. Kings derive their absolute power from the affections of the people, but even the best king will want to use his power to do not only good but also evil. Thus, the king will want to keep the people weak and miserable, so that they will lack the power to resist. The apologists of royal power, Rousseau argued, will accept it without murmuring, as the chastisement of Heaven. Thus, for Rousseau, the whole principle of monarchy is deceptive. "What should we say to a physician who promises miracles, but whose whole art is to exhort the sick man to be patient."

In the French Revolution's "ideology," the State and indeed all deliberative public power could easily be explained away. These were processes thought to be explainable by man's natural constitution; since society was an abstract individual "writ in large," and man was thought to be related directly to the "powers of Nature," the intervening governmental mechanisms became unnecessary. Thus the perplexing indifference of many of the thinkers of the French and British Enlightenment toward the actual forms of government. Any form of government, they thought, would be workable if it relied on sound reason and obeyed Nature.

If one accepts, in the manner of the Hispanic philosophers, the common-good theory of the State, the problem is then one of explaining in what precisely the common good resides. More often than not, the State policy was associated with the ideal of grandeur, expansion, and progress—this then became the cushioning motive that made up the ethos of nationalism. Few men in the history of the Iberian nations have applied the promise of grandeur and welfare in the cushioning function as effectively as did the Marquis of Pombal (1699–1782), the prime minister and dictator of Portugal. It was under Pombal that the Jesuits were banished (for intriguing and rivalry against State power), the sway of the Inquisition was broken, elementary education was established, the army was reorganized, agriculture and commerce were advanced, and the colonization of Brazil was greatly bolstered.

What then was, in Pombal's own view, the particular pride of his benevolent dictatorship? The national worth of Portugal has been restored, he claimed. Those people who have denigrated Portugal have been proved wrong—those who, "with arrogance, vainglory, and imaginary superiority, have hitherto regarded the Portuguese people as ignorant, rude, inert, and destitute of all the elements and principles of the mechanical and liberal arts." [55] By now, Pombal added, the Portuguese not only are on a par with those nations, but they surpass most of them. The common good, in other words, consists of promised national grandeur, which alone makes individual fulfillment possible. The rationale of nationalism, which during the Renaissance replaced medieval Catholicism, made obsolete Catholicism's cherished motif, *memento mori* (remember that you will have to die). From the notion of government as a necessary whip there was a transition to the notion of life-giving government. Power was now to be reconciled with the principle *juvat vivere*: "It is a pleasure to be alive!" The power of commanding, correcting, and chastising was to be based not only on the alleged weakness, immaturity, ignorance, and ill will of the people but also on the wholesome, prideful effect that goes along with nationalistic regime. Adam's fall and man's corruption and viciousness were not the only reasons that the use of power was necessary; men were compelled toward a power-bound social order because in it they found the only rationale that makes progress possible.

Hobbes and Locke, in the history of modern political thought, represent those who commend the life-giving potentiality of the body politic; for them, as Hobbes describes it, the pacts and covenants which constitute the body politic resemble nothing less than the creative act whereby man in the true sense came into being. The "ideologists" of the French Revolution, the nineteenth-century liberals, and the evolutionists, however, destroyed the common-good notion of political power and erected in its place the notion of the "spontaneous forces of society." Common good, the new doctrine held, resides in the civil sector, not the polity. Society, in the words of Herbert Spencer, "goes on without any ministerial overseeing." In the Western thought, political power in fact became increasingly suspect. The nineteenth-century liberal tradition outspokenly linked government with coercion, bureaucratization, corruption, pettishness, and the manipulation of mass sentiment. "In every political personality," Gustav Ratzenhofer wrote in 1892, "by virtue of their political position, absolute hostility must prevail. The masses will never fully support political causes which will offer them no visible and tangible benefit." [56]

Whereas the Anglo-Saxon liberals decried political abuse, governmental intervention, the social-class bias of governments, and the inefficacy of public action, Latin American social thought inherited from the Iberian model of benevolent despotism an optimistic notion of elite guidance. It was believed that, through this guidance, the conflicts of class interest, ruralism and urbanism, federalism and unitarism could be overcome in a beneficial harmonizing national synthesis brought about by the new-found national association and national consciousness. These are the ideas that predominate, for instance, in the writings of Esteban Echeverría (1805–1851), the Argentine founder of the Asociación de Mayo. Responsible national leadership, this view implies, cannot be abusive; its role is analogous to that of Platonic philosopher-kings. Political union and harmony in nature are thought of in similar terms. Power is seen in its tutelary function, disciplining and refining the instincts of the masses for their ultimate benefit. The "reason of the people" must be recognized as a potentiality that may eventually be granted to all social classes. For the time being, however, reason must be exercised by the prudent and rational elements of the society.

Latin American political thought, from the elitist philosophy of the era of Independence to the positivism of the late nineteenth century and to the technocratic *desarrollismo* (the ideology of developmentalism) of the mid-twentieth century, tends to separate, analytically, the command from above from the spontaneous initiatives and pressures from below, and to proclaim the virtues of the former. Unlike liberalism and Marxist socialism, Latin American thought is suspicious of attempts of the civil sectors to define themselves in spontaneous action. Liberty must not be confused with license, the Latin American tradition holds. On the positive side, the tendency that Latin American philosophy demonstrates to separate legal imperatives from social norms renders it more sensitive to the political components of change, in comparison with the Anglo-Saxon tendency toward apolitical sociologism.

Whether the Latin American cushioning tendency to justify public action is warranted or not cannot be immediately decided. Most social analysts would agree, however, that in a society where spontaneous growth is arrested by structural marginality inherited from the past, some coercion and cushioning are required to overcome the obstacles to social mobility. In Latin America, a Perón or a Castro derives his appeal not only from the cult of person, from the attraction that a charismatic leader displays, or from some other political idiosyncrasy of the Latin American politics. He derives his appeal also from a realistic notion that power is urgently called for in a society getting rid of the segmental power of the landed classes and other inherited class privileges; and that only a strong man has the capacity to terminate the dependence of these societies on the advanced industrial-center powers of the world. The role of coercive politics, in Latin America, is seen in its capacity to uplift the lower classes, to implement social justice, and thus to enforce the totalizing promise that cushioning entails. Most Latin American political thinkers agree on the singular importance of governmental power as a progressive tool, and the fact that many Latin American strong men have failed to live up to their totalizing promise has tended only to sensitize public opinion to the use and abuse of power.

Whether cushioning is an undesirable element of public action cannot be immediately decided. Political promises and cushioning, one might say, do not in themselves make public action wrong. They may impart a sense of security, commitment, nationalistic zeal, and responsibility; and these are political amenities that no government can forego. Although the cushioning aspect of public power may appear as an illusory, sham ideology, people may need the opportunity for public commitments that the politics of cushioning provides, the rallying points that bring them together and move the civil sectors toward cooperative effort. The politics of cushioning is simply the power holders' mode of obtaining political support by projecting a future full of promise and by laboring to prove themselves the "servants" of the people who must work to bring about this future.

On the negative side, cushioning stands for a search for certainty which can never be fully established. It necessarily leads to official hypocrisy. On the positive side, it is a political must. It requires the projection into the future of end-states and the proposal of workable means of obtaining them, end-states and means that will move people into action within the system and keep them from leaving it or combining in alliances against it. Any sociopolitical power involves both a coercive aspect and a protective charitable one; by cushioning the system, the holders of power endeavor to strike a balance between these aspects, in order to appear to the people as a benevolent life line rather than a hateful Leviathan.

Education as an Aspect of Public Policy. Overlapping in practice with the cushion response, education as an aspect of public policy (*Figure 3*) involves the notion of improvement in the powerless role *B*, guided by principles derived from the ideological superstructure Z, which supports the powerful role A. The gate-keeping mechanism in the power system *P-M* is open, but permanent modifications in *B*'s output *b* are expected to occur. This is the idea of education as a ladder, eventually leading to social and political competence and equalization. Education was fully exploited

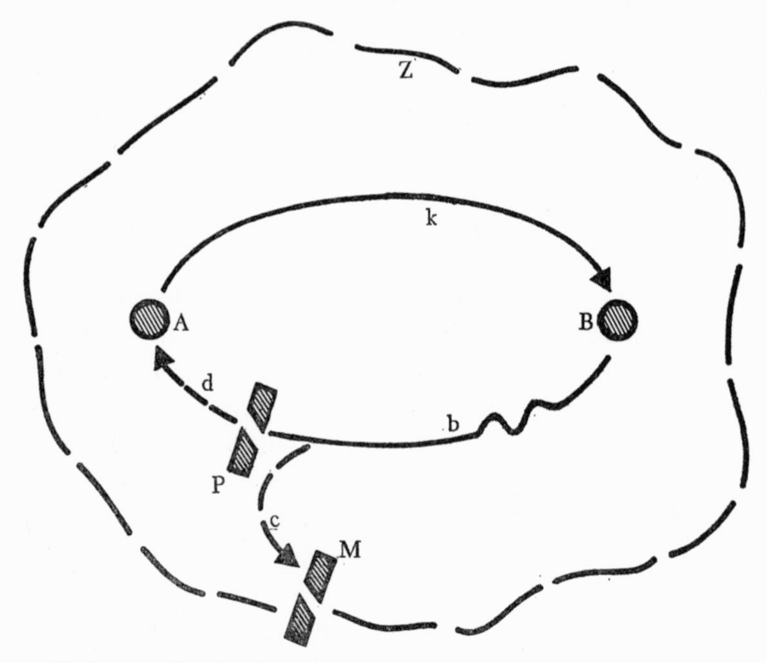

Figure 3. The education response in a power system

in Sepúlveda's design for encomienda; in Las Casas it was modified, and included such things as the training of the Indians, and the weeding out of non-European ways of life. Education as an established type of action "from above" must be distinguished from socialization. By the socialization of an individual, we mean his absorption of normative influences through his experience in the pluralistic group life that his activities impose upon him. Education as a gubernatorial activity involves the cultivation, by the appointed guardians, of people's skills, morals, and loyalties, their training for new duties, their counseling; education also involves the establishment's function in given areas of legally substituting its judgment for that of the private citizen, and the function of informing the civil sector of the rights and amenities that legitimately belong to it.

A publicly sponsored school system labors to combine the guidance quality with the initiatives arising from the civil sectors, in a more or less precarious balance. In Latin America, the centralized quality of guidance traditionally prevails over the civil initiative, but attempts to reverse this within the so-called "community-school" system have gained support since the 1950's. Community school, ideally, is the one reflecting the interests and needs of the local communities and thus emerging as an instrument of the grass-roots movements promoting social change.

This ideal of a community school, however, is rarely achieved; in Latin America the rural schools especially are at best service institutions; they impart skills and values reflecting standards that are alien to the peasant. The failure of the public schools to bridge the gap between public ideals and grass-roots realities is even more remarkable if one considers the prominent role education has traditionally been given in Latin American thought, as the prime mover of progress and as one of the most agreed-upon strategies for dealing with the Indian issue and with that of the lower classes in general. Since the days of independence, the rhetorics of education occupies in Latin American ideologies a role analogous to the missionary motif of the colonial religiosos. The first generation of intelligentsia in the independent republics, men like Argentina's Esteban Echeverría, propounded the salience of education and the need "to toil over the masses." Argentina's educator-president Domingo Faustino Sarmiento, in the late 1860's, described his country as one "where education is everything, where education has succeeded in establishing true democracy, making races and classes equal." [57] In the late nineteenth century, both liberals and conservatives in Latin America hailed public education as the panacea for social ills; and the positivists in Mexico and elsewhere since the 1870's considered education the main instrument of their policy of "order and progress."

It was only in the 1920's that Peru's writer José Carlos Mariátegui and some others realized fully that the modern public school, even if it could keep pace with the increasing number of rural children of school age, is incompatible with *gamonalismo*, the rural power system of latifundio. "The mechanics of servitude," he said, "would completely annul the action of the school. . . . The school and the teacher are irremissibly condemned to become deprived of their true nature under the pressure of the feudal environment." [58]

The theory of power brings this fundamental Latin American dilemma into focus. The major power systems in rural Latin America, in this theory, are seen to represent variants of a confrontation pattern. The official educational ideology, endorsed by the rural teacher, emphasizes the role of education as the principal avenue to social mobility within the national system, whereas the hacienda owner (who frequently finances the school) adheres to the principle of an occupationally immobile labor force. In these circumstances, the rural teacher is definitely out of place. She is trained to focus on skills demanded mainly outside the school locality; she will probably have an urban background, and she will probably live in a nearby town. After the children have learned the "four R's" (the basics in reading, writing, arithmetic, and religion), both the peasant parent and the patron will want them to drop out of school to assume their roles in the labor force. Education in birth control would have, incidentally, about the same chances of success in the peasant communities. Even if the spiritual and moral restrictions on birth control were removed, the peasant head of the family, the wife's sometimes narcissistic self-pity notwithstanding, will represent the power principle in matters of sex; he will consider the economic advantage involved in having many children: they can be employed in outside labor, and they constitute the principle source of security for their parents' old age. In these areas as in general, while the functionalists study the "whole" educational institution in relation to the "needs" of "the society," studies oriented to power exploit the notion of divergent ideologies and counterideologies within the various system levels.

That localistically oriented power systems in the area of education can resist the official system despite improvements in overall efficacy seems indicated, for example, in the case of Cuba in the first half of the twentieth century. The ratio of teachers to the number of children of school age was doubled in Cuba from 1902 to 1952, and an effort was made to modernize education by, among other things, doubling the ratio of the class rooms per teacher; yet, school attendance rose only from 51 to 54 per cent during the same period.[59] The quality of education undoubtedly improved, but, within the rural power system of plantation economy, education did not correspondingly penetrate the society.

Administration as an Aspect of Public Policy. Administration is concerned with the application and channeling of the established ideology through the delegation of duties of public nature by instituting a legal network of subordinate power. It includes replacements in administrative duties and personnel, sanctioning, new definition of administrative roles, appointment and promotion, the creation of new public roles and the elimination of others, jurisdic-

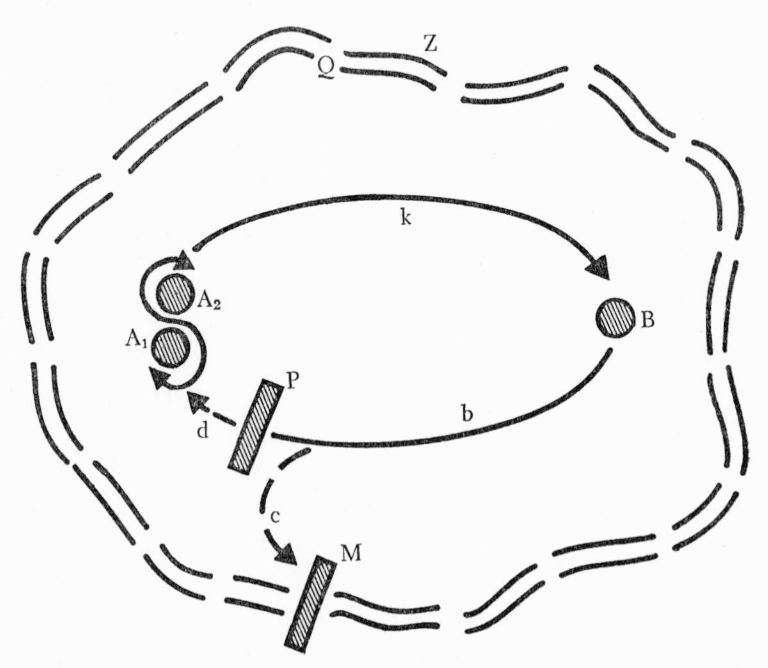

Figure 4. The administrative response in a power system through changes in the command role

tional changes affecting the boundaries of the target populations, and such reorganization and allocation of resources as land reforms. An example (*Figure 4*) is Las Casas' proposal to replace Spanish encomenderos A_1 by administrators A_2 appointed by the Crown. Another example (*Figure 5*) is Las Casas' proposal to replace Indian labor B_1 by slave labor B_2 and thus to obtain an administrative overhaul. One of the key issues in administrative response is the increased complexity induced "from above," that is, through controlled planning, in the structure of the official network of relationships of command. On the level of ideologies, the redistribution of political duties involves splits Z-Q and increasing specificity in responsibility within the initially

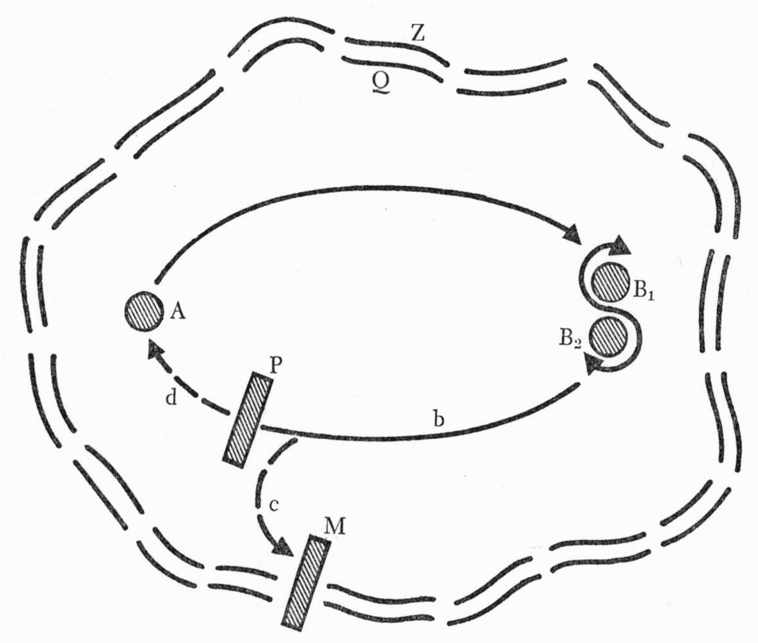

Figure 5. The administrative response in a power system through changes in a powerless role

unified systemic ideology. Las Casas' plan to isolate Indian areas from the power of the encomenderos, for example, implied a split between the spiritual and the exploitative spheres of responsibility regarding the European penetration in the New World.

The administrative response is concerned when the power holder modifies or widens the institutions through which his mandate is being implemented and diffused. It includes, as in Locke's and Montesquieu's models for the State, the separation of executive, legislative, and judicial powers. When the power holder thus creates an institutional frame to implement his power, Adolf A. Berle observed, he becomes "responsible" to his creation; institutions inevitably exert influence over him; he must take them into account in everything he does. If he fails to keep them in working condition or alienates their personnel, or if his actions are contrary to the principles upon which the institutions are founded, he may weaken their effectiveness.[60] There are, moreover, several other consequences that ensue from the creation of mediating institutions: the duplicity of function—very much in evidence in colonial Latin America; the difficulty in keeping family responsibilities apart from loyalties to the Nation (the problem of nepotism); the tendency of the administrative personnel to proliferate out of all proportion and to become riddled by graft and corruption, and their commitment to self-perpetuation instead of to the initial ideology. In colonial Latin America, corruption, the duplicity of function, and bureaucratic rivalry became suffocating. Several institutions created at different times were in competition with one another, Indian leadership conflicted with the authority of the European administrators and judges, Crown authority conflicted with that of the Church and the military, the visiting investigators interfered with the function of the viceroys and the royal courts, and toward the end of the colonial period Creole enterprise militated against Crown monopolies. The administrative mode of yielding, one might say, totally failed in the colonies; power was not successfully delegated; overcentralization resulted in administrative overreaching, with the colonial administration endeavoring to have a say in every little detail and the Creole landowners gaining in actual fact in power.

The ill effects of public administrative practice have prompted some social philosophers to devise a model for the State in which the institutional delegation of power is virtually nonexistent. Rousseau's was such an early model. No man or administrative body, for Rousseau, can have the right to make laws and to carry out executive action in the place of the body of the citizens at large. Their constant participation in the immediate exercise of their inalienable sovereignty is necessary to keep the State machinery in operation. Although only the Greek city-state or other small political units of the same sort could follow a model like Rousseau's, it has had appeal, in Latin America particularly, among the advocates of direct democracy and citizens' direct political action, in the nineteenth and twentieth centuries.

The delegated authority belonging to the administrative personnel, by its very nature, is conservative rather than innovative. It is not the function of the power holder's representatives to modify the established ideology; their function is to implement it in an impersonal and unchanging manner. Kings' ministers claim merit not for innovation but for their staunch loyalty. The lower echelon of public administrators, therefore, becomes the natural target of popular discontent. In Latin America, the oppressed focused their ire on the corregidores and on the lower officials in the colonial bureaucracy rather than on the monarch. Insurrectionary movements such as the one launched in the early nineteenth century in Mexico by Miguel Hidalgo characteristically derived their striking force not from anti-monarchist feelings but from the peasants' and the Indians' desire to come to the defense of the king against bad administration.

The basic weakness of the colonial regime in Latin America arose from its inability to implement in full the administrative response to pressures from below throughout the system. Regional strong men remained in a power position autonomous enough to challenge the central government. Gamonalismo (from *gamón*, a parasitic plant), the rule of local aristocracy, became predominant; it enabled the landlords to maintain their small realms within the larger political units, to command the labor force, to monopolize the peasants' political affiliation, to deprive men of their land, and to compel them to sell their labor. The kind of interception of administrative response that gamonalismo and latifundismo represent was not corrected in the independent republics; quite the contrary, it was reinforced by the principle of federalism, which coincided with the localistic interest of the self-acclaimed power holders. Gamonalismo and latifundismo in Latin America therefore resulted from a power deficit which, except in those countries where basic social revolutions have occurred, still keeps the Latin American political system in a state of immaturity and stagnation. Administrative weakness is perpetuated by the frequent coups —forms of administrative yielding which may bring another strong man or another faction into office, with the replacement resulting in no substantial change of policy.

Partial Release. Partial release is the type of public action that legally exempts from control certain areas of function or certain segments of population in an effort to respond to the pressures from the field by permitting new degrees of autonomy to the civil sectors. It entails the recognition of the legitimacy of popular claims for liberation from earlier dependence. This type of disposition to yield (*Figure* 6) is exemplified by Las Casas' design for the restoration of caciqueship, and by his design for the restitution of free Indian farming. In *Figure* 6, the powerful role A has only segmental control over the surplus output *d* from the power-

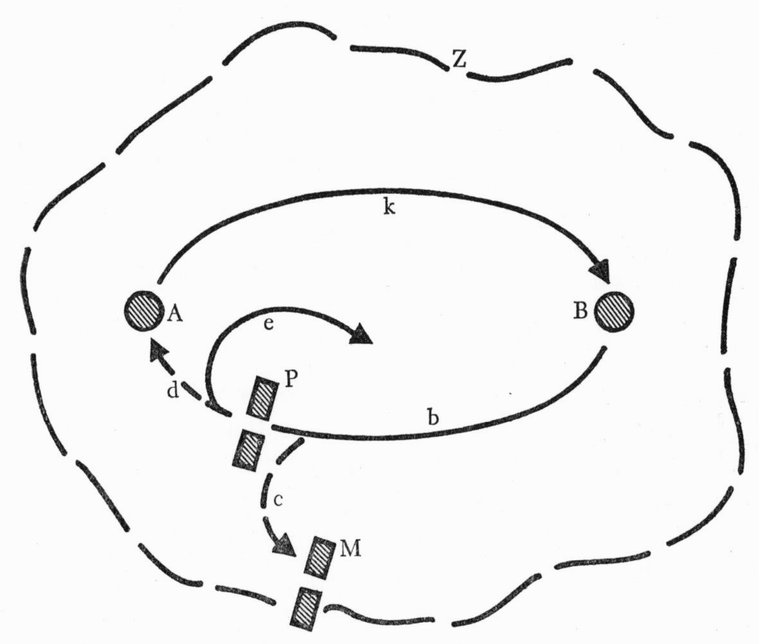

Figure 6. Partial release in a power system

less role *B*. Part of *B*'s output *e* is released from public regulation, to permit segmental self-sufficiency and some self-management independent of the gate-keeping mechanisms of *M-P*. Actor *B*, who represents the civil sectors, is given legal right to freely make use of some benefits of his effort that were inaccessible to him before. The areas of independence, however, are still defined by the powerful role A, and the spontaneity permitted is still within the context of the single ideology Z of the official system.

In colonial Latin America, partial release was sparingly applied. Laws on vagabonds tied the Indians to total dependence, and only Indian communities in the most remote areas could remain outside the European patronage, as pockets of escapees from the colonial system. Censorship and cultural isolation were imposed to curb ideological contamination and the traffic of ideas. Commercial dealings were restricted, and the relaxation of colonial monopoly was considered when it was too late to pacify the anti-imperialistic feelings that it had stirred. The holders of power looked at the sociopolitical structures as if the tendency toward self-sufficiency and liberation did not exist and as if the movement toward self-organization and independence could be kept forever under control.

There are two ways in which the power holders may apply partial release to relax the tensions within the sociopolitical system. Either there are relaxations of some specified controls over the target of power, relaxations such as constitutional guarantees of the freedom of religion, speech, and assembly, or some sectors of the target population are totally disengaged from their legal responsibility to the public sector. The latter type of release permits the formation of breakaway groups, sovereign states, and groups of political exiles. Public power by definition works against breakaway tendencies of this kind, and a drive toward large-scale political disengagement of subunits, such as occurred within the Spanish empire in the early 1800's, will inevitably lead the system to a civil war.

In the colonial system, total allegiance to the central authority, spiritual, political and economic, was exacted on all levels. The *patrón-peón* relationship became one of diffuse, all-encompassing loyalty and dependence. There were always words and phrases—the fight against anarchy, lack of discipline, immorality and vice, vagabondage, the defense of law and order—that could be fitted into arguments against the drive toward partial release.

Upon the collapse of the colonial controls, the first generation of Latin American intellectuals relished the newly acquired self-rule. They dramatized the intellectual break with the past that the Independence entailed, indulged in explorations of the uniqueness of the American freedom, and of the ethos of individualism on which it would be founded. The revolutionary task was seen to consist of combatting the vestiges of the Old Regime, which must be stamped out to free the Latin American thought from the shackles of the commitment to the European ideal of *imperium unum*. Democracy in America was to be founded on the right that everyone had to grow, unhindered by outside authority. The revolts in the mid-nineteenth century Europe captured the minds of the militant young liberals in Latin America, and "revolution" was the catchword that inspired the Creole intellectuals who erected altars to the Goddess of liberty in Buenos Aires and staged abortive coups to overthrow despotism in Lima. Liberty would embrace the new republics lovingly in her bosom.

This ferment of liberalism, however, occurred at a time of political disorder, when elitist factions fought one another for power and the unity of the public frame was lost. The liberal regimes instituted in the new capital cities were crippled by lack of funds, lack of administrative experience, and the hostility of the strong men of the hinterlands. In the faction-torn situation, peace and order were endangered, and many deplored the liberal doctores' propensity to seek remedy in education and philosophic phraseology rather than effective discipline. Caudillismo emerged in these circumstances, not merely as a "deplorable" trend in politics, as critics of the Latin American political systems would call it, but as an alternative response to the insecurities arising from the reshuffling of the power structures after Independence. Beginning with the Argentine writer Domingo Faustino Sarmiento (1811–1888), most Latin American intellectuals have adopted the term "barbarism" as the accepted characterization of the Latin American strong men's politics of power. Liberalist tradition in Latin America has continued to belittle the caudillos' effort to find a substitution for the centralizing power that formerly belonged to the Crown and considers it as a mere reflection of the destructiveness of the Latin American character. There is an impasse between those who insist that development basically consists of setting free the spontaneous initiatives of the people and those who insist that basic reforms in Latin America cannot be carried out in the populist fashion, without resort to power. In recent years, this impasse has resulted in the intellectuals' rejectance of the strong-armed solutions that the military-technocratic governments in various Latin American countries have sought to find to the problems of modernization.

The controversy between the liberals and the technocrats over matters of development thus arose in Latin America along with Independence. The intellectuals generally believed that "education in liberty" and the full recognition of man's natural faculties would spontaneously usher in a new moral order; and that whatever had been obtained by liberal populist policies in Europe would serve as a model for Latin America. The caudillos instead claimed that the termination of the Spanish rule in America had left a vacuum, that the European experience in Latin America was useless, and that the power vacuum involved could be filled, not with abstract notions of the "ideas-forces" hidden in man, as the French-inspired liberalists maintained, but with an agrarian-oriented economy and the pragmatic rule of a strong-willed man. Independence only increased the insecurities to which the Latin Americans were exposed, Argentine caudillo Juan Manuel de Rosas (1793–1877) argued in 1820. "The benefits of association have cruelly vanished." The solution, therefore, was not to be found in liberal egalitarianism or in more freedoms. This only would lead to anarchy. In the political system that Rosas imposed upon the Argentines, consequently, no release existed, and the head of the State had "faculties as unlimited as is necessary in order to erect and effectively organize the walls of respect and security." [61]

Some prominent ideologists of Latin American independence, such as Fray José Fermín Sarmiento (1772–1812) of Paraguay, had proposed what they called "the theory of reversion," implying that sovereignty, in the absence of a monarch, must revert to the people from whom it emanated, and that a Constituent Assembly must be called for all the emancipated people, as the only possessor of legitimate power. Emancipation would then be carried out through a single body to whom all political power would belong.*

No unbroken transfer of power to a single holder could be achieved, however. Bolívar was fully aware of the "differing conditions, opposing interests, and variations of characteristics" that divide the Latin Americans. But he did envision a Confederation of Latin American nations (excluding the La Plata region, Chile, and Brazil), which would reinforce and solidify independence. In a Confederation of this kind, Bolívar

* Herein lies, in fact, the kernel of the controversial issue of the Latin American unity. Such a unity must be assumed to exist, initially at least, since the independent Republics emancipated from the rule of the same monarch. Brazil and Haiti are the most notable exceptions.

believed, Mexico could assume a leading role. Quite soon it became apparent, however, that internal disputes would prevent the Confederation from materializing and that even Bolívar's ambition to create a permanent union between Colombia and Venezuela would be eventually frustrated. The first Hispanic American Congress (an idea originated by Bolívar) was called to meet in Panama in 1826. The agenda dealt with items such as legislative unification, the settlement of disputes, and the creation of a common army. Only a token success was attained, with Gran Colombia alone ratifying the very limited agreements made. The invitations extended to the United States, Great Britain, and Holland to send their delegates to Panama changed the nature of the Congress at the last moment from a Latin American affair into a Panamerican and an international one.

No political supersystem analogous to the power of the Crown came into existence in Latin America; in this sense, the individual nation-states emerging, with all their weaknesses and internal splits, were "released" from the previous supranational bond, free to direct their own destinies. The issue is important because the failure of the Latin American unity to materialize in political terms made it possible for the Monroe Doctrine of 1823 to take its place. This was the principle, unilaterally declared by the president of the United States, "that the American continents . . . are henceforth not to be considered as subjects for future colonization by any European power," and that the prerogative and responsibility of hemispheric defense henceforth belonged to the United States.

A special case of partial release in colonial Latin America was the granting of legal privileges such as the *fueros*, legal exemptions, to the colonial clergy and the military. The monolithic political component was hereby fragmented to serve segmental interests, which at the time seemed essential for the totality but later on became obsolete. Political concessions of this nature reflect a power deficiency rather than populist interest in enhancing political participation or self-determination. In theory, as the early liberalists in Latin America would assume, the assignment of responsibilities to organizations below the State level may serve as an antidote to totalitarianism. In reality however, precisely the contrary occurred. The fragmentation of the totalizing governmental power in Latin America offered an open invitation to caudillo federalism to enter through the back door.

Creative Response to Resistance. The public sector learns, collectively, by admitting and actively acquiring information feedback from the field, and by processing, evaluating and interpreting this information in the light of the ideological guidelines underlying the existing policy. The sector's full cycle of collective learning is completed in the decision-making processes that will be devised to enact legitimate social change. The public sector has priority in the interpretation of the legitimacy principle and consequently may introduce amendments in it, but the civil sectors must be advised of any changes in the legitimacy of a set of practices that are publicly introduced. Otherwise initiative for change undertaken by the public sector would appear as arbitrary to the sectors subject to public power.

The various aspects of the sort of collective learning discussed here may be illustrated in *Figure* 7. The public sector A declares publicly its intention to enforce a change in the programmatic guideline Z. A corresponding change is made in the concrete commands by A to the subject actor B. Policy changes are linked up with a set of principles transcending the particular situation. The new mode of command is thus justified in the light of preceding modifications of the public rationale Z. Command is given "in the name of something," or "for the sake of something," with the transcendental element of public ideology aiming at a new totalizing goal for the collectivity. In all this process, the public sector A maintains its preferential initiatory access to the interpretation of

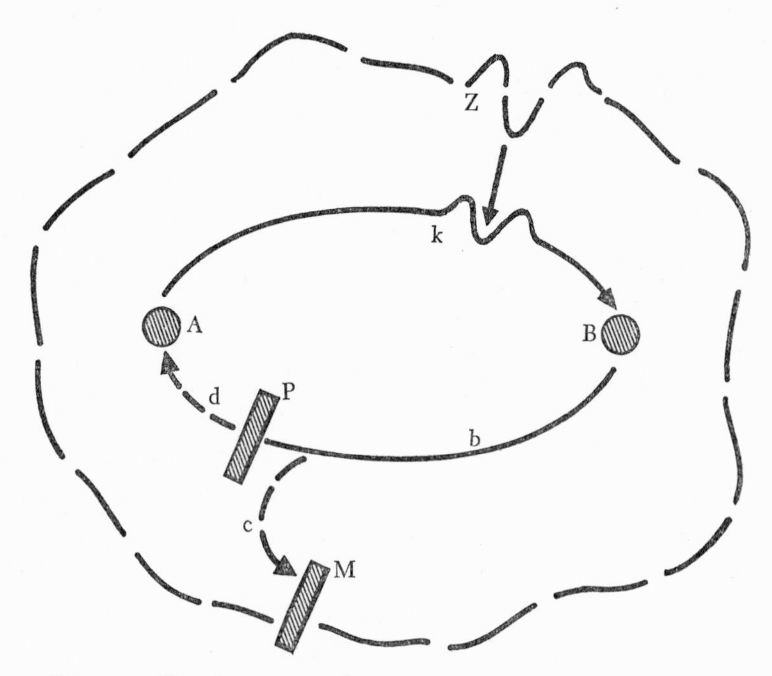

Figure 7. Creative response in a power system

the totalizing principle Z. It thus manages not to appear as arbitrary to the private sector B, not to cut loose from the system's tradition, and not to act from weakness. Only in the case of revolutionary modifications of the ideology Z do the groups brought to power in contested upheavals draw upon their public commitment to the principle of total overhaul of basic arrangements rather than upon the continuity principle.

The expected result of the modifications in Z obviously is *A*'s gaining of control over the exploitable portion *d* of *B*'s total output *b* and the lessening of *B*'s escapist liberation tendency *c*. A policy guideline is modified to the degree the public sector senses the necessity of yielding in order to soften the coercive impact of the sanctioning system *M* and thereby to reduce *B*'s withdrawal tendency *c*. In describing this type of structural modification by public action as a "creative" response to pressures from the civil sectors, we simply mean that the logic of the situation forces the policy makers to launch programs which are untried within the system, thus rejecting the more-of-the-same principle of conservation.

Decisions to launch creative public action to solve political dilemmas are made at formal meetings or otherwise in an official setting, and they are issued in an explicit manner. The issuance of the modifications of public commitments and demands consequently occurs in an abrupt and formalistic manner, not in the gradual and imperceptible manner in which norms and values undergo changes within the civil sectors. Thus we may use the term "great leap" to describe a large-scale attempt at a creative modification of a public-policy orientation. The creative response that the public sector labors to achieve to check resistance from the civil sectors involves the effort to find a new way to fit public goals to existing realities which have become increasingly difficult to handle. This response involves an officially endorsed disposition to yield in matters of principle, to produce a new formula for coordinating collective action in circumstances where the empirical situation has become resistant, menacing, and full of counterevidence that invalidates the old ends-means correspondence. Thus creative response in public action reflects authentic learning, introducing a change in the quality of public life. It involves the application of power in its unmechanistic quality of erecting-plus-destroying, building-plus-undoing, in order to "save" the collectivity at a time its unity is threatened by split, polarization, and dissent. New theories to validate public action are produced in the process, and the holders of power will make an appeal to the people to gain their commitment to these theories. The processes that go on in the minds of the makers of public policy are separate from the processes that go on within the civil sectors constituting the system. The policy makers reinforce the aims expressed by popular sentiment but the action of the policy makers usually claims priority over the sentiment of the people and tends to regulate it rather than conform to it.

A creative kind of response to the power dilemma is seen in Las Casas' rejection of the hortatory catechetics of the old and his adoption of the Erasmian appeal to sentiment in Christianization. The commitment to a new set of principles implied a new voluntaristic concept of man and a new understanding of the meaning of Christianity; it therefore represented something more than a mere change in procedure. In a more general sense, Las Casas' willingness to experiment with diverse alternative arrangements to handle the Indian issue and his criticism of the encomienda represented a creative disposition to adopt a modernizing policy implying a new concept of the Indians' collective rights and a recognition of the legitimacy of their demands.

Since the processes occurring in the minds of the policy makers are separate from those occurring within the civil sectors, the explanatory task is one of finding a link between these two levels. The functionalist sociologist's manner of dealing with this problem consists of efforts to explain sociopolitical change solely in terms of the properties of the system. Social change, in the functionalist sociological approach, is seen to flow from impersonal system variables; the sociologist in this tradition views the system in its capacity for self-regulation, or in its capacity to adjust to the environment. Public action introduced by the polity is seen as the direct function of the demands and the support flowing to the political sector from the intrasocietal and extrasocietal sources. The public sector is thus focused in its machinelike capacity to convert supporting feedback into action output.

The historian rejects the assumption of systemlike actors vested with impersonal and universal qualities of self-sufficiency. He stresses the uniqueness of the persons vested with the responsibility of decision, who turn the tide of events by virtue of their contribution. Political insiders, in the historical interpretation, are seen to force the system into change, and the personal motivations of the great men are stressed. The historian's task involves an "individualizing" motive that makes him sensitive to the exceptional performance of the leading political actors, yet the historian must also bring within the scope of his inquiry sensitivity to the regularities and patterns that describe the ethos of the times and entire cultures.

Sociologists have a handy answer to those critics who blame them for overlooking the personal element in explanation. After all, sociologists say, the system produces the roles that are filled by great men. Great men are products of the system; their individuality matters less than their system-bound performance in roles provided by the system. If this answer is accepted, then creative sociopolitical change is viewed as another system property that is predictable on the basis of whatever information we may have about the system variables pressuring toward change.

This is not the implication of the personal-power model proposed in the present essay. The personal-power model stresses the importance of dissenting men who are *not* immediately offered legitimate roles within the system to capacitate them for the implementation of innovation. An innovator in fact steps out of his ascribed role and thus becomes a rebel or insurgent in the eyes of officialdom; he bears the stigma of insubordination until the holders of power heed his warning, establish a rapport with innovator, and eventually create the new role urged by the latter. Roles as such are void of analytic power as far as sociopolitical change is concerned. All sociopolitical power is ultimately of a personal nature. Roles only explain permanence and stability; an ability to explain how people overcome the limitations of roles is indispensable in attempts to understand change.

The theoretical guidelines of public action called ideologies are not mere abstractions or generalizations extrapolated from an enumeration of the attitudes, values, motives, and strivings of the people within given geographical boundaries. People, if by this word we mean an anonymous population, do not produce ideologies in the sense of public blueprints. People do support ideologies; they are exposed to programmed efforts to implement them. People express different degrees of subjective commitment to whatever they know about the public ideologies. But in the legal sense people *are* committed to the official ideologies irrespective of what they know about them. People act but are also acted upon, in the sense of being forced to act within the boundaries of an ideology prescribed for them by a relatively few known individuals who formulate the framework within which public action will take place.

Creative intellectuals, when innovative response is in the making, may withhold their approval of some fundamental principles on which the social order is presently founded; they may expose the gap between ideals and reality, and the hypocrisy of public policy; or they may capitalize on the issue of injustice and martyrdom that the present course of action induces, in order to inflame active counterideals and to call for a reexamination of the ideological core elements that the system embraces. No government can remain entirely unresponsive for long to cries for "justice," and the chief executive, earlier than the lower echelon, may be inclined to listen to the dissenters for insight and advice in anticipation of an ideological bankruptcy he senses may be coming. The power holder who turns a deaf ear, at this point of widespread discontent and of cravings for new collective orientations, will show that he has exhausted his ability to produce a creative public response to the crisis. This was precisely the fate of the colonial government in Spain in the late eighteenth century.

One of the common fallacies in interpreting Latin American intellectual history is to place it in periods or stages. A typical set of stages posits the sequence of romanticism, liberalism-conservativism, positivism, and antipositivism. This kind of periodicity in explanation violates the historical sequence of events and makes idea systems appear as if they were independently evolving congeries which will exhaust themselves after a given period of time. The practice of looking for periodicity in social thought ignores the actions that shape ideologies during their formulation, their adoption, their execution, and the revision forced on them by the obstacles met during the process. Thus the explanatory model of stages, if applied to the Latin American history, fails to consider the strategically central role of the Latin American influential thinkers and their mediating role in politics as they have voiced the cries of injustice and introduced ideological innovation from abroad. In the Latin American area, one is impressed by the affinity of philosophy and politics, by the realization, as W. Rex Crawford has expressed it, that the Latin American thinkers interpret the whole social reality about them, seeking its roots in the past and looking "with grave concern for their country and for America into an unknown future." [62] A quality of prophecy and doomsday-calling permeates the pensadores' lifework and gives it a moralizing tenor. This tenor derives from the pensadores' closeness to the sources of power, from their ambition to be a part of politics, instrumental in reloading ideologically and inspirationally the political system to which they belong. In the Latin American context perhaps better than elsewhere one will realize how social thought moves between the poles of fact finding and ideology making, between an interest in presenting things as they are and an interest in moving them in the direction in which they ought to move. Latin American social thought is relatively less concerned with value-free descriptions of social situations and more concerned with arguments on the justification of public commitments. Instead of isolating themselves in academic research positions the Latin American historians and social scientists, successfully or not, strive to blend their labors with the political issues of the day.

There is a concurrent tendency among the Latin American power holders to pursue a course of action derived from scientifically formulated technocratic principles. The positivist statesmen in the late nineteenth century were already laboring to combat the "fossils" they considered the Latin American nations had inherited from the Hispanic tradition. Like Porfirio Díaz in Mexico, they aimed at producing a new generation of scientifically trained leaders sufficiently versed in the application of universal methods—men who would no longer speculate, as the Thomists did, on the question of why things occur the way they do but on that of *how* things arise and evolve. These were the positivist leaders who wanted to sacrifice ideology altogether, except for the ideal of rigor that exists in the scientific method itself. Government, in the positivist view, should find a justification as *science,* on the grounds of its practical utility in obtaining progress, not as the protector of any branch of metaphysical thought.

It is a mistake, then, to look for the transition from romanticism to positivism in the Latin American intellectual history, for the culmination of positivism in the governments of "scientists," as Díaz' government in Mexico was called, for the failure of positivism, and for the wave of antipositivism since the 1920's. Also it is a mistake to consider that positivism in Latin America was a short-lived intellectual orientation introduced in Latin America as a novelty during the second half of the nineteenth century and dramatically dying away since the 1920's. In a broader perspective, Latin American positivism represents a continuity of the policy of "enlightenment" of such colonial reformers as Portugal's Marquis of Pombal and Governor-Bishop Abad y Queipo in New Spain. In an interpretation derived from the model of periods of thought both these men come out far ahead of their times, representing the ideals of scientific management characteristic of the positivists of the late nineteenth century. In the interpretation followed here, their efforts are taken as attempts to implement through official channels a creative response to political failure, involving the new ideology of labor mobility, economic efficiency, modernization, and self-sufficiency in the colonies, thereby sacrificing, or coming dangerously close to sacrificing, the mercantile principle of colonialism in order to "save" the imperial unity of sociopolitical order. Both Pombal and Abad y Queipo thus labored to implement from within the system a creative mode of response to the dilemma imposed by the increasing political unrest in the colonies. They worked for a policy of committing the resources of the colonial subjects to progressivism without severing the colonial ties. Abad y Queipo's efforts, in the wake of the movements of independence, were too late to save imperial unity; the Marquis of Pombal, instead, succeeded in consolidating royal control over Brazil and contributed to the postponement of the independence movement there.[63]

III

Hidden Challenge to Public Power

Continuities of Indianness

In the preceding chapter, the power component was considered from a point of observation located within the conquering Spanish system; we concentrated on the types of yielding to resistance and on the institutionalized practices and commands ensuing from these. We shall now examine the implications of power from the opposite perspective, as they are evident in the subjected and nearly destroyed marginal "outgroup" of the Indians. First, we shall discuss briefly the pre-Colombian history of the Aztec and the Inca Empires.

Do the two Americas have a common history? In his well-known thesis, historian Herbert Eugene Bolton proposed in 1932 an affirmative answer to this not entirely rhetorical question. Isolationist, nationalistic, and chauvinistic historical writing deserves to be replaced by a broader treatment of the "epic of greater America," common to both Americas, Bolton maintained. In the New World, discovery was always followed by exploitation and colonization; it was "not a matter of one nation, but of many." [1] Bolton's thesis attempts to shift the historian's view from the immediacies of New World existence to its European origins, which then become the great common explanatory background.

A position different from Bolton's is taken by those who,

like Frank Tannenbaum, find similarities in the world view of the people of the two Americas—similarities which Tannenbaum traces back to the Americans' common experiences "with the Indian, the Negro, the open spaces and wide horizons, the unique role of the horse . . . , and the experiences of the farm life." [2] But they nevertheless find the decisively Latin American mode of life embedded in the *continuities of Indianness* and in the persistent mutual attrition of the aboriginal and the European culture. Those tensions, as Tannenbaum seems to sense them, affect not only selected sectors like the agrarian structure, but also even cultural and ideological totalities.

It is in the light of the latter kind of tension model and liberation model that I have interpreted Latin American history in the present book. Action on the lower levels of the system, it is held, cannot be adequately explained by expectations, on the level of the colonizing and expansive whole, of "needed" supportive action, or by the actual gaining of such support. Rather, one will have to focus on the readiness of the subjected sectors to break for freedom from imposed guidance and exploitation, if an opportunity for doing so arises. In the world view of the marginal individual who is molded to an overmastering will from the outside, power looks like a prison: something to be either avoided or escaped from; or something oppressive, the injustice of which the victim of power can denounce only through his own martyrdom. Those who are victimized and who render appeal and protest derive hope, however, from the thought that the powers *above* the immediate masters—the supreme holders of power such as the king, government and, ultimately, God—appear benign and approachable.

The gubernatorial model is not one which would explain social change by public action alone; rather, it sees that the grass-roots resistances and attritions are constantly exposing the shortcomings of the official beliefs, ideals, programs, and propagated ideologies and forcing changes in them. The ideals in Latin America that once inspired the men at the top of the hierarchy, we have seen, relapsed into double standards, into a loss of identity, into conflictive allegiance, into sham piety and empty promises, making it increasingly difficult for the Europeans to maintain a firm sense of the success of their universalistic mission. There ensued dogmatic relaxation, quarrels, secularization, and bureaucratization. The thought systems of the founding fathers of the colony—Vitoria, Sepúlveda, Cortés, and Las Casas—and the very ideology of a universal Christian crusade would soon divide the public sector as well as unite it. There emerged the task of keeping popular thought in line with officialdom, and the law-and-order task of preventing the "masses" from building up reactive rules and standards of their own.

One difficulty in translating the theory of living militant Indianness into broad explanatory programs arises from the internal inconsistencies of the *Indianismo* theme itself. The Aztec ideology, for example, immediately before Cortés' arrival had, among the nobles and the priests, reached a point approaching a fatal disharmony; it reflected a mounting suspicion of the validity of the very basis of the traditional social order. More was involved, it seems, than mere resentment of the excesses of the odious, imposed Aztec rule: the opposition to the established "grand design" and to the older Aztec ethos of military performance and aggrandizement stemmed from the subversive impact of new ideas that gave man a voluntaristic, individually responsible, and pacific role in the universe and nurtured the feelings of guilt and self-incrimination.

During their nomadic period and long after the founding

of their permanent settlement in Tenochtitlán (now Mexico City) in A.D. 1325, the Aztecs (the *Méxica*) were a backward tribe of defenseless newcomers—suspected, harassed, and persecuted by the earlier more advanced peoples of the Valley of Mexico. Yet, they seem to have been possessed by the singular vision of a chosen people: "You will conquer the four corners of the world," their oracles foretold, "you will win and subjugate peoples. . . . It will cost you sweat, labor and sheer blood, but you will attain and enjoy the finest emeralds, precious stones, gold, silver, fine plumage in many colors, delicious cacao brought from faraway places, cloths in many tints." [3] A class of priesthood (ideology makers and ideology propagators) was formed, which saw to it that in every new place where the tribe took residence a cave temple with a *cú* (altar) for Huitzilopochtli, God of War, was built. The tribesmen were herded into the temple, and from the cú, "with the Mexicans not seeing but understanding," the voice of the priest-God could be heard.

This, one may say, was the voice of the government, in a system which had become organized into a State. You will win victories, the voice would tell, "*because* you have founded and erected your own head, body, government, republic, a very strong nation in this place of Coatepec." Practical advice would mix with promise for the future. The voice told the Mexicans to dig wells, to plant fruit trees and sugar cane. It advised them in the art of fishing. It also stressed on the symbolism of continuity: a colorful bird, Izcahuitl, plentiful in the area, the priests told, was the incarnation of Huitzilopochtli, and should be worshipped.

The promised grandeur eventually did come about during the second half of the fifteenth century. By then the Aztecs had advanced from a feudal tributary clan under the Tepanec to an autonomous, tribute-collecting state and had assimilated much of the superior culture of their neighbors. They were erecting a capital city—the most conspicuous token of their success—of a splendor and architectural massiveness which at the time of the arrival of the Spaniards in 1519 made some of Hernán Cortés' soldiers wonder whether this exotic metropolis, the immense pyramids, the floating gardens, palaces, and plazas were a mirage or perhaps a part of their dreams. By this time the Aztec empire extended from Central America far into the territory of the present-day United States.

One of the old Aztec legends dating from nomadic times portrays a split between Goddess Malinalxoch and her younger brother Huitzilopochtli. The powers of the former stemmed from her skill in black magic. She was believed to be in alliance with snakes, spiders, and beasts; she would turn animals against man; and she would cast an evil eye on a person who, the day after, would die and whose living heart she would devour. Huitzilopochtli's authority, again, was derived from the rationale of military performance and conquest. "My office is war," he declared, "and with my heart, head and arms everywhere I have to carry out my office. . . . I have to sustain many peoples and to give them food and drink, to watch over them and to join them together . . . and this not too gently."[4] Malinalxoch was superseded, and the once primary preoccupation with the biophysical environment was replaced in the Aztec ideology by a new concern with system building: with the sociopolitical prerequisites of survival and imperialistic expansion, and with the issue of oneness.

The cult of the multiform Quetzalcoatl, the Feathered-Serpent divinity coming from the Toltecs, however, represented values antithetical to those associated with the worship of the great War God. In one of his many guises Quetzalcoatl was identified with the pacifist king of the Toltecs, Topiltzin,[5] who was born either A.D. 935 or 947. This "ugly, long-faced and bearded" [6] ruler—whose identity has baffled generations of archaeologists—mastered the art of smelting ore; he and his vassals polished diamonds and lived in houses inlaid with precious stones and oyster shells. During his reign, maize gave abundant harvest, fruit grew large, and cotton grew in many colors. The capital of the Toltecs, Tula, achieved an unprecedented degree of prosperity.

Quetzalcoatl-Topiltzin practiced penitence, brushed hemp plants with blood from his self-inflicted wounds, and bathed at midnight in the springs of Xippacoya.[7] He abstained from intoxicating drink and sex until his adversaries—who seem to have preferred the worship of the Soldier-God Tezcatlipoca [8]—cunningly trapped him into indulging in both. Overcome with repentance, according to one romantic tradition, Quetzalcoatl decided to abandon his kingdom; he burned down Tula, sank his treasures in the bottom of a river, and destroyed his magnificent gardens. Quetzalcoatl-Topiltzin, this line of tradition puts it, left for the east, with a promise to return. When the Aztecs first received a message of "towers" or "mountains" approaching by sea from the east—the arriving Spaniards—Emperor Montezuma, a man deeply influenced by Toltec tradition, accepted with fatalistic conviction the idea that the conquistadores were the forces of Quetzalcoatl now returning to rule over the Aztec lands.

One outstanding theme in the Aztec philosophy maintained that history underwent a succession of "ages," or "Suns," each characterized by a rationale of its own. The age of Quetzalcoatl was one of movement and of fulfillment of the historical destiny of the Aztec people.[9] The ages apparently did not follow each other in a deterministic fashion;

rather, man was instrumental in keeping the cycles in motion by invigorating the Sun with offerings of a life-maintaining substance—human blood. Universal continuity was bought by human sacrifice; there was a link between cosmological processes and human action; and human sacrifice was "necessitated" by the burdensome, yet glorious historical role imposed upon the Aztecs.[10] Heroic martyrdom was built in to the Aztec system to guarantee its longevity.

As a part of the nation-building efforts of the great Aztec leader Tlacaelel (d. 1475 or 1480), the doctrine of human sacrifice led to the institutionalization of the practice the Spanish chroniclers called *guerras floridas,* that is, wars whose principal purpose was to obtain a supply of prisoners for sacrifice. The tribes subject to this abuse and those forced to pay tribute to the Aztecs developed what seems to have been a genuine fear of the master race; they formed sectarian, Messianic movements cherishing the expectation of mankind's eventually being delivered from its obligation to human sacrifice. The Sun, in one Totonaca tradition, would send his Son to redeem the world from this intolerable burden and by this act of divine grace would usher in a new, happier and more prosperous era. Protesting Aztec imperialism and degrading its symbols, Texcoco king Nezahualcoyotl (1418–1472), who had been obliged to erect in his city a temple and a statue of the Sun-Huitzilopochtli, built in front of it an even more sumptuous temple dedicated to the unknown god of the Toltecs.[11]

The Franciscan friar Bernardino de Sahagún (1499?–1590) has recorded a wealth of data which give us insight into the conflicting, duty-bound, yet often self-accusing ethos of the pre-Colombian religions in Mexico. Prayers to the Warrior-God Tezcatlipoca, as handed down by Sahagún, picture an individual who—in the words of his apologist, the Aztec priest—is caught between the demands of the official ideology and his individual dispositions, embedded in his "natural state," and predestined in the "signs of his birth." The individualistic principle of free will—a voluntaristic image of man—blends with the principle of responsibility, thus producing a rationale in which meaning is attached to such notions as sin, divine wrath and forgiveness.[12] The principle of voluntarism, however, is never carried so far as to disregard the external, collective, and uncontrollable prerequisites of morality. Poverty, nakedness, hunger and weakness—physical and moral—are seen merely as mitigating circumstances of sin. They do not wholly explain or justify the individual's revolting against the system itself.[13]

The Aztecs also practiced what seem to have been equivalents of Christian communion (paste shaped into the image of Huitzilopochtli was ceremonially consumed), baptism, confession, and penance. These were institutionalized responses to what was thought of as man's moral obligation to establish and maintain his particular place in the divinely ordered world, which extended to the life after death. However, ritual was clearly not enough. In the Nahuatl literature of the Toltecs, the Aztecs, and several other peoples in central and western Mexico, man was depicted as being compelled by his nature to be actively in search of his *ixtli*—his "face," "heart" or "person."[14] True, the *tonalpohualli* (augural calendar) marshalled individual destinies, from birth to death, into such broad categories as those of good or ill fate. But man was also thought to be capable of *monotza*, "invoking or calling himself," mobilizing his inner forces in order to gain control of his heart and his destiny; and he was expected to pay heed to the teachings of the *tlamatinima*, the savants and "masters of truth," whose function it was to "admonish" and to "humanize the wills of people." [15]

From the Aztec history one learns how the initial command action indeed produces effects and also side effects, errors, problems of identity, and dilemmas of duty. In the case of the Aztecs, it was their cult of war, the terror incited by imperial tax collectors, and the human sacrifice "necessitated" by their ideology which made their "empire" (actually a triangle of semi-autonomous empires) decline. At the time of the arrival of the Europeans, the Aztec power was nearly exhausted. The fear associated with the prospect of losing power, losing systemic oneness of empire, was expanded, it seems, into a dogma, propagated by ceremony, asserting that the continuance of the existence of the whole world was indeed endangered at the time one cycle by Venus count changed into another. George C. Vaillant tells how the Aztecs, during the five final days of the outgoing cycle, let their fires go out and destroyed their furniture. People fasted and lamented; the pregnant women were shut up in granaries, so they would not be changed into wild animals. At the sunset on the final day, the priests scanned the heavens from the temple on top of the Hill of the Star.

At the very moment when [certain stars] passed the meridian the priests seized a wooden fire drill and kindled a new fire in the open breast of a victim freshly slain for the purpose. The populace—priests, chiefs, and commoners—thrilled to great happiness. Runners lit torches from the new fire and rekindled the altars in the temples of every town and hamlet, whence the people bore the flames to their hearths. . . . The darting torchbearers sped through the night, bringing the promise of new life to every man, woman, and child. With the dawn, . . . the populace rallied, renovating their temples, refurbishing their houses, and making new utensils for temple and household use. There was feasting on special food, and sacrifice, both by personal bloodletting and the immolation of captives, betokened the measure of popular gratitude.[16]

This kind of officially propagated fear of discontinuity apparently served the Aztecs as an ideological device for correcting the failure of the power center to carry its command throughout the empire.

One source of friction between the Europeans and the Indians involved the cognitive discrepancies of their respective grand designs. The early chronicles abound in data, strewn as marginal trivia in the dogmatic context, suggesting the overriding significance of the fact that the respective ultimate and relevant "wholes" of the Europeans and the Indians, upon which the destinies of men were believed to depend, were critically different. The Indian view, paradoxically enough, in some ways came close to the modern empiricist "middle-range" outlook. First, the ultimate explanatory principles associated by the Indians with the sun, the moon, the earth, and the forces of nature, were assumed to represent diversified, not clearly hierarchical qualities, as opposed to the monotheistic Christian assumption of the ultimate singleness of quality and the hierarchy of "essence." Second, in the Indian view, the so-called locus problem, that of selecting the level of abstraction in conceptualizing the most relevant ultimates, was solved in an immanent and concrete manner. The ultimate explanatory principles were vested in observables. Immediate nexus, even at the expense of painful sacrifice, was expected to exist, concretely and unequivocally, connecting events in the individual and public life with the events of nature and of the visible universe. For the Indian, the separation between theology and morality was alien; divine and imperial demands were conjointly mediated. It was impossible for the Indians to think that life-giving processes, in a universe which was orderly to them as it was to the Europeans, could somehow be derived not from the vital events around them but from events remote in time and space. Nor did the distinction between natural and supernatural exist for them as it did for the Europeans. Some Guaraní Indians, for instance, were reportedly highly depressed at the thought of an omnipresent and all-seeing God who would watch their every step. The deductive chain from ultimates to immediate moral imperatives was continuous, and consequently the elaborate symbolism involved in the Spanish concept of abrupt Christianization and baptism was meaningless to them. The Indians assumed that the European observing his compass was receiving instructions from his Deities. Their close analogy between diverse natural events and meaningful and moral human action did not imply the logical necessity of faith in its Christian sense of total custody, nor that of lengthy indoctrination, or conversion. According to one illuminating anecdote, an old Indian from the Andes "infuriated" the missionary and the accompanying hacendado by requesting to be excused from baptism because he was unable to retain "long things" in his memory. Both the Europeans and the Indians adhered to a collective thought model emphasizing dependence, responsibility, and submission to the group. They both assumed that life processes "ought to" proceed not arbitrarily or in an isolated manner but within a limited independence always measured with duty; that partial processes are always reminders of totalities. One important difference in the religious sphere was that the dogma of Christ as the single link between God and man made no sense to the Indians.

Christian symbols, for the Indians, were reduced to signs in the sense of being conceptually, morally, and ideologically undefined before they had been applied in concrete life situations. This perhaps explains the complaint of a cacique who claimed that the "word" of the Spaniard, capricious in meaning, becomes "law" for the Indian, the further claim being that the Indians' vices—their drunkenness and laziness—reflect their failure to read meanings in the sociopolitical world. Cognitive confusion was aggravated by the fact that the Europeans did not appear to the Indians so committed to efficient unitary moral standards as their grand design implied. "Who is a Christian, who are these Christians?" a Central American tribal chief demanded. "They exact corn, honey, cotton, women, gold, silver. They do not work; they lie and gamble; they are wicked, and they swear."[17] As a part of the immediacy principle, the Indian concept of shared divine patronage was associated with localistic and tribal Deities, a practice in conflict with the Christian principle of universalism. "How is it possible," one cacique queried, "that after I gave you my friendship without doing you any harm . . . you wanted to destroy me, your friend and brother. You gave me the cross to defend myself against my enemies, and by the same cross [obviously given by the priests to an enemy tribe as a token of Christianization] you wanted to kill me."[18]

In spite of their adherence to the model of undefined numbers of ultimate divine properties and the principle of immediacy, the Indians' point of view differed from the modern, scientific-experimental view in another dimension. The Indian thought sought the validation of the truth not only in the power of an ideology to produce progress and in its efficiency but also in its power to maintain stability and to contribute to the earth-bound security of a frictionless society and of the citizens. The Indian view held work in esteem not for the economic values it produced but for the community experiences and actual enjoyment derived from it; work therefore was considered the pivotal element of life. The Aztec ethos of aggrandizement, it is true, derived its expansionist dynamic force from a militant religion; and the Toltec counterideology of technological advancement was linked with an antiwar religious credo. But these were either transitory themes or latent undercurrents in the main stream of established Indian thought, which was committed to the ideals of "necessitated" collectivism, stability, regulation from above, castelike divisions, bonds with the soil, and the overall permanency of the existing social order which thrived on work and duty.

The Indian's intimate relationship to the land, his finding the principle of motherhood in the earth, and the psychological impact on the Indian of the immense mountains and plains of a contrasting and impressive geography, have given rise to writings on the particularly Indian mystique of land. Involved as the issue of land tenure was with religious sentiments, it nonetheless was, among the Incas and the Aztecs, one of the most articulated and formalized aspects of a bureaucratic, institutionalized, and centralized practice. All land, in the concept of both the Aztecs and the Incas, ultimately belonged to the emperor by virtue of his alleged superior origin or by the title he obtained to it as the head of conquering forces. In an arithmetically determined proportion, the lands were distributed by locality among the royalty, the nobility, the priesthood, and the commoners, with the royal lands being used as a reserve from which new land grants could be drawn. The Aztec *calpulli,** meaning

* For discussion on calpulli, its transformation to Spanish *sujeto* (town) and its persistence through colonial times, see Charles Gibson, *The Aztecs under Spanish Rule* (Stanford, California, Stanford University Press, 1964), pp. 34, 152f.

the *barrio* (neighborhood) of the "known people," that is, individuals (nonslaves) accepted by virtue of consanguinity or the length of residence as co-villagers, through communal administrative channels, took the responsibility of annually revising the titles to the use of land; whereas it was up to the imperial administration to revise the exterior boundaries of the lands thus redistributed.

Similar rules obtained in the Inca empire. The *ayllu*-lands available for cultivation by commoners were distributed into *sayanas*, a Quechua word that possibly had the connotation of "representation," or "standing up" in defense of the user's legitimate access to their cultivation.[19] Neither the Aztec nor the Inca system permitted the splitting of the lands by generational succession: at the death of the principal user the land returned to the commune for redistribution. To suit the Inca's policies, entire ayllus were occasionally transplanted; but such mass movements did not affect the individuals' benefits from the use of land. In both systems, working days demanded from the commoners were proportionately divided among teams working on each category of lands, including the communal lands, the *ejidos*, as they became known in New Spain, and the *altepetlalli* of the Incas.

This was an authoritarian, deductive, security-oriented rationale, but it did provide for yielding on matters of access to land: some sort of demographic lever was placed in the hands of the power holders, which would solve, for the time being at least, the Malthusian predicament. The Western values of individual freedom, social mobility and civil equality were de-emphasized. Land was held as the source of family subsistence, never as the means of speculation or of social mobility. Military bravery and civic performance could bring promotion to the privileged caste (the former even to "Heaven"), a promotion which had concomitants in relation to land tenure; and the caste position was generally hereditary. Differences of status, on the other hand, were quite marked among the barrios. Thus only the big urban barrios accumulated collective property, built large temples, maintained military schools and welfare institutions; and some degree of individual advancement was probably provided by permitting individuals to move from one barrio or village to another. Wars could ensue from such inequalities on the level of the barrio and the subtribe, but by political and military means the emperor would labor to mobilize and maintain a sense of oneness to keep the subjects under the same global control.

Indian Systems of Power

Of particular interest in the preceding section is the mechanism of power involved in Malinalxoch's rule. Malinalxoch, the legend puts it, was in alliance with snakes, spiders, and beasts—principal killers of the nomadic tribes who had not yet achieved defense against the hazards in their biophysical environment. The female ruler was able to maintain the unity of the migrating tribe by virtue of her ability to control the environment—a skill which apparently implied considerable knowledge of medical practices and of other skills to ward off death induced by animals and microorganisms in an unknown environment. This skill she used both as a tool of defense against the enmity of her tribesmen and a barrier inhibiting their escaping her rule. As far as the legend goes, hers was an unyielding rule indisposed to change: characteristically, the legend has Huitzilopochtli escaping his sister's rule at a moment the female despot was asleep. The rationale of her rulership, one might say, involved no myth making. It simply made use of the bare essentials of survival; it relied on life-saving knowledge about what kinds of food to eat, what kind of animals and insects to avoid, what kind of instruments to use, and how to fish and hunt. The element of sociopolitical ideology was absent in Malinalxoch's system and, since the tribe she ruled was probably small in size, she could deal with each one of the tribesmen in a one-to-one manner.

Huitzilopochtli induced modifications in the Aztec system and tentatively accentuated the motif of change. The cushion response was applied: the Aztecs were promised prosperity in exchange for allegiance to the propagated ideology of militant aggrandizement. Human sacrifice became the ritualistic showy symbol of the Aztecs' allegiance to their nationalistic calling. The education response was applied. Aztec leaders attempted to induce, for example, epidemiological controls within the huge empire,* including mosquito control; they encouraged bathing and other forms of cleanliness.[20] Administrative response included the emergence of an elaborate system of governmental bureaucracy and the division of public rights and responsibilities among the king, nobility, and priesthood. As contrasted with the direct monolithic rule of Malinalxoch, structural differentiation was thus introduced.

Along with the sociopolitical element that had now been added to the Aztec mode of thinking, myth-making developed. Remaining together was recognized as a prerequisite of collective goal attainment; the sweetness of collective glory and the allurement of external conquest were realized. The one-to-one manner no longer sufficed for dealing with

* The term "Aztec empire" presupposes a high degree of unity within the system. Modern historians prefer to describe the sociopolitical situation in Mexico before Cortés as one of a tribal hierarchy of power and status, with a "triple alliance" among the most powerful tribes, the Méxica, the Acolhuaque or Texcoco, and the Tepaneca.

tribesmen in different positions, geographically and functionally; it would be necessary to produce some kind of global blueprint for living, an ideology, and to propagate it as a formally recognized set of explicit, a priori core principles of a contractual nature to guide collective life. The simple rule of trial and error was replaced by the more sophisticated guideline of certainty and promise vested in political guidance; the principle of threat was replaced by imperial promise; an appeal was made to human desires for a better collective future. Long-range collective goals were hailed as legitimate ordering principles to which individual cravings must be sacrificed. Power was now meaningful not in the instrumental sense of applying skills to the immediate biophysical environment to one's proven advantage but rather in the public and institutional sense of promoting collective beliefs and designs. These implied that the sociopolitically organized group itself provided public means to an end and that the collectivity, consequently, was in some sense an end in itself.[21] History might prove these grandiose designs illusory; for the time being, however, the attraction and repulsion they exerted on the people must be taken into account as a collective device shaping the destinies of the group.

The ideological and administrative processes involved in the management of power, however, create a tendency to overreach, some kind of "ideological surplus," a tendency to promise too much, and a tendency to take the initial overcommitment of subjects breaking away from their previous (trial-and-error, biophysically bound) power systems at its face value. When such overreaching occurs, alliances within the imperial system will tend to crumble, ideological undermining occurs and, accelerated ideological mobilization notwithstanding, unless some core items are discarded, power will come to an end. The power holders will then be expelled by means not contemplated in the established administrative structure[22]—by revolution, coup, foreign conquest, or by absorption into emerging higher-level systems representing a new intersystem (international) hierarchy of control. Levels of command may overlap in some of these cases of power deficit, just as they had in the Aztec empire, in which rival kingdoms rose to power. This kind of split involves a process essentially different from the in-system processes of stratification.

As in any changing system, the problem of fitting together mutually inconsistent ideologies existed in the Aztec world. The melioristic, pacific ethos of Quetzalcoatl ran counter to the warlike ethos of the tradition of Huitzilopochtli; the Texcoco (Acolhuaque) king Nezahualcoyotl challenged openly the legitimate hegemony of the God of War. There can be no doubt that at the time of the Conquest, the ideological crisis within the Aztec world had become profound enough to produce in the ruling sector what we have called a creative response to a deficient power situation: an essential loosening up of the overreached ideology and a disposition to yield in matters of the imperialistic principle. Montezuma's surrender to Cortés suggests strongly that the Aztec king by that time was convinced that the yielding response had been too slow in coming and that the imperial Aztec system was irretrievably doomed to perish. The conquest of Mexico proved easy for Cortés; the marginals and the oppressed elements within the empire willingly offered their services to a conqueror determined to march on the capital city that was the glory and the showpiece of the imperialistic achievement.

Ideologies of a Caste Society

As conflicting as the Spanish ideologies on the European penetration in the New World seemed, in practice they fused into an effective ideology that reduced the Indians to subjection. The more militant policy makers, following Sepúlveda, held it only reasonable and commendable that the flag-bearers of the civilized world bring the bestial and naturally servile aborigines to civilized ways, by force if necessary. This became the dominant expansionist rationale; it survived throughout the entire colonial period and later was unquestioningly accepted as the philosophical point of departure by many first-generation pensadores of the independent republics. But even the more liberal philosophers, Vitoria, Las Casas, and their followers, failed to work out ideologies essentially more favorable to the Indians. Vitoria argued that the Indians were obliged to *hear* the Gospel and that force, therefore, could be used to make Christianity freely accessible to them. In practice, this doctrine came to justify the forceful pacification of the Indians as a first step prior to missionary work. Las Casas expected that the Indians would gravitate to Christianity by their own deliberate choice. Once they were converted, he thought it necessary to impose European patronage upon them, to improve and to educate them, and to keep them from drifting back to paganism. In practice, this doctrine came to justify coercion and exploitation as the second step, once the Indians could be considered formally Christians.

The subjugation policy was reinforced rather than reversed by defining the Indians as "free vassals of the King." This euphemism (a core item of the ideology), it is true, formally contradicted the popular concept of the Indians as bestial, childlike, or unable to govern themselves. It also, in theory, helped the Crown keep the Indians from falling prey to the conquistadores and settlers. On the other hand, it established the right of the Crown to levy tribute and to use the right of taxation as the rationale by which the Indian was permanently placed under obligations expected from a subject of the empire. It established the legal and moral right of the Crown to annex the new territories, irrespective of the atrocities committed by the conquistadores: the Catholic kings, under the vassalage theory, had extended their rightful political dominion into the New World bona fide, respecting the rights of the Indians and recognizing them as equals, ignorant of the excesses and usurpation on the part of the captains of the conquering forces. As new vassals of the king, the Indians (unlike Moslems and other infidels) were nominally entitled to preferential treatment after the war; previously free Indians, for example, could not normally be branded as prisoners of war. Yet the tribes who refused to accept vassalage, or those who rebelled or committed particularly heinous offensive acts, could be taken prisoners in a "second war." [23] They could be subjected to slavery and, as in the case of the Caribs of Puerto Rico in the 1530's and later the undefeatable Araucanos in southern Chile, could be classified as "enemies of Christendom"—another core item implying a warlike situation. The presumption that the Indian could choose whether or not to become a subject of the Crown and whether or not to accept Christianity was a myth.

The colonizing enterprise was launched under the auspices of the State, with the Crown directly financing the first expeditions. The private sector gained in scope during the penetration into the mainland under Hernán Cortés. In the 1530's, tension developed between Cortés and Antonio de Mendoza, the first viceroy in the Indies. This development illustrates the precarious balance of power between the private sector of military settlers and the representatives of the empire. In general, the fusion between private and imperial motives was systematically maintained in organizing colonizing expeditions. The soldiers were privately recruited and were expected to supply the arms, equipment, and even the food necessary to make the trip. The financing of the shipment, again, was commercially arranged by the head of the expedition, who also acted as a mediator between the individual participant and the State and as a "minister of His Majesty" in his dealings with the Indians. The Conquest consequently assumed the powerful triple aspect of a ruthless private venture in exploitation, a Christian crusade, and a State-regulated militaristic and mercantile undertaking. The New World was opened up not only for the "hunter of the souls" and the conquistador but also for the miner, the seeker of El Dorado, the settler, and the merchant—barring only such "public enemies" as Moslems, Jews, and individuals condemned by the Inquisition. Profits could be reaped, after the military phase of the Conquest, which far surpassed the unglamorous economic chances of the family farmer, fur trader, or the haggard gold digger of the English colonies. The Crown's take in the Spanish colonies, in turn, consisted initially of a royalty of one-fifth of the yield of gold and silver mines, of a tribute paid by male Indians between eighteen and fifty years in age and, later, of certain excise taxes, export and import duties, and revenues from monopolies of gunpowder, tobacco, salt, and the like.[24] This revenue the Crown used not only to finance the ambitious building projects in the colonies and to pay for the upkeep of a heavy colonial bureaucracy but also to serve its monopolistic interest in accumulating new wealth, vitally needed at the time to consolidate State power in its domestic rivalry with the nobility and the Church. Later it helped to finance the European wars in which Spain became involved.*

* Earl J. Hamilton has discussed the discovery of America and the flow of American gold and silver to the European market as one of the most important sources of modern capitalism. An increase in

To identify the Spanish colonial policies with a simple expansionist rationale involves the risk of oversimplification. The pure type of expansionist economic and political growth, Bert F. Hoselitz says, "implies the consecutive incorporation of new territory . . . either through colonial settlement or by a process of creating new political units which become politically and economically coordinated on a basis of equality with the older portions of a country." [25] During the Conquest, the idea of territorial expansion was, of course, present. But the efficiency of the expanding colonial system in Spanish America was not dependent on the creation and the spread of new, self-sufficing and egalitarian political units in a social and geographical vacuum. Instead, there developed a rationale of arrogant parasitism, justifying the formation of social polarities, making the conquered pay for the success of the Conquest, allowing castes which would divide the conqueror and the conquered. The Indians were to remain marginally attached to the colonial nuclei, to be collectively employed as a menial instrument to correct the colonial institutions' intrinsic lack of functional self-sufficiency, to provide for manual labor in mining, farming, and building, and generally

---

price was associated with this flow. Merchants and industrialists were able to make unexpected profit; wages in manufacturing increased. In Spain, Charles V (1516–1556) and Philip II (1556–1598) opened an era of imperialistic and religious wars that undermined the economy. During the reign of Philip III (1598–1621), Spain suffered severe inflation, and the State assumed enormous debt. The monetary disorder continued up to the late seventeenth century. Thus, the *Edad de Oro* (Golden Age) of the sixteenth century was followed by *Edad de Plata* (Silver Age) and *Edad de Bronce* (Bronze Age) not only in arts and letters but also in the health of the economy. See Earl J. Hamilton, *El florecimiento del capitalismo y otros ensayos de historia económica* (Madrid, Revista de Occidente, 1948), pp. 6ff, 19, 121ff. Hamilton's explanation differs sharply from the Weberian view on the origins of capitalism.

to serve as an equilibrating mechanism between the emergent colonial society and its physical environment. The Indians became an essential link between the Europeans and the biophysical resources available to them.

The effort to gain manipulative control over the intermediate human resources deterred the development of task-oriented skills among the colonizers themselves. Idleness on the part of Spaniards was considered pardonable, and the penniless adventurer could obtain free food and lodging from a compatriot. Pioneering work meant not the conquest of nature but the conquest of human Indian resistance. Once this task was completed, the colonial society, and subsequently the Creole society, maintained an unchanged exploitative pattern and was unable to substitute machine technology for free or cheap manual labor. The Indians were ascribed their extractive roles in a manner which froze the whole colonial society into underdevelopment.

The issue of European dominion in the New World is more complex than that implied by the familiar image of aristocratic tradition, depreciation of manual labor, and feudal heritage in Latin America. These verbalizations underscore the mental and attitudinal correlates of domination and underdevelopment. The European domination had, however, as André Gunder Frank puts it, its "cash nexus and the hard economic reality behind it, . . . the structuraly produced concentration of ownership, control, and accumulation of capital which also concentrated land, encomienda labor, commerce, finance, and civil, religious, and military office into few hands. Capitalist monopoly power reigned supreme from the very beginning just as it continues to reign today." [26]

The mechanism of colonial domination and its economic impact have been the topic of longstanding, heated arguments from early colonial days to the present. In the first half of the eighteenth century the French Académie Royal de Sciences, authorized by Philip V of Spain, sent an expedition of scientists to the viceroyalty of Peru. By orders of Philip V, two young officers of the Spanish navy, Jorge and Antonio Ulloa, joined this expedition. Their "secret mission" was to report directly to the Court about the social, political, and military status of the colony.*

The picture given by them is one of unscrupulous exploitation, opportunism, and lust for riches: "The tyranny which yokes the Indians is born in the insatiable hunger for riches taken to the Indies by those who go there as rulers; and since the latter have no other means to obtain riches than by oppressing the Indians. . . they use all modes and attacking them everywhere with cruelty exact from them more than they would from their slaves. It is true that repartimientos † have not been established in the Province of Quito, but the corregidores have so many other ways of doing it." [27]

The exploitative mechanism was implemented under circumstances in which no effective alliance and no effective communication existed between the high-level power holder (the Crown) and the Indian communities; information from the field did not easily reach the power holder; and the high-level ideology of colonial equality ("vassalage") was thwarted and challenged by quasilegitimate ideologies on the local level.

* The accuracy of this source has been questioned, needlessly, it seems. In the scope of the first-hand observations, statistical information, and practical insight presented, it commands acceptance. The writers of this report not only explain but also evaluate. Unless we recognize in the main as authentic the bitter account of colonial abuse in this document we find it difficult to explain the Indian uprisings later in the eighteenth century.

† *Repartimiento:* The institution of rotating Indian labor, created in response to a shortage of manual labor. Repartimiento was generally initiated around the mid-sixteenth century. See Charles Gibson, *The Aztecs under Spanish Rule* (Stanford, California, Stanford University Press, 1964), pp. 224ff.

The colonial administrator and the entrepreneur measured the Indian for what he was worth in manual work and by and large found him obstinate, lethargic, and lazy. Echoing Sepúlveda, a hard-line ethics of caste-bound discipline developed. Remesal has recorded the contemptuous outburst of a Spanish patrón at the mere thought of a more egalitarian treatment of the Indians. An encomendero had blurted out, about 1550:

There are two species of people in Castile, the nobles and the plebeians, *hidalgos* and villains. The hidalgo, the noble, wants to be taken by love and gentleness, to be treated with respect and courtesy and with good reasoning and on honorable terms; they can make both the wax and the wick, as they say in our country. But the laborer, the villain, is hard and stubborn; and since he has more of feeling than he has of reason, four strokes with a stick work better on him and persuade him easier than all the discourses of Aristotle. This difference God took away from the natives of the Indies; every one of them, everywhere, in every occasion and in every kind of business are of the second class; they are sons of servile fear; they want to be taken by rigor, to be shown an ominous mien; they do not want to be heard or listened to, not to be paid attention for their services; and whenever they fancy that their services have been major, they have to be paid with a slap on their faces; it is better for them to be punished so they understand that they have sinned; and the whip and the stick should first hang above their necks to admonish them for their delict; because in this manner they turn solicitous, diligent, cautious, without getting ideas; and they carry out a command sooner than it takes to give it. On the contrary, if they are taken with gentleness, love and affection, they do nothing; they are careless, lazy, idle; they depreciate the one who is in command; they think that they are being treated gently for lack of strength, and with this fancy a thousand grievances will rise.[28]

The mestizo could not be treated with similar arrogance. He frequently was the interpreter of thought and language the Spaniard needed to deal with the Indian. He was much more versatile than the Indian. Like the Indian, the mestizo was nevertheless forbidden, for example, to possess arms, to ride a horse, or to employ Indians to carry loads; he was not entitled to hold an office, and he could not be ordained priest. Many principles of the sociopolitical order that were initially applied to the Indians were similarly applied to the peasant, thus making the paternalistic subordination of the peasant sector a permanent consequence of the "vassalage of the Indians."

The first generation mestizo was often abandoned, even sacrificed, or unwillingly reared by his Indian mother. Discriminated against by Indians and Spaniards alike, dissenting, and gravitating away from the agrarian structure, the mestizos concentrated in the urban ghettos, which became flaws in the rigidly planned Spanish-style cities, or they were collected in orphanages and hospitals. The mestizo was regarded as a disturbing latent element prone to contaminate the disciplinary order imposed on the Indians: "They all turn ill-mannered and obdurate in vice, to make one afraid of them and the Negroes. They are too many to handle by correcting and punishing them or to treat by ordinary justice. The mestizos live among the Indians; and since their blood is half Indian, the latter conceal mestizo children, and feed them; and from the Indians learn bad examples and pernicious habits." [29]

The American-born Spaniard, the Creole, did not face the same prejudices and deprivations as the mestizo; but he did experience the fear that his claim to the "purity of blood" could be easily questioned; that prestige and positions were discriminatingly preserved for the *peninsular*, the newcomer from Spain, who "on the account of being a Spaniard only had to arrive at the shores of Vera Cruz to find everything to his liking, not wanting in anything; and this was the beginning of his fortune, for in a short time his wages were raised; soon he became a partner, and finally there was the marriage with the patrón's daughter to crown his bliss and to place him into the possession of the house and the property." [30]

Within the religious and cultural order, the Spanish missionaries spared no effort to weed out pre-Colombian traits. They used persuasion, intimidation, promise, punishment, official prohibition and, in the case of Europeans and Creoles, the Inquisition. The renegade Indian was publicly whipped, chained, excommunicated, or exiled from his community; the more humane priest would indicate his displeasure to the petty sinner by refusing to talk to him or by refusing to receive his gifts. Not only were the sacred objects of the Indians destroyed wherever they could be found and the old religious practices censored, but the religiosos, by way of diffuse generalization, attacked virtually anything non-European. The Indians were forbidden to engage in such a harmless diversion as the *palo volador*, a sport in which young men tied up to a tall pole whirled around it in spiral flight. Musical instruments were taken away from the Indians; their *fiestas* and family celebrations were strictly supervised. Native dance, when tolerated, was permitted only if the participants wore no body paint or if they were dressed in the style of Castilian peasants.

The marginality of the Indians was an intractable feature of the colonial system because it was sustained both by attitudes and institutional practices, both by subjective and objective mechanisms, both by civil sectors and public sectors. In this sense it represented the vicious circle that Gunnar Myrdal and others have described.[31] The society as a whole, Myrdal holds (leaving thereby the meaning of "society" unclear), has no built-in mechanism of self-stabilization; on the contrary, it is "constantly on the move away from such a situation." Governmental power, this view implies, represents a device which must be employed in order to bring such a polarizing cycle to an end. On the one hand, the Indians were oppressed *because* the Europeans found them, not only in the colonial times but also in the modern era, lacking in initiative, vicious, and even animallike. On the other hand, the Indians did lack in initiative, they did indulge in alcohol and coca, they did withdraw from participation, and they did behave in a manner below the Europeans' concept of dignity * *because* they were legally and privately discriminated against and were made not only second-rate citizens but reified instruments of the Europeans' aspirations to wealth.

Social Class in the Colony

Class, Power, and the State. In functionalist sociology, social class is ordinarily understood in the frame of reference of an underlying status continuum or stratification pattern consisting of status dimensions such as prestige, income, level of education, and occupation; or of combinations of these—"life chances," as Weber calls them. Class as opposed to stratification is assumed to exist, in this view, when individuals in approximately the same strata share a common set of class sentiments, value attitudes, and ways of life to a degree that makes them a distinguishable subculture within the general culture. The sociologist who has adopted the vertical model

* Harold Osborne suggests that the Indians *in their own environment* are different beings from the Indians who are in contact with whites. See Harold Osborne, *Indians of the Andes* (London, Routledge & Kegan Paul, 1952), p. 211. Such a view, it seems, is in agreement with the one presented here. In their own sociopolitical environment the Indians are "released," somewhat at least, and they will have to be explained by different commanding totalities.

of stratification implies thereby that there is an analytic continuum from the upper strata through the middle levels to the lower strata and that this continuum provides for a conceptual pattern in which social mobility may be conveniently studied. The functionalist sociologist will then proceed by splitting the vertical dimension of status into upper, middle, and lower levels within the stratificatory scheme, and these levels he terms classes. Unlike the Marxian theory of social class, the Weberian theory is consequently unconcerned with structural class properties such as concentration of power, subjection to power, permanent dependence, exploitation, or the access of the powerful actor to a monopolizing position.

Those who accept the model of a vertical continuum as the frame in which they explain social class implicitly assume that social-class structure is something that can be adequately understood in terms of individuals' achievement and performance on the level of infrastructures, and that the sociologist who wants to describe social class in a given society may do so by extracting his classificatory criteria from individuals' responses to questionnaire items, from the class sentiments the respondents express, and from their socioeconomic attributes and possessions. Apart from his commitment in principle to the notion that social class is basically an attribute of the society, not of the individuals, the functionalist sociologist proceeding in this fashion falls back on behaviorist methods implying that the individual in abstraction is the ultimate unit of analysis.

This stratificatory model of status continuum presupposes two things: (1) Individuals are seen, if one accepts this model, as being involved in a choice-making process whereby they weigh one alternative outcome of their action-output against another; and (2) they are seen consistently, in other words, throughout the society, at any level, to choose the same alternative. These two presuppositions, to paraphrase Russell L. Ackoff,[32] define a meaningful situation where the range of obtainable benefits is regulated only by the individuals' mobility and his fitness in a competitive society, by his ability to interchange and to cooperate with others, and by his ability to handle interpersonal conflicts arising from this interaction on the infralevel.

In contrast, those who accept a power theory of social class focus on the intentional origin of social inequality as a built-in feature of the politically organized system. The Marxian power theory of social class, for instance, does not consider the more–less continuum of Weberian "life-chances" but rather the have–have-not dichotomy of exclusive access to the means of production. More generally, a macrosociological theory of power focuses on inequalities, hierarchies, castes, and restraints on mobility in terms of features induced by the public sector to promote and support a given political design of ideological nature. Marx spoke of the State as an idea system embracing the aspirations, desires, and virtues that the ruling class has projected into it. The State, Marx said, represents the "heaven" of the ruling class; the capitalist State represents the "heaven" of the master class of manufacturing capitalists whom the Industrial Revolution created. In a similar manner, if we emphasize the role of power in the creation of inequalities, social class appears in its origin as reflecting the necessity of priestly, administrative, military, jurisdictional, educational, and other public roles as organizational steps toward the building of the State apparatus. Social-class differences exist, if the role of power is emphasized, because they are the outcome of willful policies enforced by an ideology-bound public sector which aims at the efficiency and permanency of the sociopolitical arrangements. Social classes cannot be sufficiently well explained by either individual differences or some apolitical system prerequisite, such as the necessity for a stratificatory system to test individuals' competence.

In the power theory, social classes assume, then, the same analytic quality as the State; they are in fact seen as direct consequences of the mobilization processes leading to the formation of a permanent sociopolitical unit. The current voluntaristic-interactionist theory of social stratification displays the same explanatory incapacity as does a theory aiming at analyzing the origin of the State in terms of automatically emerging mutual transactions, without considering the political elements of circumscription and coercion that are essential to its formation. The crux of the problem of sociological theories of the origin of the State seems to be that no lasting form of organization rendering a unit autonomous in its dealings with other similar units can be explained on the basis of a give-and-take pattern of reciprocity alone. A lasting sociopolitical organization requires the formulation and the programmation of an ideology that is restrictive and that in its restrictive capacity imposes a political responsiblity upon those subjected to it. This public ideology represents a pivotal element, linking public intentions and blueprints to the private activities of the participants and giving the reasons why such a linkage should exist. The public sector may use various degrees of coercion, persuasion, promise, and discipline in imposing the public commitments upon the recipient people, but the net effect of this politicalization process is a legitimate circumscription of the participants' lives. Unless the participants succeed in moving out completely, they will have to accept the legitimacy of the sociopolitical arrangement, not only because it is actively imposed upon them by the public sector, but also because the participants by not breaking away from the system render themselves subject to the sanctioning power that the public sector legitimately has.

Whereas the continuum model of social stratification may be helpful in gaining understanding of the short-term dynamics of mobility and change in open industrial societies, its limitations are obvious if the model is applied to agrarian societies undergoing change. It fails to account for social-class demands as these challenge existing political priorities and, importantly, it fails to bring home the point that social-class differences can be regulated by public action. The issue of social class, as I have examined it here, is the outcome of some type of collision of ideas as these emerge from the aspirations and projections of the public sector and become increasingly divorced from reality, which will force yielding action from the public sector. To an important degree, public policy as such aims at the regulation of social-class relations and at their restructuring over time.

In order to properly focus on the global (political) quality of social classes one might be well advised not to use the misleading word "class" at all. The admittedly vague term "operating unit" could perhaps be applied to refer to the structured power formations below the State level that the politically oriented sociologist has in mind. These operating units reflect responses to the restraints and distributive mechanisms that belong to the State. By replacing the term "social class" with the one "operating unit," the sociologist acknowledges that no power formations within the political entity can be fully free from State power, and also that the State power is continuously contested by such powerful subunits as the military, the cliques of a few families who may own most of the arable land, the Church, and the various movements of counterpower that may exist in latency.

Richard Adams in his study on Guatemala examined

"operating units" of this sort; he pointed out that the changing of the bases of the power may be contingent upon the access these units have "to derived power sources," in the manner the *finquero* (farm owner), for instance, may control his land directly but still depend on his annual credit, extended to him by a bank.[33] Power, in this view, can never be reduced to one-to-one statements of "who commands whom"; a full explanation of it requires also a reference to the institutionalized network of standards and practices that make up the political climate. Thus power, although it is basically personal in nature, can only be exercised in an institutional setting. The State provides a single set of standards that are accepted as legitimate, whereas social classes reflect the existing cleavages in people's demands and expectations from the public sector and in their access to the public sector. Social classes are consequently not merely clusters of individuals with similar attributes; they are alliances formed by groups of individuals in the struggle for power that goes on within the system. The State's function is to regulate this ongoing struggle, in order to carry out a moderating role that cannot for long belong to any particular segment of the system. The operating units that succeed in gaining control of the legitimacy principle may sponsor revolutions, as in the case of the Creoles overthrowing the Spaniards, thus establishing a monopoly on the State function. It seems that no single segment or operating unit can permanently monopolize the legitimacy principle. The State then becomes an idea system in the name of which demands for social justice will be made and shifts in ideology and in the access to power will be induced.

Subordination en Masse. In Aztec society prior to the Conquest, as Charles Gibson has pointed out,[34] a major social-class criterion reflected the differential status of the commoners (*macegudles*) and the subordinate peoples (*tlalmaites* and *mayeques* in Hispanized Nahuatl). The former owed indirect tribute, ordinarily paid in labor, to the communality and to the elites of kingdom, the nobility and priesthood. The latter owed private personal tribute and did not have tenure to the land they cultivated. Spanish colonialism removed this differentiation of status and placed all Indians under a single condition of powerless subordination.[35] Although the Spaniards in Mexico for a time recognized the upper-class ranks of Indian *tlatoques* (caciques) and *pipiltin* (relatives of the caciques), they did not recognize the line of efficient command from caciques to Indian commoners; this line of command was intercepted and replaced by a new one from encomenderos and corregidores to the Indian populations en masse.

Social classes in colonial Latin America evolved in circumstances that may be characterized as a contest between the royal power and the localistic power of the Spanish colonists over the efficient command of the Indians. The encomienda system involved a temporary concession to the colonists; it was progressively discontinued, however, by the mid-sixteenth century, and replaced in many areas by the system of corregimientos, a centralized system of government and tribute collection under the Crown.[36] Hacienda, on the other hand, emerged from the early *mercedes de tierra* (land grants), from land purchase, and from land concentration, as the principal institution absorbing and monopolizing command over Indians and over the use of their labor.

There were, then, two major power systems and thus two different orders of social class that evolved in Latin America from the Conquest (*Figure* 8). One was the official *urban* social-class structure, consisting of the hierarchy of upper-class

Spaniards (peninsulares), the middle stratum of American-born Creoles, and the lower-class mestizos in cities and towns. The other was the unofficial (from the point of view of the Crown) *rural* social-class structure, which evolved from concessions permitting the semifeudal landowning oligarchy to maintain jurisdiction over the Indian populations and over

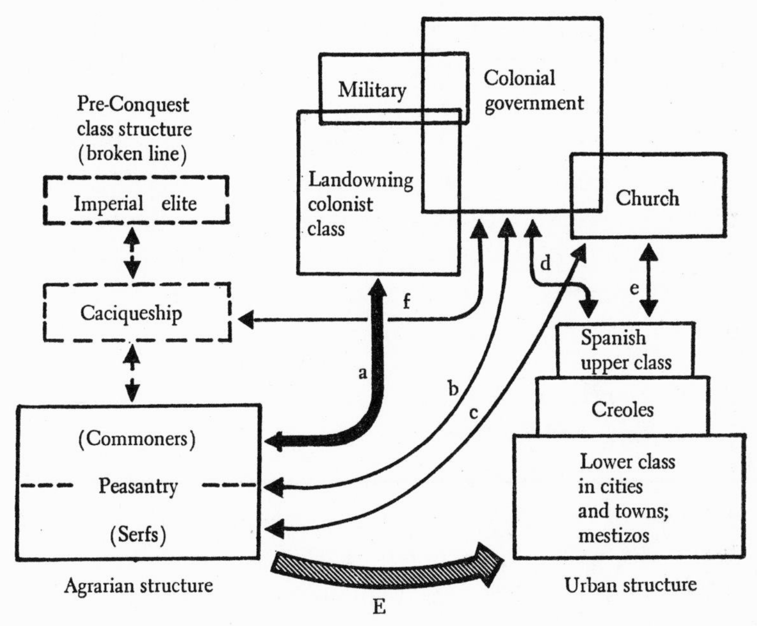

Figure 8. Colonial social-class structure in Latin America

the peasantry. The important status criteria in the urban social-class structure were ethnicity (*limpieza de sangre* or racial purity) and participation in administration within the colonial government *d* and the colonial Church *e*. In the agrarian social-class structure, in turn, the most significant status distinction related to the personal patrón-péon relationship *a* between the landowning colonist class and peasantry. Participation by the peasantry in administration within the colonial government *b* and the colonial Church *c* was minimized, and it was mediated by the patrón, and the role of preconquest caciqueship in adminstration *f* was only nominally recognized by the colonial government. In all essence, the absence of political participation and the lack of "nationalization" or "politicization" among the Latin America peasants, noticed by present-day observers of the Latin American scene, reflected the monopolistic distribution of power involved in the rigid patrón-peón relationship *a*, the absence of middle strata in the agrarian social-class structure, and the consequent absence of upward mobility within the agrarian structure. The pressures created by the rigid agrarian structure were released (and are increasingly in the twentieth century), in a disproportionately high rate of rural exodus *E*, with its compound side effects of slums, unemployment, and underemployment in the major cities.

Overcommitment, Avoidance, Ritualism, Fatalism, and Martyrdom

Previously we examined the types of error-regulating mechanisms that the wielders of power may apply in an attempt to lessen the pressures arising from the tension inherent in a situation where there are two political actors: the power holder and the victim of power.[37] We turn now to an examination of the responses of the latter. The question arises, What are the consequences to him of being power bound? What are the consequences, as far as he is concerned, of living in a protracted situation in which his spontaneous response to command is filtered, intercepted, anticipated, and expected to conform to a binding pattern?

By and large, the social scientist is concerned with collective movements insofar as these pursue a "cause" and possess a distinct counterideology of their own, and also insofar as a movement results in uprisings and authentic revolutions introducing permanent change in the social structure. It is my intention here to broaden the typology of reactive collective behavior and to propose that, besides collective movements and revolutions, there are several latent moods which do have explanatory significance in the sense of evoking unplanned change in the nature of public action. Revolution itself, I believe, is no unique turning point reversing the previous course of events, but it is preceded by collective danger signals that range from easy enthusiasm and passive withdrawal to militant resistance. Revolution is thus inseparable from the prerevolutionary and postrevolutionary processes that normally take place within any sociopolitical system. It is, in fact, the core of all social change. It does not necessarily involve bloodshed, military confrontation, or other violence. It does imply, however, an awareness on the part of the people of something that Chalmers Johnson has called "power deflation," [38] the evaporation of the confidence people had in the current power rationale. In the case of power deflation previously latent, unnoticed collective tendencies come into the open and are exploited by the agents of counterpower. The weak will seek alliance, in the case of a power deflation, in order to be able to confront the strong, and eventually these countercurrents will force change in the established governing principles themselves.

Overcommitment. One of the first of the collective reactions to power is overcommitment. This entails servility, overly easy compliance with a command, and a kind of initial fervor or sometimes an awe which is evoked by the presence of the commander or by one or another impressive aspect of the power system. Overcommitment may involve exaggerated feelings of loyalty in the newly initiated participants, especially if these are escapees from other systems, or it may involve a tendency toward uncritical and sometimes unsolicited adoration of the person of the power holder—Latin American *personalismo*. Overcommitment may also manifest itself in obstinate loyalty to a sacred cause to which the actor pays tribute irrespective of changes in the distribution of power. An example is Durkheim's notion of altruism, which means a state of personal sacrifice willingly assumed by the individual who has strong feeling of solidarity toward the group.

Examples of easy compliance with power are the Indians' gift-giving at the early stage of the Conquest, and their joining Cortés' occupying forces by the thousands. Overcommitment may thus fuse with an opportunistic desire to side, in a power contest, with a stronger party against a weaker wielder of power. The Indian women, to find a different example of overcommitment, were sexually attracted toward the Spanish and Portuguese conquerors, an attraction which resulted in a large mestizo sector.

Overcommitment on the part of the victim of power may evoke the tendency of the power holder to accept the credit for overfulfillment actually due to extraneous circumstances.[39] Overcommitment is a concept useful in explaining shortlived successes in planned change, and in explaining an ostentatious affectation of loyalty to a cause that is only vaguely understood. A false sense of security and a blind belief in "the cause" are derived from working together with people who never say "no." An example of such an ostentatious affectation is the blend of reverence and fear with which the Latin American peasant today regards religion. Orlando Fals Borda in his study on the peasants of Saucío, Colombia,[40] has given an interesting account of the timorous undertones in peasant religiosity; of the peasants' fearful attitudes toward the holy sacrament and toward the chance of excommunication (becoming "orphan of the Church"); and of the overcommitment to the cause of religion characteristic of an over-pious *lambeladrillo* (literally, a brick-licker).

In political analysis, overcommitment is important because it entails the unverified disposition of trust without immediate proof of the efficiency of the proclaimed policy. Either the people may enthusiastically confer decision-making powers on a strong man, who will then give his word that he will act in a manner worthy of their trust, or the power holders may adhere to an imagery of sociopolitical order, implying that history moves toward the realization of a cause to which both they and the people will rally in an overcommitted manner. In times of crisis and power deficit, overcommitment to person may prevail. Thus, in the first decades of Independence, the Latin American caudillos were more than a match for the idealistic "doctores" who wanted to foster a sense of sociopolitical order as derived from constitutionalism, positivism, and other "isms" which they imported from Europe. The former would speak of efficient action, the latter would speak of "truth." In either case, overcommitment from the people was expected.

In times of tranquillity, one learns from Latin American history, impersonal "truth" and what the Latin Americans call *principismo* may indeed carry weight. But at a time of crisis and transition it is no longer the truth that inspires political enthusiasm but the pull linked with the name of a strong man; thus *Rosismo* (from Juan Manuel de Rosas), *Peronismo*, and *Fidelismo*. It follows from the Latin American inclination toward liberalistic idealism after World War II that these personalistic "isms" are most often associated with a "cynical" argument in politics. Yet, one will ask, what do people place high, to what are they overcommitted, not only in Latin America but in any political tradition—glorious causes or personalistic leaders capable of assaulting at least some of the limitations of tradition, fossilized systems of ideas and morals, and decadent bureaucracy?

Avoidance. Victims of power may react in another way: they may show avoidance.[41] This involves evading responsibility, defensive fear, withdrawal, the lack of participation, isolation, refusal to take sides on controversial issues, and keeping one's mouth shut in public places. Frank Tannenbaum speaks of the "voicelessness" of the Indians in Latin America;[42] the expression *huelga de brazos caídos* has been used in reference to the Indians' basic attitude of impassive escapism. In all its briefness, a laconic anecdote from Bolivia before the 1952 revolution describes avoidance:

> Patrón: "It seems we will have rain soon."
> Peón (glancing at the cloudless sky): "*Sí, señor.*"

Apathy and inactivity associated with avoidance introduce a vicious circle of mutual distrust between the power holder and the victim of power. In colonial Latin America, the Indians' desire to have no part in the "different freedom" prescribed for them by well-meaning European reformers contributed to an image of the Indians as inherently incapable of self-government. The predominant attitude of the Europeans and the Creoles toward the Indians entailed the notion of the latter as incorrigibly "irresponsible" and infantile, and as "necessitating" permanent tutelage. Typical in this respect was Bolívar's position on the Indian issue.[43] The Indians only wanted peace and solitude, Bolívar held; they were easily assuaged; they had no ambition to impose their will on others, even if they were in majority. The Indians, consequently, could be discounted as a political factor in Latin America. The basic dilemma in the new Republic, for

Bolívar, rested on the divergence of opinion among the ruling European minority.

Fatalism. The fatalism of the victim of power can be best clarified in conjunction with the companion concept of *anomie.*[44] According to the original elabortion of these concepts by Emile Durkheim,[45] anomie is a mode of personality adaptation to a situation "disturbed by some painful crisis or by beneficent but abrupt transitions." Economic disasters, Durkheim says, suddenly cast individuals into a state lower than their previous one; individuals are "not adjusted to the condition forced on them." Anomie is the type of personality adaptation induced by societal crises and major societal transformations such as industrial revolution. The society's capacity to allocate benefits to its members has increased, and the "share of each class of producers" will have to be redefined. Time is required to reclassify men and things. "All classes contend among themselves because no established classification any longer exists." Permanent poverty, instead, "protects" individuals against suffering and against the feelings of deprivation they may develop as a consequence of competition and of being led to believe that they depend on themselves only. Self-incrimination, in other words, accompanies anomie; blame for failure is sought in oneself, not in others. Society is not effectively "present" in individuals; * the individual is left to his "individual passions."

Against this background, Durkheim briefly sketched his analytic counterpart, *fatalism,* but left it conceptually incom-

* Durkheim's notion that anomie may cause the individual to withdraw from normative conflict has inspired the more modern "cross-pressure" theories on political apathy and political participation. See S. M. Lipset, *Political Man* (London, Mercury Books, 1963), pp. 203ff.

plete. Fatalism is the kind of personality adaptation that occurs when the futures of individuals are "pitilessly blocked" and their passions "violently choked by oppressive discipline." Blame for failure is sought in others, not in oneself. Slavery is, for Durkheim, the prototype of fatalistic situation; by and large, fatalism for him has only historical interest, and examples of it are "hard to find."

Taking their lead from Durkheim, most contemporary sociologists have focused on anomie. Fatalism, thereby, has been either ignored or it has become conceptually fused with the master concept of anomie. Dorothy Meier and Wendell Bell have stated that "anomia is not necessarily confined to the city dweller. In fact, we may expect considerable despair in the near future among members of agricultural, nonindustrial, nonurbanized populations with low living standards —the densely settled 'undeveloped' areas." [46]

The problem is that "despair" of the dependent marginal people, the victims of a subsystem of power, has qualities which make it essentially different from the anomic despair of individuals competing for jobs and striving for security in the industrial labor market. For the latter, a degree of ego involvement is present. Individual achievement, competence, education, and other individually acquired assets may significantly add to the individual's strength to negotiate, to plan ahead, and to advance. Alternative opportunities of work may be available, and moving from one employment to another or from one type of employment to another may actually serve as a ladder.

The plight of farm laborers in Latin America does not look like this. Their careers are immobile from one generation to the next. A peón has little chance to get more wages by moving to work for another hacienda, since wages are not competitive. The only way for him to increase his wage returns, in today's rural Latin America, is to work extra hours, if this is possible, and, particularly, to increase the sold labor force of his family. A family's loss of labor force is linked with its social decline; a large family is an economic asset; the schooling of children beyond the minimum of the three R's is wasteful; and adolescent children, by moving to the city, may drive the parental generation to disaster. Social immobility, in fact, becomes a condition necessary for maintaining the family status quo of minimum subsistence.

The signficance of "not leaving the field" is enhanced by the fringe benefits of the *colono* (a sharecropper who receives in exchange for his work a small tract of patrón's land to cultivate). The colono, typically, is entitled to production in the tract assigned to him; he may build his house out of whatever materials are available; he may have right to pasture and irrigation water; and he may be allowed to gather firewood in the patrón's property.[47] Although a diversity of statuses in farm labor exists throughout Latin America, and the particular norms of the relationship between patrón and peón may vary greatly from one region to another, the *total* dependency of the peón and his family on a single employer still remains basically unchanged.

Thus the patrón, now as in the past, may tighten at will his hold on the peón or the colono, since the latter cannot relocate without accepting a risk that will affect deeply the traditional structures on the family and the community level. In order to move to the city, it commonly is necessary for the family to split up, so that the employable members will settle there first. The earlier communal structures, similarly, will barely survive in the city.

In terms of social structures, fatalism is produced by the unprotested phasing out of systems unsupported by official policy and exploited by other systems above them. These systems are unable to compete with the structures sponsored by those who have some sort of monopoly on public power. One complicating factor involved in producing fatalism seems to be that some elements in the old structures will refuse to have anything to do with the new superimposed structures, and refuse to compromise, despite an overcommitment to innovation on the part of some other elements in the same structures. For example, the tradition-bound elements in Latin America may look with suspicion upon technology, despite overcommitment to it on the part, for instance, of those who are committed to the ideal of *desarrollismo* (developmental policy). Structurally, fatalism thrives when officially backed systems are prospering and the voiceless systems are being exploited and crushed. Charles Gibson in his study on a late colonial hacienda in Mexico has shown how the hacienda's failure to make a profit immediately caused a lowering of the peones' wages and how, in a larger scale, the system of hacienda developed and prospered at times that were critical for the economy of the Indian towns.[48]

One point to make here is that the alleged inability of the Latin American nations to assimilate their rural lower-class populations into a modern nation-state,[49] if this is meant to imply irrational resistance by the "backward" sectors, is misleading. It is much more to the point to say that those who are subject to an overwhelming power, which they feel to be inimical, may altogether avoid the opening of any discussion, if they feel that it might lead to a change. In their experience, *any* change affecting their dependence will be for the worse. Herein lies the "conservativism of poverty," the unwillingness of the dependent to experiment with novelties, and their reluctance to accept any innovation, even though it has been allegedly introduced "in their favor." "It has been tried so many times," the Latin American peasants are likely to say about improvement, "and nothing good has ever come out of it." The fact is, at a time systems other than the peasants' prosper, they may be right.

The same kind of fatalistic tendency to completely ignore some large-scale problems that seem near bursting may also be characteristic of the holders of power. In Latin America, the issue of land tenure has over time become such an "unspeakable" topic. The breaking down of the latifundista pattern through drastic land reforms would bring immediate economic disaster, not in the first place to the landed groups but to the urban centers; it would endanger the national export economies based on the single-crop production of the large haciendas. Insofar as these nations depend on agricultural exportation for their economic equilibrium and self-sufficiency, the social immobility of their rural sectors is indispensable. The hacienda is a "closed" monolithic system because, being unmechanized, noncompetitive, and nonmodernizing, it makes use of a permanent stock of cheap labor, and in spite of its shortcomings its present functioning is vital to the national entities. The Mexican anthropologist Rodolfo Stavenhagen has made a similar point:

What is important is not the mere existence of two "societies," or a "dual society"—two contrasting poles at the end of a socio-economic continuum—but rather the relationships that exist between these two "worlds" and that bind them into a functional whole. To the extent that the localized development of certain areas in Latin America is based on the use of cheap labor . . . , the backward regions—those that provide the cheap labor—fulfill a specific function in the national society and are not merely zones in which, for one reason or another, development has not taken place. Moreover, the archaic zones are generally exporters of raw materials to the urban centers of the country and abroad. . . . The developed areas of the underdeveloped countries operate like a pumping mechanism, drawing from their backward, underdeveloped *hinterland* the very elements that make for their own development. This situation is not new to the underdeveloped countries. It is the result of a long historical process that began with the expansion of mercantilist and colonialist Europe.[50]

The efforts of social planners, now as in the colonial times, have been concentrated on finding ways to end the total dependency of the peasantry on the hacienda structure. On the one hand, some of the planners envision the masses of peones and colonos being converted to commercial farmers; sweeping land reforms would give them ownership of idle and undercultivated lands, expropriated with recompensation from their present owners. The weakness of the approach is that despite the gradualness of the contemplated land reforms, *ultimately* they are likely to throw the hacienda system out of balance, by reducing the number of wage-earning farm laborers and thereby enforcing competitive wages for farm labor. The conservative wing of planners, on the other hand, concentrates on enforcing minimum wage laws for farm labor, and on other legislative improvements in farm work. The weakness of the approach is that it leaves the structural marginality of the rural sectors essentially unchanged.

In contemporary efforts to increase social mobility among peasants, land reform and wage increase have priority; in the colonial society, on the other hand, improvement was sought through legislative policy obliging patrones to pay wages in cash instead of in kind. Portugal's Jesuit Court-Preacher António Vieira, for example, in the mid-seventeenth century fiercely attacked the slavery of the Indians, even though its abolition, he said, would force the colonists' wives and sons to "fetch a pail of water," or "carry a load of wood," or "grind the manioc."[51] The Indians living in "King's villages" (in which they alternated two months of hired work for the Europeans with two months of their own labor and received seven feet of cloth a month for hired work) should receive their wages in cash, Vieira demanded. Like Las Casas, Vieira insisted that freedom for the Indians could best be obtained by importing more slaves from Africa.[52] His proposals, like those of Las Casas, were met with hostility among the colonists and suspicion among the friars of the Mendicant orders and among the Crown's officials. Facing the risk of being manhandled or lynched, Vieira and his associates were for a time deported to Portugal in 1661.

Fatalism, seen as a state of mind, is associated with a permanent state of society in which the actor's self-generated efforts to improve his lot are futile and the impulses for change "from below" are inefficient. Social change and improvement, in the fatalistic disposition, are induced from above if they are to occur at all. Outside determinants—the will of patrón, government, king, president, church, and ultimately God, and their mutual alliances, are given primacy. Actor-centered sources of social change such as learning, individual adaptation, self-help, self-efficiency, and voluntarism are minimized. The individual interprets his life experiences as dependent on extrasystemic distant agents largely unknown and unreachable by direct contact. Individual achievement, self-generated regulation of error in response, planning, and individualism in general are de-emphasized, and conformity is emphasized. The peasant does not compete over issues that he knows he cannot win or even influence; he may be aware of a larger society, which he is "in" but not altogether "of."[53] Causation is seen in terms of forces at play above the actor's ability to interfere. For the Latin American peasant, "God gives the harvest, God takes it away," and epidemics may be divinely willed, thus making vaccination inappropriate.[54] "Usurpation goes well as long as God wills," an old Indian proverb from Colombia tersely states.

Recognition of this basic weakness of the Latin American society is only the first step toward its correction. To some, fatalism means the simple issue of mental dispositions such as the absence of achievement motivation. In this interpretation, it may be best combatted by educating the affected individuals. Just who is capable of undertaking this enormous and anomalous task remains unexplained. To others, fatalism signifies the impersonal workings of "laws of history" such as the "contradictions of capitalism." In this interpretation, no effort short of overthrowing capitalism itself can restore the Latin American peasants' confidence in their individual achievement.

An intermediate position is taken in the present essay. Fatalism among the Latin American peasantry, it is argued here, is associated with the peculiar marginality produced since the Conquest. It is a state of mind *and* a state of policy orientation bent upon conquest. Two major power systems evolved: the official imperial system of power predominant in the urban sectors of the colonial society and the localistic unofficial counterpower of the landowning colonists, predominant in the rural parts. There was a confrontation between the two, hostility between what José Luis Romero of Argentina has called the "small fatherlands" of the localistic nuclei of power and the innovating power vested in the governments of the emerging nation-states.[55] The national governments of the metropolis underestimated the power of the landowning elite, or were dominated by it; above all, they overlooked the fact that the ideals of political equality, social mobility, and an open society could not be obtained within the latifundista system which, on the other hand, was the economic backbone of the independent republics. The liberal doctores advocated the ideal of liberty at a time the peasants had already been forced to accept dependence on the landlords and the commitments involved in a rigid agrarian system, and at a time this rigidity of structures had become indispensable for the national system. The peasants' mobility was thus sacrificed to the greater good of national wellbeing. Individualism and voluntarism were taken as explanatory principles where fatalism prevailed. To break down the vicious circle creating fatalism is, of course, not impossible, but it involves ideological innovation, high economic cost, and powerful means to implement a significant policy of equalization.

Martyrdom. One primary reaction to power, when it is felt to be overbearing, is the attempt to defy it, even though the fatalistic actor must know that his defiant act will be punished, or that uprising is hopeless, or that there is no escape from reprisals except at his own risk and ultimately in death. Some kind of martyrdom is the logical consequence of fatalism. If the actor perceives a world controlled by outsiders, and if this world is seen as changing from bad to worse, then one meaningful thing to do is to blame his misfortune on someone else. If the actor's known protest motive is publicized, an aura of martyrdom may be created which, again, may heighten the mobilization effect of protest ideologies to come. Martyrdom, it is true, means escape, but no longer a defeatist escape for those who bear witness to it. It is a glorified kind of escape, involving penalty or suffering accepted by a person whose lawbreaking or fault exists only in the eyes of the establishment and whose action the protesters expect to be eventually justified by all. A martyr does not necesarily advocate resistance, yet he is no longer harmless to the establishment, because he, in dissenting, has opened up the possibility of new identity and new affiliation among the people along the lines of "they" and "us." Martyrdom by its weight may precipitate overt reactions such as open protests, appeals, and revenge. It marks the beginning of self-organizing countermovements which will serve as a warning that the latent resistance is gaining increasing strength.

Martyrdom derives its unique power from the fact that it may be achieved either by a single dissenting subject or by an anonymous mass of victims of the system; for instance the people in poverty-stricken areas may be victimized collectively by factors beyond their control and be unable to move out, for lack of economic means. The Latin American novel provides descriptions of peasant movements culminating in martyr action of this kind. One example is Euclides da Cunha's *Rebellion in the Backlands*, a book that labors to demonstrate how despondency is transformed into heroism in reaction to government attacks and how fully organized guerrilla communities have their origin in fatalism. Government reprisals in Latin America tend to intensify the power of the protest movements and to widen the gap between the government and the people and create symbols whose example may spread to other situations. Martyrdom personifies and concretizes the unexpressed desires of the oppressed people, reinforces them in the drama of the martyr's sacrifice, and attracts the uncommitted to the cause of the dissenters. It is therefore the necessary link between the collective and the individual levels of action. Although martyrdom may signify defeat, it will have demonstrated to the power holders and the people alike that a single individual, in principle at least, has the capacity to challenge principles upon which the system is based and that his example may live on. The power holders are forced to handle would-be martyrs as explosive elements whose impact far exceeds their organizational strength and who may be indicative of important things to come. By publicly taking sides with the martyrs of the past, again, the power holders can explicitly indicate that they have sanctioned the ideological innovation which the victimized prophets of change heralded.

In the colonial Latin America, two men attained martyrdom of lasting significance: Father Miguel Hidalgo (1753–1811) in Mexico and José Gabriel Tupac Amarú (1742?–1781) in Peru. Both of these men led revolts against the Spanish and lost their lives in these. Hidalgo's martyrdom reflected the spirit of French Enlightenment and mestizo-Christianity, and the revolt he led aimed at the elimination of social inequalities and caste privileges. The Hidalgo revolt was philosophically derived from the principle of equality; it was inspired by the notion that in the ideological struggle for power the legitimacy of the forces from the civil sectors must be recognized. Hidalgo labored for a new conception of social justice, implying that the Indians should be told of the injustice and cruelty by which they had been conquered and deprived of their lands, and they should be urged to fight back to reclaim their lands and their rights. This was an egalitarian revolution designed to reverse the results of the Conquest and emancipate the oppressed classes. For this equalizing effect, Hidalgo's was an ideology the newly established Mexican State could endorse; and it did so, immediately after independence was won. Tupac Amarú's rationale, although it did emphasize assimilation between the two cultures and although it recognized the legitimacy of the royal power, failed, even after independence, to attract the Creoles, who had ambition for achieving leadership in the new republics without giving the Indians any effective power. Consequently the symbolism associated with Tupac Amarú could not be endorsed by the newly established Peruvian State, and the revolt that Tupac Amarú led still maintains the aura of illegitimate uprising. The urban guerrillas in present-day Uruguay, in fact, name their rebel movement after the famous eighteenth-century martyr of Indian resistance.

Publicity accompanying the deeds of these men is paramount in the perpetuation of the counterpower involved in martyrdom. Few people knew of Tupac Amarú's martyrdom, whereas every Mexican schoolboy now learns the history of Miguel Hidalgo. There were scores of unpublicized Negro slaves in the West Indies in the eighteenth century who, as in Haiti, poisoned cattle, killed their fellow slaves, committed mass suicide, or ran away in panicky flight after they had killed their masters, only to wait tremulously in hiding places for their recapture. Still, none of these runaway slaves and forerunners of the "Black Revolution" of 1790 in Haiti gained the personifying publicity that politically effective martyrdom requires. The Voodoo religion, although it fed on oppression and slavery, did not officially nurture the memory of these early victims to raise them to the public counterpower that martyrdom may entail politically. Also, although the initial phase of the 1790 revolution in Haiti was plotted by Voodoo priests and other authentic Negro slave insurgents, Haitian independence, when it was finally obtained in 1803, was no longer inspired by the spirit of Negritude. Rather, it was inspired by the Westernizing ideals of men such as Pierre Dominique Toussaint L'Ouverture (1746–1803), who believed in the "educability" of the Negro, deeply admired the French culture, and was convinced of the superiority of Christianity over Voodoo. Thus, in Haiti as in Peru, the deeds of the early martyrs of independence were not officially recognized as a part of the patriotic folklore of the emergent nations.

Martyrdom, thus, fulfills several kinds of functions. It sometimes serves as an early reminder to the establishment that the existing official power system may be vulnerable. As Origen (185?–253?), a Church Father from Alexandria whose own father suffered martyrdom under Septimius Severus aptly put it, the martyrs "despoil . . . the principalities and powers . . . which you will soon see conquered and overcome with shame."[56] In the same way that power is personified in the ruler, counterpower may be personified in the martyr. In this meaning, martyrdom may have latent impact in a prerevolutionary situation. Martyrdom may also offer the liberation leaders themselves the ideological backdrop necessary for carrying on the unfinished task and mobilizing courage in combat. In a postrevolutionary situation, finally, the deeds of the martyrs, insofar as they have a totalizing impact upon the system ideology, will be officially commemorated. They will then serve as inspiring models in efforts at politicization. A new set of heroes recognized by the establishment indicates that a reassessment of priorities has indeed occurred.

IV

Toward Overt Resistance

The Virgin of Guadalupe

The prevailing theological doctrine, until the middle of the eighteenth century, generally held that conversion represented an "absolute rupture."[1] The doctrine regarded pagan civilizations and pagan religions as completely corrupt, uncultivated, and unworthy. The past was to be totally wiped out. Conversion was to mean a clean break with the individual's former environment; no valid elements were found in the past that could serve as a bridge to the future, and there was, therefore, no room for accommodation. In all this can be seen the medieval attitude of horror toward making a pact with the devil.

In New Spain, the ability of the religiosos in spiritual accommodation came to test soon after the Conquest. In 1531, the time-honored legend goes, Virgin Mary appeared to a humble Indian convertite, Juan Diego, at a mountainside at Tepeyac, a few miles outside Mexico City. It was the wish of Virgin Mary that a church be built at the site of her appearance, and Juan Diego was to relay this message to the archbishop. Unable at first to understand and to believe the Indian's report, Archbishop Juan de Zumárraga, however, was impressed when two days later Juan Diego returned to tell of a second appearance, and an image of the Virgin

Mary—later known as the Virgin of Guadalupe—was found imprinted in the folds of his *tilma*, or shoulder cloth.

Tepeyac, it happens, had traditionally been an important center of religious pilgrimage where, before the arrival of the Spaniards, an altar had stood in dedication to the Aztec Goddess Tocí, Mother Earth. Tocí's face had been painted half black and half white, and she had worn an elaborate crown not unlike the one worn by Virgin Mary in Christian art. As a consequence of the old tradition's blending with new symbolism, the name of Mother Earth became confused with that of the Virgin of Guadalupe in the native tongue. On the other hand, the Virgin of Guadalupe, with her coppery complexion, was depicted as a captivating mestiza, not as the blond medieval European madonna; unorthodoxically, she did not carry the holy child in her arms. The Indians found their dethroned Mother Earth in the new guise of the Virgin of Guadalupe; a vigorous cult of the mestiza-Mother sprang from the legend of the apparition, and the pilgrimages to Tepeyac were resumed.

The new cult may at first have escaped the attention of the religiosos; Archbishop Zumárraga, for one, made no reference in his memoirs to the miracle of Tepeyac. During subsequent decades, however, the legend gathered impetus, and the healing powers ascribed to the Virgin of Guadalupe attracted untold numbers of Indian and lower-class believers. A royal decree issued in 1551 barred Indians from membership in the *cofradía* (brotherhood) of Guadalupe.[2] In 1556, Fray Francisco de Bustamante, in the presence of high colonial officials, unleashed in his sermon a scathing attack against the revival of idolatry that the cult represented. He grimly warned that it endangered the fruits of missionary labor and excited the fancy among the Indians that a picture "painted by Indian Marcos" would have miracle-making powers.[3] The mestizaje motive of the cult of the Virgin of Guadalupe was fully appreciated only much later and it was made their foremost symbol by the revolutionary independentists in the early nineteenth century, when Miguel Hidalgo chose the Virgin of Guadalupe for patron guardian. In the postrevolutionary republic of Mexico, the subversive edge in the tradition of the Virgin of Guadalupe had finally worn off, and the cult became "respectable." In 1940, it become associated with right-wing patriotism, when Manuel Avila Camacho, a conservative candidate, replaced the socialist Lázaro Cárdenas in the presidency. At this time extremist opinion demanded that loyalty to the cult of the Virgin of Guadalupe be considered a test of patriotism and that nonbelievers be subject to persecution.

In the rest of Spanish America, visitations by the mestiza Mother of God followed the Mexican pattern. As in Mexico, apparitions were perceived by the people; miracle-performing objects were found and their powers testified to by Indians, caciques, mestizos, mulattos, and "humble laborers"; and, again, the eyewitnesses projected their own racial features upon the divine agents who appeared.[4] The Indians and the mestizos did not respond to the unyielding doctrinal and hortatory approach of the first missionaries, an approach which demanded the passive acceptance of the new religious system as an unmodified whole. The rhetorical "spiritual conquest" of the New World never occurred in the expected preprogrammed pattern. Instead, Christian doctrines were modified to fit the pagan mold. In the emergent mestizo Christianity, God did not descend upon the earth; nor was the divine principle accepted as such from the European theology. The Indians clamored for their right to partnership in erecting a supreme divine symbol, one which would embody an aspect of their past, of their own values and aspirations. No spiritual shift occurred in the manner of cultural diffusion from the conquering system to the subject system, but the conquered insisted on their right to spiritual self-organization, which would enable them to find "us-ness" in the religion replacing the old one. To the extent that the divine principle was shared, it became a protective and life-giving symbol instead of a threatening *memento mori*. The Indians' claim of their right to share the ultimate power principle and to creatively modify it is the key to an understanding of the rationale of the Indian uprisings in the eighteenth and nineteenth centuries. These uprisings were liberation movements the legitimacy of which rested, in the Indians' conception, not on the naked power of the insurgents, but on their demand for legitimate access to the ultimate power principle. They were movements directed against those who abused authority in the lower echelons of the colonial establishment, not against the supreme royal or divinely ordained authority.

Mestizo-Indian Protest

Among other colonial designs that had as their purpose the preservation of Indian culture were various formulae for preferential treatment of the native caciques. In theory, the ancient rights of the caciques over their subjects—the *macehuales* or commoners—were to be respected; normally the caciques could be prosecuted in the superior courts only; the sons of the caciques were to be free from *mita* (forced labor in mining). During the first decades after the Conquest, the caciques were entitled to demand tribute and services from the macehuales—a prerogative that commonly resulted both in a double tax burden imposed on the common Indian and in frequent disputes over the legitimacy of the claim of a tribal Indian leader to a caciqueship.[5] On the other hand, the Spanish corregidores (local administrative officials and judges) could interfere with the caciques' decisions. Thereby the caciques were reduced to minor administrators under the corregidores and mayordomos, who were the foremen of the encomiendas, until the last vestiges of their authority evaporated.

A new mestizo intelligentsia, however tentative and quietist, did come into existence even under colonial chaperonage. In Peru and in Mexico, many of the descendants of indigenous ruling families affected noble ways of life, even to the point of ostentation.[6] They did benefit from their European-style education at the missionary colleges; and, at times, combined the material wealth inherited from their conquistador fathers with the exotic prestige carried by their maternal families. Some mestizo writers earned distinction as historians of the pre-Colombian past and as chroniclers of the events of the Conquest. Their treatises blended latent nostalgia for the pre-Colombian past with voluble admiration for the Spaniards and for their Christianizing acts. For this they were censored and ordered to make their writings conform to the European view of history. Chronicler Garcilaso de la Vega Inca (1539–1616), the son of an eminent conquistador and of a niece of a deposed Inca ruler, dutifully promised that he would "not write novelties unheard of heretofore, but the same things that the Spanish historians have written . . . , citing their very words whenever convenient, so that it could be seen that I am not relating fiction in favor of my parents but saying the same as the Spaniards said."[7] In New Spain, the gubernatorial committee which authorized in 1608 the publication of the historical works of Fernando de Alva Ixlilxochitl (c 1568–1648, direct descendant of the last king of the Texcocans) found it to the author's merit that his famous ancestor had been a staunch ally of Hernán Cortés. This ancestor fought against his own uncles and brothers and delivered his older brother, a renegade, as a prisoner to the hands of Cortés.[8] The writer himself admiringly narrated these events in homage to Christian soldiership.

The first documented expressions of colonial protest came from the ranks of the mestizo intelligentsia. In 1748 Fray Calixto Tupac Inca, a lay brother, clandestinely distributed among the principal caciques in Peru his *Veracious Representation and Meak and Lamentable Exclamation All the Indian Nation Makes to His Majesty the King of Spain and the Emperor of the Indies, Don Ferdinand VI, Asking for His Attention and Remedy, to Take Them from Their Shameful Ignominy and Debasement in Which They Have Lived for More Than Two Hundred Years.*[9]

The Indians are now Christians, Fray Calixto claimed in this intense document; and yet they are excluded from priesthood and from full secular status. They have to pay the Spaniards in order to be mistreated by them; and they have to pay for the wood on which they are crucified. They are ruled by viceroys, governors, corregidores, and judges who are nothing but His Majesty's servants, but who, in the colonies, have transformed themselves into kings by their own right. Fray Calixto assured the king of the loyalty of the Indians and brushed aside a contemporary Indian uprising (1742–1753) as a mere skirmish incited by a "few barbaric and rustic Indians, naked and without military concert." He particularly insisted on the right of the Indians to be heard by the king. Why should we be your vassals, your subjects, your tributaries, your sons, Fray Calixto queried, only to serve, to fatten the royal treasury with the fruits of our sweat? Only because we are Christians. Recognize us as such, get to know us, take us into your presence and listen to us!

Fray Calixto demanded that the canons of the Roman Catholic Church and the laws and decrees of the Court be fully enforced in the colonies and that obsolete laws be repealed. He called for the right of the Indians to hold property, engage in commerce, and manage their own farms and institutions; also he demanded the right to substitute Indians for the Spaniards and mulattoes as administrators and foremen in agriculture. He demanded the abolition of debt peonage and of the free services imposed on the Indians, he requested that the Indians be taught how to read and write and that they be accepted at colleges and seminaries. He petitioned the abolition of the mita, the commending of the Indians to the Spaniards, and the replacement of Spanish corregidores by Indian officials. As elsewhere in the Spanish empire, only the positions of viceroy and governor should be reserved exclusively for the Spanish. And he recommended the establishment of a joint high tribunal, composed of Spanish authorities and Indian nobles and mestizos, as a replacement for the Council of the Indies.

The *Exclamation* was intended to express the anxieties and wishes of the "Indian Nation" to the king in person, without passing through the hands of the colonial administrators or the Council of the Indies. After nearly a full year of risky, unauthorized travel, Fray Calixto arrived in Madrid in 1750, where he was refused an audience with the king unless the matter was first discussed by the council. Determined not to let this happen, with his trust in the good will of the king unshattered, Fray Calixto followed in the trail of the royal party on a hunting trip and, the opportunity arising, rushed through the retinue of soldiers and tossed the document into the king's chariot. Though the king was said to have read the manifesto, Fray Calixto's subsequent discussions with the members of the council proved fruitless. By

1756 Fray Calixto, back in Peru, was active in organizing subversive juntas among the caciques; he was apprehended and exiled to a cloister in Spain.

An emancipation movement aiming at the restoration of the caciqueship and the abolition of the caste barriers imposed on the Indians, as it soon became evident, was highly disagreeable to the Creoles. Although they nursed a bitter hatred for the Spaniards, they pictured themselves as heirs to power and wealth rather than as champions of popular revolutions. Colonialism thus bred longing for independence as well as class tensions. Appointments in administration, church, jurisdiction, and army were made in Madrid; the Spaniards formed alliances to keep Creoles from being nominated as directors of educational institutions; and "any barber of the Court could be assured of seeing his son appointed, at least, the administrator of a major customs house." [10] As the Creoles became more affluent and better educated, their intolerance of colonial abuse grew to bitter antagonism. Yet, whereas the Indians and mestizos aspired to freedom from local exploitative practices, the Creoles favored the maintenance of a social infrastructure in the form of an oligarchy, transferred to them from the Spaniards.

The so-called Tupamarista revolution (1780–1783), the last and most violent of the Indian uprisings in South America, illustrates these contrasts. It was instigated by José Gabriel Tupac Amarú (1740–1781), another educated mestizo who traced his genealogy on his mother's side back to the last Inca. Like most of the mestizo elite, Tupac Amarú was a devout Catholic and a genuine admirer of the European culture and Spanish legal system. Authorized cacique since 1776, familiar with the problems of the Indians and particularly concerned with the wretched conditions of the miners working under mita at Potosí, he became an advocate of far-reaching reforms. His demands, as he expressed them in his letters to the viceroyalty and in his edicts to the caciques, were virtually identical with the ones made by Fray Calixto a generation earlier: the abolition of the mita and of the forced transplantation of Indians from their villages; the substitution of the corregidores by locally elected alcaldes; the examination and amendment of the practices of taxation and land distribution; the elimination of the obligation of the Indians to buy at stores owned by landlords; the abolition of the practice of expropriation of the lands of the Indians who were unable to pay their debts; and the correcting of the mistreatment of Indians working for haciendas. "The hacendados (large landowners) treat us worse than slaves," Tupac Amarú complained; "they make us work from two o'clock in the morning to the rise of the evening stars; they pay only two *reales* a day; on Sundays they make us to do extra work, on the pretext of needing us there to check our work records." And: "The corregidores are such great chemists that instead of turning gold into blood to sustain us they take our blood to nurse their own ambitions; . . . they torment the priests to the point of shedding blood; they profane holy images; and they prohibit the Indians from taking part in the divine cult, on the pretext that it would add to their poverty . . . , they intimidate priests and stifle in them the love for God and His Saints." [11]

It was Tupac Amarú's intention to provoke what he considered a morally rightful uprising against bad administration and, particularly, the corregidores, not against any specific ethnic group. His revolutionary appeal was summarily addressed to "Spaniards, Creoles, mestizos, *zambos* [mixture of Indian and Negro] and Indians." [12] The ensuing hostilities, nevertheless, assumed the character of a caste war, with the *realistas* commanding the support of most of the clergy (who organized in Cuzco military companies of their own), of the majority of Creoles and mestizos, and of a considerable number of loyal caciques and their men. The few Creoles and priests who initially cooperated with the revolutionary forces soon backed out or remained in contact with Tupac Amarú only in order to spy on the movements of his troops.

In the mining city of Oruro (in present-day Bolivia), the Indian revolution, for a brief, tumultuous period in 1781, took a different turn. With mining operations on the decline, the leading Creole families here had suffered heavy economic losses. They had failed to obtain from the realistas either capital for investment or political concessions to escape complete ruin. A Creole clan, probably inspired by Tupac Amarú's edicts, plotted a conspiracy against the *chapetones* (Spaniards). They called for the Indians, mulattoes, and mestizos who worked in the mines, and the Indian peasants to assist them in insurrection. The Indians responded readily, started pouring into the town, sacked European businesses and houses and took over nearby farms. In an attempt to control the Indian mobs, the Creoles, at one critical moment, urged them to enter the church, where a priest handed over to them some weapons of the Europeans as a token of surrender. But when he began to give advice to them, the Indians forced him to come down from the pulpit and scoffed at the holy images which had been hurriedly carried in a procession arranged by the priests to distract the Indians. Soon vandalism, plundering, and killing went beyond anyone's control. Lacking food supplies, threatened by the Indians who, after withdrawing from the city held it in siege, the Creoles decided to seek the assistance of their former enemies, the realistas, who had been in hiding in Cochabamba. Beginning as an attempt at a Creole revolt, the

Oruro uprising furnished dramatic proof of the inability of the Creoles and the Indians to unite in a common front against the Europeans.[13]

Impulse for Change "from Below"

In the previous discussion (Chapter III), overcommitment, ritualism, avoidance, fatalism, and martyrdom were outlined as early modes of adjustment, or latent resistance, by Indians and peasants, to powerful command. All these modes have in common the assumption of an unpreparedness on the part of the "victims" of power to actively participate in the morphogenetic processes underlying social change. They accentuate the dependence, the inertia, and the silence of the peasant class, and the conventional view that significant historical events occur at a level above the limited world of the peasant's earthbound routine.

This version of history is obviously simplified. "No longer is it possible to take seriously the view that the peasant is an 'object of history,' a form of social life over which historical changes pass but which contributes nothing to the impetus of those changes," Barrington Moore, Jr., remarked.[14] The problem is how to assess peasant contribution; how to explain peasant unrest, peasant rebellion, and peasant revolution; and how to incorporate the study of peasant movements and peasant activism into a treatise of the sociopolitical events within the larger system. In the broadest sense, the question is: How does one explain social change when the dependence of a silent sector upon an active and powerful one is the salient feature of the situation?

The classics, one might note, related the problem of dependence (or power) not to change, but rather to stability. In an ideal society, Plato held, the individuals would be divided into those who worked, those who performed military service, and those who ruled. Dependence was necessary and natural. The State should concentrate on an educational effort to improve the capacities needed for individuals to fulfill their functions in their respective places.

It was Hegel who introduced the truly revolutionary theory associating dependence not with stability, but with impending change and revolution. In the long historical perspective, Hegel held, power and dependence do not last, They are doomed to dissolve in the dialectics of the World Idea as it unfolds in history.

One approach to Hegel's views is his *Phenomenology of the Mind* (1807), a book by which Marx, among others, was deeply impressed, and which he called the "true birthplace and secret of the Hegelian philosophy." This book includes a chapter on "Independence and Dependence of Self Consciousness: Lordship and Bondage," [15] a treatise on power and cognition.

Hegel's starting point is extremely abstract. What happens when one self-consciousness encounters another self-consciousness? Two things. First, he must undertake to "nullify" the other independent being, to eliminate his own double, in order to secure a self-identity of his own. Second, he must "nullify" himself, for his "other being" is, indeed, "self." The same process of emergent self-consciousness occurs within the other. "Each sees the other self do what it does itself; each itself does what it demands from the other; and so does what the other does, but only insofar as the other does the same." One-sided action, Hegel explains, would be useless.

Thus, he continues, the relation of the two self-consciousnesses is determined by a struggle for life and death." The two must enter this struggle, for only by testing can they gain the certainty of themselves. It is only by risking one's life that the immediate experience of being oneself is obtained. "The individual who has not staked his life may well be recognized as a person, but he has not grasped the truth of this realization." Similarly, each must aim at the death of the other: the "outer-self being" (*Aussersichseyn*) must be negated.

Yet, for Hegel, the relationship as it now unfolds is not symmetrical. Unlike today's "symbolic interaction theorists" and "exchange theorists," Hegel did not speak of the individual, in abstraction, interacting with another individual, in abstraction; nor does he speak of "ego" interacting on equal footing with "alter." For Hegel, there exists a built-in inequality on the conscious level. The master's is the consciousness that "exists for itself." It is, however, a consciousness which is projected toward the exterior world only through the efforts of the other, the bondsman or the slave. Moreover, "the master relates to the servant by way of the independent Being, for that is precisely what keeps the bondsman in thrall; it is his chain, from which he could not disentangle himself in a struggle." That is why the bondsman proves himself dependent, and he proves his dependence by becoming a thinglike being (an object of "reification"). Thence, the master relates to exterior reality through the servant, whereas the latter can express his individuality only by working (*bearbeiten*) upon the exterior reality. It is the master who exploits this arrangement, Hegel held; yet, fatally for himself, for he has interposed the bondsman between himself and the unfolding existence. His immediate mastery and control over the existence are curtailed.

In serving and toiling, Hegel went on, the bondsman passes from a negative relation to the object into a meaningful relationship with it and into a command of the "form" of the object. He now becomes aware of himself, *in* himself, as being factually and objectively self-existent. "In fashioning the thing," Hegel expressed it, "self-existence comes to be felt explicitly as its own proper being, and it attains the consciousness that itself exists by its own right and on its own account." It is precisely in labor that the bondsman becomes aware of being himself—an independent being. In work and through work the servant acquires a mind and a self-consciousness of his own.

To the modern reader, Hegel seems to say two things. First, all enduring interpersonal relationships are power oriented, with the power holder deriving his relative autonomy (for the time being) from his access to a general principle or ideology in which both actors are enclosed. Second, power becomes exhausted. The actor subjected to power, through the very process of carrying out his commanded and initially routine work, will gain self-sufficient mastery over the environment, which eventually liberates him from his instrumentlike (reified) existence into a free and self-conscious existence. He will then challenge the existing power relation. The "principle" which in the past justified the master's superiority has lost its thrall and its overall validity within the system. The slave, on his part, has discovered a way out of his objectlike existence, and he will now face up to the challenging and wonderful reality of his existence with new courage and hope.

Similar notions underlie the theories of Marx and Engels. The industrial revolution, they held, has created a master class of large manufacturing capitalists, but also a laboring class, a far more numerous one. The latter's destinies, at first, depend on the capitalists' design, but the laboring class will gradually increase in numbers, and this numerical increase will awaken the workers to a realization of their power and push them toward self-organization. Whereas official class ideology, in the capitalistic society, distorts reality by adhering in symbolism that is historically out of phase, the exploited classes will eventually challenge the "truth" of the official establishment and doubt the long-range "stability" of existing institutions. New truth, in these circumstances, is created through revolutionary praxis.

The peasant as a sociopolitical type would seem to defy the Hegelian-Marxian theories of conscious emancipation. His life style is marked by ritualistic overcommitment, conformity, and fatalism. His appears to be the belief that the will of God has made the world such as it is; that the determinants of an individual life cycle are "given" from above; and that "learned" determinants (such as good administration of one's affairs, or planning ahead) do not shape the destinies of man.

There is, however, a rebellious and explosive element involved in the peasant outlook. Fatalism produces a state of mind whereby a distant *outside* (extrasystemic) frame is employed to explain change: God, king, government, or patrón. Now, whenever the fatalistically oriented peasant feels that things are changing from bad to worse, he will lay blame not on himself but on the holders of power above him, on those agents with whom he is somewhat but not completely familiar. Aggression rather than self-incrimination is the concomitant of fatalism. Those Latin American writers are right, I believe, who depict the Indian, and the peasant, in terms of heroic passivity instead of submission. The Indian was reduced to his present "animality" by the inhuman exploitation to which he was subjected since the Conquest, the Bolivian writer Alcides Arguedas (1879–1949) maintained. But whenever suffering becomes intolerable, he will make an uprising; he will follow his heart full of hatred, vent his passions, Arguedas said; he will then rob and kill with a blind fury. Authority, patrón, power, priest no longer exist for him.[16] Latent resistances come into the open in an abrupt manner.

There are less violent responses to subjection, however, which may occur before the "blind" peasant fury will erupt. Those who want to avoid the rigidities of the agrarian structure may "escape" to the cities. Since colonial times, the exodus of displaced individuals rather than feudalistic immobility has in fact been characteristic of many rural areas in Latin America. The consequences in large cities have been disastrous. Baron von Humboldt, for one, when visiting Mexico City in the beginning of the nineteenth century, was impressed by the mass misery he saw and by the sight of the numbers of Indians sleeping off their drunkenness on the streets, then piled up in carts and taken away as if they were human garbage.

Appeal to a source of power above one's immediate master is another nonviolent response to oppression. Appeal aims at proposing a charitable undertaking, or a correction on behalf of the subjects victimized by the system. It involves the proposal that showy action and promise be redeemed in corrective action, and it often points out the ways in which this should be done. It is an attempt to identify the guilty party when marginality is the issue, by accusing the one responsible for the deprivation; in this accusation an appeal may link complaints with names of individuals and practices, thus bringing latent issues into the open and submitting them to the attention of the gubernatorial sector. Grievances are thereby documented. It is noteworthy that in the colonial system the audiencia real was supposed to serve as the court of appeal, particularly for the "humble classes," yet it signally failed to do so. The Indians, for one thing, were afraid that resort to the audiencia would bring reprisals from the corregidores. Outside the audiencia, again, the channels for bringing complaints to the Crown's knowledge were blocked; the Indians were even prohibited from unauthorized travel outside the territorial limits of the corregimiento. Fray Calixto's adventurous travel to Madrid represented, therefore, something more than a legitimate meek appeal. Being unauthorized and secret, it disregarded the official power hierarchy: it was a subversive act, therefore, and a protesting act.

Another element in Fray Calixto's mission made it distinctly subversive. His *Exclamation* did not aim at the remedy of individual abuses by bringing these to the king's knowledge. Rather, it was derived from the plainly revolutionary notion of an Indian "Nation" demanding its rights. A degree of self-organization, illusory or not, was implied in the protest. The head of an allegedly organized unit, in Calixto's reasoning, was approaching here, with nonviolent intentions, the head of the imperial power. This kind of appeal enunciated in the name of others, tacit protest, and claim to the right of self-organization and to the sharing of power arise from the following rationale: the ultimate holder of power can, if he so wishes and if he is informed of the urgency of it, undo the bureaucratic bottlenecks which keep the total system from becoming open, or continuous, from top to bottom and so can eliminate the States within the State which capitalize on such thwarting marginality.

There was one more subversive element of awakening resistance involved in Fray Calixto's and particularly in Tupac Amarú's appeal. They wanted to create and publicize an image of the mass power behind their demand. This power was based not on mass support actually mobilized but on an anticipated widespread alliance among those who would have similar complaints. A call was made upon the "victims" of power to join, in spite of dissimilarities, in collective and coordinated action for revolutionary ends, to bring about the downfall of the oppressive infrastructure. In such instances, self-organizing individuals seeking alliance with their fellow victims become what they are by radical and cognized refusal of the image into which others have made them. They use terms like "the people" to stress the unanimity of the self-organizing elements which seek liberation, recognition, and new identity. Protest, at this point, will ramify in a downward direction; it will prompt the formation of a network of alliances extending throughout the entity and exploring the power sources on the outside which might be sympathetic to the cause. The polarization that has occurred between "them" the enemy and "us" the underdogs helps to erase hostilities which up to now have kept the eventual allies apart. That alliances of this kind were concerned in the Tupamarista revolution becomes apparent when we consider that this movement affected Indians in a vastly heterogeneous area from present-day Argentina to Venezuela—it is not known whether the Jesuits, for instance, would have appeared as "outside" allies. What could *not* be achieved was an alliance with the Creoles.

One might think, besides, of a more militant type of move against oppressive power, one which uses the techniques of disruption. These are techniques designed to throw gravel into the machinery through which legal authority is implemented, to sabotage the system without escaping from it and without the prospect of an open revolution. The literature on colonial times does not delve much into the techniques of disruption that the Indians may have employed; yet, guerrilla attacks and the slaughtering of landlords and minor officials were common events. Stealing was practiced. In some areas Indian parents taught their children that whenever they were traveling they should stay overnight in the homes of the Europeans, but that upon leaving in the morning they should pilfer something, even if it were only a knife. The slaves, on the other hand, used disruptive techniques widely; in Haiti, for instance, they sabotaged the economy by poisoning cattle and by killing their high-priced fellow slaves.

There is, also, the hard-to-define massive, assertive divorce of vast civil sectors from their political allegiance at a time of crisis. This is the ultimate manifestation of resistance against the sway of public power. Examples of a large-scale political disenchantment can be found in France by 1789, in Czarist Russia in the late nineteenth century, in the Weimar Republic in Germany, or in Batista's Cuba. Although some accelerators may push certain revolutionary groups into action at a time of such a massive disaffiliation, this by no means is a collective mood predictive only of a revolution from below. The polity, too, has mechanisms at its disposal which are designed not only for manipulating the collective mood but which actually permit and cater authentic ideological change. Thus, at the time of large-scale disaffiliation, ideological alternatives are brought into relief; they are openly discussed; a time for big decisions is known to be at hand. If some ideological core items are "debunked" in the process, this may lead to nothing more spectacular than a change in personnel or the coming to power of an opposition party, such as was the case of the gradual loss of ground of the Christian Democrats in Chile in the 1960's and the victory of the socialists in the elections of 1970. Or, regressive movements may emerge at a time of general disaffiliation, demanding that the spirit of the fatherland be substituted for the spirit of disillusionment and crisis; or the military may offer their services, as they commonly do in Latin

America, to secure law and order at a time no common vision guides and unites the masses. *Any* ideology, one might safely generalize, will be threatened in the long run by the pluralistic mentality, deviance, and empirical inapplicability that will weaken it; and any ideology will become increasingly suspect. In modern Latin America, this has happened in the case of Christian democracy as well as Marxism; the controversy between these two ideological contenders has in fact become an insolvable one concerning the nature of man and society. Whenever the gods of any ideological denomination fail, the pragmatic principles of technocracy and scientific management in politics will have an upper hand. It is this search for a new basis for legitimate power not in the realm of abstractions but in the realm of workable solutions to social and technological problems that lately has become characteristic of the Latin American political practice.

As far as the times of the colony were concerned, Tupac Amarú's movement came closest to producing an ideology truly cynical about the current application of power and truly capable of producing an ideological alternative: Indian nationalism. Significantly, Tupac Amarú opened his earlier edicts with the words, "The King has given me the orders" or "I have received superior instructions." Yet later on, after the outbreak of the revolt, he would introduce himself as "*El Señor* Don José Gabriel Tupac Amarú Inca, the Descendant of the Natural King of the Realm of Peru and Its Only Regent." It was this break from loyalties that the Spaniards could not tolerate; it was as unthinkable to them as the hideous "novelties" of the "naturalist philosophers" of the French Revolution.

There was, also, the intriguing history of the Virgin of Guadalupe in New Spain and the emergent mestizo Christianity it represented. In more than one sense this movement looms important in the colonial history. It was essentially pacific; it entertained the illusion that no inequality regarding the allocation of power will ultimately exist. It definitely created something novel on the level of symbols; it remained vigorous throughout the colony, despite authoritative measures undertaken to stamp it out; and it is still very much in evidence in Mexico. The cult of the Virgin of Guadalupe, in fact, stood for something different from the Tupamaristas' efforts at liberation and government creation. It represented a movement designed to remove the cognitive discrepancies between the immanent nature-bound world view of the Indians and the transcendental world view of the Europeans. For the Spaniards, the movement represented an ill-directed heresy "from below"—a threat to the colonial unity, to the good that flows from unity and to the Crown that serves this good. In Hegelian terms, the slave had undertaken here the task of relating himself to the independent reality. This was a task that could belong to the master and the ideology maker alone. It is essential to the power system that changes in ideology, although they may arise from crisis situations and "from below" in the populist spirit, be subsequently legitimized by the supreme holder of power. In-system arguments within the establishment, whenever major issues are concerned, must be settled before decision making will be channeled into programming and into administration. The establishment, from the moment of reaching a decision, must be able to display a united front. A complete reversal of roles of the kind involved in Hidalgo revolt, for instance, would violate the very foundation on which the power system is built.

In Latin America, from colonial days to the present, the question has remained: Shall the government be the sole generator of innovation and change, or shall it only assume the role of a bureaucracy, receiving impulses for change "from below" and legitimizing them in public action? In today's political vocabulary, other more specific questions arise. Can some form of parliamentarism be expected to supplement and eventually replace the executive office in producing and executing ideologies? Perhaps one should seek some sort of historical explanation for the existence of political power, instead of an analytical one? The executive function was established at a time the parliamentary system was still unborn, this view would imply, or when there was no confidence in it. In the course of history, it will phase out. Legislative function will absorb totally the executive function.

As far as Latin America is concerned, however, the trend is not toward the dissolution of personal executive power. Both unguided populism and parliamentarism have gone into a decline. The Latin American political models tend to be totality oriented, hierarchy oriented, guidance oriented, and person oriented. Historically, these models were based upon traditions that were taken from Catholicism, and the gospel, the Church insisted, ought to be applied "not according to man." For better or worse, the idea of democratic freedoms was never amplified to include the freedom of the people to dictate public beliefs. Even in times of ideological change, the Latin American view holds, a revolutionary intelligentsia will be necessary to guide the developments, or, in an alternative version, a revolutionary military will accomplish the transition. It is the legacy of the Church tradition to insist that divinely revealed law, as revised by a responsible inner circle, and this alone, will determine the major developments that occur within the polity. The hierarchy of the polity "commands" the people on issues of fundamental doctrine, not for the sake of staying in power but for the sake of complying with the superior order of things.

The "divine" principle, it is true, no longer inspires these processes. Secular technocrats and intellectual revolutionaries no longer take their cue from Catholicism. In the late eighteenth century, in fact, the Iberian technocrats assumed independence from Rome, and nationalistic statism was introduced not only in the Iberian countries but also in Latin America. An assertive pride in "principle," as opposed to British empiricism, was nevertheless to remain the essence of the Ibero-American nationalism. Government must frequently go against popular trends, the enlightened technocrats' rationale underscored. Empiricism and populism as guides for government are not only untried but threatening and perverse—unpatriotic. If there is alleged "progress" in England, France, and elsewhere, Pompal exclaimed, then "let them fly those novelties with which unpracticed men seek to improve what is good, in the hope of making it better. . . . Such innovations . . . eventually lose the good they once possessed, to the irreparable ruin of the crown they serve, and of the subjects they govern."

Split within Hispanic Christianity: The Jesuits

As the most important agent of popularly acclaimed authority in the colonial era, the Church asserted prerogatives which often interfered with colonial policies. Tensions broke out between viceroys and archbishops, between the secular branch of colonial jurisdiction and the Inquisition, between corregidores and parochial priests, and between missionaries and colonizers.

Much of this conflict, especially before the eighteenth century, hinged on the determination of the boundaries between secular and religious authority, not upon far-reaching ideological divergences. To cite one bizarre instance, a violent clash of ambitions occurred in the 1620's in New Spain between a newly appointed viceroy set to curb administrative corruption and an archbishop apprehensive of infringements in Church affairs. The ecclesiastical leader, the report of this episode goes,[17] plotted against the viceroy who planned to investigate the affairs of an alcalde accused of unscrupulous exploitation of the Indians in his jurisdiction. To strengthen his position, the archbishop appealed to popular sentiment and mobilized crowds in his defense, humiliating the viceroy and forcing him into hiding. The mobs, strengthened by a procession of torch-bearing Indians, jubilantly escorted the archbishop on his victorious return to the capital city.

Within the non-Indian sectors of the colonial society, the Inquisition was the guardian of the purity of the faith and orthodoxy, chastity, and race.[18] The Inquisition proposed to eradicate not only heresy but also any type of rebellious or critical thought in politics, all impurities. In the heyday of the Inquisition, nobody was permitted to leave the ports of Peru without the authorization of the Santo Oficio. The agents of the Inquisition were present at the arrival of every ship to find out what the travellers had said during the voyage. Since a relative, or a fellow religioso could be an informant for the Inquisition, no one escaped suspicion and no one could be assured of the loyalty of his intimates. A careless comment on socially or politically sensitive issues could be incriminating. Artisans, merchants, and priests were brought before the Inquisition for having remarked that the "gospel of the wealthy is a tragicomedy," that "many people gather in front of the altar and have their hearts with the Devil" or that "God has paid in full for the Indians." A clash between the Inquisition and audiencia real was inevitable. In the words of an early eighteenth-century viceroy of Peru, the Inquisition made a claim of "superiority and control" and "offered heavy competition to the audiencia real, on which it always imposes as a big brother." [19]

Much vexation among the colonial administrators was occasioned by the bid for power of the Jesuits. In fact, some of the members of the Inquisition itself, in the early eighteenth century, gloomily alleged that the Holy Office was infiltrated by Jesuits. The strength of the Jesuits came from their organizational discipline, their often aristocratic backgrounds, their superior learning, and their exclusive recruitment policies. These recruitment policies discriminated against the Creoles, but helped to guard against the general ignorance and degeneration which many wary contemporaries saw as undermining the authority of the colonial Church and the older religious orders.

The Jesuits disallowed private property but were active in accumulating their collective wealth. In philosophy, they adopted the doctrine of probabilism, which in its essential consequences challenged the validity of the one absolute, preexisting, and unquestioned truth and, particularly, the interpretation given it since the middle of the eighteenth century. The doctrine made a prudent concession to sound opinion, experiential proof, science, and Cartesian philosophy. By making a distinction between the tentative category of probabilistic truth and unattainable absolute truth and by permitting action based on the former, their approach to decision making became flexible; doctrinary yielding was legitimized. Innovation was no longer rigidly identified with heresy and apostasy, as it tended to be among the scholastic philosophers and other religious orders. A further concession to pragmatism was Jesuit casuistry, the practice of solving problems in an ad hoc manner in the context of reasoning, the laws of the society, the church canons, and documented divine laws. In order to validate a decision, the Jesuits maintained, only the "external probability" of its soundness was necessary; in other words, it had to be supported by at least one eminent authority. By a master stroke of compromise between the exigencies of dogmatic continuance and efficient leadership, a single "external authorization" was thus determined to prevail over the opinions of even several authorities of the past. Public action, in specified circumstances, could be modified in the course of its execution.

Education, missionary work, and the Indian policies became the particular concerns of the Jesuits; and it was their stand on the Indian question that aroused the most vehement controversy. On this, the Jesuits went as far as to dispute the encomenderos' right to collect tribute.[20] For their frontier missions, they demanded freedom from interference, a demand in opposition to the official colonial strategy in which the Jesuit settlements were viewed as a transitory step toward the final conquest.

The missions founded in the early seventeenth century among the Guaraní of the region of La Plata (parts of present-day Brazil, Paraguay, and Argentina) attained a permanence and prosperity that brought them to worldwide attention. The "Jesuit State of Paraguay" was an agglomeration of thirty to thirty-six missions, reaching, in the 1730's, a peak population of about 140,000 natives. Initial penetration into the area was secured in a quasimilitaristic effort; *ladino* (Europeanized) neophytes were used to attract the Guaraní, and additional members for the settlements were obtained by purchasing them for slavery. Life in the settlements was strictly regimented: church bells marked the hour for work teams to start field work and to return home. Singing and music—liberally applied by the padres as lubricant —were pedantically scheduled, and even the children's plays were regulated.[21]

Some of the Indians found the discipline tyrannical; there is, for example, the report of an Indian who abandoned the commune in exchange for the "life of gaiety" in Buenos Aires. The deserter promptly adopted the ways of ladino. Having a musical talent, he "never missed a banquet." He even distributed (obviously with the assistance of the enemies of the Jesuits, settlers in Buenos Aires) a circular in the Guaraní communes, describing his mundane exploits and unceremoniously calling his former countrymen "barbarians" and "idiots."[22] The Jesuit drill made use of the docility of the Guaraní and yet covertly developed and exploited attitudes of dissent as well as an individualistic attitude of achievement. Attitudinal change of this kind is part of the same drastic and abrupt shift in total world view from fatalistic traditionalism to the mestizo-style modernism that is today found to accompany some of the more successful community development projects among Indians in Latin America.[23] The shift from the tribal clans into the totalitarian Jesuit system entailed overcommitment to the new system and a desire to defend it.

Every adult Guaraní had access to a plot of land, the produce of which was used for family subsistence; everyone was to serve one-half of his time in teams working the communal lands. Tools, cattle, and horses belonged to the commune. The commune provided for free educational, medical, and recreational services; laws were applied vigorously, yet apparently without arousing resentment. The priests reestablished caciqueship but never delegated to the native officials more than minor subsidiary authority. With the exception of trade trips by the Jesuits, the communes were hermetically closed against the outside world. Visits by Europeans were forbidden. A defensive spirit was fomented and an impressive defensive capacity maintained during the bloody, prolonged raids that the settlers of the São Paulo Province periodically launched into the area.

It was their economic success in isolation that made the missions a focus of polemics. Rumors were spread of the Jesuits' having found immensely rich gold mines. This argument was first advanced by the Dominican archbishop of Paraguay, one of the many bitter opponents of the Jesuit State among the clergy. Gold-hungry settlers fancied that the padres were guarding the gates of the elusive El Dorado and shipping vast treasures to Rome. Another line of argument attacked the Jesuits for bolstering principles and practices which ran counter to the colonial order: scores of Indians—potential field hands badly needed to work on plantations of the coast—were kept "in idleness." This was viewed as wasteful and as establishing a dangerous example for the rest of the natives. Up to the founding of the Jesuit State, the relations between the Portuguese colonial administration of Brazil and the Church had been relatively relaxed; in fact, the parallelism of the spiritual and secular conquests had not occasioned here the same kind of contest for power that it had in the Spanish colonies. The autonomy of the Jesuits in the hinterlands, however, became increasingly irritating to the "enlightened" colonial administrators, who were concerned with political consolidation, centralism, the Crown's monopoly of trade (as against the Dutch, the British, and the Jesuit trade), and increased economic productivity. With the colonizing frontier being steadily pushed toward the interior, public opinion turned against the Jesuits and eventually led to the suppression of their State.

The attitudes toward the Jesuit undertaking among the

European social philosophers of the time, particularly among the philosophers of the Enlightenment, ranged from unqualified admiration to total disapproval. Montesquieu (1689–1755), in spite of his insistence on the principle of separation of church and state, elevated the Jesuit State into the elite rank of the republics inspired by "virtue." The Jesuit effort, he said, "will be ever a glorious undertaking to render a government subservient to human happiness"; it showed how the "idea of religion joined with that of humanity"; and it drew "wild people from their woods, secured them a maintenance, and clothed their nakedness." [24] This statement in essence marks the beginning of the apologetics of colonial intervention and protectionism in France. Voltaire (1694–1778) found nothing but clerical-militaristic tyranny in a scheme concocted by the Jesuits, and he was satisfied with no less than having his disenchanted Candide stab to death the German father-commandant of the Jesuit State. In Voltaire's Paraguay the "padres had everything and the people had nothing"; visitors had to wait three hours before they were allowed to kiss the spurs of the father-commandant, and the natives, out of sight of the priests, gave up their intention to eat Candide only after they were convinced that he was not a Jesuit.[25] A middle course was taken by Guillaume Raynal (1713–1796), the French writer and polemist who in his popular history of the Indies lauded the Jesuits' skill in pacifying the Indians, their moral stamina, and the fact that they had accomplished in a short time more than had been accomplished in two hundred years of colonial rule. Yet all of his effort was wasted, Raynal concluded. Instead of serving the common good of the New and the Old World, it served the exclusive good of Rome and the corrupt, power-hungry and philosophy-hating Jesuits.[26]

What was, then, the Jesuit rationale for the communes?

Since the regime was institutionally and rationally planned by the disciplined and well-trained members of a world-wide ecclesiastical bureaucracy and did not thrive on the indigenous leadership of men with prophetic vision, it cannot be conceived of as a classical "charismatic" theocracy. It was socialistic or communistic in a limited sense only: money did not circulate within the communes, the price and market mechanism did not operate domestically; and export crops—*yerba mate* and cotton—were grown on lands that were collectively owned. But unlike socialism or communism, it did not represent a social-protest response. It did not attack the mundane ills of a society polarized into contrasting social classes or the ailments of an alienated or exploited class. Alienation was part of Jesuit thought but in the spiritual sense only. Many of the regime's assets were capitalistic as opposed to those, for example, of the primitive communism or primitive socialism of the Incas. Its success depended on an unhindered capability to market and compete externally, and on the availability of capital for re-investment. It made use of induced skills and of its access to free submissive labor. Technological advancement was stressed but not acknowledged as an ultimate value. Technology culminated in the manufacture of textiles, firearms, ammunition, and gunpowder, and in book printing. Internally it was a caste-divisional welfare society providing for each one according to his needs. There was no tendency toward a distribution of the communal income among the population, nor were there any incentives to stimulate social mobility. No Indians were admitted to the priesthood. Instead, Indians received their training exclusively in view of their prospective roles within the commune. The missionary motive of Christianization, of course, was predominant. However, unlike Las Casas (whose settlements, in spite of his aversion to the enslavement of the Indians and the shedding of Indian blood, were to blend into the colonial structures) the Jesuits conceived of a system that combined the functional self-sufficiency necessary for survival in a hostile environment with dependence on a high-level outside authority of a specifically spiritual order, all uncontaminated by mundane laxity and vice. The commune was basically a parallel total organization, a State within the State or an agent of counterculture on the community level. It departed from the view that the Christianizing motive of the penetration into the New World must be differentiated from the Westernizing motive. The original alliance between the two was broken, insofar as the Jesuits were concerned, to sharpen into an ideological confrontation of two divergent total perspectives, the universal-papal and the national-monarchist.

Latin American Enlightenment

From the 1770's on, the Santo Oficio became increasingly involved in the uncontrollable invasion of foreigners into the Spanish colonies. Lutherans, Calvinists, Freemasons, Jansenists, and freethinkers infiltrated the professions, the commerce, and the army. They belittled the religious deeds of the Spaniards, scorned their fanaticism, called them idolaters, boasted of "rather leaving religion alone and preoccupying themselves with eating and living," or with the "diseases of the potato rather than indulgences." [27] More alarmingly, French revolutionists were caught conspiring with Creoles. Political pamphlets were circulated, which encouraged insurrection under the protection of the Parliament of England, or exploited the long-standing "black legend" of the Spaniards' cruelties, or extolled the Jesuits' work in Paraguay.

The most formidable ideological force behind the agitation, in the eyes of the realistas, were the apostles of "anti-Christian naturalism," the French philosophes. These, the royalist organ *Gaceta* of Mexico proclaimed in 1790, were the "new race of philosophers, men of corrupt spirit . . . who, under the alluring title of defenders of liberty, actually plot against it, in this way destroying the political and social order and hence the hierarchy of the Christian religion . . . and pretending to establish upon the ruins of religion and monarchy the imagined liberty which they imprudently say made all individuals equals or independent from each other." [28]

The hostility with which the royalists viewed the French Enlightenment grew out of ethnocentrism, religious zeal, and authentic ideological disagreements. In Spanish political theory, it is true, since the Jesuit philosophers Francisco Suárez (1548–1617) and Juan de Mariana (1536–1624), Aristotle's doctrine of the "naturalness" of social association had been expanded into a Catholic version of the theory of social contract. But there were critical differences between the Spanish contractualists and the "enlightened" French and British philosophers who used the model of social contract to stress the legal, conditional, and voluntaristic aspects of the body politic and, consequently, its dissolubility under popular resistance.

In the first place, the Spanish contractualists made use of the model mainly to justify the rights of individuals who adhered to a minority religion, specifically Catholics in Protestant countries.[29] Besides, the Spanish version of the contract theory was firmly linked to the ideal of monarchism, whereas the "enlightened" French and British contractualists of the generations following Hobbes generally were partisans of the idea of the separation of republican governmental powers. Also, the Iberian view of the social contract was patently restrictive in delineating the limits of permissible resistance to misrule. There could be no right to revolution. The right to resist tyranny, and the right of opposition, according to the Iberian view, belonged either to a legally constituted permanent body or, in the case of extreme abuse, to the select few who declared their intention to restore justice and order. It should never spread to popular movements threatening with anarchy the continuity of the existing order. The legal use of the right to ultimate disobedience, Mariana maintained, consisted of the comparatively painless and antiseptic act of tyrannicide planned and committed by a group of the most respected citizens.

The major difference between the Iberian and the French-British views relates, however, to the issue of equality and power. In the philosophy of the French Revolution ("ideology," as it was called), moral sciences must be founded on sound firsthand knowledge of man's natural constitution: on knowledge of his organic functions, which concur with the formation of his thought and will, and on knowledge of the natural processes by which man influences other men in the social whole. The model, one will notice, was similar to the one of the modern-day functionalists: for the purposes of the analysis, men are viewed in their freewheeling capacity to influence one another in any direction. Their contacts will follow the simple law of individual pleasure and pain: whenever their interests are in conflict, men will in a natural manner stop at the "resistance" they encounter in one another's wills. The "inevitability of order" in society is based on the uniformity of the human mind. Only the perpetuation of bad habits can deter progress. This is a psychologized and ahistorical view of man and society. The society is seen as built upon man's nature. There is a natural inclination in man toward sympathy, the view implies, linking the self and other beings. Society thus arises from the series of bilateral transactions, in which the public sector is irrelevant.

The Iberian conception, in contrast, considers equality in

its dependence on power. Power creates inequalities, this view holds, but it reduces them, too. Political power is there, the Iberian view implies, to allow or to deny segmental demands; power cannot be exhausted altogether, although it may be transferred, willfully toned down, and shared. The power principle itself may be modified in the process, to fit the particular equalizing or inequality-creating tasks that the power holders confront. Ideally, power will be thinly distributed among the "people," so as to make the whole community, if possible, copartners in its use. However, the extent to which power is delegated will always be determined by the power holders themselves. Only power can make itself extinct.

Man, in the Iberian view, is placed at the center of meaningful relationships, all of which radiate out toward living humanity, whose existence is an accepted belief. The universal ordering principle must be seen "first," for men to be able to properly focus the scientific enterprise, or to wisely exercise statesmanship. The study of nature, the Iberian view holds, cannot be separated from the study of man, for both are derived from the same highest principle.

These are some of the philosophical guidelines of the Iberian philosophy, many of which were in France much later and independently incorporated in the so-called positivist philosophy by Saint-Simon and Comte. The Iberian "positivism" and the Latin American positivism (although the latter was formally taken from Comte) were of much earlier origin than the 19th century positivism in France. Whereas the French positivism wanted to replace the Thomist four-fold system of lawfulness with a scientifically "verifiable" system, and whereas it was consequently hostile to Catholic-inspired traditionalist thinking, the original Iberian "positivism" grew out of the Catholic tradition itself. It labored to save those elements of Catholicism which were thought to be indispensable in creating a power-centered sociopolitical order whereby private conduct could be adequately subordinated to the public sector.

The ultimate moral imperatives, the Iberian "enlightened" philosophy maintains, transcend the actor and reach toward the eternal community. As Gaspar Melchor Jovellanos (1744–1811), minister of justice under "Prince of the Peace" Manuel Godoy, expresses this notion of transcendentalism:

> One might now say that the law and the norm of our actions must be embedded in our soul, and that the soul contains in itself knowledge of those, so that it would be self-sufficient for the study of our being. But you will have to realize that this norm is not born along with us mature and developed, but it is our spirit which is born with the aptitude necessary to know the moral norms and to discern their dictates, and to direct our conduct accordingly. . . . (In himself) man sees the relationships which exist between the Supreme Being and other beings which surround him, and he sees the place and the functions assigned to him in the general order of creation. From this he deduces knowledge about his rights and obligations, and he concludes that only by fulfilling faithfully his obligations and being careful not to transgress his rights he can obtain perfection and happiness, for these are contained within the same system of order.[30]

One difference between the "naturalist" view and the Iberian view relates to the perception of the wholes. In the "naturalist" view, there were none beyond the individual. The Iberian, on the other hand, was the grand view, focusing on the universal human system hierarchically organized, in order to give man his place, his belongingness, and his responsibilities. The grand system could not alienate, although an individual could alienate himself from it, and he would have to be brought back. Sciences, too, could become alienated from their duty, which was to bring isolated discoveries to bear upon the larger context.

Power, analytically, means oneness in the Iberian view. It is ultimately vested in the universal order. True power does not lastingly reside in individuals, not even in the preeminent ones who mediate it, but in the order they stand for. Power was established because it is necessary, and because it is in conformity with the nature of man. The polity is indeed based, the Iberian philosophy implies, upon an a priori arrangement that, in its origin, transcends all existing systems. Power must exist prior to politically organized society itself, and the maxim that "all power comes from the people," if by "people" we mean the present population, must be heretical and essentially atheistic. The power holder's is a service unlike any other in the society. It is designed for the highest political, judicial, economic and military functions, and it is above all these.

In spite of the conservative tenets in the Iberian social thought, the empirically and individualistically oriented Enlightenment reached Spain and Portugal and their colonies during the second half of the eighteenth century. In Spain a dissident Francophile minority among the intellectuals and devotees of natural sciences challenged the alleged *obscurantismo* and charlatanism of the Spanish legacy, and decried the scientific gap isolating Spain from the rest of Europe. At the same time, profound structural changes affected the previously static Spanish society: mass migrations to the cities, the expansion of market economy, diversification in farming and industry, and the growth of a new bourgeois class. These changes came too late and were too slow to save the Spanish society from a drastic decline; but they did contribute to the downgrading of the nonutilitarian hidalguía and to the enhancement of the value of manual labor and competence.

In England, such processes of modernization took place at a much faster rate, yet at the cost of extreme misery among the workers. There, an ideology was embraced which was suspicious of governmental guidance, and which substituted for it the operations of a metaphoric, self-generating "invisible hand." In contrast, the secularizing break with the past in Spain was a programmed, machinated, yet heretofore untried act of governmental planning. It was the "enlightened despots" of the House of Bourbon, with Charles III (1759–1788) as their most outstanding champion, advised and assisted by their physiocratic ministers (some of them foreigners), who opened the strategic gates for the middle sectors, who admitted them to membership in the various royal councils, who eliminated the required proofs of limpieza de sangre, and who stipulated—by the decree of 1783, which in Spain has been called the "most revolutionary measure of the century"—that individuals entering business or industry did not lose thereby their title to hidalguía or their eligibility for municipal employment, as they had before.[31] The most important civic movements that appeared during the second half of the eighteenth century and soon reached the colonies were the technologically oriented *Sociedades Económicas de Amigos del País,* which were created largely by royal decrees. Colonization of empty lands and educational and administrative reforms were similarly sponsored by the State.[32] Whereas in England the government much later, in the late nineteenth century, undertook the task of remedying the ill consequences of the industrial revolution and of arbitrating the agitation, violence, and protest occurring among factory workers, in Spain the role of government was perceived in terms of anticipatory action against privileges and in favor of a cautious policy of equalization through education. Political power, in the Iberian view, is not in theory supposed to maintain a wholly unrevolutionary society. It is expected to assist in removing the obstacles to equalization, and in this its justification rests. Enlightened revolutions launched from the office of the monarch were to modernize, not only to remedy; they were to inspire advancement in science and welfare.

The institution of enlightened revolutions "from above" was not confined to Spain. Frederick II of Prussia, Joseph II of Austria, and Catherine II of Russia belonged to the socially conscious and sober generation of monarchs who sought justification of the use of their absolute power in their role as the first servants of their people. They attempted to establish a society on the egalitarian principle of natural law, to remove some of the most offensive feudal privileges of birth, and to eliminate injustice and corruption.

The "enlightened despotism" of this period was an admixture of the old principle of hierarchically imposed order, the new populist principle of private progress, and the scientistic principle of the inevitability of progress. In spite of the antimonarchical strains often involved in the ideology of the Enlightenment, many of the most influential philosophies of the time seemed to assume that human improvement could occur, as it were, in a political, structural, and institutional vacuum. The physiocrats—proponents of the doctrine of "rule by nature"—had utmost confidence in the creative capacity of human reason to directly act upon physical nature and to exploit the soil, in the winning parallelism and combination of the "infinite power of nature"—as Montaigne had already called it—and the equally infinite power of human intelligence. The philosophes of the *Encyclopedia* believed in the power that comes from the accumulation and diffusion of knowledge, irrespective of existing political forms. It was indeed characteristic of them to expect that the progress of backward people would be even more fantastic than that of the civilized people, because the former would effortlessly benefit from their access to the ready-made pool of knowledge available to them through the efforts of the advanced people. Condorcet (1743–

1794) and his followers, however, were formally opposed to monarchism, and they held to a view of history (anticipatory of Comtean positivism) as a universally unfolding succession of mental and societal stages leading from barbarism to the intellectual revolution of contemporary times. It was the development of the mind, parallel to the development of social institutions, that was thought to act as a driving force to progress, inevitably propelling humanity toward higher and higher stages of perfection. Interest, in other words, was now increasingly in change, not only in order and stability.

In Spain and the colonies, "enlightened" tasks such as the diffusion of public education, the expansion of experimental sciences, and the development of agriculture and industries were attempted not only at a time of general corruption and decline but also against the overpowering forces of institutionalized reaction. In the "rebellion against Esquilache" in 1766, the Spanish nobility and clergy joined forces against the innovations of Charles III. To overcome the resistance of ecclesiastic hierarchies, the Crown, as Portugal had done earlier, resorted to such drastic measures as the expulsion of the Jesuits, in 1767. Significantly, the Spanish latifundia proved too powerful for even the absolutist government to break up to further its apparent interest in land reforms. Under these circumstances, the idea of strong, crusading, and efficient centralism was added to the Spanish Enlightenment; and this pattern was reflected essentially unchanged in the colonies and in the new Latin American republics. In the latter, throughout the nineteenth century, progressive liberalism and reformism became identified with the principle of centralism, whereas the latifundia-backed conservativism became indentified with the principle of federalism.

The reformist disposition of the "enlightened" colonial administrators was impressively exemplified in New Spain by the bishop-governor of Michoacan, Manuel Abad y Queipo (1751–1825). Coming from a man known as one of the most bitter enemies of Miguel Hidalgo, the famous humanitarian liberal and secession leader, Abad y Queipo's reports on the ethnic and social problems of the colonial New Spain are surprisingly unorthodox.[33] The apathy of Indians, Abad claimed, their proneness to steal and to lie, their drunkenness, and their unwillingness to work are related to their being socially and economically discriminated against. He recommended that the Indians be freed from paying tribute; he attacked the lingering myth of the "natural viciousness" of the Indians; he demanded that the Indians be made eligible to hold public positions and that they be encouraged to engage in wool and cotton industries. He further urged that uncultivated and publicly owned lands be distributed among the Indians and that a general reexamination of the ownership of land be carried out. Abad y Queipo defended the political rights of the Creoles and specifically emphasized the necessity of improved educational opportunities for them. He promoted irrigation and industrialization; he suggested that the monopolistic restrictions of colonial industries be lifted and that sufficient development capital should remain in the colonies, to be used for reinvestment. He even hinted at the possibility of expropriating some of the gold and silver belonging to the Church, to subsidize colonial industries.

A spirit of liberation as bold as Abad y Queipo's probably reflected inquietudes about mounting pressures against colonial rule. As the Argentine independence leader Manuel Belgrano (1770–1820) observed in summing up his impressions of Spain in the years immediately after the French Revolution, the "court of Spain . . . wavered in the methods by which it exploited its colonies: thus we have seen liberal and illiberal measures applied simultaneously, proof of the Spanish fear of losing the colonies."[34] On the one hand, many bureaucrats and royalists of the last days of colonial rule were sincerely dedicated to the idea of induced improvements in economy, education, and the administration of justice, as well as the abolishment of social inequalities. This deduction rested not only on the political expedience of these improvements but also on the dogmatic belief of these men in orderly progress and the feasibility of economic growth of the colonies. These ideological innovators were confident that rational planning and applied science were now to replace neglect and charitable sentimentalism.* On the other hand, the American and the French revolutions established frightening precedents; their social and ideological implications were menacingly at odds with the colonial rationale of order and discipline. The destructive rebellion of the black masses against the white ruling elite in Haiti and the anarchy ensuing there toward the end of the eighteenth century forcefully demonstrated the disastrous effects of the revolutionary impulse in circumstances where the colonial masters themselves tentatively favored the ideals of tolerance and the natural rights of man, or even dreamed of political emancipation earned in alliance with the formerly suppressed classes. The abolition of slavery in France incited violence among the mulattoes and Negroes in Latin America, thus creating a political atmosphere full of fear and a preparedness for basic changes in the structure of economy and for eventual abolition of slavery despite the enormous economic loss that it would entail. Although it became increasingly obvi-

* A Spanish brand of "socialism" existed. Jovellanos laments the "melancholy state in which men are forced to die from hunger as if it were by flipping of a dice"; he notes that men are "brothers of a large family," and that the "efforts of the moralists are in vain as long as the science of customs does not have the material interest as one of its principal foundations." From Medardo Vitier, *Las ideas en Cuba,* 1 (Havana, Trópico, 1938), 64f.

ous that the policy of censorship and monopoly was doomed to fail or, at its worst, would only have a politically explosive boomeranging effect, there could be no doubt that a sudden reversal in colonial policies would hasten the total collapse of the overseas rule.

The Creoles shared the economic optimism of their political opponents, the royalists, and expanded it into a physiocratic vision of Latin America as El Dorado reduced to bondage. The notion of Latin America as a vast continent with unlimited resources was typical of Simón Bolívar and others who were profoundly impressed in this respect, among others, by Humboldt's convincing and favorable appraisals. From Adam Smith the Creole economists accepted, as can be seen in the writings of the Argentine Mariano Moreno (1778–1811) on the eve of the *Revolución de Mayo*, the notion of an international division of labor, the notion that the power of exchange is limited by the extent of the market alone (and not by structural imbalances, such as those involved in the terms of trade or in a farming economy versus a manufacturing economy), and the liberalist expectation that the removal of colonial restrictions of commerce would bring immediate, overall benefits to the obstructed economies.* If there is a warning in Adam Smith's *Wealth of Nations* that national prosperity cannot be built on farming as it can on manufacturing, this warning was certainly disregarded.

The gains from free trade between the Old and the New World, as Moreno saw it, would be reciprocal and compound:

* Preceding Moreno, the Argentine patriot Manuel Belgrano (1770–1820) denounced in his writings the economic ills that plagued the colonial commerce: lack of initiative, lack of skills, idleness, and waste. Influenced by the ideas of Condorcet and Adam Smith, Belgrano proclaimed in 1806 that Mother Nature had invested the province of La Plata with infinite means of wealth, which were left unexploited only through ignorance.

My imagination is captured by the multitude of goods which an active public income must produce towards our happiness; tranquillity would settle over our hard-working people among whom no vice could find its way, vice which is born only in languor; the vivifying breath of industry would animate all reproductive seeds of the nature; cultures would be advanced by the creation of a spirit for new goals; our harbours would be filled with innumerable ships, and their continuous returns would form a viable bridge to augment our communication with the metropolis; by a thousand canals the seeds of population and abundance would be implanted among us. Such is the image of commerce.[35]

The bourgeois romance with world trade, the political ambitions of a Creole class enjoying increasing affluence in landed property, overcommitment to the ideal of political freedom, and the impact of international events in Europe leading to the downfall of the regime of Charles IV of Spain were the animating themes of the Latin American emancipation movement. Ideological problems were involved in the transference of sovereignty to "the people," a term which was interpreted narrowly to include only the politically active and meritorious patriots of the colonial cities, merchants, lawyers, physicians, landowners, clerks, military officers, and public functionaries. The earliest demands for emancipation juntas—in Montevideo—orginated in the desire to create an American counterpart to the anti-Napoleonic royalist juntas in the cities of Spain.* Possible anarchy, regional divisions within the American province, and divisions between provincial capitals and their hinterlands loomed as larger problems than the need for equalizing institutional changes. If the issue of the injustices of colonial institutions arose, the emancipation leaders either opted for

* In contrast, the *Cabildo Abierto* (open junta) of Buenos Aires, which constituted the nucleus of the Revolución de Mayo of 1810, voted in favor of the cessation of viceroyalty.

continuity and strengthening of the hierarchical social structures inherited from the Spaniards or recommended the postponement of reforms until efficient constitutions were organized. "Maintain if you wish the very abuses of the obsolete institutions," the Argentine Assembly of 1813 ambiguously declared in a proclamation meant for other provinces as well, "providing only that any decision-making receive its noble character of public consent." [36] Vested interests rather than the voice of the people determined the way the transference of power was accomplished, and the activist Creole elite now held in their sway all the institutions they inherited from the colonial regime. The maintenance of stability, from the early days of independence, weighed more than equalization. The independent republics inherited the Hispanic principle of nonrevolutionary systems; individuals would be assigned their places, populist movements would be efficiently kept under control, and the power holders would act as instruments of change, mediating between the principle of common good and the needs of the people as defined by the elite.

Legalism and Anarchy: Hidalgo

Even the most erudite defenders of equality and human rights rarely voiced arguments and their arguments were unconvincing. Francisco de Miranda (1750–1816), the ill-fated Venezuelan veteran of the French Revolution who in 1806 set forth on a military expedition to Caracas to assist the American people in shaking off their chains of oppression, vaguely envisioning an American monarchy headed by a nominal "heir of the Incas," * was received with not only suspicion and hostility but derision.[37] His failure was precipitated by tactical

* The title was chosen for the showy effect it was expected to have upon the Indians who, it was thought, would dislike the deflated title of "king."

blunders and by the alienating impact of his troops, who were Anglo-Saxons. Miranda saw in the American Revolution of the North an "infallible preliminary" of similar developments in the South; he confidently transcribed the old doctrine of "natural gravitation" toward Christianity into a secular doctrine of equally effortless and inevitable gravitation from despotism to equality, prosperity, and freedom. In the words of one of his British captains, he saw "fifteen millions of people, released from colonial dependence, and the system of monopoly and restriction it involved; enjoying a free government; elevated from their depressed condition; commanding the ample and inexhaustible resources derived from Providence; made happy in themselves, and connected with the civilized world, by direct and extensive commerce." [38]

Yet, Miranda was clearly apprehensive of "anarchist convulsions" in America. He recommended that efficient measures be taken against the "subversive French system," and even declared that the "principal object" of the Spanish colonies was to work out a solution "diametrically opposed" to that of the French. Miranda, Belgrano, and other Creole leaders of the transitory period, Salvador de Madariaga comments, defined liberty as noninterference by arbitrary laws given by irresponsible kings; by equality they meant their due claim for maturity and parity in an upward direction; and the third component in the formula of the French democracy, fraternity, they replaced with the notion of the supremacy of security and property.[39] And the Creole design had a fourth component, religion, which was to be salvaged in the transition. Mariano Moreno, the translator of *Contrat Social,* characteristically deleted Rousseau's "delirious" paragraphs dealing with religion. Simón Bolívar, in a letter of 1828, candidly stressed the expedience of religion as the core instrument to ward off social dissent: "Religion is the great enthusiasm I want to reanimate to use it against all passions of demogoguery." [40] For the delaying action that the wielding of power implies, religion would offer the master strategy.

The insurrection movement launched by Miguel Hidalgo y Costilla (1753–1811) in Mexico came closest to the devastating, Haitian-type "black revolution." Only superficially can this movement be reduced, as some have tried, to something hardly beyond a major orgy of sacking and burning by "ignorant Indians," aroused by a frustrated parish priest with no talent for leadership, and foredoomed to fail since it estranged, in a shock reaction, the predominant Creole opinion. In the social context, in its nature as a class war, the ideological roots and implications of the movement are far wider.[41]

Hidalgo was a nonconformist, an idealist, with no obvious or persistent ambition to undermine religion or the public order. In religious circles he was known to be a freethinker, a man of erudition who had translated Molière, who occasionally liked to ridicule, in the company of his colleagues, the Immaculate Conception (this brought him to the attention of the Inquisition), or to make fun of the priestly calling; and who praised the French Revolution and explained the mechanism of the world "like a philosopher." Embarrassment was caused, locally, when he recognized his two illegitimate children and purchased in his name and acceded to community use his former priest house at San Felipe—"Little Paris" or "Little France," as it had become known among the parishioners, in reference to "the equality with which everyone was treated" there.[42] In like manner, in the rural town of Dolores, after 1803, Hidalgo kept the doors of his residence open to the "Creole as well as the mestizo and the Indian"; but—his intimates observed—he was at this time intensely immersed in reading and planning.

Gradually Hidalgo's social evenings were transformed into

community action projects. A manufacturing plant including facilities for work in clay and brick, leather, metals, timber, and textiles was built by Indian volunteers. An irrigation plant was installed. A garden of mulberry bushes was planted, and a colony of bees obtained from Cuba. The parishioners were advised to grow grapevines in their patios, until this practice was suspended by authorities as violating the colonial laws of monopoly. Classes in manufacturing skills and alphabetization were given in the evenings; newspaper reading was encouraged; and an orchestra was founded. Impressively, the cooperative prospered. Soon work in porcelain was added. Furniture and such textiles as silk were produced. Tradesmen from Dolores peddled the wares produced in village markets, making their visits coincide with major fiestas, and coins were cast to facilitate business transactions. Hidalgo gave up his vicarship and applied for government support to expand the extension activities. The application was rejected; but a vocational training school, the first in Mexico, was founded at Dolores.

In the meanwhile, Hidalgo became engrossed in wider schemes for revolutionary action and independence. A tentative conspiracy in the nature of a coup d'état was designed by the wealthy army captain Ignacio de Allende; the plan attracted Hidalgo, and his popularity with the Indians and the castes brought him leadership in the plot. Whereas Allende was agreeable to the idea of recruiting a striking force from among the Indians, he was obviously not prepared to partake in a social revolution of the scope that Hidalgo envisaged. The Indians were to be told, Hidalgo projected, about the cruelties and wrongs their ancestors had suffered from the Spaniards and about the conspiracy by which their lands were taken away from them and abused. An uprising would be justified, they were to be told, to free the lands for redistribution and to throw off the chains of oppression. Hidalgo anticipated a *Reconquista.*

In secrecy, the work plant at Dolores produced weapons: a cannon, bows and arrows, and machetes. Insurrection plans crystallized into formal conspiracy, and the famous *Grito de Dolores*, which Hidalgo issued on September 16, 1810, marked the beginning of the War of Independence.

Like those of the earlier Indian uprisings, the movement's political objectives were ill-defined. According to some of the witnesses of the Inquisition Hidalgo desired "French liberty"; others claimed that he had spoken in favor of republicanism. The elusive manifesto of Hidalgo, published at the outset of the revolt, promised the establishment of

> a congress composed of the representatives of all cities, towns and localities of this kingdom, with the principal object of maintaining our Sacred Religion, and to dictate mild and beneficent laws appropriate to circumstances in each locality; they will then govern with the sweetness of fathers, they will treat us like brothers, they will drive off poverty, impeding the devastation of the kingdom and the extraction of its money, foment the arts; and the industries will come to life; we will make use of the abundant products of our fertile lands, and within a few years their inhabitants will enjoy all the delicacies with which the Supreme Creator of the Nature has filled this vast continent to overflow.[43]

The rebellious crusade proceeding from Dolores swelled within weeks to an avalanche of 80,000 Indians. They advanced, shouting *vivas* for America, for the Virgin of Guadalupe (Hidalgo, on an impulse, chose the Virgin as the protective symbol of the rebellion), for the King,* and death to the *Gachupines* (Spaniards). Looting and drunken celebration of victory broke out in the towns conquered; on the other

* Allende tells in one of his letters that "as the Indians were indifferent to the word liberty, it was necessary to make them believe the insurrection was being accomplished only in order to help King Ferdinand." Hugh M. Hamill, Jr., *The Hidalgo Revolt: Prelude to Mexican Independence* (Gainesville, Florida, University of Florida Press, 1966), p. 113.

hand, the movement was planned to subsist on captured ammunition, cash, and supplies, and much of its effect would depend on the vindictive fury of the Indians and on the terror it caused among the Spaniards. Bishop Manuel Abad y Queipo was the first one to raise the voice of the Church against the "perturbers of the public order, seducers of the people, the sacrilegious and perjured"; the Archbishop of Mexico joined in and excommunicated Hidalgo and his captains. Hidalgo "is courting you with the allurement of promising you the lands," the Archbishop proclaimed in his *exhortación*. "This he will never do; he will take away your Faith; he will impose tributes and personal services on you, because otherwise he cannot subsist at the elevation he aspires for; and he will shed your blood and the blood of your sons to defend and aggrandize his glory, like Bonaparte." [44]

The issue dividing Hidalgo and Abad y Queipo was one of anarchy versus legalism—it was an ideological one concerning the legitimacy of power. The two had been friends, to the degree even of sharing an interest in growing mulberry trees. Philosophically, the two men were still close. They both believed in the natural equality of men and in the equal rights of men to progress. But they differed on the issue of how to promote these ends. For Hidalgo, equality entailed the right to insurrection, the right to remove the power holders who were not up to their equalizing task. For Abad y Queipo, legal "enlightened" leadership alone was to serve as an instrument of progress, and the necessary transformations were to be produced from within the system.

Numbers of Creole officers and members of the lower clergy joined the insurgents; whereas the higher clergy, landed aristocracy, high-ranking military officers, and realista bureaucracy joined forces in the defense of the capital city. On the initiative of the viceroy, backed by pious *señoras* of high society, the

Virgin of Remedios, pictured as a striking Spanish beauty and carrying the crowned Holy Child and reigning over the symbols of the Spanish Reconquista, was proclaimed the patron saint of the royalists.*

For reasons that have not been established,† Hidalgo's forces—reduced to 40,000 men now because they had suffered casualties and because many Indians had simply preferred to return home—never entered the capital city, although the royalists anticipated a murderous onslaught. After two days of camping on the outskirts of the city, Hidalgo and his troops marched toward the interior. Guerrilla battles and uprisings broke out in the provinces, as Hidalgo had expected; and the viceroyalty was thrown into economic chaos. Acting with the authority of the head of a State and assuming the title of generalissimo, Hidalgo abolished slavery (actually, slavery had already been outlawed in Mexico), sent an envoy to the United States (who was probably killed on the way), and formed a government.

The first leaders of the revolution were captured within

* Too much symbolism should not be attached to this act. The viceroy wanted to bring *both* images of the Virgin into Mexico City, to associate the royalist cause with the religious one. Since Hidalgo's troops advanced toward the capital from a direction opposite to the location of the shrine of Tepeyac, the statue of the Virgin of Guadalupe was left unmoved. *After* these events, it was the Virgin of Remedios who was praised for delivering the capital city from the insurgents. Hugh M. Hamill, Jr., p. 161.

† Hugh M. Hamill, Jr., proposes that the retreat from the gates of Mexico City was in recognition of defeat. Efforts to arouse the villages of the Valley were unsuccessful; the number of casualties and desertions was overwhelming; Hidalgo feared that his horde would disperse in plunder in the capital city, and no discipline would be possible. A few insurgents had sneaked ahead of their army to steal the Virgin of Remedios from her shrine in Totoltepec. Since the royalists had removed the statue, superstition was added to produce a depressing effect. Hugh M. Hamill, Jr., p. 178f.

months, through the treachery of one of their colonels, and were executed. José Maria Morelos assumed leadership. Proclaiming himself "The Servant of the Nation," he abolished all caste privileges in the districts under his control, confiscated the property of the rich, broke up large haciendas and distributed the land among the peones.[45] On the war front, Morelos enforced military discipline and organization, and he introduced ingenious guerrilla tactics but, like Hidalgo, failed to enlist the Creole support. With the revolutionary fervor of the Indians dissipating over the years, the royalists succeeded gradually in regaining control. Creole-backed Augustín de Iturbide, whose revolutionary action by 1822 formally represented the fulfillment of Hidalgo's and Morelos' aims insofar as political independence was concerned, was dominated by the ambition to accomplish independence without permitting changes in the internal structure: the Mexican institutions were to duplicate their Spanish models, and the military was to watch over order during the transition. "Be surprised, countries of the civilized Europe," Iturbide declared, "to see that (Mexico) was freed without shedding a single drop of blood." In the Hidalgo movement, he continued in an organic analogy, "the acids left the stomach where they belong . . . and poisoned the heart and the brains. . . . The single and immanent passion that ought to exist, in order to compete, in the center of the society, in noble deeds, in virtue, utility and charity, has degenerated and left the center where the all-knowing Creator has destined it to belong."[46]

The Legacy of Catholicism

In the world view of the medieval theologians and scholars, all things were in relation to their ultimate, divinely established purpose, to the end toward which they were necessarily striving and moving. In order to understand and to know, it was necessary to go beyond the immediately visible; truth was not derived from the limited observation of the contemporary and the proximate. Generalization from isolated facts alone would not lead to knowledge: *Scientia non est particularibus.* The principles of explanation were transcendental; they could be practiced only by reliance on the "eye of the soul," which, in turn, took the realm superordinate to man for granted. The ultimate principles transcending observation were thought to be revealed in history and in dogmas; they were codified and authoritatively transmitted. Since each thing was assumed to possess an entelechy according to its nature, classification by broad essences was the first tool of systematization. The essences of things were ranked in hierarchies of classes, and gradation or overlapping was not expected to occur. The natural scientists, for instance, conceptualized in terms of the known essences of earth, air, fire, and water; and up to the scientific revolution of the early nineteenth century, some of them still looked for the life-preserving, rejuvenating "fifth essence."

Like any other thought system the scholastic one, however, was torn by internal divergences. The "realist" position (which is somewhat confusingly called "idealist," for its insistence that "ideas are real") could be traced back to some formulations of Plato, and it made up the traditionalist wing among the schoolmen. On the other hand there were those who agreed with Ockham that generic "being" is nothing but a notion formed in our sensible experience of the particular instances of being of which the world consists—we are thus concerned, this so-called nominalist position implies, not with "real" substances but with the names that are given to such notions. But there was also the extreme empiricist viewpoint, quite influential by the time of the Renaissance, claiming that universals (ideas, generic notions) are posterior to observation (*universalia post rem*). If the empiricist view be accepted, then all our theories, notions of right and wrong, and generic principles would be extracted from the data we have observed, in the manner of generalization.

As the so-called Neo-Thomist branch of philosophy has explicated in full, Thomas Aquinas offered in fact a solution to these problems of essence and existence (theory and empiricism). "Essence," Aquinas held, must be examined in its three "states": by postulating what is *prior* to "existence," by contemplating what is *in* it, and by retaining what is *posterior* to it. Essence, then, can be viewed in these three dimensions, and there exists a relationship of analogy from one state to another. If the more familiar word "structure" is substituted for the scholastics' "essence," Aquinas would then seem to say that structure is (1) something that anticipates observation, or something that we must have *before* the collection of our data; that it is (2) something embedded *in* our data; and, finally, that it is (3) something derived *from* data, in an analytical effort posterior to the collection and manipulation of the empirical data.

Within the human class, in the scholastic view, ill will and ignorance made for a gradation, not however in the individuals' inherent worth as humans, but in their actual stage of reaching toward what was essentially human. Individuals could be, as it were, more or less removed from the single path toward their perfecting goals; they could have frailties, become animallike or renegade. It was up to the Christian polity to firmly bring them back to the category of being to which they belonged as the possessors of reason and an immortal soul. The medieval view, furthermore, recognized man as the carrier of the burden of original sin transmitted to him from the time of the Fall. Man's sinfulness thus necessitated government, laws, and institutions, but they constituted, in the Aristotelian sense, the "natural" context in which alone it was possible for man to realize himself. There was, in other words, a penal effect of power as it was exercised by governments, but there also was a life-giving effect. Power had its threatening aspect and its loving aspect. Social duties were there, but benefits could also be expected from political organization. Hierarchy was thought to be necessary in order to institutionalize the system of disciplinary responsibilities and areas of competence. In this sense, inequality was involved, but this was the kind of inequality which could serve no other purpose than that of the natural fulfillment of man, in the Aristotelian sense.

The principle of power, in Hispanic America and elsewhere, thus took on a dual aspect. Because men are corrupt and vicious by nature, and so have separated from their great natural Community, they must, through "positive" laws, be assembled in smaller political units. Within these, the penal power purpose must prevail; crimes must be punished and evil must be combatted. This threatening aspect of power is very much in evidence in colonial statesmanship. Yet, there also must exist a second power purpose. Some life-giving common good, some security and promise of improvement must be derived from a politically organized arrangement whereby men have given up their citizenship in the "natural" great community of men. Liberation from the lower-level penal power purpose and joyful association with the higher-level power purpose, then, must be the goal.

In political analogy, this is tantamount to a vision, very characteristic of the Latin American thought, of something beautiful and of true benefit that would flow from a future union of the liberated Latin American nations, as opposed to the slavery, dependence, and impotence that the politically fragmented arrangement entailed. "Bolívar's Dream" is one way to describe this disposition, although it came in several disguises. It involved the idea that, once independence was achieved, the Latin American nations would rally around ideal polities and uniting causes capable of truly replacing the frustrating and exploiting unity that had once existed under the colony. This is one aspect of principismo in Latin American thought—the search for the principle, for new synthesis, and for new self-identity. It clashes, now as in the past, with the pragmatic theme of personalism or caudillismo. As Frank Bonilla has pointed out about Venezuela and Bolívar, the far-sighted leaders of Latin American independence would soon realize that the key to the formation of postrevolutionary political systems lay not in grand theories of ideal politics but in the will and capacity of the chiefs of grass-roots revolutionary armies, who were sympathetic to the cause of independence and had gained command and respect among the rural "masses" and the Venezuelan plainsmen (*llaneros*).[47] Upon these men the maintenance of law and order in the countryside would ultimately depend. The way to build up a political linkage to these fierce men and thus to fill the power vacuum left by the Spaniards was not through high-sounding ideals, as the doctores attempted it, but through the indispensable mediating action of the caudillo.

Along with the Enlightenment and the statism that it entailed in late colonial Latin America, it became evident that the Church would be inefficient in producing anything beyond vague millenarianism; and the clash between the Jesuits and the secular authorities, on the other hand, demonstrated that the State would no longer tolerate rival visions from the Church. Social thought, too, became secularized, but it did inherit from Catholicism the transcendental pattern and the tendency to assume that Ibero-America was an enclave of civilization thrown up in the sea of barbarism,[48] and that it was up to the select few to create and propagate a universalistic vision which would save the people from localistic barbarism. This is the Biblical notion of "where there is no vision, the people perish," but in Latin America it sounds particularly ominous because it explicitly denies the merits of the impulses from the masses.

The economic theorists of the era of transition, men like Mariano Moreno and Manuel Belgrano in Argentina, and José María Luis Mora in Mexico placed their confidence not so much in developing internal resources but in the benefits from an unrestricted international trade and in the power of commerce which would make everyone partake in boundless abundance. The same emphasis on unrestricted world trade was maintained up to the end of the nineteenth century, after which it was slowly replaced by economic protectionism and economic nationalism.

Besides universalism, the Catholic legacy stressed hierarchy and one voice in command. In medieval social thought, man's earthly wants and desires, and his endogenous capabilities were suspect; freedom was not seen as a wise solution for men whose inner nature was thought to be weak and failing. Individual choice making was not seen as a safe standard of good and bad; deviation was suspect and was understood as a failure to conform to the ubiquitous will of God. Freedom, in Catholic-inspired thought, is indeed an innate quality of man, but it always carries overtones of the duties and responsibilities with which it is associated. These will carry a binding command. There is, moreover, the sacrificial component of action, in the Christian model, and the tendency to explain partialities from eternal wholes, suggesting that man is a participant in the process of erecting the City of God, a true communitarian existence enhancing sociability, altruism, charity, and integration.

In the medieval connotation, policy making as such carried moralistic overtones. Any given policy orientation was seen to be either based on divinely established principles and serving the City of God, or else not deserving to exist. The sharp focusing of the notions of good and evil as something "essentially" different in spite of sometimes "apparent" similarities was the core of the medieval intolerance. Glory and achievement meant nothing if they were seen to serve wrong ends; on the other hand, proper ends sometimes justified the use of imperfect means. There was fascination over the pending greater enemy and the greater catastrophe from which the defenders of the public moral order would save the people. In this sense, scholasticism, as Alejandro Korn puts it, "always assumes to be the master of universal norms, always subordinates the individual to the collectivity, always smothers the personal expansion in order to bring it to the context of the common orientation. Thus, it is always intolerant." [49]

The Catholic-inspired tendency was to think in terms of irreversible contrasts of just and unjust, legal and illegal, on an abstract level. This attitude is very different from the modern one, in which failures to conform to the varying demands and norms of a pluralistic society are viewed singly—or segmentally—and in which an "objective" explanation of the etiology of some of the failures to conform may result in their being stripped of their moral implications.

The experimental sciences in the West, in the seventeenth and eighteenth centuries helped destroy some of the medieval certitudes. Predictive capacity, efficiency, inventiveness, and the power to control the physical environment were enhanced, the new sciences demonstrated, when the criterion of validity for the acceptance of truths was lowered from transcendental God to the impersonal authority vested in guided observation and empirical verification—procedures which could be learned, improved, accumulated, and checked. Doubt, disagreement, counterargument, and the postponement of judgment now could be interpreted as virtues; and the system of rigid boundaries between teleologically "necessary" classes blended with the notion of dovetailing boundaries which were circumstantial and which separated categories different from each other in degree. Truth could no longer be intuitively grasped or authoritatively handed down. In the Lockean empiricism man no longer appeared as inherently corrupt but rather as inherently receptive to the influences of his immediate environment, in his creative capacity to achieve improvements over his natural condition. Moral responsibility was no longer derived from a single source; it now appeared problematic, disputable, pluralistic, and self-asserting. Society, not polity, became relevant in explaining moral dictates. Along with this "socialization" of moral notions, political responsibilities, too, were transferred to the multiplicity of groups and associations within the civil sector; the political component in its global sense thus became emasculated and even unnecessary for explanatory purposes; power as a generic property belonging to the polity was questioned. The French revolutionary philosophers' conception of a deist universe proposed no counterpart to a supreme creator-destroyer analogous to personal God. Whereas the theist God-Creator also knew how to undo, the God-Architect of the deists, upon designing the universe, left it alone and, in that sense, he only knew how to make "more of the same."

It was not immediately clear upon the dissolution of the old regime what should be placed at the apex of the sociopolitical order once the model of personal power (the willfully creative-destructive power) was abandoned. The French Revolution's "ideology" proposed that nothing at all should be substituted for personal power—this kind of political individualism would lead to a "direct democracy," or to "anarchy." The utilitarians in England replaced the willful element of power by psychologized notions of the benefits that could be derived from a lawful system, benefits that had to be maximized. In Latin America, both of these thought currents had an impact, and they led, after the first half of the nineteenth century, to the Latin American liberalism. The idea that polity—the government—must somehow "hold together" civil life was increasingly challenged; it appeared backward or "political superstition," as Marx called it. The ethos of duty fell out of favor, and the polity was increasingly viewed as simply serving the civil sector.

Government, on the other hand, ceased to be a mere instrument of order and prohibition; it acquired more of the nature of a manmade agent of improvement. It was seen not not only as a necessary whip imposed from above but also as useful in its function of reconciling individual autonomy and the common-good requisites of societal progress. Positivists, utilitarians, and Marxists alike recognized manmade laws as the major instruments for obtaining man-related goals, calculated by lawmakers rather than deduced from their essences. They all, on different grounds, considered these laws to be subject to change, relativistic, and demanded modifications in them.

Spain exported to the colonies the medieval moralizing grand view of universal organic hierarchy and the destined cosmological singleness of purpose. Differences between the Europeans and the natives were interpreted not as relative to each cultural and geographical setting and not as related to the structural marginality planfully imposed on the natives by the conqueror but as relative to the divine grand setting. Unfamiliar traits assumed a sinister character. The immense task of Hispano-Christian penetration, it soon became obvious, could be successful only if the tentative liberal ideas of peaceful interchange were sacrificed in favor of coercion. Failure to achieve unity and to diffuse Christianity resulted in a vicious circle of intensified Indian militancy and Spanish retaliation. Assimilation—mutual racial and cultural diffusion resulting, even in those strenuous circumstances, in new blends such as mestizaje and the cult of the Virgin of Guadalupe—contradicted the logic of purifying forms; and, since they could not be arrested, they were seen as sources of anarchy and threat. In his worth as a member of society, the Indian was reduced to an inferior status as merely the impersonal object of colonial exploitation; and the rationale of parasitism and exploitation was generalized across the blurred ethnic boundaries to include the masses of *campesinos* (peasants) who became instrumental in maintaining the system of latifundia, and whose "necessary" status, in the large context of the societal and economic logic, thus became permanently fixed.

The cultural isolation of Spain from continental Europe in the seventeenth and eighteenth centuries perpetuated the scientific lag in Latin America, as did the policy of colonial closure, in spite of increasing infiltration from the outside. The expulsion of the Jesuits, in a way, blocked another bridge to Europe: the Jesuits were not only the progressive wing of scholasticism but also the avant-garde of Cartesianism and the Newtonian natural philosophy, and pioneers in experimental science. The economically and politically chaotic "era of the caudillos," following an intellectually barren war period, further slowed down modernization. The universities inherited from colonial times, with some notable exceptions, were embedded in the scholastic tradition; and the theological and juridical knowledge acquired at them drew only a little upon research and upon growth from within. Ideological authority among the Creoles characteristically belonged, on the eve of independence and in the new republics, to institutionally unattached, self-taught pensadores. The pensadores' creative fervor was aroused by their observations abroad, during travels in Europe and in the United States; and their political and philosophical premises often rested on an intuitive, diffuse, overcommitted, and conversionlike conviction of the superiority of the foreign culture.

The historical sequence of events—the priority, both in time and in legitimatized authority, of the Christian grand view over the segmental, efficiency oriented, scientific-experimental view—helped to build upon the vestiges of Catholicism the peculiarly Latin American mode of social thought, *traditional idealism.** Catholicism in the colonies did not simply petrify into an empty faith and passive ritualistic participation. Nor was its role limited to theological matters alone, for the Catholic thought pattern with its emphasis on the permanence of essence, transcendentalism, and orderly progress was transferred from the sphere of religious matters to the sphere of politics. Thus, the Latin American philosophers who borrowed the Catholic pattern and applied it to secular political thought arrived at their peculiar compromise—traditional idealism. Traditional idealism in Latin America means the mediating pattern of thought between the Christian grand design and the rationale of the Creole rule. It

* The Cuban philosopher Rafael Montoro (1852–1933) defines idealism as the conviction implying that "even though experimental knowledge is one of the functions of spirit, it is not its only function nor the most important one, since there are in the world things which our sense cannot reach nor perceive . . . ; behind the stage on which the drama of history is presented, and behind the spectacle of nature exhibited, there lies a hidden invisible cause, a mysterious author—*Deus absconditus*—who has determined in advance the action and the changes occurring in it." Quoted from Medardo Vitier, *La filosofía en Cuba* (Mexico City, Fondo de Cultura Económica, 1948), p. 189.

should not be confused with pejorative word-labels such as the "speculative" strain of Latin thought, Latin "logolatry," "romanticism," "emotionality" or other expressions which suggest that the "Latin mind," and the Latin American culture patterns reflect unpreparedness, or idiosyncratic and whimsical separation from reality, or lazy unconcern with the effort of cognitive systematization. To explain away the emerging idealistic thought as an uncritical mimicry of foreign ideas is not helpful. The Creole pensadores of the nineteenth century *were* concerned with their domestic "realities," but reality for them did not mean solely what was empirically observable and testable. In the traditional idealistic view, passing, as it did, through the secularizing and formalizing process of the Enlightenment, the Platonic and Christian idea of the transcendental realm of absolutes was "saved." Truth, good, and virtue were seen as descending deductively and authoritatively from above upon lower-level orders. Social institutions were to mirror the vertical world rationale. As an organizational principle, Latin American transcendental idealism implies a conviction that cosmos will ultimately triumph over chaos, despite the fact that the ordering principle may transitorily be threatened, and that humanity will ultimately triumph over self-interest, class interest, fractionalism, nationalism, and imperialism. The Latin American transcendental view draws a distinction between the manner in which political action may be justified and the scientific processes whereby assumptions are merely verified. The analytic necessity of the essentially value-bound, undeterministic and willful gubernatorial principle is recognized, in Latin American thought, as something different from the objectivity principle in the empirical sciences. Intellectuals have their prerogatives; their voices are listened to and their proposals carry more weight than those of the general public. Although the intellectuals have no decision-making power, they are thought to influence the destinies of their nations through their crucial impact on the spirit of the collectivity. They are able to rise above party politics and comprehend the synthesis that must be breaking in.

Transcendental in theory, Latin American traditional idealism became diffuse and ambiguous in its consequences: it involved poetic imagery as well as the dullest inventories of social ethics, revelries in the "logic of love" as well as bureaucracy and militant intolerance. It involved a predisposition to theorize in abstractions and see reality in total perspectives, and an unwillingness to compromise between conflicting total views. A Brazilian saying expresses this disposition: "Ou oito ou oitenta" ("Either eight or eighty"). The postulates underlying the grand design tend toward extremes. The preference is for ideal rather than possible courses of action.

Emphasis on power and hierarchy,* taken from the grand Christian context, was projected by the Creoles onto the emerging institutions. The Latin American thinkers, past and present, have accepted the notion of a vertical relation of cause and effect, of essence and existence, and of a whole and its parts. Dialectical contradictions between these are recognized to exist. Power represents the pivotal willful (personal) element which must be there to solve these contradictions. Without it, the base of social existence, in its essential nature of subordinated existence, would be endangered: either the autonomy of the parts would be imperiled or a single part would take over the totality. Power will cease, in this conception, when the subsidiarity principle involved in sharing power no longer exists. The totalizing effect must prevail; the totality has priority; a synthesis must follow from contradictions;

* Examples of the hierarchical dualities proposed by the scholastic philosophers were the relationships between accident and substance, existence and essence, matter and form, and actuality and potentiality.

and oneness must prevail over dispersion. In Latin American political thought, executive power on the State level is not considered to be limited to specific areas such as war or foreign policy. It is thought of as a necessary essence, not a historical phase-out, with even the Latin American Marxists clamoring for such personalistic revolutionary leadership as Perón's or Castro's.

Hierarchy is taken for granted. "For the Latin American," John Gillin comments on traditional social-class structures in Latin America, "the universe, including human society, has traditionally been arranged in a series of strata, and the culture is still strongly influenced by the values which he attaches to this hierarchy." Emphasis on hierarchy, Gillin goes on, does not contradict the value attached to personalism and inner uniqueness: . . advancement in hierarchy may come, although not necessarily so, as the result of fulfilling one's potentialities."[50] The affinity between the Latin American concept of social mobility within the limits of ascribed status and the Christian concept of individual advancement within the spiritually preordained hierarchy is obvious: classes of individuals have their castelike "natural" places in the society, with "necessary" differences of essence; individual advancement is relative to the limitations imposed by the "grand view." Liberty must be distiguished from license.

Thus Esteban Echeverría (1805–1851) of Argentina, one of the first thinkers of the independent Republics, spoke of the blind, capricious, and irrational collective "will," which was to be replaced by collective "reason." Democracy, to him, ought not to become the absolute despotism of the masses. The "reason of the people" must be exercised by the prudent and rational elements of society. "The ignorant part remains under the tutelage and safeguard of law dictated by the uniform consent of the rational people."[51] Government must make available to the masses the means of their own emancipation, first by elevating their levels of living and next by educating them. Masses only have instincts, Echeverría holds, they have to be instructed, systematically, to distinguish their own good. During the period of transition, their "collective" political rights must be revoked while their individual natural rights are recognized. Equality of social classes within a new totalizing synthesis is the supreme, but distant, goal. José Enrique Rodó (1871–1917) of Uruguay several decades later found that utilitarianism and mass democracy destroy hierarchies without erecting new ones. The moral influence of "spiritual selection," the life of sublime disinterest, good taste, and the arts are lost when social equality is made the rule. The democracy of mediocrity and the consecration of the pontificate of "Anybody" impose a regime that hates merit as if it were rebellion.[52]

Emphasis on pure types is another instance of the transition of Latin American thought from Catholicism to traditional idealism. Value is attached, in the traditional idealism, to the individual's becoming more sublimely true to his essence. The pensador is not to assume the pedestrian task of investigator.* "Real" politicians, Esteban Echeverría said, are opposed to the pedestrian *maniobreros* ("technicians") in politics. The former are placed at the apex of directive thought; from their lofty perspective they not only determine what the

* José Gaos supplies a definition of Latin American pensadores: (1) renowned philosophers; (2) renowned cultivators of jurisprudence, sociology, economics and other human sciences; (3) historians whose works have special relevance or contain "general ideas"; (4) cultivators of exact sciences whose inspiration has benefited the whole culture, especially when it has resulted in wide reforms and (5) literary and art critics of particular literary merit. José Gaos (ed.), *Antología del pensamiento de lengua Española en la edad contemporanea* (Mexico City, Seneca, 1945), pp. 15f.

society is like, but also what it needs. Technical efficiency is suspected of violating the autonomy of spirit. *Machismo*—unabashed maleness—carries prerogatives which are beyond challenge. A true leader is not obliged to consult or listen. Purity of race becomes a value: fights over the limpieza de sangre kept the courts busy for almost the last two hundred years of colonial rule. It was only in the 1920's that the pensadores in Mexico and in Brazil erected the countermodel of the "cosmic race," a round-about way of regaining conceptual purity. The purity of language is jealously guarded under the surveillance of the Academia Española. Contrary to the model of Adam Smith and to that of the evolutionists, traditional Latin American idealism suggests the ultimate reduction of types rather than functional differentiation and specialization, thereby reinstating the scholastic position. The ideal destiny of man, similarly, is thought to consist in harmonizing all the separate ends of his being, in gaining integrity, and in defending his inherent dignity and human worth: the overall purity of the human condition. José Vasconcelos (1881–1959) of Mexico spoke of the "miracle of creation" acting toward its own completion in Latin America. Social processes are thought to be neither arbitrary nor mechanical. Guided by the dynamic and living logic of the spirit, the creative *ordo amoris*, (order of love) produces transition from multiple forms to integrated forms.[53]

Protracted Parasitism: Latifundismo

The chaotic state of sociopolitical affairs following the collapse of the European rule has been called, with some justification, the Latin American "Middle Ages"—a regression to the feudal times. The new governments were economically crippled and lacked the respectability needed to obtain credit from foreign sources. The only available resource of significance, the public lands, were haphazardly sold to the moneyed landowners and speculators, a policy which rapidly added to the latifundista pattern.[54] The politically active groups were split over issues of regional interest and over the controversy of centralism and federalism. The provincial landlords acquired an unprecedented position of power. Ernesto Quesada, describing the situation in Argentina after the 1820's, tells how

> each successful caudillo considered the region or province he dominated as his fief; in effect, the country was divided into great earldoms, inhabited by vassals and subject to true medieval lords, whose system of justice was based on the gallows and the knife and who exercised even the most fantastic rights of feudal potentates. They did not have recourse to the special forms of feudalism and did not swear fealty to an overlord, preferring to cloak themselves with the external forms of republican government, but the result was the same as in Europe: the masses supported and followed their caudillos because they protected them and guaranteed the precarious tranquillity which they enjoyed.[55]

The Spanish monarchs, however, had been able to combat the excesses of latifundismo by making an alliance with the *municipalidades*, a new and vigorous political entity which stood for a more egalitarian principle of land tenure. This strategy of counteracting neofeudalism by reinforcing rural power groups other than the hacienda owners was not open for the republican governments of Latin America. The rural social structure, as it emerged from the colonial epoch, conferred unrestricted political monopoly on the hacienda owner: the rural *cabildos* (municipal councils), after the withdrawal of the corregidores and other colonial authorities, were little more than nuclei of class-conscious Creole elite; and rural politics were solidly controlled by their interests. The Latin American hacienda assumed not only political functions but also economic, juridical, and social functions which elsewhere might belong to the community * or to the family. These included building of roads and schools, the duties of the peones to work on the hacienda in exchange for a plot of cultivable land and a building site, disciplinary matters, problems of sickness and death, the exacting of personal services, dealings with immigrants, credit, the observance of religion, and the rallying for reprisals against rivals.

By successfully warding off "social convulsions" of the French variety, the Creole leadership not only saved but reinforced the status of the landowning oligarchy. In France—a country whose intellectual contribution has been much in evidence in Latin America—a combination of urban and peasant uprisings, oratory, and ambiguous parliamentary action during the last decade of the eighteenth century brought about the abolition of serfdom and the personal servitude imposed upon the villains, and the revision of feudal property rights. The "interpenetration" of national and local institutions was thus realized, structural marginalities were removed, and the

* Local idiomatic expressions, in present-day Latin America, are revealing of the absorption of the community by the hacienda. Unable to find local equivalents to expressions such as "community leaders," and determined to treat Latin American *aldeas* (towns) and villages as basically autonomous entities, the extension workers versed in community development techniques have been forced to introduce the neologisms of *líder* and *liderazgo*, monstrosities to many an idealistic ear. The Spanish language has a perfectly adequate equivalent for "community leader": *dirigente comunal* or *dirigente de la comunidad*. The neologism líder, used not by the people but only in the context of community development programs, is an example not only of the influence of the English language but also of the tendency for the real "influentials" in the rural communities in Latin America to be the big landowners. The word líder serves its purpose in a community-development context, because it creates an image of community power other than that of the landowners. In the Philippines, by the way, *lider* connotes a local politician.

French peasantry tasted the experience of participation in high-level policy making. In Latin America, latifundia remained as the intercepting mechanism, keeping a barrier between the secularizing, politicizing, ideologically divergent, individuated urban sectors and the compliant, apathetic, nonparticipating rural sectors.

The thesis of uncritical commitment, among the first generation of Creole leaders, to the cause of the landed aristocracy and the status quo should not be overstretched. Independence, for the Creoles, carried with it the ideal of justice and of a government conscious of its duty to work for the general welfare, as historian Charles C. Griffin reminds us.[56] Bolívar more than once expressed his impatience with the tame compliance of the peasantry and with their indifference to national issues. But the Creole leaders' interest in championing modernization and in sponsoring policies aimed at the destruction or restriction of the latifundista power was tempered by their desire—and need—to fully exploit the economic potentialities of the hacienda, the physiocratic honeycomb for governments anxious to join in international commerce. The single-crop economy of the hacienda, shaped under the auspices of colonial mercantilism and "enlightened" developmental policies, was the organizational prerequisite of a nascent national economy striving for immediate participation in world trade.

But, to repeat, the hacienda was more than an economic institution. It was the bulwark of family tradition, privileged life style, and luxury. It represented insulated hidalguía. In this sense Eric Wolf has called it a "retreat from Utopia," the refuge the strong found in his ability to control men at the time the mystique of El Dorado had dissipated and the external markets had been dried up by an economic depression.[57]

The hacienda system produced a landed aristocracy which

showed no interest in industrial investment and took a dislike to the governmental designs for *fomento* (promotion of industry), for fear that along with industries a strong new upper class would be brought into being. The system's rationale was derived not wholly from the task of maximizing the production of export crops by the use of cheap labor, but also from the task of safeguarding its autonomy and legalizing an isolationist hands-off policy toward the State. In this dimension, the hacienda appears asocial, since it induces discontinuity between local and large systems. Instead of copying the voluntaristic, secular interpersonal bonds of a business enterprise, the hacienda copied the paternalistic, authoritarian, and personalized bonds that have been documented mostly in somber contour in the Latin American social novel. Bonds of this kind are akin to those of the family. They follow the overriding principle of solidarity, with the concomitants of "closure" toward the outside, the sharp duality of ascribed power and status, diffuseness, the lack of commitment to businesslike efficiency, and the indivisibility of command.

In this historical and structural setting, where does the latifundium belong as a theoretical construct?

The sociological and anthropological tradition of the West had adopted a conceptual model proposed by classics such as Emile Durkheim, in which societies are seen as gradually moving away from the predominance of normative control by small, homogeneous, and traditional sectors—the family and the local community—toward the predominance of norms derived from the groupings of functionally differentiated individuals interacting in a mutually complementary, open, and impersonal pattern. The base of social solidarity, in the Durkheimian model, shifts from the "mechanistic" subordination of the individual and the predominance of the "collective conscience" to the predominance of the competitive and adaptive spontaneity characteristic of the emergent "organic" solidarity.

Obviously, this model is concerned with *unhampered endogenous growth* within a single social system. Durkheim himself, in a crucial paragraph, explains that the "division of labor (functional differentiation) can be effectuated only among members of an already constituted society." He cannot conceive of a situation where relations of pure hostility "*without the intervention of any other factor*" would be transformed into social (interchanging) relations.[58]

It was the coercive character of the institutions of encomienda, agregaciones, corregimientos, misiones, mercedes de tierra (land grants) and latifundium that made them such an intervention. These institutions grew out of the Conquest; and they represented what Amitai Etzioni calls the encapsulation of conflicts: processes by which tensions are modified to rule out the use of arms, and whereby some other modes of conflict are legitimized (bringing the complaints to the audiencia, for example) but which do not solve the conflicts in the sense that the parties become pacified.[59] Modeled after grand designs, divine, imperial, mercantile, or physiocratic, the colonial institutions purported to accomplish unilateral integration at the expense of the autonomy of the preexisting primary groups. The theories implying that the Conquest and its aftermath meant the relatively easy substitution of the "King of Spain for Inca," or other indirect attempts to explain away the far-reaching consequences of the European intrusion and its feedback effect, do not help in understanding the rural grass-roots movement of colonial protest, which invariably hinged on the issue of access to land and labor and on the strategic issue of regaining functional self-determinacy for localistic power groups other than the hacienda.

With their roots deep in colonial history, the Latin American rural communities, except for the *minifundista* (subsistence farm) societies of parts of Paraguay, Haiti, Bolivia since 1952, and of Colombia, do not simply fall along the line of varying degrees of traditionalism, sacredness, homogeneity, isolation, and other variables customarily taken to measure the hypothetical "rural-urban continuum." [60] This polar-type model of society stresses the contrasts between archaic and modern, static and dynamic, subsistence economy and market economy, without duly considering the *processual nature* of the relationship between the peasantry and the governmental groups *as mediated by the latifundia.* The Latin American peasantry is exposed to the demands made upon it indirectly by the established power structures, demands which reduce it to a fatally marginal position. The peasant marginality, in briefest expression, reflects a lack of security, a lack of autonomy, a lack of mobility for the family, and a lack of capacity for change. It implies dependence on the single patrón, the necessity of employing family labor for work on the hacienda, the need to maximize family income by maximizing the number of family members with outside jobs, the need to minimize the period of schooling for children, the inability to improve one's socioeconomic status by moving to better positions along the fictitious "agrarian ladder." In political terms peasant marginality involves inflated urban power over rural power. The relationship between the modern and progressive and the old and stagnant, thus, is less that of two parallel, coexisting worlds of development than it is that of an imbalance of terms of trade, resulting in prosperity for one at the expense of another, a parasitic situation created with the implicit backing of the official ideology.

V

A Totalizing View

The Relevance of the Whole

The essay delves into questions of legitimacy, power, systematic change, and resistance. An explanation of social order and social change is given which is different from the impersonal sociologism of Max Weber and the functionalists.

The historian and the social scientist must account for the specific character of the social arrangements that they are concerned with, not only in the atomistic sense, by explaining everything possible about the behavior of the component parts, but also contextually, by relating the particulars to the systems, wholes, or orders on which they are seen to depend. The explanation is understood not in terms of singling out associations between selected variables or events but in terms of pointing out the mediating power mechanisms vested in "wholes." Guiding functions are seen to survive, on some level at least; and they are seen to service, to equalize, and thus to affect the action of all the units that belong to the whole and depend on it. In one way or another, the totalizing and moderating power of the sociopolitical whole entails the capacity, as Jean-William Lapierre puts it, "to *decide for* the entire grouping." [1]

The meaning of the high-level "wholes," however, is highly ambiguous. It implies in fact nothing less than a full-fledged theory of history. Weber wanted to explain historical change by universally increasing rationalization. In his view, actors ascribe legitimacy to a social order by virtue of (1) tradition, (2) affectual faith, (3) expediency and legal enactment. Legitimacy, in this outlook, is derived from a voluntary agreement of the interested parties and is imposed "by an authority which is held to be legitimate and therefore meets with compliance." [2] Social order, in the Weberian view, flows from the spirit of Christianity and Hellenism, and it ushers mankind toward the "iron cage" of bureaucracy. Power, in this view, is a personal quality, but *as such* it is also a residual category in history. Relationships between individuals are seen to be increasingly dictated by the profit motive, by impersonality, and by the maxim "more of the same." Individuals on all levels of society, irrespective of their access to decision making, are seen first of all in their capacity to make voluntaristic choices, weighing one course of action against another. Weber was aware, it is true, of the fundamental importance of the economic factor in social arrangements; on the other hand, he was convinced that men are disposed to adopt increasingly rational conduct, which then constitutes the essence of legitimacy. Men's action, with Weber, is consistently overt, meaningful, self-directed and oriented toward calculated interest. Also, in the Weberian sociology, the system is seen as *one*. Confrontations, for instance, between two power systems or two ideology systems, or confrontations between the official system and the challenging quasiofficial systems (either residual or revolutionary) are not vital to Weber's explanation: the processes described are automatically unifying ones. Thus, the Weberian sociology is insensitive to situations where the oneness of the system is either debatable or virtually breaking down.

In the so-called American sociology, however, both rationalism and the tendency toward individualism are pronounced. Explanations are sought as if official norms and dictates flowing from an established decision-making body did not exist at all. The emphasis lies then upon informal group influences, social norms, value consenus, culture, group of reference, meaningful others, mores, or folkways. The role of the State merges with that of any other "reference group" defined in ex post facto analysis to explain certain aspects of individual action. The pioneering sociologist William Graham Sumner (1840–1910) was an exponent of this "groupist" approach.

In the struggle for existence, Sumner explained, each profits from the other's experience. Everyone will eventually adopt the same efficient ways. Thus, through the frequent repetition of petty acts the folkways are born. These are uniform, universal within the group, and imperative. Yet, in time they become more and more arbitrary. Soon, people do not even know why their folkways exist. Things are done in a certain manner because they have always been done in that way.[3]

Folkways, the building blocks of action, exert a pull on the individuals within their range; that is why they become impelling "societal forces." They are made unconsciously and are adopted by imitation. They initially tend toward improvement and consistency; they contribute to the erection of an invisible barrier between the "we-group" and the "others-group," and they nourish ethnocentric feelings. "Stronger minds," Sumner admits, produce folkways, which pass by suggestion from mind to mind.

When folkways touch upon the welfare of men and society, Sumner goes on, when they involve philosophical and ethical generalizations with respect to societal welfare, and when they concern vital issues that men must deal with in common, we call them "mores." These are taboos concerning the sexes, property, war, or killing. The mores are backed up by some kind of philosophy. There are protective taboos and destructive taboos, all relating to societal welfare.

This is the gist of the Sumnerian sociology, which has remained, since the turn of the century, the sociological ABC for the freshman student in the West. Its contention becomes clear only if one examines the medley of things Sumner included in his "mores." A random selection will suffice here. In the Middle Ages, it was the "mores" that determined the ecclesiastical and hierocratic forms of government. Slavery was founded on "mores." The isolation of Russia belonged to the realm of "mores"; Peter the Great, however, terminated the isolation, a countermores action that Sumner leaves unexplained. The Renaissance represented an "unsuccessful" attempt to adopt the mores of another period. Sumner's "folkways" are fully as comprehensive as his mores: language is a folkway; so is magic; so are manufactured artifacts, methods of fishing, weapons, money and its use, notions of labor, and class privileges. The list could be made endless. What appear to be neither mores nor folkways, and are consequently not considered by Sumner, are (1) policy-making actions flowing from official decision-making processes, from legislation, judicial processes, and administration; (2) entire thought systems (theories, and ideologies) produced by intelligentsia, by men whose names usually are known, not only by "stronger minds" in abstraction; (3) public plans and programs that are made legitimate for the entire political entity, not unconsciously but purposefully, either produced endogenously or borrowed from without; (4) abrupt ideological transformations arising from revolution or from the fear of revolution; and (5) revolutionary theory making consciously aimed at debunking some prevalent practices, with the holders of power turning *against* some "mores" or "folkways" in order to eradicate them.

Viewed in this light, Sumner's theory of folkways and mores is nothing but an apology for a model of social change (and history) minimizing the innovative action of the government and the legally binding quality of public action; minimizing the theories, ideologies, and scientific orientations *from which* (rather than from immediate experience) both the mores and the folkways may actually be deduced; minimizing the analytic distinction between command and consensus, and the distinction between influentials in opinion formation and the official ideology makers to whom the holders of power listen; minimizing the guiding role of elites and of great men in history; minimizing the importance of the splits among the ruling elements that originate in differences of ideology and theory. Sumner attempted to write history in the spirit of anonymity and impersonality, to identify society with polity and thus to overemphasize the role of consensus formation in a politically leaderless, politically amorphous cultural entity. In Sumner's social "groups" there are no rules that *must* be observed because they are dictated from above; there is no law enforcement, no power of the government to make certain things available or unavailable to people; no conflict of basic aims, or their arbitration; no stipulations involving social control. Nation (even culture, or group), in Sumner's theory, becomes synonymous with State (and sociology may indeed do well without the notion of the State!); folk action becomes synonymous with State action. His is a politically emasculated model.

Sumner's inspiration, again, came largely from Herbert Spencer (1820–1903), the evolutionary theorist who explained social change by a constant process of "differentiation" which resulted in the emergence of internally cohesive groups with more and more specific functions. Thus, the "regulative classes" (governmental, administrative, military, ecclesiastical, and legal) appeared, the several "bonds of union" that they had in common making them "subclasses." "Evolution then,

. . . is a change from a less coherent form to a more coherent form, consequent on the dissipation of motion and integration of matter." [4] Evolution means the transition from the simple to the compound. Every new order of aggregation initiates a new order of "rhythm." That evolution leads from a state of homogeneity to a state of heterogeneity must ultimately arise, Spencer concludes, "from the exposure of (the system's) different parts to different aggregates of forces." Thus, with Spencer, subclasses are formed from classes, and subsubclasses are formed from these, *ad infinitum*. As society is separated into subgroups, these groups lose their cohesiveness and are themselves internally split. Power, if one means by it power applied from above, thus ceases to affect "subclasses." Individuals will become increasingly self-sufficient agents or "islets" of energy interchange; society as a whole will resemble an "anarchic" agglomeration of loosely associated individuals; education will become irrelevant, along with public services; the State will be reduced to a subsystem within the "society," which the individual may or may not join. This is, in fact, what Spencer maintained *must* happen. If three individuals discuss, he once pointed out, whether they should accept the State to promote their interests, and if A and *B* agree on accepting membership in the State but C disagrees, then the dissenting individual has a perfect right not to enter the agreement and not to become a member. The logic of voluntary association, in other words, is applied here to politically organized power systems. Spencer pays no attention to the consequences of *C's* refusal: he will either become the target of politicization efforts by the polity, or he will be forced to completely move out.

Before evolutionary theory influenced it, sociology in America had been profoundly affected by the ideology of the French Revolution. American social thought took shape at a time progressive philosophers were anxious to erase the legacy of the medieval authoritarian models. The medieval notion of man and society, as the Scholastics elaborated it, was taken from the Greek classics, the Bible, and the Church Fathers. It attributed all lawful power to a single source which was personal in nature. "All law," Thomas Aquinas (1226–1274) declared, "proceeds from the reason and will of the lawgiver; the Divine and natural laws from the reasonable will of God; the human law from the will of man, regulated by reason." [5] Man, the Scholastics taught, lost his original grace and freedom in the Fall, in a generic way, with Adam's disrespect for God's "binding" command. Hence, men must be subject to rightful guidance and to a legislated law which rules them with a penal effect and curbs their sinful nature. Besides, man has organs (the heart and the genital member, for instance) which disobey the command of reason.

What the Scholastics called the law of nature John Locke (1632–1704) translated into the binding quality that men in civil society (as opposed to the state of nature) must ascribe to the law. The law of nature cannot be pinned down to a single principle, he argued. Nor is man's heart inherently prepossessed by the natural law, for there are no innate ideas. Man acquires his knowledge of the natural law by his natural faculties, by sensation and reasoning. The souls of men, Locke declared, are at birth nothing but "empty tablets" (*tabulas rasas*), capable of receiving all sorts of imprints but having none stamped on them a priori. Man's reasoning, simply and naturally, proceeds from "things known to things unknown." Thus, the whole of human knowledge, including man's moral concepts, rests on sense experience. By associating simple sensations man arrives at complex notions.

Lockean associationism had a particular appeal to the men who hailed the 1789 revolution in France. What they needed was not a philosophy of rightful guidance from above but a theory declaring the old regime obsolete, propounding the felicity of life without political restrictions on man's "natural" freedom, and telling that man would be able to make the best of his natural endowments if left to his own devices. From Locke and Condorcet they accepted the principle of empiricism; from Voltaire their disgust for theology ("schools of cooking disputing over recipes"); and from Helvétius their "materialism." No longer was it acceptable to parrot "knowledge" from Aristotle or other authoritarian sources. Destutt de Tracy (1754–1836) demanded an entire new apparatus of thought, a veritable *novum organum* such as Francis Bacon had envisioned. Ideas must be studied in the same manner that species are studied in zoology. We arrive at general ideas, de Tracy explained, by combining pure and simple sensations, by "recalling," "relating" and "classifying" them.

There is only one law of nature, the French philosophers of revolution insisted: the law of pleasure and pain (a notion that Bentham embodied in his utilitarianism). The desire to obtain pleasure and avoid pain, rather than any lofty principles, leads men to judgment. The "inevitability of order" in society, de Tracy explained,[6] cannot be deduced from the religions that philosophers have concocted and poets and orators have popularized. It simply arises from a series of accommodations and transactions whereby one links oneself to other beings. It rests on man's natural inclination toward sympathy and on his disposition to settle the conflicts arising when his will encounters the "resistance" of another's. The settlement will benefit both parties. Not surprisingly, the philosophes, following closely in Adam Smith's footsteps, extolled the "power of production": they had full confidence in a smoothly operating free economy in which the income would automatically be distributed in the most profitable manner and in which the profit made one year would the following year buy a little more labor, which would be a little better paid. "What is our industry altogether," Jean Baptiste Say (1767–1832) exclaimed, "but the simple employ, more or less understood, of the laws of Nature? It is by obeying Nature . . . that we learn to command it." [7]

In the United States, these individualistic ideas met with ready acceptance. The laws of society, it was thought, must reflect the laws of the single individual. "What is true of every member of the society individually, is true of them all collectively," Thomas Jefferson declared, "since the rights of the whole can be no more than the sum of the rights of the individuals." [8] We may imagine, he went on, a whole generation of men to be born on the same day, to attain maturity on the same day, and to die on the same day, leaving the next generation all together in their mature age. Could the senior age, then, impose its will upon the succeeding one? Obviously not. One generation cannot bind another; dead cannot govern the living. "Society" is tantamount to the living, to whom "the earth belongs in usufruct."

When the French Revolution was still young, some of the activitists, Thomas Paine (1737–1809), Baron "Anacharsis" Cloots (1755–1794) and Pierre Samuel Du Pont (1739–1797), approached in 1789 the Irish party leader Edmund Burke (1729–1797). Was not the revolution exportable? they asked. Would not Burke, champion of minority rights and foe of British imperialistic policies in India, lend his support to the cause of *liberté, égalité, fraternité?*

Burke not only refused to collaborate; he vehemently denounced the "abstract metaphysics" underlying the French Revolution. The revolutionary zealots had created a void, he warned, by "throwing off that Christian religion which has hitherto been our boast and comfort." The triumph of the revolution had unleashed regicide, massacre of innocents, and cries that all the bishops be hanged on the lamp posts. The revolutionary ideologists had moreover failed to notice that a certain *quantum* of power must exist in any political community, "in some hands, and under some appelation." Religion, morals, laws, prerogatives, privileges, liberties, rights of men may be pretexts. Very well, change the names of these pretexts, yet some binding principle beyond the mere "rights of man" must remain. Considerate people, Burke says, before they commit themselves, will want to know what use will be made of power, particularly if they are dealing with new power vested in new persons. For the State, indeed, is something better than a partnership agreement in a trade of pepper and coffee, calico or tobacco. It must be looked on with other reverence. It is "not a partnership in things subservient only to the gross animal existence of a temporary and perishable nature. . . . It is a partnership in all science; a partnership in all art; a partnership in every virtue, and in all perfection. As the ends of such a partnership cannot be obtained in many generations, it becomes a partnership not only between those who are living, but between those who are living, those who are dead, and those who are to be born. Each contract of each particular state is but a clause in the great primaeval contract of eternal society, linking the lower with the higher natures, connecting the visible and invisible world." [9]

Generations of social and political philosophers since Burke have unfortunately floundered in the analytic confusion involved in mistaking Burke's for a *conservative* (pro status quo) view of society. It is a view which advocates continuity in change. But it focuses on the kind of contextual explanation of social change in a politically organized system in which the coercive, accelerating, modernizing, or utilitarian forces operating are seen to be totalizing, produced neither by "group experience" nor "stronger minds" but by the officially established government. It is a model for long-range social change from above. As such, it does have analytic merit.

The de-colonization experience in Latin America and elsewhere has showed the fallacy of adopting the notions of liberalism and conservatism from Western social-philosophical usage and projecting them as such upon the nations struggling for emancipation and modernization. In the "developed" nations which make up the colonizing center, it is true, progress may ensue from a liberal regime that leaves the citizens to their own devices. Yet, as the failure of the liberal philosophies of President Bernardino Rivadavia (1780–1845) in Argentina, educator-author José de la Luz y Caballero (1800–1862) in Cuba, and innumerable others has fully demostrated, the doctrine is outworn which repudiates all coercion and tutelage applied from above within a system striving toward modernization or finding its way out of a colonial situation. De-colonizing struggles and modernizing struggles must be oriented not only *for* something but also *against* something. They call for a militant philosophy of liberation, whether from feudal patterns of power or from the colonial yoke, from the spiritual tutelage of an ultramontane Church or from foreign hegemony. In the Latin American experience, men with a totalizing political philosophy, who work within the establishment rather than against it, have indeed accomplished structural, modernizing change. Pombal and Abad y Queipo were such men in the days of the colony. José Gervasio Artigas, Juan Manuel de Rosas, Antonio López Santa Anna, and Juan Perón come to mind as more recent "modernizers." The liberalist solution to the dilemmas of development consists of prescribing a remedy *as if* the equalizing and liberating social transformations had already occurred, *as if* dependence, marginality, and structural bottlenecks did not exist. The totalizing philosophy of change, again, recognizes that these bottlenecks are still there and that they must be traced back to their historical-institutional origins, so as to remove them efficiently in an administrative and ideological act of transformation. Only the State can offer the power base necessary to move *against* these traditional strongholds of power.

Why the word totalizing in describing the philosophies of these structural reformists? Their view is derived from the claim to primacy that the totality, the system, has over the individual; from the belief that human association refers not only to the voluntary act of joining but also to a preexisting corporate body in which the individual is born and which will survive him. This body politic, in the totalizing view, asserts prerogatives which private interest is not allowed to challenge. There is, in the first place, the constant danger of total breakdown of the established order, of rebellion spreading into anarchy. The totality, then, must be "saved"; salvation can be obtained only by projecting (promising) and ultimately carrying out equalizing societal surgery that will necessarily hurt somebody's segmental or private interests. Centralized power, in the philosophy of equalizing statism, is a precondition of further democracy.

There is, in today's Latin America and elsewhere, a scandalized outcry against alleged totalitarianism, that is, against philosophies teaching that the body politic is capable of producing some "mystical" good that the individual is unable to produce. This is a sham ideology, for the polity *is* indeed capable of producing the only structural context within which administration, laws, equalization, education, and basic reforms become possible. Any Nation-State is totalitarian to a degree. It limits the choices and the mobility of the citizens. Any Nation-State labors for systemic integration, continuity, and defense. To decry the violence and the strongarm measures oftentimes involved in totalizing efforts in Latin America may be tantamount to a failure to notice that violence will eventually be the outcome of the liberal policy of inertia as well as of the policy of centralized reformism. In the so-called developing countries, Latin America among them, power must be seen not only as personal power, or lust for power "blown up." Analytically, it must be seen as a sine qua non of induced change. To borrow here a terminology commonplace among the New Leftist writers of Latin America today, the totality must be entrusted with enough catalytic dialectical sway to overcome the dualities, contradictions, and polarizations.

The totalizing and transcendental theory of the State, on the philosophical level, may be traced back to Aristotle. With the classics and with the Iberian authors, it presupposes that the State indeed is a "whole" not visibly present but nevertheless a frame from which both change and stability will flow, a corporate body which by its nature is prior to the individual ("man is born in the society") and which will remedy man's inherent weakness. The body politic, in the Iberian theory, is seen to be neither immediately subservient to the individuals' short-range needs or demands, nor to immediate utilitarian values. According to this view, its present component parts do not explain it. Only in a transcendental State-whole, this theory implies, the partial may be truly discernible, truly understandable, and truly predictable. Man will be defined and recognized only within a larger context, which makes for an analytic counterpart of "God" in the scholastic theory; *by* this vertical context of guidance, not only in the immediate, empiricist and atomistic horizontal context of the "now" generation. In this way, the Spanish philosopher Juan Luis Vives in the early sixteenth century explained the analytic necessity of "wholes." Wholes are something more than the sum total of their parts, in this view. They are not singly and successively affected by small-scale changes in the parts. Wholes are forged together in different ways: by their "constitution, connection, subjection, joining, admixture, or accumulation." [10] Whatever the case, it is the nature of the whole, Vives said, that we must understand first, in order to understand the nature of a part. The global power-component sustaining the systemic unity through periods of change, in other words, is analytically necessary, irrespective of the way the system was originally forged togther. The fact that the Latin American nations emerged from a conquest may make the power component more visible in them than in some other Nation-States. Yet, it is always there, within the present regime of nationalism.

The transcendental model of man and society is remarkably unpopular among the social scientists. It is often wrongly associated with the ideal of status quo; and it is just as confusingly associated with the ancient notion of divine rights. The model lacks the operational demonstrability, concreteness, and surface credibility of theories of human behavior based on paper-and-pencil study of the "regularities" of mostly verbal behavior, and on answers to questionnaire items that the behavioral scientist scrambles up. Historically, as we have seen, the transcendental theory of power has its roots in Platonism, Aristotelianism, and Thomism—in the kind of "metaphysics" that the behavioral scientist may thoroughly detest. The Thomists, it is true, made the political reality contingent on a deductive system that ultimately led to the lofty heights of cosmology. By the time of the separation of State and Church, the nature of the ultimate "whole" from which the rulers' and the lawgivers' power emanated was no longer clear; and the vertical contextual explanation fell into disfavor among those who wished to introduce a new science of man. The social scientists face the necessity of bringing back to their studies an efficient notion of the power holder as juridical person mediating between the ideals and the reactions of the pluralistic, powerless but explosive civil elements.

The Power Model in Social Analysis

The workings of power must be more closely analyzed. By power I mean the capacity of the person or known party in command to unilaterally impose on what appear as anonymous others rules and principles that initially regulate their response (with or without their knowledge) in social interaction and thus restrict their choice making. Escape is made difficult for the people, or the people initially lack the means for mobility that escape involves. The public sector stresses the need for systemic oneness to ward off disunion and collapse, and it seeks ideological justification for the use of power. This justification is sought not in the immediate and verifiable consent of the people but by enforcing upon the entity a single legitimate ideology which conveys a promise of reward and stirs pride among those who, by not escaping the system, commit themselves to responsibility to it. Ideology of some sort is consequently a necessary element of any attempt of the public sector to explain large-scale change to the civil sector. An ideology serves to mobilize, to hold the system together, and to maintain continuity in change. It must be specific enough to serve as an a priori guide for determining the legitimacy of particular social acts, and it must not lose its credibility. It also must be periodically redefined.

This notion of power differs from that applied in the so-called American sociology. In Robert K. Merton's formulations, for instance, the postulate of the functional unity of "society" cannot be determined in an a priori manner. It is up to the researcher, Merton advised, to extract *from his data* the totalities to which functions are imputed. There must exist, Merton assumed, "standardized, patterned and repetitive" items—social roles, institutional patterns, social processes, cultural patterns, culturally patterned emotions, social norms, group organization, social structure, devices of social control, and so forth—to which functions may be imputed.[11] The researcher is assigned the option to choose among these, as he is in need of a structural totality that will serve as an explanation for the body of data at hand.

I propose that, contrary to Merton's argument, there *are* important functions that can indeed be determined and commanded in an a priori manner and that the intentional nature of the a priori mechanisms of guidance is an inherent aspect of the sociopolitical organization. The function that the law has is one example of the verticality of causation that command-bound action entails. The long arm of the law reaches everyone within the predetermined sphere of its jurisdiction but no one beyond it. An extension of a law across the jurisdictional boundaries would be tantamount to an intended act of conquest. This is why it was expedient for the Spaniards to postulate the vassalage of the Indians as a prerequisite of subsequent Indian laws. By making the Indians vassals of the king, the Spanish lawmakers created a situation in which their commands regarding the Indians would no longer be considered interventionism but a part of legitimate public action. The same a priori quality belongs to administrative measures, which have binding legitimacy within the whole administrative territory but none beyond it. Ideologies are similarly system-bound, along with the functional consequences for the system they may imply. Public services, foreign policy measures, issues of national defense, transitions from one regime to another, revolutions, coups d'état are among the many further instances of issuance and transfer of societal functions that affect the actions of the citizens and that are still a priori strictly system-bound. The social scientist can either promote research "as if" these dictates from power-holding layers did not exist at all, or he can elaborate models that take them into account. The American sociology, up to now, has opted for the former alternative. It has thereby become more utopian than the classical utopias. The old utopias, from Campanella's *Civitas Solis* to Fourier's *phalanges,* however impractical and inefficient, would prescribe a social order only in circumstances where certain legislated laws would be binding.

My second point is that these binding principles cannot remain unchanged for long. Here again, a comparison with the American sociology is called for. Talcott Parsons has made the point that every system will have to face up to essentially the same kind of general problems, which he calls system "imperatives." All systems must solve the problems of how to "make a living," how to achieve the "consummatory state" that is aspired to, and how to make adequate use of the external resources. This problem solving is the system's imperative of (1) *goal attainment.* Again, the system must be able to mobilize its internal resources in order to secure goal attainment. The necessary skills and specializations must be developed. This development of skills refers to the imperative of (2) *adaptation.* Also, the system must have enough cohesion and solidarity to function. There must exist a system of social sanctions, and there must be special agents (schools, religion, psychotherapy, and so forth) which engage in (3) *integrative action.* Finally, the conflicts that appear must be adequately handled; and there is the problem of recruiting and training new personnel, and the problem of carrying the system through relatively inactive ("latency") periods; there must be an adequate network for internal communication. Problems of this latter type belong to (4) *"pattern maintenance and tension management."* [12]

One unwarranted tenet of reasoning runs through all of Parsons' system imperatives. They take it for granted that the system as it stands will continue as it is, with only gradual adaptations and modifications, since it ultimately rests on some principles that have been established for all time to come. These principles can all be traced back to the single process of *verification.* Once we accept the idea that the ultimate principles on which the group life is founded are sound, it necessarily follows that all the subsystems involved must reach their goals, mobilizing their internal resources to obtain them, maintaining the requisite solidarity and the continuity of pattern, and managing tensions. Parsons' imperatives preclude all in-system criticism of the basic policy orientation and all in-system splits and warfare. They take it for granted that any evolving system will promote integration, succeed, and survive, through solid consensus and tension management; that there is no subsystem whose vital interest contradicts the public sector's policy of equalization. All of Parsons' system imperatives, moreover, are in line with the notion of linear progressivism. They do not admit that public policy may be discontinuous, that some vital principles of policy making may be drastically revised, that systems may form new alliances, that they may merge, or that a supersystem may impose its imperatives upon the present ones. Parsons' are, then, merely defensive imperatives, designed to reflect a stable unrevolutionary situation within its present boundaries and in the frame of an unchanging ideology.

A social science laboring to explain sociopolitical change in terms of progressive self-sustained equilibrium indulges in the fallacy of misconceived stability. By emphasizing the importance of self-sustained equilibrium and continuity one will easily come to the conclusion that all social processes are governed by some universal laws reflecting an invariable regularity of successive and synchronic events, and that our theory making will gradually gain in accuracy and predictive power. Now, social science, looked at in this light, becomes essentially an accumulative process whereby generation after generation of empirical scientists, all starting from the same hypotheses, will indefinitely "add" to our knowledge of historical events.

If one wishes to make use of the concept of universal "system imperatives," there is, then, a fifth imperative, which one may call the imperative of forced *yielding*. The holders of power must be prepared not only for partial failures and partial successes, but also for complete failures endangering some core items in the established system. Unless there is yielding, the holders of power may be confronted with resistance and tensions beyond their capacity to manage. The imperative to yield, therefore, is implemented by the holders of power (or by those who have carried out a coup) who foresee the kind of trouble that can no longer be contained by conducting business as usual or by increasing the efficiency of the established controls, but only by recognizing that some earlier principles and practices, including the principle of the inbreeding of the holders of power, "must go." In this sense, there is a dialectical element involved in yielding.

Yielding, however, is a one-piece operation only during an authentic open revolution. At other times, it involves preliminaries. There is the cushioning response by government to civil resistance. This may involve showy displays of power or charitable public action. The regalia of officialdom, ceremonies, titles, promises, propaganda, and attitudes such as machismo reflect the showy aspects; concern with welfare and with the needs of the "humble" classes, or concern with social justice and charity are examples of the charitable softening mechanism. Whatever is showy undoubtedly must sooner or later be replaced by useful and meaningful public action; both stick and carrot are called for. In this sense, the early American sociologist Lester Ward (who was Sumner's opponent, and whose influence in the American sociology has been negligible) spoke of "attractive" State action and "attractive" legislation, which will strive, not toward irritating prohibitions, but toward channeling social forces toward useful ends. Mere promise will be insufficient unless the notion of common good is concretely sustained; Judge Holmes once tersely summarized the modernistic principle of promise: "With taxes I buy civilization."

Closing the system to the outside is another preliminary to yielding. The colonial regime endeavored to isolate the colonies from religious, political, and ideological corrosion from abroad, and to keep them from trading with other countries. The Indians' physical mobility was restrained; the doctrine of the oneness of the system was applied to justify the exclusion of ideas from the rest of the world. The Creole intellectuals in the time of the late colony knew amazingly little about the rest of the world. Those few revolutionary Creole intellectuals of New Spain who managed to come to the United States to escape the Inquisition were profoundly impressed by the wholesome cooperation they found, in Louisiana, for instance, between government and private farmers; and those many who went to Europe were exposed to something of an intellectual revelation. Colonial Latin America, Bolívar held, was planfully kept in a state of political infancy. The holders of power who closed the colonies, however, did not anticipate the consequences. Unwittingly, by permitting a select few to travel freely and relish the taste of the foreign, they created an intelligentsia who, once permitted back, tended to propagate the most resolute counterideologies. This is why closure, contrary to the design of the power holders, actually entails a step toward yielding.

Education, planful politicization, brainwashing, and other techniques of molding individuals' minds may be substituted for naked power and coercion. Since the Latin American Enlightenment, education has been passionately emphasized; it is still officially recognized as the key to progress *par excellence.* The Enlightenment abolished the black-and-white distinction between spiritual good and evil. Yet, the moralizing distinction between the perfect "pure" forms and the empirical "frailties" survived as a legacy of Catholicism, and education was now seen as the principal tool to cure all impurities. A secularized theory of the perfectibility of the individual was adopted. This led to efforts to establish formal schooling; but it also led to acts of extreme intolerance. Whatever stood in the way of progress must be crushed, the new educational policy in Latin America implied. Thus, for instance, the pitiless suppression of Indian institutions by the "positivist" governments in Mexico and Argentina toward the end of the nineteenth century.

Power may be yielded through administrative measures, too; through the separation of powers (executive, legislative, and judicial), through the delegation of power (whereby we arrive at the concept of "authority"), and through administrative shifts. Yielding through administration represents a conscious, planful attempt to cope with the problems arising; it therefore entails concomitant refinement in ideology. The French-inspired system of intendants, for instance, was attempted in the late eighteenth century to "save" the colonial system from the ills of the corregimiento. The separation of State powers, in many Latin American countries, has remained incomplete up to the present time; "government by decree" (presidential government) is still predominant, or the president may revoke the legislative powers in times of crisis. One-party politics, in many Latin American countries, tend to give policy making its undivided, heavily centralized character.

Partial release may be attempted to alleviate tensions within the power system. Whereas the colonial system permitted release only in a very narrow sense (by tolerating pockets of Indian communities, by permitting trade with European nations other than Spain and Portugal, and so forth), in the latter part of the nineteenth century most of the new constitutions, drawing on the doctrines of liberalism, proclaimed the customary freedoms of speech, assembly, and property. On the issue of religious freedom, however, there was considerable hedging and delay. In practice, even the nonreligious freedoms in Latin America have traditionally represented no more than cushioning devices, which are, besides, frequently revoked through "preventive" military coups or state-of-siege measures.

The power holders, finally, may yield in matters of principle by attempting to formulate or to accept from others a new set of basic rules or principles, still without relinquishing power. On the State level, government then becomes something of a catalyst; it supplies the society disillusioned with the dogmas of the past with innovative ideas, thereby taking into consideration pressures from within and international developments. In this role, government attempts something beyond solidifying the institutions already in existence. It becomes the agent for the *undoing* of items that have become a barrier to social mobility and modernization. Some of the technocratic military governments today have assumed this creative role. Although most of them revert to the cushioning technique of unredeemed promise, the tremendous potentiality that these governments have for creative social transformations should not be overlooked. When governments have assumed their role of undoing social structures, it no longer makes sense to look at the past or at some "structural variables" in an effort to understand what may happen in the future. The workings of power rather than the anticipated recurrence of events becomes the explanatory frame.

On the other hand, the power system may be studied in the perspective of the anonymous subjects of power, of the growth aspect, the civil sector as Marx called it, or the unconscious social genesis as Lester Ward has it (in contrast to government-inspired "telesis"). In this dimension, power appears in its acted-upon quality of imposition, in different types of accommodation to it, in resistance to it, and in counteraction. These responses vary over time, reflecting the intensity of the pressures within the system and the degree of success of the holders of power in legitimizing, routinizing, and institutionalizing public action.

There are some latent types of resistant reaction by the civil sectors. Those subject to power may try to leave the system altogether whenever an opportunity arises. The participants may withdraw cooperation to avoid responsibility, but they also may exaggerate their show of allegiance. Discrepancy may occur, in this case, between the lipservice the public sector may enlist from the people and the latent tendency of the people to disobey. Relatively apolitical aspects of life may become explosively loaded with tense overtones, and people's actions will be severely judged as reflecting their loyalty, or the lack of loyalty, to the public ideology. Overcommitment thus reflects a state of latent discrepancy between ideology and reality, involving either exaggerated enthusiasm or a cult of person, both characteristics of a collective mood that the powerbound Latin American systems seem to foster. Imposed apathy, fatalism, and ritualism are further instances of resistance which is hidden. Resistance of this kind will become meaningful only in the power context, and it must be explained in terms of dependence and liberation.

Some other types of resistant accommodation force themselves upon the attention of the power holders. These include acts of martyrdom, planful acts of violence, strikes, sabotage, guerrilla actions, political kidnapping, and other types of disruptive techniques by the dissenting civil sectors. Appeal may be made to a higher power, or in today's Latin America the threat of violence, public demonstrations, rallies, manifestoes and antigovernment literature may replace direct appeal. Self-organized countermovements seek increased power for the resisting sectors, and along with subterranean organizations an actively rebellious leadership may develop. The term "the people" may be used by the rebellious leaders as an open invitation to join a protest cause. At this point, dissent may ramify into counterideologies and into new alliances within "powerless" sectors, or into alliances with what to the establishment looks like the "enemy." Although ideological infiltration does sometimes take place, Latin American history offers abundant evidence of fully endogenous reactive leadership capable of producing efficient countermovements. Unless movements of overt resistance are blocked or pacified (this occurs when the high-level holders of power and the intermediate power holders, former ideological foes, enter a common front, or an international alliance is made) they may result in rebellion, or in an authentic social revolution "from below." Haiti, Mexico, Bolivia, and Cuba, in Latin America, have undergone the full cycle of civil upheaval some time in the past. It would be erroneous, however, to maintain that only these four countries have undergone social revolution. Uruguay, Chile, Argentina, and other countries have carried out modernizing social revolutions, with more or less success, *from* the office of the President, and many more countries are now desperately attempting to do so.

The modes of yielding to pressure, on the part of the holders of power, and the modes of reactive accommodation and resistance to the exercise of power, on the part of the victims of power, are summarized in *Table 1*. Both the establishment's yielding responses and the civil sectors' reactive response may bring permanent structural change, either directly or indirectly. However, in traditionally power-oriented systems like those in Latin America, most change comes from the governments' yielding action. The role of the government in general

Table 1. Modes of yielding and reactive accommodation

Yielding	Reactive accommodation	
1. Cushioning response to resistance a. Showy display of power (incl. "keeping distance") b. Charitable yielding 2. Closure, censorship, secrecy prior to decision making 3. Education (political mobilization, motivation) 4. Administrative yielding 5. Legislation 6. Partial release (freedom of opinion, speech, assembly, mobility, syndicalism, *etc.*) 7. Creative yielding (incl. the removal of obsolete institutions, bottlenecks, and ideologies)	1. Escape, withdrawal of cooperation, avoidance 2. Overcommitment (initial enthusiasm, cult of person) 3. Apathy, fatalism, ritualism	Latent
	4. Martyrdom	
	5. Techniques of disruption (sabotage, inertia, strike, guerrilla action) 6. Appeal to a higher power, protest 7. Self-organization (possibly underground) 8. Counterideology (incl. dissenting elites) 9. Alliance (with other powerless or with the "enemy") 10. Disenchantment, credibility gap	Overt

is more vital to the developmental processes of the nations aiming at modernization than it is to the functioning of socio-political systems based on industrial ways of life.

Obviously, however, the easy concreteness of the typology here presented is an illusion. These are merely *analytical* dimensions of the yielding of power and the resistance to power. In empirical fact these modes appear in combinations. While the rank-and-file are engaged in disruption and protest, the leaders may be meeting with policy-making bodies and determining post revolutionary goals. The holders of power may simultaneously apply different modes of yielding "from above," so that one mode ramifies into another. What initially was intended as a mere charitable response may over time transform into an established form of public service; education may transform into an emphasis on freedom of thought.

Also, some types of reactive accommodation may appear "as if" the power arrangement were terminated and, indeed, reversed. Self-organized reactive groups may in times of power deficiency stage displays of power and threats of violence; they may induce terrorism or, within their respective spheres, assume all the appearances of power. Just like the sectors in power, a militant underground may make use of promises, slogans, or other symbolisms of power. If such self-organizing resistance succeeds, the establishment, on the other hand, may choose the role of martyr, and the chief executive may offer his resignation; or the confrontation will reach the dimensions of a civil war, and the establishment will extol loyalty in terms similar to those the resistance applies to martyrdom. Or the power holders may seemingly withdraw from activism, as Eric Wolf puts it, "into the protective carapace provided by the administrative machinery," content to "keep their ear 'to the ground' through the use of police spies and informants, not to cope with the causes of unrest, but to curtail its symptoms." [13]

Social stagnation and "encapsulation" then become the prevalent pattern, a pattern that is perpetuated by many a strong man and hacienda owner in today's Latin America. Graft and bribing are further instances of the power effect in reverse; they imply a cushioning attempt by the powerless. A person with the right connections may capitalize on his knowledge of the loopholes he detects in the bureaucracy, in order to find his own means of escape from the prerogatives of officialdom.

In a significant reversal of role, power-holding groups tend to form alliances and "national fronts" during radicalist disturbances. Some of these conservative pacts may, in fact, assume the appearance of an underground front. Thus, a constitutional government may withdraw into a token parliamentarism, into an alliance with the military, who will be prepared to step in whenever the need arises. Some types of governmental action, again, represent anticipatory moves to ward off expected spontaneous self-organization within the civil sectors. Thus, governments (or employers) may introduce workers' syndicates as extensions of their own power, in order to prevent a politically more explosive syndicalism.

Power relations cut across several system levels. On the family level, they represent the relationship between the powerful parental generation and the relatively powerless younger generation. The patrón, the government, the solitary strong man, the rural caudillo and the Church may represent significant powerful roles in Latin America. On the international level, the United States has played an important power role there. With respect to ideological systems, traditional idealism has supplied one of the most important sources of the logic of power; as such, it apparently continues the old Spanish ideal of benevolent dictatorship, and the positivistic ideal of an alliance between military and scientific power, between "order and progress," or (as in the original motto of the Republic of Chile) between "force and knowledge."

Their ability to confer or withhold legitimacy serves the power holders as a means of establishing the oneness of the system in situations where the pluralistic civil sectors "below" exert rival pressures for change. The power holders will need to justify their totalizing action. The issue of power cannot be indefinitely reduced to the simplified formula of "who . . . whom," who commands whom, who employs whom, or who, ultimately, kills whom. It also involves the issue of "why" or "for what?" The use of power must be justified as a way of promoting Christianity or inducing order, security, progress, Westernization, industrialization, lasting peace, autonomy, nationalism, antiimperialism, anti-Yankeeism, or internationalism. The holders of power rarely justify their power without seeking support for their ideologies from some segmental pressures or populist movements "from below." Initiatives toward unguided new self-organization, new alliances, and new attempts to reverse the power order, nevertheless, are invariably restricted; on the other hand certain archaic alliances (between government and the big landowners, for instance) are tolerated, and they enable some type of residual quasi-legitimate subsystemic power systems to remain latently efficient within the large power system. Latifundismo has been described here as such a typically Latin American lower-level system of power, mediating between peasantry and the central government. It "protects" the peasantry but also restricts their mobility, demands overcommitment, and dictates its terms in high-level politics.

Although the most common, latifundismo is by no means the only case of mediating subsystemic power in Latin America. Peasant uprisings in the Andean region, guerrilla "States" in Colombia, the eighteenth-century communities of runaway slaves in Brazil and in Dutch and British Guiana, the peasant-led sectors of the Mexican Revolution of 1911 and similar peasant-led rural syndicate movements in Bolivia after 1952 have demonstrated how the allegiance of the peasantry and other marginals may be diverted, in times of turmoil, from their former patrons and legitimate holders of power to the caciques, guerrilla leaders, and syndicate leaders who, temporarily at least, assume a mediating role and even autonomy of command. In general, such quasilegitimate subsystemic nuclei of power may result from the military or sanctioning weakness of the central power; from its impracticality and idealism (as was the case of the Constitutionalist "unitarians" in the early Republics); from its inability to end concessions intended to be temporary; from its need to tolerate a strong rival power for the sake of internal peace; or from the fact that the economic functions of a subsystem of power, for the time being, may appear vital to the welfare of the large system. The last-mentioned has been the case of governments in Latin America, which have tolerated the exploitation of Indian and peasant labor out of economic necessity since the early days of the Conquest. In many of the Republics, this situation remains essentially unchanged as far as the peasantry is concerned. An alliance between the legitimate holders of power and the quasilegitimate holders of power may then emerge on the level of national politics; the two may merge; or quasilegitimacy, latifundismo, for example, may take over central government. This means a reversal of the base of power; in the language of Latin American liberalist-constitutionalist writers of the first decades of Independence, "barbarism" takes over "civilization."

The notions of power, subsystemic power, alliance for power, and yielding to reactive pressures are useful in clarifying the position of the marginal sectors within the sociopolitical entity. The marginals do not simply represent lower readings on a unidimensional scale of prestige, socioeconomic status, income, education, or other valued attributes; nor can their marginality be explained in terms of their drifting down, their lack of achievement motivation, lack of initiative, or laggardness. Although marginality may be measured in these terms, it is not thereby adequately explained. Within the framework of social stratification and socioeconomic differentials, marginality, in fact, would create an image of a society which is open for advancement from top to bottom and in which individual choice making, equal on all levels, would be of strategic importance. In the power frame, marginality is seen as the outcome of historical morphogenetic processes whereby some subject sectors of the sociopolitical entity remain essentially within the domain of subsystemic nuclei of power, taking their command not from the overall legitimate holders of power but from the lower-level quasilegitimate order of power, whose domain is merely tolerated by the supreme holders of power. Escape from marginality, when this is the case, will depend less on the ability of the individuals to improve in efficiency, education, or achievement motivation than on their collective ability to attract intervention "from above" in their favor, to collectively withstand their immediate masters, to organize against them, or to otherwise move from latent to overt modes of reactive group-action. In this frame, marginals are seen to be receptive, among other things, to the possibility of an alliance between themselves and the sectors of the social system close enough to the legitimate power holder to have access to him. Thus the Indians were receptive to the efforts of the religious orders to mediate between themselves and the Crown. In more recent times, peasants have been receptive to the efforts of progressive student groups and progressive priests to the same effect.

As long as governmental power rests on an alliance of powerful segmental interests and thus has a social-class basis, structural "bottlenecks" (subsystemic nuclei of power) are likely to persist. But how do these dissolve? On this issue, one will notice, both the traditional Latin American philosophy and Marxism propose a dialectical solution; yet the dialectics in each case is seen in a different light. Karl Marx proposed that social classes emerge in history as the principal carriers of power. A constant class struggle is going on in society, he argued, and as a side product of the struggle (in the capitalist society) an initially dull and passive working class will develop. The authorities in the polarizing society simply have the task of reinforcing the ordinary run of things, or the "business as usual" rationale. The intelligentsia, again, have the task of explaining away the contradictions of capitalist production in the apologetic terms of "natural laws of production," which only serve to justify the parasitism, dehumanization, and class antagonisms involved. The intelligentsia within the capitalist system, according to Marx, are assigned the disgraceful task of defending a rotten system and serving as lackeys to the capitalists. They represent, to him, a false moderating power, because the capitalist State is nothing but a capitalist "heaven," a biased projection of the capitalists' aspirations. In the Marxian view of society, moreover, the element of impersonal inevitability prevails. The initial principles, whenever they are externalized, will inevitably turn into something different, and against themselves. Man, in the capitalist society, "externalizes" his labor, which will be estranged from him so that it will be reduced into a means of mere survival. It thus turns against him, and turns man into a being alien to himself. Not only his fellow man becomes a competitor for survival, but man's spontaneous labor, through a relationship of market exchange, becomes wage labor. Now it no longer stands in immediate relationship to his needs or to his status but is determined by social-economic forces alien to his labor. Furthermore, the buyer of the product himself is not productive, for he only exchanges what others have produced. What used to be the domination of one person over another (under feudalism) has now become the domination of the *thing* over the person, of the product over the producer. Man, Marx holds, is alienated from the product of his work, from the instruments of production, from the act of producing, from his own human nature, and from direct social relationships with others. The society becomes permeated by impersonal alienation, which is apparent not only in the fact that the worker's means of life belong to someone else but also in the fact that the system at large will be ruled over by an "inhuman power." [14] The capitalist society will become ungovernable. Revolutionary praxis will then in a dialectical fashion introduce a transformation that will bring concrete intelligibility into social relations.[15]

In contrast, the tradition of Latin American dialectics comes from Catholic sources. Society, this view holds, can never "exploit" and never "alienate," if it is ruled by just laws in accordance with the transcendental principles of eternal, divine, and natural laws. If there is an "exploiter" at all, the Catholic-inspired view holds, this must be humanity itself through the demands it makes upon the individual. Yet, membership in humanity is a liberating and inspiring experience that involves "real" freedom. Nor does the Latin American tradition accept the notion that inhuman powers rule over historical change, for power, in this tradition, appears as a personal quality. "Things" cannot dominate over persons. Intellectuals and, in a different sense, caudillos, too, are totality-bound, not in the sense of deriving their appeal directly from the forces operating within the totality, but in the system-building sense of serving as a totalizing and moderating power which can stage a revolution as well as prevent one. Revolutions, in the Latin American view, do not flow from the impersonal sources of class war, but they are inaugurated by the personal will of the "real" revolutionaries, who can be either intellectuals or caudillos. A revolution of either kind does not elevate a proletarian class into power, as the Marxists have it, but it is considered as one more step in the equalizing process toward social justice, and it helps in overcoming past mistakes.

I do not intend to go into these problems any further than is necessary to place the traditional Catholic-inspired Latin American social philosophy of totalizing moderating power in contrast with the social-class models of power. Catholic thought emphasizes the universal association that Nature has established among all men (*inter omnes homines cognatio*). It is a universalizing model, regarding the society as an assemblage of reasonable beings, as St. Augustine has it, who are "bound together by a common agreement as to the object of their love." It is inconceivable, in this model, for any social class to exploit another, for any inhuman power to gain upper hand. The liberating synthesis, in one way or another, is pressed from above; and this above-dimension is seen to absorb the individual in a march of humanity akin to the Christian crusade. It is no wonder, then, that in the Latin American Christian Democracy particularly the totalizing effect is still seen to be mediated by the Christian vision of oneness. "In the midst of misery, confusion, strife, and disillusionment," Ivan Vallier puts it, the Latin American Catholics "look for a convincing eschatology and for membership in some beautiful crusade." [16] Something of an essence will always remain unaffected by accidental change, and totalities will thus be forever preserved.

The Catholic reformists (since Las Casas, in fact) recognize the problem of marginal populations (slum populations, peasants, and so forth), but they emphasize that the forms of self-help arising from among the marginals must merge, in an integrative, populist, moderating, and conciliatory manner; with the marginals accepting the assistance extended to them from the centers of power in downward direction. Only recently, since the mid-twentieth century, attention has been called in Latin America to the vicious circles which may be supported from the outside, in an alliance, for instance, of domestic strong men and foreign business interest, which may induce marginality of a kind that does not dissolve in a smooth integrative manner.

The moderating power, in the Catholic-inspired Latin American view,* cannot be vested in a class but is vested in the autonomous command which the legitimate holders of power wield and which is derived not only from the "community" (the civil sectors) but also from transcendental sources of political vision. There must be a way, in the Latin American view, to integrate intelligence and action, and naked power and action. The moderating power has its spiritual, intellectual, and military manifestations. Since these three moderating elements cannot belong to any single segment or class, they are considered to be sociopolitically free-floating; they do not fit the stratificatory concept of class at all. Although

* Brazil was made an empire independent of Portugal in 1822 and it was governed under the monarchical constitution of 1824 up to 1889, when it finally was made a republic. By 1824 the formula of "moderating power" was devised. It meant initially the power belonging to the emperor, which would prevent supreme power from falling into the hands of aristocracy or some other segmental interest. After the second empire was dissolved it no longer was clear to whom the moderating power should belong.

the relative strength of the three moderating powers may vary over time, they all strive, through different methods, toward the totalization of the polity-society complex.

Their common aim also explains how the three moderating powers may at times appear interchangeable. Ivan and Vivian Vallier observed how the military in Latin America, for instance, may assume functions that are properly religious, concerned with the guardianship of values, whereas the Church frequently assumes functions that are properly political.[17] The army, one may add, has also assumed duties such as road construction, resettlement, and even education; the army-supported social science centers in some Latin American countries have assumed what was formerly the normal function of social scientists, who may want to have nothing to do with the resurrection of the positivistic alliance of "force and wisdom." Although the Latin American pensador, unlike the Anglo-Saxon social scientist, seeks a place in policy making, he is presently inclined to be an antipositivist and an antimilitarist.

Totalities, in the Latin American view, are fighting a winning battle against segmentalities. Social change is seen to occur in a dialectical manner, and a permanent revolution is thus seen to be in the making; but no single class, in the Marxian sense, can be considered the revolution maker. The ultimate revolutionary potential is lodged in humanity—in the past, present, and future of mankind. Latin American humanism, as its apologists see it, is a revolutionary force which will relentlessly push toward a just society, in which the exploitation and dominion by the privileged groups is made impossible. In the Latin American humanistic view, whenever humanity is in charge there are no exploiters and exploited: the whole society, so to speak, will be the exploiter, and economic loss and risk, in this visionary view, is seen to be evenly divided among all. This leads to the abstract ideal of Christian-inspired communal living—a Latin American notion, which in European thought may be traced back to such writers as Constantin Pecqueur (1801–1887). The primitive Christian communes, a related Latin American line of thought implies, were indeed the highest expression of social justice. Civilization and industrialization, the Latin American thinkers warn, move toward fragmentation and the exaltation of self; only the ethos of humanity renders man truly a man, in the grand context of the timeless totalizing supersystem that humanity is.

The totalizing power, the Latin American outlook implies, belongs not to an impersonal institution or group such as a class, "the people," or the bureaucracy, but to a willful, decision-making agent who must have the autonomy of action which will allow him to face his responsibility to humanity. The personal nature of power, the Latin Americans insist, does not make it fragmented or arbitrary. But it does imply the ability of the holder of power to counteract segmentalism, to set his weight against those who oppress and exploit others —the ability to forcefully destroy the obstacles to unity, not merely to produce a *promise* of unity. Thus the Latin American political thought focuses on a sort of guided democracy aiming at governmental interference for the benefit of the lower classes.

This notion of equalization by autocratic means is one of the deepest tenets in the Latin Americans' power-oriented political philosophy, a philosophy that has its roots in the Catholic and positivist traditions. There will come a time, the Latin American philosophers concede, when power will be relaxed and people will be ready for a democracy of the European kind. The course of history will consequently lead away from the use of force, in the direction of scientific principles of government. Did not Comte propose a "law" which would admirably apply to the history of the Latin American nations, namely, that human mind, science, and history must pass successively through the military-theological, the metaphysical, and the final altruistic-positivistic states? In the positivist state, planners will be substituted for political rulers, and methodical verification for political ideology. This is how the Latin American positivists interpreted Comte, and this is how the present-day antiromantic technocratic social planners justify their effort to promote pragmatism. Power is a part of the historical scene, the Latin Americans hold; it was heavily applied in the colonial situation; and it must still be applied in some situations. Thus, the military must intervene whenever pressure for anarchy seems to threaten the sociopolitical order. The Latin American tradition admits that the sword was wielded too freely when the cross failed and that in the hands of the military (and frequently enough in the hands of churchmen) power has assumed its naked and brutal aspect. Yet, the abuse of power will lessen in an increasingly participant system.

What will replace power on the State level? Unlike the Europeans, Latin Americans rarely propose the substitution of parliamentary for executive power. In their experience, a parliament is unable to solve such issues of marginality as land tenure. With the exception of student groups, the Latin Americans rarely believe that political power will, or should, dissolve into an anarchist "social power" emanating from the civil sectors. There is, in Latin America, belief in a communitarian-type collective power vested in corporative groups; and the Marxian ideal of ultimate "consumers' association" may have impact. By and large, however, Latin American social thought is less interested in finding substitutes for personal power than in demonstrating the logical necessity for it in *any* circumstances. Power may lessen, the Latin American tradition holds, yet a minimum of it will remain, for it is in the essence of things. Without personal power in some form, order would be impossible.

The logic of personal power—spiritual, intellectual, or military—implies the preparedness of the power-holding actor to deduce from experience *and* from some preexisting principles, "known" to him but unknown and not immediately available to the powerless actors, guidelines for a yielding action. These guidelines cannot as such be verified. They imply emphasis on the "ought-to-be" nature of moral order, on moralizing, on totalizing, and on long-term rather than short-term objectives. In Latin America, the logic of power blends with an emphasis on idealism, transcendentalism, and with the elitist emphasis on necessary hierarchy. It would be unreasonable not to recognize the remarkable potentiality that a personalistic wielder of power may have not only for maintaining stability but also, as in the case of some of the modern-day military technocrats, for undoing some of the most blatant forms of protracted parasitism which affect the rural populations, and for curtailing some of the inequalities flowing from this source. Demographic pressures may invite in Latin America the application of a strong-arm revolutionary power that some of the new technocratic-military governments possess. Marginality may be increasingly recognized as a vicious circle, with its roots in history, which spreads rather than withering away and cannot be eliminated by civic action without heavy technocratic intervention "from above." Whereas a parliamentary government usually proceeds by issuing agrarian and other "laws," to be applied nation-wide, a military government has the advantage of reformist operation by presidential decrees. The latter approach makes it possible to obtain land reform without upsetting the economy and without endangering the food supply for the urban centers. In Peru, such a technocratic transformation is being attempted, by introducing basic land reforms in a few inland provinces first, and by attracting domestic capital from investment in land to industrial investment. Technocratic solutions are thus more flexible and experimental than parliamentary solutions.

The in-system splits among the diverse moderating powers, the neomilitaristic technocrats, the intelligentsia, and the Church, constitute one significant aspect of the sociopolitical history of Latin America. The enmity between the technocratic "colonels" and the intelligentsia, in countries like Brazil, Peru and Bolivia, seems particularly crucial. Most Latin American miltiary-dictatorial wielders of power, the majority of intellectuals will remember, have acquired notoriety not only for their bloodiness and caesarism but also for their readiness to serve the interests of the dollar-imperialists. The military, under whatever disguise they come, are highly suspect; and an alliance between the technocratic pragmatists and the intellectuals is slow in forming. This particular cleavage between the intelligentsia and the military-scientific governments dates back to the antipositivist thinking which has been widespread in Latin America since World War I.

Yet, it is one thing to decry the abuse of personal power and another to come to grips with the problem of the analytical role of personal power in the sociopolitical processes and in social explanation. Sociopolitical order and changes in it cannot be fully explained by correlating one impersonal variable to another. Nor can social norms fully explain it. "The norm," Theodor Geiger said, "is no command or imperative." [18] Command and imperative invariably imply the existence of some kind of central power, which assumes a monopoly on initiating and legalizing sociopolitical change. The central power must be considered as the "order-supporting" group for the entire system. This order-supporting group will assume responsibility for all the items listed in the left-hand column of *Table 1*. Unless we recognize the logical role of sociopolitical power in our analyses, we will need to assume that all social change is essentially revolutionary "from below"—which it is not, for much of it flows from anticipatory yielding action.

The morphogenetic guiding action from above, consequently, is an indispensable element in jurisprudence, statesmanship, and in social control. It is, moreover, indispensable in any attempt to explain change within sociopolitical wholes. Explanation of change must also attempt to describe how individuals influence one another in a reciprocal manner, how deliberate designs play crucial roles in the gubernatorial control and direction of enduring sociopolitical entities, and how every crude attempt initially undertaken to this effect will eventually lead to further measures, critical and corrective, whereby these attempts will be constantly revised. The gubernatorial function is concerned with the conditionally autonomous command function on the level of wholes. Thus F. S. C. Northrop speaks of two fundamentally different kinds of social "theories": (1) the "factual social theories" that attempt to give a systematic conception of "what is," and (2) the "normative social theories" that give the laws with which the judge, the lawyer, and the statesman are concerned. These not only record "what is" but aim to modify certain existent social facts.[19] Power entails theories of the latter kind. It defines and transforms into public action the salient motifs of the times, as the holders of power and their ideology makers (favorite writers, and so forth) perceive them. These motifs are treated, in the processes of power, as promising, totalizing, or necessary givens, which may derive their mobilizing effect from being either in favor or against (either verifying or falsifying) some specific large-scale alterations in the system of government. Power is implemented by pursuing these motifs at the risk of short-term expenses, tensions, resistances, exploitation, inequalities, injustices, and even brutalities, up to the point where resistance reaches some kind of societal limen of tolerance and martyrdom. At this point, the possibilities of yielding in the traditional direction have become exhausted. Ideological creation and replacement become necessary.

Notes

I. *Introduction*

1. Allan Nevins, *The Gateway to History* (Garden City, N.Y., Doubleday, 1938), p. 335.

2. Warren B. Walsh, *Perspectives and Patterns: Discourses on History* (Syracuse, N.Y., Syracuse University Press, 1962), p. 1.

3. Folke Dovring, *History as a Social Science: An Essay on the Nature and Purpose of Historical Studies* (The Hague, Martinus Nijhoff, 1960), p. v.

4. Amitai Etzioni, "Toward a Macrosociology," in *Macrosociology: Research and Theory*, ed. James S. Coleman, Amitai Etzioni, and John Porter (Boston, Allyn and Bacon, 1970), p. 112.

5. Max Weber, *Schriften zur theoretischen Soziologie, zur Soziologie der Politik und Verfassung* (New York, Burt Franklin, 1968), p. 89.

6. See Paul Honigsheim, *On Max Weber*, trans. Joan Rytina (New York, The Free Press, 1968), pp. 116ff.

7. For sources on modern systems theory and the gubernatorial approach, see Walter Buckley, *Sociology and Modern Systems Theory* (Englewood Cliffs, N.J., 1967); James S. Coleman et al.; Eugene J. Meehan, *Explanation in Social Science: A System Paradigm* (Homewood, Ill., Dorsey, 1968); William A. Gamson, *Power and Discontent* (Homewood, Ill., Dorsey, 1968); Amitai Etzioni, *The Active Society: A Theory of Societal and Political Processes* (New York, The Free Press, 1968). The following points rely heavily on Buckley's formulations.

II. *The Principle of Power: Oneness*

1. Rafael Altamira, *A History of Spain,* trans. Muna Lee (Princeton, New Jersey, D. Van Nostrand, 1966), p. 98.

2. *Ibid.,* p. 103.

3. Claudio Sánchez-Albornoz, *España: un enigma histórico,* II (Buenos Aires, Sudamericana, 1956), p. 45.

4. José Antonio Maravall, *El concepto de España en la Edad Media* (Madrid, Instituto de Estudios Políticos, 1954), p. 555.

5. Franciscus de Victoria, *De Indies et de ivre belli relectiones,* ed. Ernest Nys (Washington, Carnegie Institute, 1917), p. 127.

6. *Ibid.,* pp. 129 ff.

7. *Ibid.,* p. 144.

8. *Ibid.,* p. 153.

9. *Ibid.,* p. 155.

10. *Ibid.,* pp. 157 f.

11. *Ibid.,* pp. 160 f.

12. *Ibid.,* p. 162.

13. Karl Popper, *The Logic of Scientific Discovery* (New York, Science Editions, 1961), p. 40.

14. See Paul Meadows, "The Metaphors of Order: Toward a Taxonomy of Organization Theory," in *Sociological Theory: Inquiries and Paradigms,* ed. Llewellyn Gross (New York, Harper & Row, 1967), pp. 77 ff.

15. Karl Mannheim, *Ideology and Utopia* (New York, Harcourt, Brace, 1936), p. 194.

16. *Ibid.,* p. 195.

17. Theodor Geiger, *Aufgaben und Stellung der Intelligenz in der Gesellschaft* (Stuttgart, Ferdinand Enke, 1949), pp. 66 ff.

18. Franz Adler, "The Range of Sociology of Knowledge," in *Modern Sociological Theory,* ed. Howard Becker and Alvin Boskoff (New York, Holt, Rinehart, and Winston, 1957), p. 418.

19. Juan Ginés Sepúlveda, *Demócrates segundo o de las justas causas de la guerra contra los indios,* ed. Angel Losada (Madrid, Consejo Superior de Investigaciones Científicas, Instituto Francisco de Vitoria, 1951), pp. 19 ff.

20. *Ibid.*, pp. 22 f.

21. *Ibid.*, p. 29.

22. *Ibid.*, p. 78.

23. Toribio Motolinia, *Motolinia's History of the Indians in New Spain,* trans. and ed. Elisabeth Andros Foster (Berkeley, California, The Cortes Society, 1950), pp. 18 ff.

24. Charles Gibson, *The Aztecs under Spanish Rule* (Stanford, California, Stanford University Press, 1964), p. 78.

25. See Silvio Zavala, *New Viewpoints on the Spanish Colonization of America* (Philadelphia, University of Pennsylvania Press, 1943), p. 81.

26. Juan Ginés de Sepúlveda, *Tratado sobre las justas causas de la guerra contra los Indios* (Mexico City, Fondo de Cultura Económica, 1941), p. 173; Teodoro Andrés Marcos, *Los imperialismos de Juan Ginés de Sepúlveda en su "Democrates Alter"* (Madrid, Instituto de Estudios Políticos, 1947), p. 182; Angel Losada, *Juan Ginés de Sepúlveda a través de su "Epistolario" y nuevos documentos* (Madrid, Consejo Superior de Investigaciones Científicos, Instituto Francisco de Vitoria, 1949), pp. 227 f.

27. See Marc Bloch, *Feudal Society* (London, Routledge & Kegan Paul, 1961), pp. 242 ff.

28. Teodoro Andrés Marcos, p. 53.

29. Max Weber, *Wirtschaft und Gesellschaft,* 1 (Tübingen, Germany, J. C. B. Mohr [Paul Siebeck], 1956), 17, 122 ff.

30. *Ibid.*, pp. 28 f.

31. Emile Durkheim, *Suicide* (London, Routledge & Kegan Paul, 1952), p. 276 n.

32. Bartolomé de las Casas, *Historia de las Indias,* 1 (Madrid; Bibioteca de Autores Españoles, 1957), 376 ff.

33. Manuel Giménes Fernández, *Bartolomé de las Casas,* 1 (Seville; Escuela de Estudios Hispano-Americanos, 1953), 196 ff.

34. *Ibid.*, pp. 311 ff.

35. Lewis Hanke, *The First Social Experiments in America: A Study in the Development of Spanish Indian Policy in the Sixteenth Century* (Cambridge; Harvard University Press, 1935), pp. 67 f.

36. Fray Antonio de Remesal, *Historia general de las Indias Occidentales y particular de la gobernación de Chiapa y Guatemala*, 1 (Madrid; Biblioteca de Autores Españoles, Atlas, 1964), 213 ff.

37. Bartolomé de las Casas, *Del único modo de atraer a todos los pueblos a la verdadera religión* (Mexico City, Fondo de Cultura Económica, 1942), p. 7.

38. Lewis Hanke, *Bartolomé de las Casas: pensador político, historiador, antropólogo* (Havana; Sociedad Economica de Amigos del País, 1949), p. xxxvii.

39. Fray Antonio de Remesal, pp. 421 ff.

40. Ramón Menéndez Pidal, *El padre Las Casas: su doble personalidad* (Madrid: Espasa-Calpe, 1963), p. 291.

41. *Ibid.*, pp. 176 ff.

42. See Charles Gibson, p. 223.

43. Sheldon S. Wolin, *Politics and Vision: Continuity and Innovation in Western Political Thought* (Boston, Little, Brown, 1960), p. 431.

44. Condillac, *Oeuvres complètes de Condillac*, vol. 2, *Traité des systèmes* (Paris, Houel, 1789), p. 1. Italics in the original.

45. See Richard T. LaPiere, *A Theory of Social Control* (New York, McGraw-Hill, 1954), p. 248.

46. For a discussion of power as a disposition term, see Charles Kadushin, "Power, Influence and Social Circles: A New Methodology for Studying Opinion Makers," *American Sociological Review*, 33 (October 1968), 685 ff.

47. David J. Finlay, Ole R. Holsti, and Richard R. Fagen, *Enemies in Politics* (Chicago, Illinois, Rand McNally, 1967), p. 242.

48. Guglielmo Ferrero, *The Principles of Power* (New York, G. P. Putnam's Sons, 1942).

49. Bertram Gross, *Activating National Plans*, in *Operational Research and the Social Sciences*, ed. J. R. Lawrence (London, Travistock, 1966), pp. 478 ff.

50. Irving Louis Horowitz, "The Norm of Illegitimacy: The Political Sociology of Latin America," in *Latin American Radical-*

ism: A Documentary Report of Left and Nationalist Movements, ed. Irving Louis Horowitz, Josue de Castro, and John Gerassi (New York, Alfred A. Knopf, 1969), p. 8.

51. Karl R. Popper, *Conjectures and Refutations: The Growth of Scientific Knowledge* (New York, Basic Books, 1962), p. 28. See also Eugene J. Meehan, *Explanation in Social Science: A System Paradigm* (Homewood, Illinois, Dorsey, 1968).

52. See Walter Buckley, *Sociology and Modern Systems Theory* (Englewood Cliffs, New Jersey, Prentice-Hall, 1967), pp. 173 f.

53. Fernando Benítez, *La vida criolla en el siglo XVI* (Mexico City, Colegio de México, 1953), p. 42.

54. Carlo Sforza, *The Living Thoughts of Machiavelli* (New York, Fawcett, 1958), p. 92.

55. John Smith, *Memoirs of the Marquis of Pombal*, 2 (London, Brown, Green, and Longmans, 1843), 206 f.

56. Gustav Ratzenhofer, *Wesen und Zweck der Politik* (Leipzig, F. A. Brockhaus, 1892), p. 63.

57. Comisión Nacional de Homenaje a Sarmiento, *Sarmiento: cincuentenario de su muerte*, 3 (Buenos Aires, 1939), 332.

58. José Carlos Mariátegui, *Siete ensayos de interpretación de la realidad Peruana* (Lima, Amauta, 1965), p. 37 ff.

59. Calculations on basis of data from Ramiro Guerra y Sánchez, *Historia de la nación Cubana*, 10 (Havana, Editorial Historia de la Nación Cubana, 1952), 61.

60. Adolf Berle, *Power* (New York, Harcourt, Brace & World, 1969), p. 96.

61. Carlos Ibarguren, *Juan Manuel de Rosas: su vida, su tiempo, su drama* (Buenos Aires, Juan Roldan, 1930), p. 63.

62. W. Rex Crawford, *A Century of Latin-American Thought* (Cambridge, Harvard University Press, 1944), p. 4.

63. See Donald Marquand Dozer, *Latin America: An Interpretive History* (New York, McGraw-Hill, 1962), p. 168.

III. *Hidden Challenge to Public Power*

1. Herbert Eugene Bolton, "The Epic of Greater America," *Do the Americas Have a Common History? A Critique of the Bolton Theory*, ed. Lewis Hanke (New York, Knopf, 1964), p. 69.
2. Frank Tannenbaum, *Ten Keys to Latin America* (New York, Vintage Books, 1962), p. 4.
3. Fernando Alvarado Tezozomoc, *Crónica Mexicana* (Mexico City, Leyenda, 1944), p. 13.
4. *Ibid.*, p. 10.
5. Michael Coe, *Ancient Peoples and Places: Mexico* (New York, Praeger, 1966), p. 135 f.
6. Bernardino de Sahagún, *Historia general de las cosas de Nueva España*, 1 (Mexico City, Porrua, 1956), 278.
7. *Ibid.*, p. 279.
8. Michael Coe, pp. 135 f.
9. Miguel León-Portilla, *Los antiguos Mexicanos, a través de sus crónicas y cantares* (México, Fondo de Cultura Económica, 1961), p. 91.
10. Laurette Sejourné, *Burning Water: Thought and Religion in Ancient Mexico* (New York, Thames & Hudson, 1957), pp. 59 f.
11. Miguel León-Portilla, p. 116.
12. Bernardino de Sahagún, Historia, 2:77.
13. Bernardino de Sahagún, *Suma Indiana* (Mexico City, Universidad Nacional Autónoma, 1943), p. 94.
14. Miguel León-Portilla, p. 188.
15. *Ibid.*, p. 197.
16. G. C. Vaillant, *Aztecs of Mexico* (New York, Penguin, 1966), p. 204.
17. Girolamo Benzoni, *History of the New World by Girolamo Benzoni of Milan*, ed. W. H. Smyth (London, 1857), p. 146. Quoted from Lewis Hanke, *Aristotle and the American Indians: A Study in Race Prejudice in the Modern World* (London, Hollis & Carter, 1959), p. 26.

18. Gonzalo Fernández de Oviedo, *Historia general y natural de las Indias,* 2 (Madrid, Biblioteca de Autores Españoles, Atlas, 1959), 179.

19. Bautista Saavedra, *El ayllu: Estudios sociológicos* (La Paz, Bolivia, Gisbert, 1955), p. 124.

20. See Gordon Schendel, *Medicine in Mexico: From Aztec Herbs to Betatrons,* written with the collaboration of José Alvarez Amezquita and Miguel E. Bustamante (Austin, Texas, University of Texas Press, 1968), pp. 32 ff.

21. See Scott A. Greer, *Social Organization* (New York, Random House, 1963), p. 20.

22. See Adolf A. Berle, *Power* (New York, Harcourt, Brace & World, 1969), p. 73.

23. Richard Konetzke (ed.), *Colección de documentos para la historia de la formación social de Hispanoamérica, 1493–1810,* 1 (Madrid, Consejo Superior de Investigaciones Científicas, 1953), 145 f.

24. Edward Gaylord Bourne, *Spain in America,* new Introduction and Supplementary Bibliography by Benjamin Keen (New York, Barnes & Noble, 1962), pp. 239 f.

25. Bert F. Hoselitz, "Patterns of Economic Growth," *Readings on Economic Sociology,* ed. Neil J. Smelser (Englewood Cliffs, New Jersey, Prentice-Hall, 1965), p. 164.

26. André Gunder Frank, *Capitalism and Underdevelopment in Latin America: Historical Studies of Chile and Brazil* (New York, Monthly Review Press, 1967), pp. 24 f.

27. Jorge Juan y Antonio de Ulloa, *Noticias secretas de América* (Buenos Aires, Mar Oceano, 1953), p. 182.

28. Fray Antonio de Remesal, *Historia general de las Indias Occidentales y particular de la gobernación de Chiapa y Guatemala.* 1 (Madrid, Biblioteca de Autores Españoles, Ediciones Atlas, 1964), 451.

29. Quoted from P. Mariano Cuevas, S. J., *Historia de la iglesia en México,* 1 (Mexico City, Patria, 1946), 465 f.

30. D. Vincente Riva Palacio, *México a través de los siglos,* vol. 3, no. 1 (Mexico City, Gustavo S. López, 1940), 19.

31. Gunnar Myrdal, *Economic Theory and Under-Developed Regions* (London, Gerald Duckworth, 1957), p. 13.

32. See Russell L. Ackoff, Structural Conflicts within Organizations, in *Operational Research and the Social Sciences,* ed. J. R. Lawrence (London, 1966), p. 429.

33. Richard N. Adams, *Crucifixion by Power: Essays on Guatemalan National Social Structure* (Austin, University of Texas Press, 1970), p. 143.

34. Charles Gibson, *The Aztecs under Spanish Rule* (Stanford, California, Stanford University Press, 1964), pp. 152 ff.

35. *Ibid.,* p. 153.

36. *Ibid.,* p. 82.

37. See Vernon Van Dyke, *Political Science: A Philosophical Analysis* (Stanford, California, Stanford University Press, 1962), p. 142.

38. Chalmers Johnson, *Revolutionary Change* (Boston, Little, Brown, 1966), p. 32.

39. See Bertram M. Gross, "Activating National Plans," in *Operational Research and the Social Sciences,* ed. J. R. Lawrence (London, 1966), p. 455.

40. Orlando Fals Borda, *Campesinos de los Andes: Estudio Sociológico de Saucío,* Monografías Sociológicas (Bogotá, Facultad de Sociología, Universidad Nacional, 1961), pp. 272 ff.

41. See Kenneth E. Boulding, *Conflict and Defense: A General Theory* (New York, Harper & Brothers, 1962), pp. 308 f.; Bertram M. Gross, p. 477.

42. Frank Tannenbaum, *Ten Keys to Latin America* (New York, Vintage, 1962), p. 114.

43. Simón Bolívar, *Obras Completas,* 1 (Havana, Cuba, Editorial Lex, 1950), 181.

44. See Bruce P. Dohrenwend, "Egoism, Altruism, Anomie, and Fatalism: A Conceptual Analysis of Durkheim's Types," *American Sociological Review,* 24 (August 1959), 466 ff.

45. Émile Durkheim, *Suicide: A Study in Sociology* (London, Routledge & Kegan Paul, 1952), pp. 241 ff, 252 ff, 258, 276.

46. Dorothy L. Meier and Wendell Bell, "Anomia and Differ-

ential Access to the Achievement of Life Goals," *American Sociological Review*, 24 (April 1959), 201.

47. See Olen E. Leonard, *Bolivia: Land, People and Institutions* (Washington, D.C., Scarecrow, 1952), p. 116.

48. Charles Gibson, p. 78.

49. See Robert E. Scott, "Nation-Building in Latin America," in *Nation-Building*, ed. Karl W. Deutsch and William J. Foltz (New York, Atherton, 1963), p. 76.

50. Rodolfo Stavenhagen, "Seven Fallacies About Latin America," in *Latin America: Reform or Revolution?*, ed. James Petras and Maurice Zeitlin (Greenwich, Conn., Fawcett, 1968), p. 16.

51. António Vieira, "Sermon Condemning Indian Slavery," 1653, in *History of Latin American Civilization: Sources and Interpretations*, ed. Lewis Hanke, 1 (Boston, Little, Brown, 1967), 266.

52. C. R. Boxer, "A Great Luso-Brazilian Figure," in *History of Latin American Civilization: Sources and Interpretations*, ed. Lewis Hanke, 1 (Boston, Little, Brown, 1967), 248.

53. See Edward C. Banfield, *The Moral Basis of a Backward Society* (Glencoe, Ill., The Free Press, 1958), p. 65.

54. Orlando Fals Borda, pp. 276 ff.

55. José Luis Romero, *Las ideas políticas en Argentina* (Mexico City, Fondo de Cultura Económica, 1959), p. 71.

56. Origen, *Prayer—Exhortation to Martyrdom*, trans. John J. O'Meara (Westminster, Maryland, The Newman Press, 1954), p. 186.

IV. *Toward Overt Resistance*

1. Robert Ricard, *The Spiritual Conquest of Mexico* (Berkeley and Los Angeles, University of California Press, 1966), p. 284.

2. Richard Konetzke (ed.), *Colección de documentos para la historia de formación social de Hispanoamérica, 1493–1810*, 1 (Madrid, Consejo Superior de Investigaciones Científicas, 1953), 286.

3. D. Joaquín García Icazbalceta, *Carta acerca del origen de la imagen de Nuestra Señora de Guadalupe de México* (Mexico City, Paseo Nuevo No. 8, 1896), p. 13.

4. J. Fred Rippy and Jean Thomas Nelson, *Crusaders of the Jungle* (Chapel Hill, The University of North Carolina Press, 1936), p. 286; Juan B. Valladares, *La Virgen de Suyapa* (Tegucigalpa, Honduras, Talleres Tipo-Lito "Ariston," 1946), p. 93. For a study of the role of the Virgin of Guadalupe in colonial Mexico, see Francisco de la Maza, *El guadalupanismo Mexicano* (Mexico City, Porrua y Obregón, 1953).

5. Silvio A. Zavala, *La encomienda Indiana* (Madrid, Centro de Estudios Históricos, 1935), p. 151.

6. See John Howland Rowe, *Colonial Portraits of Inca Nobles* (Chicago, International 29th Congress of Americanists, Proceedings; 1949).

7. Garcilaso de la Vega Inca, *Páginas escogidas* (Paris, Biblioteca de Cultura Peruana, 1938), p. 96.

8. Don Fernando de Alva Ixtlilxochitl, *Obras históricas de Fernando Alva Ixtlilxochitl*, ed. Alfredo Chavero (Mexico City, Nacional, 1952), p. 465.

9. Francisco A. Loayza (ed.), *Fray Calixto Tupac Inca*, Los Pequeños Grandes Libros de Historia Americana, series 1, 15 (Lima, Peru, 1948).

10. Gregorio Weinberg, "Nota del Editor," in Jorge Juan y Antonio de Ulloa, *Noticias secretas de América* (Buenos Aires, Mar Oceano, 1953), p. 344.

11. Boleslao Lewin, *La rebelión de Tupac Amarú y los orígenes de la emancipación Americana* (Buenos Aires, Librería Hachette, 1957), pp. 473 f.

12. Daniel Valcarcel, *La rebelión de Tupac Amarú* (Mexico City, Fondo de Cultura Económica, 1947), p. 106.

13. Lillian Estelle Fisher, *The Last Inca Revolt 1780–1783* (Norman, Oklahoma, University of Oklahoma Press, 1966), pp. 140 ff.

14. Barrington Moore, Jr., *Social Origins of Dictatorship and Democracy: Lord and Peasant in the Making of the Modern World* (Boston, Beacon Press, 1966), p. 453.

15. Georg Wilhelm Friedrich Hegel, *Phänomenologie des Geistes* (Berlin, von Humblot, 1832), pp. 140 ff; G. W. F. Hegel, *The Phenomenology of Mind*, trans. J. B. Baillie (London, Swan Sonnenschein, 1910), pp. 175 ff.

16. Alcides Arguedas, "Pueblo enfermo," in *Antología del pensamiento social y política de América Latina*, Introduction by Leopoldo Zea, selection and Notes by Abelardo Villegas (Washington, D.C., Unión Panamericana, 1964), p. 545.

17. Hubert Howe Bancroft, "The Struggle between an Archbishop and a Viceroy in Seventeenth-Century New Spain," in *The Conflict between Church and State in Latin America*, ed. Frederick B. Pike, (New York, Alfred A. Knopf, 1964), pp. 78 ff.

18. For a study on the role of Inquisition in promoting Catholic racism, see Boleslao Lewin, *La inquisición en Hispano-america* (Buenos Aires, Proyección, 1962).

19. José Toribio Medina, Apéndice documental, *Historia del tribunal de la inquisición de Lima*, 2 (Santiago, Chile; Fondo Histórico y Bibliográfico, 1956), p. 387.

20. Magnus Mörner, Introduction, *The Expulsion of the Jesuits from Latin America*, ed. Magnus Mörner (New York, Alfred A. Knopf, 1965), p. 13.

21. Leopoldo Lugones, *El Imperio Jesuítico* (Buenos Aires, Arnoldo Moen, 1970), p. 159.

22. P. Domingo Muriel, *Historia del Paraguay desde 1747 hasta 1767, Obra Latina*, trans. P. Pablo Hernández (Madrid, Librería General de Victoriano Suárez, 1918), p. 323.

23. See Mario C. Vázquez V., "Changes in the Social Stratification of an Andean Hacienda," *Contemporary Cultures and Societies of Latin America*, ed. Dwight B. Heath and Richard Adams (New York, Random House, 1965), pp. 405 ff.

24. Baron de Montesquieu, *The Spirit of the Laws*, trans. Thomas Nugent (New York, Hafner, 1959), pp. 351 f.

25. Voltaire, *Candide ou L'optimisme* (Paris, Libraire Nizet, 1959), pp. 134 ff.

26. Guillaume-Thomas Raynal, *Histoire Philosophique et Politique des Etablissement du Commerce des Européens dans les Deux Indes*, 5 (Geneva, Jean-Léonard Pellet, 1781), 20 ff.

27. José Toribio Medina, *Historia del tribunal del Santo Oficio de la Inquisición en México* (Mexico City, Fuente Cultural, 1952), p. 292.

28. *Ibid.*, p. 335.

29. See John Plamenatz, *Man and Society*, I (New York and San Francisco, McGraw-Hill, 1963), 163.

30. Gaspar Melchor Jovellanos, *Obras escogidas* (Madrid, La RAFA, 1930), pp. 287 f.

31. Fernando Díaz-Plaja (ed.), *La historia de España en sus documentos, El siglo XVIII* (Madrid, Instituto de Estudios Políticos, 1955), p. 324.

32. Juan Regla y Santiago Alcolea, *Historia de la cultura Española, El siglo XVIII* (Barcelona, Seix Barral, 1957), pp. 75 ff.

33. Lillian Estelle Fisher, *Champion of Reform: Manuel Abad y Queipo* (New York, Library Publishers, 1955), pp. 64 ff.

34. Manuel Belgrano, "The Making of an Insurgent," in *The Origins of the Latin American Revolutions 1808–1826*, ed. R. A. Humphreys and John Lynch (New York, Alfred A. Knopf, 1965), p. 277.

35. Mariano Moreno, *Escritos políticos y económicos* (Buenos Aires, Orientación Cultural Editores, 1961), p. 135.

36. Narcisco Binayan (ed.), *Ideario de Mayo* (Buenos Aires, Editorial Kapelusz, 1960), p. 69.

37. Ricardo Becerra, *Vida de Don Francisco de Miranda*, I (Madrid, Editorial-América, 1896), p. 250.

38. James Biggs, *The History of Don Francisco Miranda's Attempt to Effect a Revolution in South America in a Series of Letters* (London, T. Gillet, 1809), p. 256.

39. Salvador de Madariaga, *De Colón a Bolívar* (Barcelona, E.D.H.A.S.A., 1955), p. 266.

40. Quoted from Ruben Vargas Ugarte, *De la conquista de la República: Articulos históricos*, 2d series (Lima, Compañia de Impresiones y Publicidad, 1950), p. 226.

41. See Hugh M. Hamill, Jr., *The Hidalgo Revolt: Prelude to Mexican Independence* (Gainesville, Florida, University of Florida Press, 1966).

42. *Ibid.*, p. 69.

43. Vicente Riva Palacio, *México a través de los siglos*, vol. 2, no. 1, *El Virreinato* (Mexico City, Gustavo S. López, 1940), p. 95.

44. *Ibid*, vol. 3, no. 1, pp. 130 f.

45. See Donald Marquand Dozer, *Latin America: An Interpretive History* (New York, McGraw-Hill, 1962), p. 215.

46. Carlos Navarro y Rodrigo (ed.), *Vida de Agustín de Iturbide y Memorias de Agustín de Iturbide* (Madrid, Editorial América, 1919), p. 285.

47. Frank Bonilla, *The Failure of Elites* (Cambridge, Massachusetts, The MIT Press, 1970), p. 43.

48. *Ibid.*, p. 56.

49. Quoted from Medardo Vitier, *Las ideas en Cuba*, 1 (Havana, Editorial Trópico, 1938), 44.

50. John P. Gillin, "Some Signposts for Policy," *Social Change in Latin America Today*, ed. Richard N. Adams, John P. Gillin, Allan R. Holmberg, Oscar Lewis, Richard W. Patch, and Charles Wagley (New York, Harper & Brothers, 1960), pp. 34 f.

51. Esteban Echeverría, *Obras completas* (Buenos Aires, A. Zamora, 1951), p. 256.

52. José Enrique Rodó, *Ariel*, ed. with Introduction and Notes by Gordon Brotherston (Cambridge, Cambridge University Press, 1967), pp. 41 ff.

53. José Vasconcelos, *Bolivarismo y monroismo* (Santiago, Chile; Ediciones Ercilla, 1937), p. 45.

54. Jacinto Oddone, *La burguesía terrateniente Argentina* (Buenos Aires, Ediciones Populares, 1956).

55. Ernesto Quesada, *La época de Rosas: Su verdadero caracter histórico* (Buenos Aires, Arnoldo Moen, 1898), pp. 62 f.

56. See Charles C. Griffin, "Further Reflections," in *History of Latin America Civilization*, 2 (Boston, Little, Brown and Company, 1967), 49, from *Los temas sociales y económicos en la época de independencia*, by Charles C. Griffin (Caracas, Fundación John Boulton & Fundación Eugenio Mendoza, 1962).

57. Eric R. Wolf, *Sons of the Shaking Earth* (Chicago, The University of Chicago Press, 1959), pp. 202 ff.

58. Emile Durkheim, *The Division of Labor in Society*, trans. George Simpson (Glencoe, Ill., The Free Press, 1960), p. 275. Italics added.

59. Amitai Etzioni, *Studies in Social Change* (New York, Holt, Rinehart and Winston, 1966), p. 115.

60. Robert Redfield, "The Folk Society," *American Journal of Sociology*, 52 (January 1947), 293 ff.

V. A *Totalizing View*

1. Jean-William Lapierre, *Essai sur le fondement du pouvoir politique* (Aix-En-Provence, Faculté des Lettres, 1968), p. 44. Italics in the original.

2. Max Weber, *Economy and Society*, ed. Guenther Roth and Claus Wittich, 1 (New York, Bedminster Press, 1968), 36. Ginn, 1906), pp. 2 ff.

3. William Graham Sumner, *Folkways* (Boston, Ginn, 1906), pp. 2 ff.

4. Herbert Spencer, *First Principles* (New York, The De Witt Revolving Fund, 1958), p. 327.

5. St. Thomas Aquinas, *The "Summa Theologica,"* 2 (London, Washbourne, 1915), 80.

6. Destutt de Tracy, *Commentaire sur l'esprit des lois de Montesqueu* (Paris, Delaunau, n.d.), pp. 1 ff.

7. Jean Baptiste Say, *Letters to Thomas Robert Malthus on Political Economy and Stagnation of Commerce* (London, George Harding's, 1936), p. 58.

8. Thomas Jefferson, *Basic Writings of Thomas Jefferson*, ed. Philip S. Foner (Garden City, N.Y., Halcyon House, 1950), p. 588.

9. Edmund Burke, *Reflections on the Revolution in France*, Introduction by Russell Kirk (Chicago, Gateway, 1955), pp. 139 f.

10. Quoted from Juan Bautista Gómis, *Criterio social de Luis Vives* (Madrid, Instituto "Balmes" de Sociología, 1946), p. 53.

11. Robert K. Merton, *Social Theory and Social Structure* (Glencoe, Ill., The Free Press, 1944), pp. 50 ff.

12. See William Mitchell, *Sociological Analysis and Politics: The Theories of Talcott Parsons* (Englewood Cliffs, N. J., Prentice-Hall, 1967), pp. 59 f.

13. Eric R. Wolf, *Peasant Wars of the Twentieth Century* (New York, Harper & Row, 1969), p. 287.

14. Karl Marx, *Early Writings*, trans. T. B. Bottomore (London, C. A. Watts, 1963), pp. 177 f.

15. See Henri Lefebvre, *The Sociology of Marx* (New York, Vintage Books, 1969), p. 53.

16. Ivan Vallier, *Catholicism, Social Control, and Modernization in Latin America* (Englewood Cliffs, N. J., Prentice-Hall, 1970), p. 22.

17. Ivan Vallier and Vivian Vallier, "South American Society," *International Encyclopedia of the Social Sciences*, ed. David L. Sills, 15 (New York, Macmillan, 1968), 64 ff.

18. Theodor Geiger, *Vorstudien zu einer Soziologie des Rechts* (Copenhagen, Ejnar Munksgaard, 1947), p. 29.

19. F. S. C. Northrop, *The Meeting of East and West: An Inquiry Concerning World Understanding* (New York, Macmillan, 1960), p. 256.

Index

POWER AND RESISTANCE

Designed by R. E. Rosenbaum.
Composed by Vail-Ballou Press, Inc.,
in 11 point linotype Electra, 3 points leaded,
with display lines in Monotype Deepdene.
Printed letterpress from type by Vail-Ballou Press
on Warren's 1854 text, 60 pound basis,
with the Cornell University Press watermark.
Bound by Vail-Ballou Press
in Columbia book cloth
and stamped in All Purpose foil.

Library of Congress Cataloging in Publication Data
(For library cataloging purposes only)

Sariola, Sakari.
Power and resistance.

Includes bibliographical references.
1. Latin America—Politics—To 1830. 2. Latin America—Social conditions. I. Title.
F1410.S25 320.9'8'01 72-4387
ISBN 0-8014-0741-9